DOING RIGHT BY
CHILDREN

DOING RIGHT BY
CHILDREN

Reflections on the Nature of Childhood and the Obligations of Parenthood

by

William B. Irvine

PARAGON HOUSE

St. Paul, Minnesota

Published in the United States of America by

Paragon House
2700 University Avenue West
St. Paul, Minnesota 55114

Library of Congress Cataloging-in-Publication Data

Irvine, William Braxton, 1952-
  Doing right by children: reflections on the nature of childhood and the obligations of parenthood / by William B. Irvine.
    p. cm.
  Includes bibliographical references and index.
  ISBN 1-55778-798-0
    1. Parenting. 2. Children--Social conditions. 1. Title.

HQ755.8 .I78 2001
649'.1--dc21
                                                          00-04168 8

10 9 8 7 6 5 4 3 2 1

For current information about all releases from Paragon House,
visit the web site at http://www.paragonhouse.com

To Jamie and to Jenny and Ryan,
without whom I wouldn't be a parent

CONTENTS

ACKNOWLEDGMENTS

I am grateful to Wright State University for granting me the Professional Development Leave during which the foundation for this book was laid. I am likewise grateful to the good taxpayers of Ohio for having funded said leave. I only hope they judge its results to be worthy.

DOING RIGHT BY
CHILDREN

PROLOGUE

America's views on the concept of childhood and the obligations of parenthood have undergone a revolution in the second half of the twentieth century. The magnitude of this revolution becomes apparent when one compares a typical childhood of the 1950s with a typical childhood of the 1990s.

In the 1950s, divorce was uncommon, and those who divorced were often subjected to a low-grade form of ostracism. It was widely agreed that children were harmed by a divorce and therefore that parents who got divorced were engaged in selfish behavior: They were putting their own desires ahead of the needs of their children. To avoid divorce, parents went to great lengths. In particular, they were willing to stay in a loveless marriage "for the sake of the children."

And if divorce was bad, having a child out of wedlock was essentially unthinkable. If you got pregnant (or got someone pregnant) out of wedlock, the only way to make amends was to get married, and even then, you would have done your best to keep the circumstances of your "shotgun wedding" a secret. To get pregnant before getting married was, after all, a shameful act, evidence that you were willing to put fulfillment of your own sexual desires ahead of the interests of any children you might create.

When a married couple had children, one parent—almost invariably the mother—typically stopped working in order to be a full-time caretaker for their children. Doing this involved a significant financial sacrifice, but one that most couples made unhesitatingly. After all, the prevailing view was that raising a child properly was a full-time job and that no one was better-suited to perform that job than the child's mother. And if the couple sacrificed money when the mother stayed home, the mother sacrificed even more, inasmuch as her departure from the labor force made it nearly impossible for her to achieve whatever career goals she might have had.

Children of the 1950s could be "delinquent," but such delinquency was uncommon, and it tended to be expressed in behaviors that were minimally injurious to others. A delinquent child might, for example, have stolen hubcaps or, in a more hardened case, might have gone joyriding.

Most children were willing to live within the rules of their society. They accepted, perhaps grudgingly, the dress codes of their schools, the intolerance for the use of profanity in public, the custom of addressing their elders as Mr. or Mrs., etc.

Those of us who were children in the 1950s and who are now raising children of our own cannot help but notice how much things have changed in the last four decades.

By the early 1990s, having children out of wedlock was commonplace, with nearly one in three American children being so born, up from one in twenty in 1960.[1] (And if the American numbers are depressing, those in other countries are even worse: In Sweden one-half of children are born out of wedlock, and in Iceland nearly three out of five are.[2] It would appear that much of the developed world is in a race to see who can first become a nation of bastards.) Furthermore, the adults of the 1990s who had children out of wedlock were not simply the poor and uneducated, but included people from all socioeconomic levels; and when they had their children out of wedlock, they often did so unapologetically.

Thus, 1998 saw the National Honor Society run afoul of changing times when high-school student Amanda Lemon was invited to join the Society, but had the invitation revoked when school authorities learned that she was an unwed mother.[3] Rather than hang her head in shame, as her grandmother or mother might have done in similar circumstances, Ms. Lemon defended her behavior: To have a baby out of wedlock, she argued, was not necessarily dishonorable. Many adults found her argument persuasive.

By the 1990s it was not uncommon for female stars to have children out of wedlock. The public seemed quite accepting of their behavior. Compare this to the public abuse heaped on Ingrid Bergman when, in 1950, she chose to have a child by a man not her husband.[4]

I recently watched a television program about professional basketball players who, despite their million-dollar salaries, had failed to make child-support payments on behalf of the children they had fathered out of wedlock. The interviewer asked many questions of the women impregnated by these athletes, but she failed to ask what, in the 1950s, would have been the obvious question: Why didn't you wait until you were married before you had sex with the basketball player? She also failed to ask what, in the 1970s, would have been the obvious question: Why, in this world of readily-available and highly-effective contraceptives, didn't you wait until you were married before you had a child by the basketball player? And the reason the interviewer didn't ask these questions wasn't that she was shy about probing into the private lives of people: The questions she did ask proved otherwise. The reason she didn't ask them was the simple fact that it would have been, by the standards of the 1990s, distinctly gauche to have done so. As far as she was concerned, having children out of wedlock raised no interesting ethical issues; it was failing to provide for the children in question that bothered her.

By the late 1990s, people were used to cases in which couples had—by 1950s standards—every reason to get married, but failed to do so. What some found troubling were those cases in which couples could have avoided marriage but nevertheless got married. Thus, when Macaulay Culkin announced his intention to marry fellow teen actor Rachel Miner, some observers reacted to the announcement with puzzlement: Why is he *marrying* her? Doesn't he realize that he's rich and famous and therefore doesn't *need* to marry her? Culkin's parents, by the way, never bothered to get married.

The no-fault divorce laws enacted in the 1970s made it possible for parents to divorce on a whim—and many did. Divorce not only lost its stigma but became commonplace, with the annual number of divorces increasing threefold between 1950 and 1993,[5] and the ratio of weddings to divorces falling from 4.33-to-1 to a mere 1.96-to-1 in the same period.[6] Indeed, many young adults came to regard divorce as the likely outcome of any marriage. The idea of staying together for the sake of the children came to be seen as sappy, if not downright stupid.

In making the above remarks, by the way, I don't mean to suggest that *everyone* who seeks a divorce does so for selfish reasons or "on a whim." It is possible, after all, to be married to a person who, because of his or her own selfishness, makes continuance of the relationship impossible—for example, being married to a physically abusive person. To seek a divorce under such circumstances would be neither selfish nor whimsical. At the same time, I would maintain that most people in America today who initiate divorce proceedings are motivated by decidedly less-than-compelling reasons, such as a desire for sexual variety.

It is also important for the reader to realize that when, in the following pages, I discuss divorce, my primary interest is cases of divorce *in which a couple has children*. Because of the children, these cases raise far more ethical questions than do divorces involving childless couples.

The combination of an increase in the number of divorces and an increase in the number of people who never bothered to get married in the first place meant that a large number of children found themselves raised by one parent. In 1950, only 7.1 percent of children under eighteen years old lived in single-parent families; by 1994, 24 percent of children under eighteen years old did.[7]

If the number of children living with one parent rose in the second half of the twentieth century, so did the number of children living with *neither* parent. Increasingly, grandparents were called on to take over the parental duties that their children were either unwilling or unable to assume. By 1996, 1.4 million children were being raised by their grandparents.[8]

In the 1950s, women who left the labor force to have children generally remained at home at least until their children were of school age: In 1950, only 11.9 percent of married women with children under six years of age worked. By the 1990s, for mothers to work while their children were young had become commonplace: In 1993, 59.6 percent of married women with children under six years of age worked.[9] Indeed, by 1995 most married women (55 percent) did not even wait a year after giving birth before returning to the labor force,[10] and married couples *with* children under six years of age were significantly more likely to be a two-income family than were married couples *without* children under six years of age.[11]

Who raises the children of dual-income families? In many cases, they are raised—together with several other children, at a day-care center—by a stranger whose reward for doing so is the minimum wage. Most parents of the 1950s would have dismissed such care as a poor substitute for the care a mother could give. Many parents of the 1990s, by way of contrast, argued that day care is actually better for children than mother care.

I remember, as a college freshman in 1970, sharing my classmates' horror at Plato's suggestion in *The Republic* that the state, rather than parents, raise the citizens' children. Three decades later, things have changed: A significant number of my fellow citizens would love it if the government provided free day care, even though in doing so, it would partially assume the role of parent.

And when parents of the 1990s did take an active role in the upbringing of their children, in many cases they raised their children differently than their parents had raised them. In particular, the 1990s saw a surge in the number of parents who handled their children's behavioral problems not by patiently investing their own time in the child—such an investment in many cases would involve too great a sacrifice—but by medication, with Ritalin being the drug of choice. Behavior that in the 1950s would have been regarded as "boys being boys" came to be regarded in the 1990s as a certifiable medical condition.

In the 1950s, a woman who found herself pregnant with an unwanted baby could "dispose of it" by giving it up for adoption. By the 1980s, many women who didn't want their babies resorted to another means of disposal: abortion. And by the late 1990s, America witnessed a new trend, as women who found themselves carrying an unwanted baby neither aborted it nor gave it up for adoption, but secretly gave birth to it and then dumped it in the trash or stuffed it down a sewer. In 1999, states reacted to the surge in baby dumpings by passing legislation that allowed mothers to legally abandon babies under thirty days old at government offices with no threat of prosecution and no questions asked. Children, it was clear, had become, for many Americans, a less precious commodity in the year 2000 than they had been in 1950.

If the attitudes of parents changed between 1950 and 2000, so did the attitudes of children.

The children of 2000 are not nearly as "innocent" as their 1950 counterparts. The average child of today knows about sex, including methods of birth control and "abnormal" sexual practices; knows about drugs and addictions; knows, and relishes in the use of, a variety of swearwords. Indeed, in many respects, the average child of today is less innocent than many *adults* were in the 1950s.

The nature of child crime has changed so dramatically in recent decades that it is a profound understatement to refer to the youthful lawbreakers of the 1990s as being merely delinquent. For one thing, today's children are 33 times more likely to be arrested for their transgressions than were children of the 1950s.[12] And not only were they committing more crimes, but the crimes they were committing had grown decidedly sordid: The children of the 1990s showed themselves to be capable of committing crimes that in the 1950s only the most hardened of adults could have undertaken.

Consider, by way of illustration, the rash of school shootings that broke out in the late 1990s, with one child killing, in a more or less random fashion, several of his classmates. As the decade progressed, such shootings were carried out on an ever-grander scale, climaxing in the shootings at Columbine High, which left more than thirty people dead or wounded. Such a crime, if committed by *an adult*, would, in the 1950s, have astonished the average citizen, and the idea of *a child* committing such a crime would have been unthinkable.

Another disturbing trend in the decade was the tendency for children to commit acts of violence at ever-younger ages. In 1996 police in California set a state record for youngest person charged with a felony when they accused a six-year-old boy of attempted murder. It is alleged that during a burglary, the boy beat a one-month-old baby with a stick and kicked it until it was nearly dead.[13] In 2000, the nation was horrified when a six-year-old boy fatally shot a six-year-old girl. The site of the killing: their first-grade classroom.[14]

The children who commit such crimes today, it might be argued, are mentally unstable, and it is their mental instability, not some change in society, that accounts for their behavior. This is doubtless true, but consider that in the 1950s, *even a mentally unstable child wouldn't have plotted to randomly gun down his classmates*. His instability would likely have been expressed in less appalling ways.

The magnitude of the change in child crime came home to me when I read, in December of 1997, that a high-school student had plotted to shoot his classmates during a Christmas assembly. What drew my attention was the location of the episode: Yerington High School in Yerington, Nevada, where I myself had graduated in 1970.

Then-and-now comparisons came flooding into mind. It is incorrect to say that back then, plotting to shoot your classmates during a Christmas assembly would have been inconceivable; it would have been *beyond* inconceivable. What was inconceivable back then was a variety of behaviors that by today's standards would hardly even count as misbehaving, for example, talking back to a teacher, skipping school, or violating the school's dress code. It was clear that something had changed.

Because child crime has simultaneously become more commonplace and more serious, and because it is more difficult than ever to characterize the crimes committed by children as innocent mistakes, there is a growing tendency in America for youthful criminals to be tried and sentenced as adults. America is almost alone in the world in its willingness to sentence children to death.

It is instructive to put the changes in our views about the concept of childhood and the obligations of parenthood into a historical context. We may think that the changes between 1950 and 2000 represent a bold leap into the future, but in fact they represent a descent into the past. A case can be made—and I will spend the early part of this book making it—that the recent "decline" of childhood simply represents a return to historical norms.

In abandoning the idea that children should be raised in innocence, Americans are reviving views commonplace in centuries gone by: At that time, few adults saw reason to treat childhood as a special, protected time of life. In calling for child criminals to be treated like adults, Americans are asking us to move back to the time, a century ago, before juvenile courts had been established. In "trashing" unwanted babies, American mothers are mimicking a practice that was commonplace in England in past centuries.

Until the seventeenth century,[15] children were treated abominably: Rather than being nurtured, they were exploited. The average child of 1500 would today count as an abused child. Back then, parents operated under what I shall call the *ownership model of parenting*: They treated their children as a form of property; and in the same way as it is left to, say, car owners to decide what uses they put their cars to, it was left to parents to decide what uses they put their children to. The view that children were created in order to be exploited was at one time taken for granted, as was the view that the interests and well-being of the child should be subordinated to the interests and well-being of his parents.

By the middle of the twentieth century, children in the West were being treated remarkably well by historical standards. The thought of putting your child's well-being at the top of your list of priorities—which at one time would have been regarded as eccentric behavior—was commonplace. The ownership model of parenting had been supplanted by what I call the *stewardship model of parenting*. The goal of steward-parents was not to exploit the children they had, but to take good care of them so they would have an enjoyable, fulfilling childhood and, when they came of age, have a good chance at an enjoyable, fulfilling adulthood. And taking care of children meant, in many cases, that parents had to subordinate their own interests and well-being to those of their children. It meant making sacrifices that parents of 1500 simply would not have understood.

Unfortunately for children, their time in the sun was short-lived. By the 1960s the status of children was in decline in America, and in subsequent decades the decline accelerated. In our treatment of children we were, for better or worse, heading back into the Middle Ages, as the stewardship model of parenting slowly but surely gave way to the ownership model it had supplanted.

It is remarkable how quickly American views on the concept of childhood and the obligations of parenthood changed. In one generation, we went a long way toward undoing the work of the dozen preceding generations in improving the lot of children.

With respect to our children, America is living what to the parents of the 1950s would have been a nightmare scenario. Suppose, in other words, that we could go back to the 1950s and describe, to the parents of that time, what America would be like in forty years. Their reaction would likely be one of horror. "How," they would ask, "did this change come about? Why did people stand for it?" That the change took place says a lot for the cumulative power of small, incremental social changes.

Carrying this line of thought one step further, consider the nightmare scenario of today's parents—consider, that is, the state of affairs (with respect to the parent/child relationship) that is so bad that the average parent would be inclined to say, "That could never happen here in America." Realize that in the same way as the previous generation of parents witnessed, in the course of their life, a gradual slide into nightmare, today's parents could, if present trends continue, witness the same. And the thought of our grandchildren being raised in what to us would be a nightmare world is a frightening prospect, indeed.

Why did we in America choose to "turn the clock back" with respect to our treatment of children? The answer to this question, unfortunately, is that we did not *choose* to turn the clock back. To the contrary, the clock was turned back as a result of other choices we made—in particular, our decision that we were not going to let the children we created stand in the way of our personal freedom. If we want a divorce that hurts our children, too bad for them: Better that they should suffer than that we should live in a less-than-ideal marriage. If by creating children out of wedlock and then departing to places unknown we condemn our children to a life of poverty with but one parent, too bad for them: Our sexual freedom comes first. If by insisting on a full-time career we deprive our children of the joys of full-time access to a parent, too bad for them: Our career goals come first.

In saying this, I do not mean to suggest that modern parents ceased loving their children. They still loved them; it's just that they grew to love something else even more, namely, themselves.

It would be one thing if, in the 1950s, we had gathered the best and brightest minds and asked them to think about what it is that children need; and if, as a result of their deliberations, they had declared it to be in the interests of children to be born to unmarried parents, to be raised by single parents or by grandparents, to be exposed to the harsh realities of adult life at an early age, and so forth. But of course no such meeting of minds ever took place. We knew we wanted freedom, and we seized it. It was only in the following decades that we came to realize that our freedom not only came at a price, but that it was America's children who were paying the greater part of the price for their parents' freedom.

In saying this, am I suggesting that American adults should

not be free to live the life they want to live? Not at all. What I am suggesting, though, is that those individuals who want to enjoy the utmost freedom that life has to offer—who want freedom to change sexual partners on a whim, who want to devote themselves to their careers, who want to spend every cent of their income on themselves—should refrain from having children, as well as from activities (e.g., unprotected sex) that make the birth of a baby possible.

If it was the increasing selfishness of adults that led to the decline of childhood, then it is reasonable to suppose that in order to improve the lot of children, it will be necessary for parents to grow less selfish and become more willing to make personal sacrifices on behalf of the children they create. Is it likely that parents *will* grow less selfish? Probably not, which means that the future outlook for childhood is bleak. But perhaps this conclusion is premature: In the same way as the rise of parental selfishness was unforeseeable, its decline might likewise take us by surprise. The advocate of childhood can only hope.

This is a book about parenting. More precisely, *it is a book about how we would parent if our primary concern was the well-being of our children.*

As author of a book about parenting, I have two serious defects. First, I myself was once a child. As such, I am hostage to my own childhood. The particular childhood I had no doubt colors my views on the relationship between parents and children, colors them in some ways of which I am aware and in many more ways of which I am utterly oblivious. Had my parents raised me differently, had I been born in a different place or time, or had I chanced to have different childhood experiences than those I in fact had, I might well have written a different book than this and drawn significantly different conclusions. Indeed, change my childhood enough, and I probably would not have written this or any other book.

The reader may be forgiving of this particular defect, since I cannot, if I am to exist as an adult, help but have had a childhood.

The same cannot be said of my second defect, though: Besides having had a childhood, I myself am a parent. In this book, I will be considering the proper role of parents. The reader might therefore worry that in my deliberations on this subject, I will deal unfairly with my own case—that I will go out of my way to reach conclusions that, quite conveniently, allow me to classify my own parenting as adequate.

If I am guilty of engaging in such a maneuver, I have done so unconsciously. And if I am, according to my own views on parenting, a good parent, I would like to suggest that it is because I have attempted to make my own parenting practices conform to the conclusions I describe and not the other way around.

Although being a parent might count as a defect in someone who would pretend to have insight into the goals of parenting, it can also count as an advantage. There are, after all, many people who have written books about children without ever having closely observed the real thing—or, more to the point, without ever having lived with the real thing, since this is a somewhat different experience than that of observing them on closed-circuit television. In many of these books, the children described seem more like theoretical entities than flesh-and-blood beings. And although it is possible to write sensibly about a subject without ever having experienced it directly and intimately, in most cases such experience is beneficial.

The reader should not, by the way, assume that the children I anonymously mention in the following pages are my own. They are not. In what follows, I have done my best to keep my own children in the background: They deserve better than to have their lives held up to illustrate this or that point.

Nor should the reader, on reading Chapter 11 (which lays out in detail the sorrows that await the prospective parent) draw the conclusion that I myself am an embittered parent. Quite the contrary. I happen to be what I term an "easy" parent—that is, someone constitutionally capable of enjoying the rewards that parenting has to offer, like witnessing first steps, going to piano recitals, and watching one's child warm the bench at Little League.

The reader is hereby given notice that this is *not* a book on child psychology. Child psychology is largely concerned with helping parents reach certain parental goals. My concern in the following pages, though, will not be with how to attain certain goals, but rather with *what the proper goals of parenting are.* A book on child psychology might offer advice on what to do if you want your child to talk back less or if you want your child to get good grades in school. This book, on the other hand, will be concerned with whether a parent *should* want his child to talk back less or whether a parent *should* encourage his child to get good grades in school. And if so, why?

The subject of this book, then, is not, How can one become a better parent? but rather, What is good parenting? What should a parent be trying to accomplish in his parenting? *What, in short, is parenting all about?*

My reason for shying away from the more standard psychological treatment of childhood is simple: My training is not in psychology, but in philosophy. If the reader is surprised that a philosopher would take an interest in parenting, it is understandable. In recent decades, philosophers have shown little interest in the topic. At the same time, one should keep in mind that this has not always been the case. In fact the first two "bestseller" books on parenting were written by philosophers John Locke and Jean Jacques Rousseau. And although centuries have passed since these books were written, there is still much—as we shall see in Chapter 9—that modern parents can learn from them regarding the proper goals of parenting.

I should caution the reader that inasmuch as I am doing philosophy rather than psychology, I tend to use the word "children" in a reproductive rather than chronological sense. When I speak of one's children, I mean one's offspring. Thus, one's children remain children even long after they have grown up. A psychologist, by way of contrast, would probably favor the chronological sense of "childhood" and be interested in dividing childhood into various stages. If my primary concern were the psychological status of children, it would be a mistake to lump, say, toddlers and adolescents together; but since my primary concern is the moral status of children, such a lumping-together is innocuous.

This book is divided into two parts.

In Part One, I discuss the evolution of the concept of childhood over the centuries. At one time, as I have mentioned, the treatment of children was abominable. Their status took a turn for the better in the 1700s. By the twentieth century, childhood had entered what was, historically speaking, a Golden Age, an age that arguably reached its zenith in the 1950s. Since then, the status of children has fallen into decline. We seem to be witnessing a return to the concept of childhood that was held in the Middle Ages—we seem to be witnessing, that is, the end of "childhood." I end Part One by asking whether it would be possible for us to reverse this trend and forestall the demise of childhood. My conclusions on this topic are not optimistic.

In Part Two, I discuss the ethical issues involved in parenting. More precisely, I describe two rival models of parenting: the ownership model, according to which children are property of their parents; and the stewardship model, according to which parents should act not as if they *own* their children and can do with them as they please, but as if they are acting as stewards on behalf of their children and therefore must do their best to look out for the interests of their children, even though doing so might require sacrifices on the parents' part. I offer reasons for thinking that the stewardship model is morally preferable to the ownership model.

Also in Part Two, I describe the goals of steward-parents and give reasons for thinking that if we accepted the stewardship model of parenting and wished to redesign the family from scratch, our "ideal family"—the type we should strive for—would be rather different from many current American families. I end Part Two by taking up what turns out to be a rather puzzling question: Why have children at all?

PART ONE

CHILDHOOD: THE EVOLUTION OF A CONCEPT

CHAPTER 1

THE USES OF CHILDREN

If we are to understand the concept of childhood, it is useful to examine the history of that concept to see how it has evolved over the centuries. Any such examination very quickly makes one thing clear: Seen from children's point of view, the history of childhood has been a prolonged ice age, broken only by one warm spell, which began around 1700. I will spend a significant portion of this book arguing that this warm spell reached its climax in the 1950s and is drawing to a close even as I write.

In this and the subsequent chapter I will document some of the uses to which children have been put over the centuries. For a use to merit mention in what follows, the use in question must have been one that, when and where it took place, was a generally accepted use of children. If the law forbade a use, the use will not be mentioned unless a case can be made that the law was not enforced or the penalties were inconsequential.

I will also center my discussion on the uses to which children have been put in Europe and America. My motive in doing so is to demonstrate that the abuses of children I am about to describe cannot be attributed to the existence of a "culture gap," as might be the case if I talked about how children were raised in, say, Central Africa or in Pakistan. To the contrary, the children I am about to describe were in many cases systematically abused by those same societies that produced what we now take to be some of the highest achievements of civilization.

Let us, then, take a look at how ingenious people have been in their answers to the question, What can one do with a child?

Exotic Uses of Children

Let us begin our discussion by examining some of the more unusual uses to which children have been and are being put.

Children's lives have been sacrificed so that adults could accomplish certain goals. Child sacrifice has been practiced by many peoples, including the Irish Celts, the Gauls, the Scandinavians, the Egyptians, the Phoenicians, the Moabites, the Ammonites, and the Israelites.[1] Some sacrifices were meant to ensure victory in battle, and others were meant to win the approval of the gods.

Children have been used to win contests. The Millar Stork Derby was the brainchild of Charlie Millar, who specified in his will that the Toronto mother who, in the ten years following his death, gave birth to the most children would win the bulk of his estate. (The will contained a variety of "practical jokes," e.g., giving brewery stock to a temperance advocate.) Mr. Millar died in 1926; by 1934, there were several women in the baby-making race.[2]

Children have been used for business purposes. In England of days gone by, arranged marriages not only took place, but sometimes involved children who were quite young at the time the marriage contract was entered into. Thus, in England in 1563, a marriage took place between a boy age six and a girl age four or five; because the girl was so young, she could not properly repeat words after the priest. A year later, a boy age three married a girl age two.[3]

In the cases just mentioned, the exact parental motives are not known. It seems quite unlikely, though, that the interests of the children were the primary concern. What advantage can there be to a child to have a mate picked out at age two? More likely the parents had their own interests in mind in arranging the marriages. If they were rich, they might have been concerned with the problem of preservation and transmission of their estates; and if they were merchants, they might have been interested in creating family ties so as to advance their business interests.

In another case of an arranged marriage, a fifteenth-century Englishman, in order to secure financing to purchase an estate, sold his son's marriage to a London merchant; the father went on to break his end of the bargain.

In yet another case, a father bemoaned the sale of his daughter in marriage; his sadness stemmed not from the fact that she had been sold, but from the fact that he didn't get a very good price for her. This same father, as it turns out, had himself been sold as a child, not in marriage, but as a ward of the king.[4] By way of explanation, there was a time when acting as guardian for an orphaned child could be a profitable business undertaking, since you had control over the child's inheritance while he grew up.[5] Adults treated guardianships as business dealings and were known to sell or gamble away their wards to others who wished to profit from them.[6]

Children have been used as props in begging. If you are going to beg, it helps to have children along, since people will be more likely to take pity on you. If your child is blind or lame, so much the better. And if your child is not blind? Steps can be taken....

Along these lines, one Anne Martin, in England in 1761, was sentenced to two years in prison for putting out the eyes of children so that they would be more effective props for begging. Her mistake, it would appear, was in blinding children who weren't her own. Had she blinded her own children, it is likely that no crime would have been committed: Parents—it was felt at that time—could do as they pleased with their children.[7]

Ancient Romans also raised and maimed abandoned children for use as props in begging.[8]

Children have been posted as "bond." There have been cases in which parents being held hostage have offered their children as substitute hostages: The parents would go free (presumably to raise ransom) while their children took their place in captivity. The hostage-taker who accepted the substitution presumably did so on the assumption that the parent valued the child.

In some cases this assumption proved to be false. One

father, for instance, told the person holding his son that he cared little if the hostage-taker hanged his son, since "he had the anvils and hammers with which to forge still better sons." Another father, having gained his own freedom by exchanging his sons, promptly broke the bargain that had been struck, and his sons were thrown in jail.[9]

Children have been used as surrogates for punishment. In some cases, children have been recipients of parental punishment—and in saying this I am referring not to cases in which children received punishment *from* their parents, but to cases in which children received punishment *in place of* their parents. Thus, when the husband of a daughter of Henry I put out the eyes of the son of one of the king's vassals, the king allowed the father of the blinded son to put out the eyes of the blinder's daughter—that is, the king's own granddaughter.[10] This punishment had its advantages. For one thing, it let the blinder know exactly what it was like to have a child blinded. Furthermore, if the parent was a loving parent, it would conceivably have been an even worse punishment than being blinded oneself. The problem, of course, is that there was no guarantee that the parent was a loving parent; and if he was not, the suffering inflicted on his child might affect him little. Furthermore, we can raise obvious questions about the justice of any form of punishment that involves an innocent person.

Children have also been used as surrogates for the punishment of other children. The most famous example of this is the use of whipping boys. In England, it was thought improper to whip a prince, even though his behavior merited flogging. Instead, another boy was given the prince's punishment. This other boy was also raised and educated with the prince; that way, the prince presumably felt the whipping boy's pain more than would have been the case if the whipping boy had been a complete stranger.

Children have been used for sexual purposes. There are and have always been adults who are sexually attracted to children. Many cultures do not allow them to act on their attraction. Other cultures allow them to act, but have rules, written or unwritten, on the manner in which their attraction can be expressed. A culture might, for example, allow consensual sex between adults and minors. (Such a culture would not share our culture's ideas about statutory rape. To the contrary, it would treat a seven-year-old girl's "consent" to have sex with a man as being no less genuine than the consent of a twenty-seven-year-old woman.) Or a culture might be indifferent to the issue of consent and take the view that an adult has a right to have sexual relations with any child; if the child does not want the adult's attentions, so much the worse for the child. And finally, a culture might forbid sex with some children but not others. Such a society would partition children into two classes: those subject to the sexual attentions of adults—perhaps for a price, paid to the child's "owner"—and those not subject to such attentions.

Looking at cultures both past and present, we find that their views on the use of children for sexual purposes can be quite complex. In ancient Rome, for example, we find adults making use of child prostitutes, with boy brothels being commonplace. We find children sold into concubinage. We also find that abandoned children were sometimes raised and placed into brothels by their "rescuers." Thus, we read, with some surprise, Saint Justin Martyr's argument against abandoning infants: His concern is not for the child who might die from being exposed or who might be forced into prostitution, but for the adult who might accidentally have sex with his own son or daughter when, years after abandoning him or her, he unwittingly pays for his or her services in a brothel.[11]

In ancient Rome, though, it wasn't just child prostitutes who were open to the sexual advances of adults. Slave children were also regarded as fair game. Indeed, problems arose when adults came across groups of naked children. They wanted to satisfy their lust, but not with a freeborn child. It has been suggested that one reason freeborn children were in the habit of wearing necklaces with golden balls is so that even if their clothes were off, adults would recognize them as freeborn and not use them sexually.[12]

According to Suetonius (who might or might not be a trustworthy source), Emperor Tiberius was particularly creative in his sexual use of children: He placed children—he called them his minnows—in his bath, where their job was to swim between his legs to lick and nibble him. He also kept children who had not been weaned to perform fellatio.[13]

Some Romans were fond of intercourse with castrated boys. To keep up with the demand for such boys, infants were castrated to prepare them for their future careers. Here is the castration process, described by Paulus Aegineta:

> Since we are sometimes compelled against our will by persons of high rank to perform the operation...by compression [it] is thus performed; children, still of a tender age, are placed in a vessel of hot water, and then when the parts are softened in the bath, the testicles are to be squeezed with the fingers until they disappear.[14]

The Romans were not alone among the ancients in using children for sexual purposes. The Greeks apparently were opposed not to the sexual use of children by adults, but to the *paid* sexual use of children. And even the Jews distinguished between sexual relations with children of different ages. The penalty for sodomy with a child over nine was death by stoning, whereas copulation with children under nine was punished only by whipping.[15]

And, of course, in modern times children are still used for sexual purposes. In the industrialized world, it is for the most part illegal to have sex with children, but this does not mean that they cannot be used for sexual purposes. A look at movies, television, and advertising reveals that in our society, many adults see nothing at all wrong with depicting a child as an object of adults' (unfulfillable) sexual desires; and many adults see nothing wrong with exploiting the sexuality of children to sell products. I will have more to say on this in Chapter 2.

In much of the developing world, the use of children for sexual purposes is widely accepted. Many of Bangkok's prostitutes are young girls. Likewise many of the prostitutes in Indian brothels are Nepali girls who were "sold" (for a few dollars) by their parents to brokers who told the parents that the children would get married or get good jobs. Instead the girls ended up in brothels, where their Mongolian features are valued. And because they have virtually no bargaining power, they can be forced to engage in higher-risk sexual acts than adults would consent to. In 1991, the average age of purchased Nepali girls was ten.[16]

In Europe the use of children for sexual purposes became a hot topic in 1996 when the normally circumspect Queen Silvia of Sweden had the audacity to suggest that Sweden's liberal child pornography laws were in need of change.[17] Although it was not, at the time, legal to publish or distribute child pornography in Sweden, it was perfectly legal to own it. This, according to Swedish police, made Sweden a haven for pedophiles.

Those who were outraged by Queen Silvia's suggestion offered various arguments against a ban on the ownership of child pornography. They argued, for instance, that such a ban would infringe on the personal liberties of adults. They also argued that inasmuch as the children featured in child pornography were not Swedish children, the production of such pornography involved "no great crime."

Queen Silvia's proposal came at a particularly awkward time, the month before Sweden was to play host for a world congress on the sexual exploitation of children.

In Japan the use of children for sexual purposes appears to be an accepted practice.[18] In Tokyo there are no laws against having sex with children over twelve, and prostitution isn't a criminal activity as long as a pimp isn't involved. As a result many Japanese men not only have sex with children, they pay the children for the privilege. Prostitution by Japanese schoolchildren has reached what Japanese police are calling "epidemic" proportions.

While in many parts of the world children are driven to prostitution to escape poverty, this is not true in Japan. To the contrary, Japanese children become prostitutes so that they can afford expensive things, like $500 purses and $350 wallets.

How do Japanese parents react to this state of affairs? Calls to outlaw sex with children have been protested by teachers' unions and mothers' groups. They argue that if sex with children were outlawed, children would have to testify against their patrons and would thus be shamed.

Children have been used for medical purposes. Children have long been thought to possess valuable medicinal properties. In medieval times, for example, it was thought that ringworm could be treated by washing one's scalp in the urine of a boy.[19] This particular medical use of children caused no harm to the children involved: Most boys, one might imagine, would be rather amused at this use of their urine.

Other medical uses of children, though, were not so benign. In the past, so-called "gelders" persuaded parents to let them castrate their boys. The gelders, it is thought, sought the testicles for magico-medical purposes. And as late as 1900 there were people who thought that venereal disease could be cured by having sex with a child.[20]

Children played a role in discovering a vaccine for smallpox and in subsequent efforts to eradicate the disease. In 1796, Edward Jenner did his famous experiment showing that vaccination with cowpox virus could make people immune to smallpox. His guinea pig in the experiment was James Phipps, a healthy eight-year-old. He inoculated Phipps with material from cowpox lesions, and then, after waiting six weeks, inoculated him with potentially deadly material from smallpox lesions. The child did not get sick. Jenner had proved his point.

Once the world came to accept that exposure to cowpox could prevent smallpox, a new problem arose. In the New World smallpox was rampant, and the king of Spain wished to protect his subjects. The question: How to get the cowpox vaccine across the sea? The answer: Use children as "hosts" for the vaccine. More precisely, twenty-two orphans were taken on board a ship bound for the New World and sequentially exposed to cowpox. At any given moment, one of the children would have the disease and could therefore be used as a source of cowpox-contaminated material.[21]

One might think that the use of children for medical purposes was a thing of the past, but this is hardly the case. Indeed, progress in medicine has meant, if anything, an increased demand for the body parts of children.

There is, for example, an ongoing debate over research involving tissue from aborted fetuses. Defenders of this research point out that such use of "children" can be justified inasmuch as the children in question were dead when the tissue was taken. The children are therefore not harmed by the taking, and others might be benefited. Surely, it is argued, this is a better use of the fetal tissue than the alternative, which is to discard the tissue in question, along with the rest of the fetus.

The opponents of such research argue that if this use of fetuses is allowed, researchers will have an incentive to cause fetuses to be brought into existence for research purposes. One can imagine, for example, a situation in which scientists pay women (perhaps women with special genetic characteristics) to get pregnant and then to abort so tissue can be harvested from the fetuses they produce.

To some extent, our views on the acceptability of harvesting fetal tissue will depend upon our views on whether or not fetuses are persons. Rather than take up this issue, I will turn my attention to cases in which "body parts" are harvested, not from aborted fetuses, but from children who have successfully left the womb. These children are clearly persons, and yet this does not stop adults from using them for medical purposes.

One such case involved Marissa Ayala.[22] When Marissa, the daughter of Abe and Mary Ayala, was fourteen months old, she became a bone marrow donor: She was anesthetized, and a surgeon put a needle into her hip and removed a cup of bone marrow.

The recipient of Marissa's donation (although it is a bit of a misnomer to refer to it as a "donation," since it was an involuntary act on the part of Marissa—how, after all, could a fourteen-month-old meaningfully consent to an operation?) was Marissa's nineteen-year-old sister Anissa, who had chronic myelogenous leukemia. What makes the case of Marissa Ayala of interest to us here is not so much the age at which she acted as donor as the fact that *she was brought into existence so that she could act as donor.* The Ayala parents had bone marrow that was incompatible with that of Anissa, and although they searched far and wide for a compatible donor for Anissa, they found none. They decided to make a baby who could serve as a marrow donor.

For the Ayalas to make a baby was no small undertaking: Mr. Ayala had had a vasectomy, and Mrs. Ayala, at age 43, was almost past childbearing age. Their attempt proved successful, though, and Marissa was born in 1990.

There was no guarantee that Marissa would be a suitable donor for Anissa: Geneticists put the odds at one in four. The Ayalas' luck held, though, and Marissa was able to play the role for which she had been created.

In another similar case, Lea Ann and Brad Curry gave birth to a daughter who had Fanconi's anemia.[23] In order to avoid a shortened life of severe anemia and possible mental retardation, she needed a transplant of stem cells. The Currys didn't even bother to look for a donor; instead, they decided to create one. Mrs. Curry got pregnant, but miscarried. She got pregnant again and had a healthy baby girl, but she proved to be unsuitable as a donor. She got pregnant again, and this time had a baby girl who was both healthy and a good match. Doctors collected stem cells from her umbilical cord and later transplanted them into the sick sister, who benefited from them.

The medical use of children, then, is hardly a thing of the past. Indeed, it looks to be a growth industry, and one that, as it grows, will leave in its wake numerous ethical dilemmas.

To be sure, the above list makes it clear that adults have been ingenious—not to mention heartless—in the uses to which they have put children. And the thing to keep in mind when thinking about the uses mentioned is that, *in the cultures in question, the listed uses of children were generally accepted.* History teaches us that it is not only possible for a "civilized" culture to neglect the interests of its children, but that cultures that refuse to exploit children are the exception.

The Labor of Children

The uses described above are admittedly exotic. Although in the history of man *some* children have been used as whipping boys, *some* children have been castrated and put into brothels, and *some* children have been used for body parts, it is safe to say that most children have not suffered these fates. In the remainder of this chapter I will turn away from the exotic and instead consider a use to which most children in the history of mankind *have* been put—namely, as laborers.

I will focus my discussion of child labor on the lives of four particular children: Charles Dickens, Sarah Gooder, Robert Blincoe, and David Porter. The first of these children is well-known to all; the other three are not. The reason for their obscurity is not that they suffered less than Dickens, but arguably because they suffered more. Young Charles Dickens was lucky enough to have been freed from his juvenile labors and sent to school; the other three children—as far as we know—were not. Had Dickens not been freed, he probably would not have gone on to become a famous writer, but would have died in obscurity, as did Gooder, Blincoe, and Porter.

A Dickensian Childhood

Charles Dickens, perhaps, is most responsible for drawing the attention of the upper classes of nineteenth-century England to the problem of child labor. Many of his novels tell touching tales of the children of London; they show that childhood can be a golden time, or a living hell. Dickens was particularly well-suited to write about the hardships of childhood, inasmuch as he himself had suffered as a child. He in fact suffered many of the same hardships as his fictional character David Copperfield.[24]

Dickens's father, John Dickens, worked for the Navy Pay Office. This job let him live a comfortable life. He kept servants, staged entertainments, and kept up his position in the community. In the end, though, he was too generous with his money: He lived beyond his means and fell into debt.

To deal with the burden of debt, John Dickens undertook desperate measures. For example, he borrowed £200, to be paid back at the usurious rate of £26 per year for life. He also extended himself financially to start a school that drew no students at all. Failure of this school meant the financial failure of the family.

In the aftermath of this failure, Dickens's father was sent to debtor's prison. Charles was sent off to live with a friend of the family and work at Warren's Blacking, a shoe-blacking business; the rest of his family went to live in prison with his father. Charles was barely twelve. For children to be sent to work at age seven or eight was not, at that time, unusual.

Dickens described Warren's as "a crazy, tumble-down old house, abutting…on the river, and literally overrun with rats."[25] Dickens's job was to cover and label pots of paste-blacking. Two or three other boys worked with him and thereby gained literary immortality. (One was Bob Fagin, whose name, if not personality, later appeared in *Oliver Twist*.) For his work, Dickens was paid six or seven shillings a week, barely enough to buy food for himself—which he was forced to do because of his parents' financial misfortunes. Later in life Dickens detailed the difficulties he had trying to make his pay last a week: He described the temptations of the pastry shop, where he often spent the money that he should have kept for dinner, and told how, when he had no money at all, he would go to the Covent-garden market and stare at the pineapples.

Although Dickens apparently had a happy childhood before being sent to Warren's, he was utterly miserable during the year he spent there. Dickens tells it best:

> No words can express the secret agony of my soul as I sunk into this companionship [with the other boys at Warren's]; compared these every day associates with those of my happier childhood; and felt my early hopes of growing up to be a learned and distinguished man, crushed in my breast. The deep remembrance of the sense I had of being utterly neglected and hopeless; of the shame I felt in my position; of the misery it was to my young heart to believe that, day by

day, what I had learned, and thought, and delighted in, and raised my fancy and my emulation up by, was passing away from me, never to be brought back any more; cannot be written. My whole nature was so penetrated with the grief and humiliation of such considerations, that even now, famous and caressed and happy, I often forget in my dreams that I have a dear wife and children; even that I am a man; and wander desolately back to that time of my life.[26]

Throughout the rest of his life, Dickens kept his childhood suffering a secret. At his death, only two people had been told, his wife and his biographer.

Dickens's father and mother had different feelings about young Charles being put to work. His father was apparently ashamed to have done this to his son. It was he who ultimately rescued Dickens and sent him off to school. Dickens's mother, however, saw no reason why he should not continue to work for a living even after John Dickens's situation had improved.

After being rescued from life as a child laborer, it took some time for Dickens to become a "child" again. In his semi-autobiographical *David Copperfield*, Dickens tells us that he had become

in the Murdstone and Grinby time, however short or long it may have been, so unused to the sports and games of boys, that I knew I was awkward and inexperienced in the commonest things belonging to them. Whatever I had learnt, had so slipped away from me in the sordid cares of my life from day to night, that now, when I was examined about what I knew, I knew nothing, and was put into the lowest form of the school.[27]

Dickens's suffering was far less than that of other children of his time. Many of these children lacked parents, a job, and a place to live; Dickens had all three. All things considered, Dickens wasn't bad off for a "deserted" child. At any rate he was much better off than the three other "deserted" children we shall now consider.

Sarah Gooder, Mine Child

Sarah Gooder worked in a mine. She was a trapper—her job was to open and close the door that controlled the mine's ventilation system. Here, in her own words, is what we know of her: "I'm a trapper in the Gauber Pit, I have to trap without a light, and I'm scared. I go at four and sometimes half-past three in the morning and come out at five and half past. I never go to sleep. Sometimes I sing when I've light, but not in the dark: I dare not sing then."[28] It is a fragmentary piece of data, to be sure, but one that conjures up a pitiable image, particularly when we keep in mind that Sarah was only eight years old when she uttered these words.

English coal mines were at a distance from the urban centers, so there was little reason for most adults to encounter the children who worked in mines. Those who did were often shocked by the "savage rudeness" of mine children. One English gentleman, visiting a coal mine in 1813, came upon a girl driving a horse that was drawing a line of baskets. The girl, he tells us, was

> covered with filth, debased and profligate, and uttering some low obscenity as she passed by us. We were frequently interrupted in our march by the horses proceeding in this manner…and always driven by girls, all of the same description ragged and beastly in their appearance, and with a shameless indecency in their behavior which, awe-struck as one was by the gloom and loneliness around one, had something quite frightful in it, and gave the place the character of hell.[29]

Mining could not have been a pleasant occupation for adults, and for children it must indeed have been a hellish existence. Children routinely stayed underground for twelve hours a day. Girls five or six might be assigned a physically undemanding job like that of trapper.[30] Boys and older girls might be assigned to fill trucks with coal, or they might drag the trucks from the coalface to the foot of the shaft.[31] To drag the trucks in question, they were "chained, belted and harnessed like dogs in a go-cart."[32]

They spent their days more than half naked, black with coal and soaking wet from the water in the mines; and since their loads were so heavy and the passages through which they moved were so low (often being no higher than 20 to 30 inches) they might have to crawl on their hands and knees to move them. These human mules might cover four to six miles each working day. And when they got their loads to the foot of the shaft, the loads, which could be quite heavy, might be transferred to the backs of girls to be transported to the surface.[33]

The mine children were not only uneducated, they were beneficiaries of none of the civilizing influences of society. All they knew was the mine and the other miners, and as a result had no idea that there was anything wrong with obscene language—or obscene behavior, for that matter.

Why children were used in mines is obvious: They were relatively powerless to resist the demands of mine bosses, and they were cheap. They were also desirable as employees inasmuch as their short stature allowed them to go places that adults could go only with great difficulty. The real question, then, is not why children were used in mines, but who allowed children to be used in mines? In particular, what parent in his right mind would let his child work under the conditions described above?

In some cases, being a mine child was a hereditary condition: If your parents had spent their childhoods in the mine, it was likely that you would too.[34] Miner-parents allowed their children to go down into the mine in part because they needed their assistance. This was particularly true of mothers whose health had been ruined by returning to the mines too soon after childbirth. Parents also needed the wages their children earned. And the prevailing view of the parents seems to have been that working in the mine did not hurt children: It hadn't hurt the parents, after all. One can picture, then, an innocent child like Sarah Gooder growing up to become the unfeeling parent who sees nothing wrong with sending her own innocent child into the mines.

Workhouses were also a source of mine children. Unlike those children whose parents were miners, children from the work-houses had no one to look out for their interests. For this reason, these children were assigned the least desirable jobs. And if a workhouse child refused to do the assigned task, he would be taken to magistrates and thereupon committed to prison.[35]

Not long after the first investigations of mine conditions, English authorities took steps to remedy the situation: They pro-hibited the employment of *children under ten* in mines.[36]

Robert Blincoe, Factory Child

Robert Blincoe was a factory child.[37] He began work in a mill at age seven. Although British law prohibited children from work-ing more than twelve hours a day, Blincoe worked fourteen-hour days (not counting overtime) and worked these hours six days a week. After four years, he was moved to another mill where work-ing conditions were even worse. Children were underfed and not given utensils to eat with. They tried to steal food from the pigs and thought nothing of eating the potato parings thrown on the dunghill. Children were not given any soap; instead they were given meal to clean themselves with. Rather than using it for its intended purpose, they quite understandably chose to eat it.

Measures were taken to educate factory children: On Sun-day they received an hour or two of lessons. The problem is that the children were exhausted by the time Sunday came around, and the teachers were not necessarily competent. More commonly, children were "educated" by beatings. During the ten years that Robert Blincoe was in the mill, his body was never free of the cuts and bruises inflicted by the beatings he received.

In the end the children paid a terrible price for their time spent in the factories. Lord Shaftesbury, a leader in trying to im-prove conditions in their lives, describes factory children in the following terms: "They seemed to me, such were their crooked shapes, like a mass of crooked alphabets."[38] And some children paid the ultimate price for their time spent in the factories: They died there. Because of the harsh conditions, disease was common among factory children. Enough children died in the mill that employed Robert Blincoe that the owner thought it advisable to split the burials between two cemeteries, so as not to become conspicuous.[39]

Englishmen of the time showed their customary sensitivity to the needs of children: In 1819 they passed a law to prohibit *children under nine* from working in cotton mills or factories.[40]

Karl Marx argued that industrialization was a big factor in the rise of child labor. In particular, he argued that the development of machinery allowed work to be done by people "of slight muscular strength, and those whose bodily development is incomplete, but whose limbs are all the more supple. The labour of women and children was, therefore, the first thing sought for by capitalists who used machinery." As a result, "Compulsory work for the capitalist usurped the place...of the children's play."[41]

Despite what Marx tells us, it would be a mistake to assume, as many people do, that the advent of child labor coincided with the dawn of industrialization. Not only was child labor common before the industrial revolution, but a case can be made that many of these "nonindustrialized" children had it every bit as bad as those children who worked in factories.

Thus, lace-making, a cottage industry, employed children as young as three to handle bobbins. Older girls were employed to make lace by hand. In one lace-making shop, seventeen girl employees shared three beds in a garret, worked from four or five in the morning until eleven or twelve o'clock at night, and sometimes worked seven days a week. Their treatment came to light only when five of them had died from overwork and ill-use.[42]

Furthermore, although industrialization initially exploited the labor of children, it was industrialization that later made childhood, in the modern sense of the word, possible: Ultimately, it was industrialization that freed children from their labors. Improved machinery did not need child attendants. Improved machinery meant greater productivity, and greater productivity meant that society could afford to let its children spend childhood at school and at play instead of having to harness the labor of its children at the earliest possible moment. This argument will be developed in a subsequent chapter.

David Porter, Climbing Boy

For one particularly horrible use of children, let us turn to the life of David Porter. "It was my lot," wrote Porter, "to be bred a chimney-sweepers [sic] boy, and to labour under the disadvantages common to the trade."[43] There were thousands of apprentice chimney sweepers, also known as climbing boys, both during Dickens's youth and the centuries before. What makes Porter special is that he not only escaped many of the calamities that could and often did befall climbing boys, but went on to become a leader in the movement—sometimes referred to as the "sooty cause"—to abolish the use of climbing boys.[44] In 1801 he wrote a history of chimney sweeping, titled "Considerations on the present state of chimney sweepers." From his commentary, together with those written by gentlemen who had taken up the sooty cause, we can piece together what the life of the climbing boy must have been like.

In the England of two hundred years ago, a room without a fireplace was, in winter, an uninhabitable room; and of course kitchens needed a fireplace not only for warmth but for cooking. This meant that houses had lots of chimneys; and because of the danger of chimney fires, the chimneys in question had to be cleaned regularly.

The use of climbing boys to clean chimneys appears to have been primarily an English custom[45] and a relatively modern one at that. The demand for climbing boys surged after the great fire of London in 1666; when houses were rebuilt in the aftermath of the fire, their chimneys were made with smaller internal dimensions, in part to gain room within houses.[46] The smaller dimensions rendered some traditional chimney-cleaning techniques unusable. These same small dimensions, however, were ideally suited for the use of climbing boys and, occasionally, climbing girls.[47]

How did a climbing boy clean a chimney? One might think that a boy would stand on the roof and lower a brush, as is now done, but one would be mistaken. Or one might think, as absurd as it sounds, that boys would be lowered into chimneys by rope, but one would again be mistaken. The awful truth is this: To clean a chimney, a climbing boy would enter the fireplace and climb up the inside of the chimney without benefit of ropes or ladders. To hold himself in place, the climbing boy would put the bottoms of his feet against one surface of the chimney and his knees against the opposite surface.[48] This would (usually) "lock" him into place and prevent him from slipping down the chimney. He would work his way up the chimney, with one arm down at his side and the other above his head, brushing the chimney above him as he went. The soot he dislodged would fall down, past his head, past his body, and ultimately into the fireplace below. The soot was put in bags and sold to farmers who used it as fertilizer.[49] By one estimate, six hundred thousand bushels of soot were gathered in London each year.[50]

To put the task of the climbing boys into true (and astonishing) perspective, one needs to consider the interior dimensions of the chimneys the boys were climbing. The *ordinary* chimney had internal dimensions of only nine by fourteen inches[51] (i.e., about the size of a sheet of legal paper), and some were even smaller, with seven-by-seven inches (i.e., about the size of a sheet of legal paper folded in half!) being the smallest chimney that one chimney sweeper said he would send a boy up.[52] In many occupations, the small size of boys was a disadvantage; in chimney sweeping, their small size was a real advantage.

Such climbing, one might think, would require protective clothing; and indeed the boys wore caps that they could pull down over their eyes and mouths. This, however, was the extent of the protective clothing. Clothing, after all, made the job of the climbing boy more difficult in that it increased his dimensions and thus made it more likely that a chimney would be impassable; notice, too, that clothing could snag on the chimney lining and cause a boy to get stuck mid-chimney. Keeping these things in mind, master chimney sweepers often made their boys climb chimneys naked, or nearly so.[53]

Climbing chimneys was physically uncomfortable: "The children are subject to sores, and bruises, and wounds and burns on their thighs, knees, and elbows; and...it will require many months before the extremities of the elbows and knees become sufficiently hard to resist the excoriations to which they are at first subject."[54] One other source of physical discomfort was the temperature of the chimney. Most of the climbing boys' work was done in the early morning, when the fires of the night before had died down. If a boy caught the chimney at just the right moment, he would be able to climb a chimney that was comfortably warm. The problem is that if he climbed too long after that "just-right" moment, he climbed a chimney that was (in winter, before the sun had risen) freezing cold. (Imagine your naked back pressed against soot-covered, ice-cold brick.) And if he climbed too soon before that "just-right" moment, he climbed a chimney that was uncomfortably warm or even dangerously hot.

Because of the frightening and disagreeable nature of the work, climbing boys typically did not want to climb. Master chimney sweepers used various forms of persuasion to get boys to go up, including beating them, pinching their feet as they were climbing,[55] poking their feet with pins, or even holding lighted straw under their feet.[56]

When a climbing boy was in a chimney, a number of things could go wrong. A chimney might collapse, either falling in on a child, or falling to the street, taking the child with it.[57] Or a climbing boy might get stuck in a chimney. This might happen if his clothing got caught on the chimney; if he slipped, so that his knees, instead of being on the chimney wall, ended up by his chin; or if so much soot accumulated in a horizontal section of a chimney that it became impassable.

Getting stuck was no doubt an unpleasant experience, but getting freed could be less pleasant still:

a chimney-sweeper, a diminutive child, about ten years of age, was sent up a chimney at the Talbot Inn, at nine o'clock in the morning, and for the purpose of lessening his size to suit the dimensions of the flue, he was stripped entirely naked. Having remained up the chimney for a very long time, it was thought that he was continuing there unnecessarily, and from stubbornness, and another lad was sent up to him; but he failed in bringing him down. After a lapse of some hours, a cord was attached to the child's legs, and several vain attempts were made to drag him down by force. In this experiment the cord was broken, and a stronger one was substituted, with no better success. The humane party then obtained a large quantity of brimstone matches—it is said three pennyworth, which were ignited, and held burning up the flue. A ladder was next procured, reaching to the top of the chimney, from whence several buckets of water were poured down upon the poor little prisoner; and a pole was thrust down to discover his position, with such force, that several lumps were afterwards found upon the poor child's head.

Finally, at ten o'clock that night, the chimney was opened and the child was released. The accident was subsequently blamed on the child, who had gone up the chimney with both arms down, rather than with one up and one down.[58]

If a child got stuck badly enough, or if falling soot accumulated around his head, he could suffocate.[59] Even David Porter, who as an adult had taken up chimney construction with climbing boys in mind, admitted that on two instances, boys had suffocated in chimneys of his construction.[60]

The dangers of climbing hot chimneys are obvious, but nevertheless children were forced to climb them, often with disastrous consequences:

A LITTLE BOY had ascended a chimney while the fire was not removed from the grate below, but merely covered over with a *gridle* [i.e., a sort of iron plate], which it was supposed would be a sufficient protection to the poor child.

The soot fell down in great quantities on the gridle, and in a little time, it ignited. In spite of every effort to prevent it, it communicated to the soot in the chimney, *which was soon in one mass of burning flames, while the poor child was pent up in the middle of it*. After a considerable time he succeeded in getting down, but when he did so, he was in a most frightful condition, *the flesh being literally roasted on his bones*, though he was still living. He was speedily conveyed to the hospital, where he remained for some time in a state of excruciating suffering—*and there died!*[61] [Italics in the original.]

Or, in another case, Philip Corbett, a chimney sweeper,

arrived at Mr. Barron's about seven o'clock, and the kitchen fire having been lighted before that hour, Corbett said it would not be necessary to put out the fire for the purpose of sweeping the chimney, as he would cover it with slack [i.e., ashes], which would prevent any injury to the boy. Having covered the fire with slack, he desired the boy to ascend the chimney, and commence operations; the boy immediately obeyed, but before he proceeded many yards, cried out that the chimney was too hot to advance farther. The master desired him to 'rattle away,' as the chimney was cool enough; the poor child continued to ascend with the greatest pain and difficulty, owing to the heat of the chimney, and the smoke issuing from the fire. Corbett then placed some straw over the fire, to keep, it is supposed, the smoke from ascending, when, unfortunately, the straw ignited, and a tremendous blaze rushed up the chimney; the little sufferer, however, succeeded in reaching the top of the chimney, and thence the roof of the house…. The appearance of the boy's body was truly distressing, having been dreadfully scorched and burned. The boy was able to speak at the time, and he said in the mildest and most affecting accent, 'O, master! what made you send me up there?'[62]

The owner of the house sent for a doctor, but before the doctor came, the chimney sweeper took the boy away. It was only that evening—twelve hours after the incident—that he sought medical help for the child, who died shortly thereafter. In this case the law did not turn a blind eye and declare the whole thing an unfortunate accident, as was generally the case, but sentenced the master sweeper to seven years' transportation.[63]

If climbing hot chimneys was dangerous, climbing burning chimneys was positively foolhardy, but children were nevertheless forced to do it. How could a child put out a chimney fire by climbing up a chimney? In the event of a chimney fire,

> [a] boy is sent up [a] chimney to sweep down the lighted soot: he is sent up blind-folded...so that he may go head, hand, and all into the middle of the soot which is on fire. Having reached it, how is he to get rid of it?... [H]e is to jump about in [the] flue like a harlequin....[64]

A human fire extinguisher, as it were.

If the reader concludes that such attempts could be hazardous to the child in question, the reader is correct. Robert Dowland, a climbing boy, was sent up a burning chimney by his master. His master subsequently

> heard him cry out he was hung to a nail; heard him crying and sobbing very much. It was said, "He will not come down;" the master said, with an oath, "Let him stop;" and at last...the flue was broken open; and the bricklayer who broke it open states "that the part of the flue where the boy was, was exceedingly hot through the stoppage, so that the skin was so scorched as to slip up with the witness's hand when he attempted to get him out; and the witness let him go, lest he should hurt him if he was alive." Sensation indeed did remain for a few minutes; but, fortunately for this infant sufferer, the hand of death speedily relieved him from his misery.[65]

In purely economic terms, it is understandable why the master sweeper would want to send a boy up a hot chimney: Clean it today and you get paid today; wait till it's cool, and you get paid tomorrow—unless one of your competitors (who is not reluctant to send his boys up hot chimneys) gets there before you. And in the case of burning chimneys, the economic motivation is likewise clear: A chimney fire puts the house in jeopardy. One can imagine that the master sweeper could command a high price for his attempts to put out a chimney fire.

Besides the physical hazards of climbing chimneys, there were a number of medical hazards as well. Climbing boys were susceptible to bone deformations, inasmuch as they were young and their nutrition was typically inadequate:

> [T]he deformity of the spine, legs, arms, &c., of these boys, proceeds generally, if not wholly, from the circumstance of their being obliged to ascend chimneys at an age when their bones are in a soft and growing state; but likewise, by their being compelled to carry bags of soot and cloths, the weight of which sometimes exceeds 20 or 30 pounds, not including the soot, the burthen of which they also occasionally bear for a great length of distance and time; the knees and ancle joints become deformed, in the first instance, from the position they are obliged to put them in, in order to support themselves, not only while climbing up the chimney, but more particularly so whilst coming down, when they rest solely on the lower extremities, the arms being used for scraping and sweeping down the soot.[66]

By the end of a climbing boy's apprenticeship, this early abuse could have terrible consequences:

> He is now twelve years of age, a cripple on crutches, hardly three feet seven inches in stature. He began to climb chimneys *before* he was five years of age, his bones not having acquired a fit degree of strength…. In consequence of this treatment, his legs and feet resemble an S more than an L.[67] [Italics in the original.]

This last comment is reminiscent of the "crooked alphabet" simile used to describe factory children.

Besides physical deformities, climbing boys were susceptible to sooty warts, also known as chimney sweeper's cancer.[68] This condition was caused by constant exposure to soot. Porter describes sooty warts in the following terms: "It affects the scrotum first by small pimples with violent itching, which is increased by rubbing, and soon becomes an ulcer, and grows into an incurable cancer: it drains the patient of his juices, and commonly terminates in his death."[69]

Actually, it was possible to treat sooty warts, but the treatment in question involved surgical removal of affected body parts, and the operation was said to "either kill or cure."[70] Understandably, chimney sweepers were reluctant to seek medical help.[71]

In its advanced stages, the disease was truly horrible. Thus, we are presented with the description of

> a man of thirty years of age, and [who] has had this affliction upon him for five years, and it has made such ravages upon his frame, as to prevent his ever obtaining an easy position for a single moment, and he may be seen for hours in an afternoon, walking up and down the miserable court in which he lives, in perfect agony. He was urged to go into the hospital, and a ticket was offered him, but the dread of the surgeon's knife has hitherto deterred him.[72]

Even when they weren't climbing, the climbing boys' life was not pleasant. They were apprentices, and as such were in the care of the master sweeper. Since, as we have seen, small size was highly desirable in climbing boys, the master had a double economic incentive to underfeed them. The typical master also did not feel it necessary to shelter or clothe them particularly well:

> If we would see this poor apprentice as he really is, let us view him in a wintery morning, exposed to the surly blast or falling snow, trudging the streets half naked, his sores bleeding, his limbs contracted with cold, his inhuman master driving him beyond his strength, whilst the pitious tears of hunger and misery trickle down his cheek, which is, indeed, the only

means he has to vent his grief; follow him home, and view him in his gloomy cell, and there will be found misery unmasked: we shall see this poor boy in a cellar, used as a soot warehouse on one side, and his lodging room on the other; I would have said his bed room, but he has seldom any other bed than his sack [for carrying soot], or any other covering than his soot cloth: in this comfortless state he shiveringly sleeps, or rather passes over the chilly hours of night.[73]

Some of the children, rather than sleeping on an empty soot sack, had the ingenuity to sleep on a full and presumably softer one.[74] Although the occupation of the climbing boy was by its nature filthy, masters typically saw little reason to keep their boys clean. It was not unheard of for climbing boys not to wash for periods of six months.[75] Thus, the life of a climbing boy was spent gathering soot when he was at work and living in soot when he was not.

Masters also typically made little or no attempt to educate their climbing boys: "[O]ut of two hundred master chimney sweepers, there are not twenty who can write their own names; and of those who can, very few have been bred to the trade [i.e., apprenticed], but have taken to it from convenience."[76]

The years of apprenticeship may have been bleak, but what came afterwards was little better. Porter describes the predicament of the ex-apprentice in the following terms:

He has learnt a trade he can no longer work at. Nature's bounty, a blessing to all other young people, (as it fits them for their different employments, by giving bulk and strength to the animal frame) is to him, in respect to his trade, of but little advantage; none but small boys can sweep chimneys in London, or any other large places in England; he is sixteen years of age, and thrown upon his own hands and the public: according to law, all chimney-sweepers [*sic*] servitude expire [*sic*] at that age, though probably the most dangerous period of their lives. He has no friends who can help him into the world, or they would have disposed of him differently; destitute of education, he is incapable of any employment which requires more than memory; uncultivated, he is unfit for any service that requires the least address; weak and stinted in his growth by his profession, he is incapable of any employment which requires strength; he is upon the whole too old and too large to sweep chimneys, and too young and too little for any thing else but a second apprenticeship; his whole fortune is at most a few shillings saved in his apprenticeship, and which is commonly spent for joy on his releasement: this is no sooner done, than he finds the period of a miserable bondage to be the commencement of a more miserable freedom.[77]

Could he not become a journeyman, as would be possible in most trades? Porter points out that "it may be his first wish to be a journeyman; but so few masters keep journeymen, or can afford to pay their wages, that there is not employment in that capacity for more than one in three of those who have served their time to the business; and the few who do keep men seldom pay sufficient wages to buy shoes and other necessaries." He may leave the city and try his luck in the country, but Porter, speaking from his own experience, points out that "when I travelled the country as a chimney-sweeper, I have been frequently hunted from those humble roofs by the suspicious farmer, or unfriendly hostler."[78]

It is hardly surprising that many of the ex-climbing-boys, finding themselves in these dire straits, turned to a life of crime. Some found that in an unexpected way, their years as climbing boys had prepared them for one criminal specialty: gaining entry to houses by means of their chimneys and then committing burglary.[79]

When the climbing boy finally emerges from the oppression of the master sweeper, he does not find joy; to the contrary, he finds, in the words of Porter, "a wide world and a narrow prospect."[80]

In England at the time in question, for a child to become an apprentice required the consent of the child's parents and the consent of the child himself. The question we are left with, then, is this: Given the hellish nature of chimney sweeping, how could masters get anyone to agree to become climbing boys?

As far as the parents were concerned, their consent could be purchased, typically for relatively small sums.[81] Thus, children were "sold" by parents and "bought" by master chimney sweepers:

> Orphans, who are in a vagabond state, or the illegitimate children of the poorest kind of people, are said to be sold; that is, their service for seven years is disposed of for twenty or thirty shillings; being a smaller price than the value of a *terrier*: but it is presumed that the children of poor parents, who cannot find bread for a numerous family, make up by much the greater part of the number of the *climbing boys*.[82] [Italics in the original.]

Since being small was an advantage among climbing boys, tiny children and ones who were delicately formed were more valuable to the master sweepers, and they paid more for these children. Of course, the purchase had to be kept a secret, or else the magistrate who had to approve of the apprenticeship would not do so.[83]

When the parents' consent could not be purchased, there were other ways to obtain the child. In some cases children were taken to become climbing boys even though their parents protested, and in other cases children were kidnapped.[84] In England at that time the law was surprisingly silent about kidnapping. Indeed, kidnapping, we are told, was not punishable at all—unless in stealing the child you also stole his clothes, this latter act being a definite violation of the law.[85] It was also possible to obtain boys from the workhouse: "There are certain individuals of great respectability in this profession, who can go to every workhouse belonging to the parish in which they happen to reside, and say, Give me boys."[86]

What about the consent of the child? The standard technique, it would appear, was to keep the would-be apprentice in the dark about the nature of chimney sweeping until after he had agreed (before a magistrate) to become one:

> No child was ever made a Chimney-sweeper by fair means,

and not a single instance could be adduced that is free from fraud and misrepresentation. Children have an utter abhorrence of the employment. The candidate is therefore kept in perfect ignorance of the trade during the time of probation or liking, which precedes the apprenticeship; and after he is bound, the mysteries of the craft are revealed to him for the first time. This explains the readiness manifested by children to become Chimney-sweepers, when questioned by the magistrates.[87]

If the use of climbing boys was difficult to defend, it became more difficult still with the introduction of "machines" that could clean chimneys, thereby superseding climbing boys. Even before 1800 there were boy-less ways to clean chimneys,[88] and in the first decades of the 1800s even better techniques (involving "machines"—i.e., brushes with long, flexible handles) were developed.[89] Master sweepers were reluctant to use the new machines, though. Some argued that the machines wouldn't work, or would work only on some chimneys. Tests showed these fears to be unfounded,[90] but the resistance to change continued.

Why the reluctance to use machines? No doubt tradition was a factor, but there were probably other, darker motives as well. For one thing, some chimney sweepers wanted to extract the full value of the boys they had bought. Also, it was argued that "the secret of the opposition [of sweepers to machines] arises from its being so much easier to sit down and gossip with the servants while the child is doing the work."[91]

One way to understand the plight of the climbing boys is to realize that they lived in a society that viewed children as a form of property. As such, it was up to the parent (or the master) to decide what use would be made of his child, much as it was up to the parent to decide what use would be made of his house or his carriage. If he chose to abuse his child, it was his business alone. Indeed, in one case of abuse of a climbing boy, the master sweeper answered protests made by those who saw the incident by pointing out that "the boy was his own child, and he could do with him as he pleased."[92]

It is instructive to compare the lot of the climbing boys with the lot of that other group of owned people, slaves. Interestingly, slaves appear to have been in many respects better off than climbing boys. One writer of the times made the following comparison:

> I do not hesitate to say, that in proportion to the number of the sufferers, this practice is even more cruel, and unjust, than West Indian Slavery itself. These objects are *all* young and helpless. Their employment is ten-fold more horrible than that of any attaching to the slaves. They are as much in the power of tyranny. A far greater number of them are crippled, and rendered deformed for life. A far greater proportion of them die in consequence of hard usage, while the horrible deaths from suffocation, burning, and other accidents, are in this case beyond measure more numerous. And all this is at *home*, within our knowledge, before our eyes, in our streets, nay, in our very houses.[93] [Italics in original.]

That slaves should be treated better than climbing boys is perhaps not surprising when we remember that whereas the working life of a slave might last sixty years, the working life of a climbing boy might last fewer than ten.

In the late 1780s, when the plight of the climbing boys became a topic of debate in England, poet William Blake wrote "The Chimney Sweeper," which begins as follows:

When my mother died I was very young,
And my father sold me while yet my tongue
Could scarcely cry *'weep 'weep 'weep 'weep*!
So your chimneys I sweep, and in soot I sleep.

When I first encountered this poem—before having researched the climbing boys—I assumed that the talk about children being sold and sleeping in soot was some kind of metaphor: Surely people didn't *literally* sell children, and surely children didn't *literally* sleep in soot. I now know better.

The poem itself shows that Blake was more attuned to the plight of the climbing boys than were many of his fellow-citizens. At the same time, the poem reveals that Blake was not sanguine that societal reforms could improve the lives of these children. To the contrary, Blake appears to have thought that only one thing—death—could free the climbing boys from their travails.

Conclusions

This chapter has presented a fairly astonishing picture of the uses to which children have been put. Nevertheless, there might be some who would take me to task for making the picture prettier than it in fact is. It might be argued, in other words, that I have not truly plumbed the depths of childhood misery.

In reply to this criticism, let me first remind the reader that my goal in the forgoing account of the uses of children was not to describe the *worst* things that have been done to children, but to describe the worst uses of children *that were generally accepted in the cultures in which these uses took place*. What I find particularly noteworthy about the climbing boys is not the extent to which they were abused—although it is a truly impressive amount of abuse—*but the extent to which their society tolerated this abuse*. It would be one thing if the climbing boys had lived off in a distant land or even if they were kept out of the sight of society. (Morally, of course, it would make little difference, but psychologically, it would.) But the climbing boys were solidly a part of their society. It would not be unusual to encounter them on the street. Indeed, a few times a year, a typical London homeowner would even have them come into his home, into his very bedroom, where, sooty, impoverished, and miserable, they would do their work. The homeowner would pay them to do it.[94]

I might also be criticized for being naive in my uncritical acceptance of stories about the uses of children. There will be those, in particular, who argue that some of the uses I describe in fact never took place, or took place in a different way than I describe them.

The problem with doing research into the history of childhood is that people in the past generally did not keep careful records on exactly how children were treated—which, by the way, is an indication of how unimportant children were in the scheme of things. It is only in exceptional cases that we have a detailed knowledge of how a particular child was raised. This means that telling the history of the past treatment of children is a risky business.

While I may indeed be mistaken with respect to some of the uses of children that I describe, this will not significantly detract from my claim that the history of childhood has been a history of abuse. Furthermore, I think that some of the most horrific uses of children that I describe above (for example, the use of children as climbing boys) are well documented.

The advent of child labor laws in the late nineteenth century put an end to the most disturbing forms of child labor. Children no longer work in mines and factories, and boys no longer sweep chimneys. This is not to say, however, that we no longer put our children to work at an early age. We do. In particular, we see nothing wrong with a child sacrificing his childhood so that we adults can be entertained watching the child do gymnastics or play tennis or perform ballet or act in a movie. Although the existences of these child stars may look glamorous, it can be argued—and I will argue it in the following chapter—that their existences have a dark side that we choose not to see, much as the London homeowner of the early nineteenth century must have chosen not to think about what became of the climbing boy when he left the homeowner's kitchen.

CHAPTER 2

CHILD STARS

In the previous chapter, we looked at some of the uses to which children have been put. In this chapter we will consider another use of children, for entertainment purposes. Whereas the children we have examined thus far were typically objects of neglect, the child stars examined in the present chapter are anything but neglected—indeed, they typically suffer from an excess of adult attention. Whereas the poor climbing boys had nothing, the child stars have it all: Many of them have mansions to live in, chauffeur-driven limousines, vast wealth, an adulating press, and an adoring public.

So why am I including child stars in my discussion of the exploitation of children? Because in many cases, these children—despite appearances to the contrary—*are* exploited. And what is particularly interesting, for present purposes, is the extent to which the public turns a blind eye to their exploitation. We assume that they are happy—that somebody, somewhere is looking out for their best interests. By examining our own tolerance for the exploitation of child stars, we can gain some insight into how it was that past generations found it so easy to tolerate the exploitation of their children.

That children can be fun to watch is something every parent knows. And many parents also know that children can be even more fun to watch if you take their natural talents and improve on them. The improvements in question can take a number of forms. The child might be given special training by his parents. Or they might enroll him in a school (perhaps far from home) where he can get special training. They might even have various surgical procedures performed on the child to increase his chances of success.

I will argue in a later chapter that one of the duties of a caring parent is to discover and develop his child's talents. Where the parents of child stars differ from typical caring parents is in the intensity and single-mindedness with which they develop their child's star-making talent. They might ignore other, less-exploitable talents that the child has. They might ignore those needs of the child, the fulfillment of which would not be talent-enhancing. And they won't just encourage the child to develop the chosen talent, but will push, prod, goad—do whatever it takes to make their child into a star.

To a large extent, the process of making a child star requires parents to discard their child's childhood: Child stars, as we shall see, become "adults" at a very early age. It is true, the star's parents generally admit, that their child is giving up something to become a star, but their child is getting something in return. To the parents of the child star, this "something" has a value far greater than that of an ordinary childhood. In the next chapter, I will return to this question of values. In the remainder of this chapter, I will describe some child stars, past and present, to show that despite the glamour of their existence, a case can be made that many of them are being cruelly exploited.

Children in the Arts

Velluti, Opera Star

Consider, to begin with, the case of Giovanni Battista Velluti, born in Italy in 1780 or 1781.[1] When he was at "a tender age" he made his first public appearance before the cardinal who would later become Pope Pius VII. Shortly after this, he was sent off to Bologna to study music. He made his operatic debut in 1800 and soon became famous. Napoleon heard Velluti sing in Venice in 1810 and was astonished by his voice. Velluti later performed before the Princess of Wales, who requested that the opera commence at the second act, against the wishes of Velluti. Velluti objected that "my throat is worth quite as much as a queen."[2] Then he cried. The princess let him have his way.

Velluti was engaged by the court theater at Modena; there he spent much of his spare time chasing the ladies of the court. He then moved on to Germany, where his singing was "acclaimed with ecstasy."[3] In St. Petersburg he not only won acclaim as a singer, but had a close relative of the Tsar for a mistress. In 1825 he went to England, where his arrival was met with great excitement. He was even described as "the best singer of his country."[4] His voice surprised the English: At his first performance, "the first note he uttered gave a shock of surprise, almost of disgust, to inexperienced ears; but his performance was listened to with attention and great applause throughout...."[5]

By the 1830s, Velluti had abandoned the stage and retired to a luxurious villa. He died in 1861.

All in all, this sounds like what one would imagine the life of a successful Italian opera star to be. What makes Velluti worthy of note in this, a book about children, is what he did to become a famous opera singer. His musical training, of course, was important, but what arguably made the difference—what made him stand out in the early 1800s as one of a kind—was the operation that benefited his voice: castration. Velluti was what is known in operatic circles as a castrato—indeed, he has been described as the last of the castrati.

Velluti's parents had at first intended him to be a soldier. Subsequently they allowed him to be castrated, and it is unclear whether the castration in question was musically motivated, medically motivated, or an unfortunate accident, with the doctor misunderstanding the instructions of the parents.

The point in castrating boys was to prevent their voices from "breaking" during puberty. As a result of castration, the castrati grew up to be men who had not men's voices, and not women's voices either, but voices possessing (at their best) a kind of unearthly beauty. Here is one contemporary description of the castrato voice:

One must be accustomed to the voices of castrati in order to enjoy them. Their timbre is as clear and piercing as that of choir boys and much more powerful; they appear to sing an octave above the natural voice of women. Their voices have always something dry and harsh, quite different from the youthful softness of women; but they are brilliant, light, full of sparkle, very loud, and with a very wide range.[6]

There are no doubt males in existence today who, because of accidents or medical misfortune, would be able to sing as castrati; they appear, however, to be keeping their talents to themselves. There are phonograph records of one alleged castrato, Alessandro Moreschi, made in 1902–3, but judging from the written descriptions of the singing of the legendary castrati, he was no match for them.[7] For the most part, then, we must leave to our imaginations what it was that made castrati so special, operatically speaking.

The rise of Christianity coincided with the rise of the castrati, inasmuch as women were forbidden to sing in church; castrati may have been used in Rome as early as the fourth century. The heyday of the castrati was in Italy in the late eighteenth century. At that point, says Angus Heriot in his history of the castrati, "Italian opera was...almost synonymous with the castrati, and...Italian opera was the opera that really mattered."[8] By the middle of the nineteenth century, however, castrati were rare in the opera, although musically-motivated castrations continued.

The motivations of the parents of the castrati were fairly straightforward: Many of them were in it for the money. Some of these parents sold their children to a teacher or musical institution. In other cases, parents themselves paid for the castration and musical training of their children, in the hope that their child would become famous and wealthy as an opera singer and would be able to provide for them in their old age. But as Heriot puts it, "why they should have expected him to be so full of gratitude is difficult to imagine."[9]

Not all the castrati came from humble families. Carlo Broschi, who went by the name Farinelli and was arguably the greatest of the castrati, came from a noble family. It could be that Farinelli was operated on for (what at the time were taken to be) legitimate medical reasons; the fact that his father had a strong interest in music makes one wonder, though, whether there might have been other motives.

How did children feel about being castrated? One suspects that in many cases, children had little or no say in the matter. (The fact that children were sold to singing masters suggests that parents of the time did not feel compelled to get a child's consent before taking steps that would have an enormous impact on that child's life.) Nevertheless, there appear to have been cases in which children *asked* to be castrated. Whether such requests can count as "consent" is dubious, though. Could a child really be expected to understand and appreciate the sacrifice he was making in being castrated?

Musically-motivated castration was forbidden, both by the church, which would excommunicate those involved in the operation, and by the state. This meant that castrations had to be carried out in clandestine fashion. According to one theory, Italian children were sent to a conservatorio to have their voices appraised; and if they had promising voices, they would be taken home by their parents to have the castration performed. The authorities allowed castrations that were performed for medical reasons. Surgeons could therefore "cover" a musically-motivated castration by claiming that it was medically motivated.

The best surgeons in Italy—and the best people to perform castrations—were in Bologna. Their fame spread to other countries, and when the Duke of Würterberg became enamored of castrati, he imported two Bolognese surgeons to help him develop his "collection" of castrati, which at one point numbered fifteen.

The operation itself was relatively refined, as castrations go. The patient was drugged and placed in a very hot bath until he had lost most sensation. Then, rather than a full castration in which the testicles or both the testicles and penis are removed, the "ducts" leading to the testicles were cut. Over time, the testicles shriveled and disappeared.

By the way, castration, while ruining the reproductive capacities of a male, does not necessarily ruin his sex life. A male can not only achieve an erection in the absence of testicles, but can maintain that erection for hours; and of course, women who have sex with a castrated male needn't fear pregnancy. Thus, a castrated male, rather than being sexually impotent, might well be a sexual dynamo.[10] This presumably helps explain Velluti's success with women.

As it happens, many of those who were castrated did not go on to develop wonderful voices. Sometimes this was because they had lacked singing ability before the castration, but had been castrated anyway in an act of wishful thinking on the part of their parents. In other cases, a child had demonstrated singing ability before the operation, but failed to develop as hoped thereafter. This meant that at one time Italy was awash in failed castrati. As one observer put it, "The number of these victims is so great, they surpass the want of singers of all kings and princes."[11]

Those castrati who became rich and famous at least got some reward for their sacrifice. And perhaps in these cases, castrati were able, in their old age, to look back and judge the sacrifice to have been worthwhile. Those castrati who did not become rich and famous, however, had sacrificed for nothing. Indeed, they often sacrificed for less than nothing, since as failed castrati, they experienced various forms of discrimination. They were objects of abuse. The Catholic Church was happy to have them sing in the choir, but would not allow them to become priests. Neither the Catholic Church nor the Lutheran Church allowed them to marry. (The reasoning of the time: The only acceptable reason for two people to get married is so they can procreate; castrati cannot procreate; therefore, castrati may not get married.) And of course, it must have been psychologically painful to be a eunuch in a time when, as Heriot puts it, "virility was accounted a sovereign virtue."[12]

Since musically-motivated castrations were not allowed by the authorities, a case can be made that such castrations were not, at the time, generally-accepted uses of children and as such do not belong in these discussions. Nevertheless, the sheer number of castrati, together with the fact that their existence was publicly celebrated, suggests that the ban on musically-motivated castrations went largely unenforced. The public and the authorities alike were quite willing to accept at face value all the stories about childhood accidents and medical necessity, if doing so meant that they could enjoy the music of the castrati.

We have, of course, abandoned the practice of castrating choirboys so that they can retain their youthful voices. This is not to say, however, that we have altogether given up the use of surgery to improve the singing of children. It was recently reported, for example, that a British choirboy had been operated upon to have his tongue "loosened." The goal of the surgery was to enable him to roll his R's so he could sing solos in Latin.[13]

Young Beethoven

Mozart was clearly a child prodigy. By age four he was playing short pieces on the clavier, faultlessly and from memory. By age five he was devising minuets at the keyboard. By age six he was playing for the aristocracy. By age seven he was more accomplished, musically speaking, than most adults can ever hope to be.

Beethoven was born in Mozart's shadow. Beethoven's father was an abusive alcoholic; his mother, who died when he was a child, was not a happy woman. Beethoven himself was a shy boy who showed no particular talent for music. But Beethoven's father apparently wanted him to be "the next Mozart"; he wanted to transform his son into a "marketable commodity," and to this end he sacrificed Beethoven's childhood.

Beethoven's father personally instructed him in the pianoforte and violin. The instruction could not have been fun: The young Beethoven was later described by those who knew him as a child as "a tiny boy, standing on a little footstool in front of the clavier to which the implacable severity of his father had so early condemned him." Another observer remembered young Beethoven "standing in front of the clavier and weeping."[14]

Beethoven's musical instruction could take place at odd hours. If his father came home from the wine-house late at night, Beethoven might have been awakened and "instructed" until dawn.

In order to realize his dream of producing a child prodigy, Beethoven's father was willing to cut short Beethoven's education. Thus, at age eleven, Beethoven abandoned all his other studies in favor of music. And Beethoven's father did not particularly care about his son's physical well-being: Young Beethoven was notable for his uncleanliness and unkempt appearance. There is also reason to think, not just that Beethoven was beaten as a child, but that his adult deafness was in part a consequence of these beatings.

When Beethoven's schoolfellows wrote their reminiscences of him, none spoke of him as a playmate, and none told stories of playing with him.[15] We are left with a picture of Beethoven, a tortured and lonely boy, paying the full price for his father's dreams of glory.

To be sure, Beethoven did, in the end, achieve musical immortality, although not exactly as his father had imagined he would.

We can ask a number of questions about Beethoven or any of the other child stars that we shall consider. Most importantly, suppose Beethoven had been allowed to enjoy his childhood. Suppose his father had not pushed him to become a child prodigy. What would have become of Beethoven?

The answer to this question, of course, lies within the realm of utter speculation. There is a chance that had he been able to enjoy a "normal" childhood, Beethoven would have grown up to be an even more astounding composer than he was. At the same time, it is possible that had not Beethoven been pushed musically as a child, he would not have displayed the least interest in music as an adult; and it is possible that had Beethoven not been abused as a child, his adult musical career—thanks to the lack of a tortured soul—would have been mediocre. In either case, the world would have been deprived of his music.

Suppose we could agree that if Beethoven had not been forced to sacrifice his childhood, he would not have gone on to compose the music he did. We are then faced with an interesting ethical question: Is it worth the sacrifice of a childhood in order to gain musical ability? What, in short, is the value of a childhood? This is a question we shall take up at length in the next chapter.

Sarah Chang, Child Musician

It would be a mistake to think that parents no longer feel the urge to transform their children into musical prodigies. The impulse is still alive and well.

In the mid-1990s, the classical music industry went into a decline. One of the few bright spots involved child prodigies. People who had little interest in hearing adults play classical music would willingly pay to hear children play—with somewhat less proficiency—that same music. Said the artistic director of the Cleveland Orchestra, "If we book them, we sell tickets."[16] And not only that, but child prodigies worked for a fraction of the pay that adult musicians required, so the profits generated for orchestras by child prodigies were disproportionately large.

According to Andrew Thomas, director of Juilliard School's precollege division, the classical music industry was "looking for tiny tots" with whom to attract concertgoers. When record companies and managers uncovered a new prodigy, they could "easily make a killing."[17]

Consider the career of child prodigy Sarah Chang. When she was four, her violinist father handed her a violin. At age six she was playing with the technical proficiency of an adult. She was taken to play for Zubin Mehta, director of the New York Philharmonic; he booked her to perform in a youth concert. At age eight she got an agent and began performing a concert a month. She recorded her first album at age nine, but her father, fearing that her career was moving too fast, asked that it not be released for two years; when it was released, it became a classical music top-seller. Then came appearances on television talk shows. And behind her, all this time, stood a "marketing machine," consisting of managers, record producers, and stylists who dressed her to maintain "the look." At age fifteen, Miss Chang was playing between 30 and 50 concerts a year.

Some critics argue that although child prodigies are technically quite proficient, they lack a genuine feel for music and are unlikely to become respected adult performers. And even those who are truly gifted might find themselves, on entering adulthood, burned out by a childhood spent touring America's concert halls. Their future prospects, in other words, are not necessarily bright.

Those children who make it as musical stars seem to realize that what makes them special is not so much their musical talent, but their talent at an early age. Said one fifteen-year-old violin virtuoso, "The one thing that makes me different is that I am young." Another child prodigy echoes this thought: "Age has lots to do with people coming to [my] concerts."[18] They also realize that their careers are likely to decline before they reach adulthood. Audiences want to see the girl prodigies wearing ruffled dresses; these dresses, which look fine on nine-year-olds, look ridiculous on fifteen-year-olds.

Joshua Bell is one child prodigy who successfully made the transition to adult musician. In an attempt to extend his time as a child prodigy, some age-changing was necessary: "I was called 14 until the age of 18." He says that as a child, he "wasn't considered a true musician, but a circus act."[19]

Gelsey Kirkland, Child Ballerina

Gelsey Kirkland (as she tells us in her autobiography *Dancing on My Grave*) was born in 1952. Her parents had high hopes for her. They enrolled her in New York's Professional Children's School so that she could work as a child. The school, notes Kirkland,

> was convenient and offered a flexible schedule, allowing aspiring dancers, actors, and musicians to satisfy the legal re-

quirements for public education. I learned how to cheat quite early, as did most of my peers. As we were bound for careers in the arts, what need did we have for books or scholarship?[20]

And to get her started on her childhood career, her mother enrolled her in ballet school—not just any ballet school, but the School of American Ballet, under the direction of ballet-great George Balanchine.

At first ballet lessons consumed a few hours a week. Then they consumed a couple hours a day. Finally they came to consume, in her words, "all my days and nights." How was dancing able to consume her nights? She had a tendency to dance—physically dance—in her sleep. Because of the rising demands of ballet, the rest of her interests began to wither away, and her studies were neglected.

Thanks to her intense training in ballet, she came to know on a daily basis pain that would previously have been unimaginable: "Pleasure and pain were inextricably connected and integral to the study of dance. When I think of how much pain and how little pleasure were involved in the next few years of ballet school, I marvel at my perseverance and clarity of purpose."[21]

Those who taught ballet realized the dangers ballet training posed to children. Here is Balanchine on the training of children:

> Even with eight- or nine-year-old children, we must always keep in mind the fact that their bones are still soft and their muscles (particularly the ones around the knee) are still unformed. For this reason one should never force the feet of children to attain perfect ballet positions, nor insist on their making an effort to turn out their legs.[22]

In practice, however, Kirkland's ballet teachers—and Balanchine in particular—tended to ignore this advice.

At age eleven Kirkland was introduced to toe shoes. She was also required to stand with her feet "turned out." The combination of toe shoes and turn-out resulted in a deformation of her feet and a severe case of bunions.[23] Her teachers' reaction to her suffering? Many of them suffered the same malady; and in any case, they argued that the presence of bunions improved a dancer's foot line: It contributed to the impression of having winged feet.

Foot pain drove her to an orthopedic surgeon who had seen the problem in ballet dancers many times. His advice—which she ignored—was to quit ballet. By age twelve the tendons in her ankles were acutely inflamed. She decided that her only option was to get used to the pain: "At the School of American Ballet, no viable alternative existed."[24] The anti-inflammatory drug Butazolidin offered some relief.

Kirkland's training regime was brutal. It could have been less brutal, but Balanchine demanded that his ballerinas sacrifice all for art. Balanchine was a man in a hurry and liked to use short-cuts in the training process. He did not like to take the time to warm up his dancers, an omission that Kirkland describes as "professionally fatal for those with chronic injuries." He required toe shoes to be worn at all times in class, even though this significantly increased the strain on the feet of his ballerinas. When Kirkland complained to him of her pain, he replied that "you're young. Young people don't have injuries."[25] His only concrete suggestion was that she try drinking red wine to ease the pain. Later on, as she grew more valuable to the ballet company, he went beyond red wine and provided her with amphetamines—he told her they were vitamins—so that she could go on stage despite being quite ill.

Much of Kirkland's ballet training consisted in forcing her body to do what it could not do naturally. The "look" of the ballerina is what mattered. On one occasion, a teacher who was having trouble putting into words what he wanted Kirkland to do, wrenched her leg into position, thereby tearing her muscles. To increase her flexibility, Kirkland would assume a position that was at the edge of her physical limitations and have a friend sit on her until the pain became so excruciating that she collapsed in tears.

Balanchine required his ballerinas to be thin: He occasionally would inspect them to see if he could discern their bones. To please him, ballerinas went on extremely restrictive diets:

Balanchine counseled them to "eat nothing." They used emetics to induce vomiting. At one point Kirkland's diet consisted of one apple per day, together with a quarter cup of cottage cheese as "dessert." The combination of poor nutrition and strenuous exercise caused her menstrual cycle to cease; it also presumably made it that much harder for her to recover from the injuries she routinely suffered. Ultimately, her obsession with staying thin led Kirkland into the nightmare of anorexia.

There were many things a ballerina could do, medically speaking, to improve her ballet. It was possible, for example, for a dancer to change the line of her foot by having her arch surgically broken and realigned. Kirkland did not resort to such extreme measures, but did (as a child) have plastic surgery and silicone injections with her ballet career in mind.

At age fifteen, Balanchine invited Kirkland to join his ballet company. She decided to quit school. Her parents acquiesced in her decision, but her father made her promise to continue to read. As the result of her childhood sacrifice—or, one might say, her sacrificing her childhood—Kirkland became a ballet star. She also became a depressed drug addict who would forever pay a price for the abuse her body had suffered.

Alexandra Nechita, Child Painter

Alexandra Nechita paints for two to three hours on weekdays. On weekends she paints all day long. She has sold her paintings—for as much as $50,000—to a variety of well-heeled individuals, including industrialist Lee Iacocca and rock star Melissa Etheridge. She is the subject of a coffee-table book. She has appeared on news shows. Her art is exhibited in galleries. She has an agent, who refers to her as "Mozart with a paintbrush"—which comment is clearly intended to be complimentary, even though it is unclear whether Mozart would have been in his element using a paintbrush. When not painting, Alexandra also enjoys doing cartwheels. That's because she was, at the time her art became famous, only ten years old.[26]

Will Alexandra grow up to be a great artist? Only time will tell. Her current works look like imitations—albeit very good imitations—of famous art of the early twentieth century. They are works which, if done (today) by an adult, would hardly be impressive. And whether Alexandra's early exposure as an artist will help or hurt her career remains to be seen. One artist/educator has suggested, though, that Alexandra's artistic ambitions would be better served if, rather than continuing to produce art, she changed her name, went to art school for a few years, and then reemerged as an artist.

One thing that is certain is that Alexandra's art is generating a considerable amount of money. Because Alexandra is a speedy painter (she can produce a finished painting in a few days' time) and because her paintings fetch so much from collectors, Alexandra's artistic endeavors racked up $3 million in sales in one nine-month period. And where does this money go? Her art dealer takes a 70 percent commission—rather than the more customary 50 percent commission. Not long ago this same art dealer had been hawking other artistic offerings—he was selling movie posters as investments—until the FTC asked him to stop doing so.

Child Actors

Shirley Temple

Gertrude Temple had wanted to become an actress or ballet dancer. On reaching adulthood with this ambition unfulfilled, Gertrude rechanneled her ambitions through her two sons, but her boys lacked both the talent and the desire to become child stars. Frustrated, Gertrude decided that she would have a third child, preferably a girl who would be easier to manage than a boy. In order to increase the chance of having a girl, her husband (on the advice of the family doctor) had his tonsils removed. They grew back, and he had them removed again. Nine months after the second removal, on April 23, 1928, Shirley Temple was born.[27]

Shirley immediately became the focus of Gertrude's life. Each morning she applied waving solution to the child's hair and wound exactly fifty-six ringlets. She also played music for her baby girl, and sang and danced for her.

Gertrude enrolled Shirley in dance lessons—not just any dance lessons, but lessons at the Meglin Dance Studio, which was arguably one of the most professional dancing schools in the country. Judy Garland (who was Frances Gumm at the time) was another student at the school.

Meglin Dance Studio was filled with the children of ambitious parents. And although the school did not like to take students under five years of age, Gertrude got Shirley in at age three.

Shirley was a talented three-year-old, but three does seem to be an early age to begin professional training, even by show business standards. Shirley's own views on her early training: "I was allowed to be a baby for about two years. So I had a couple of years as a lazy baby. I thought every child worked, because I was born into it."[28]

Gertrude never considered anything but a film career for her child, and early on, Gertrude made the rounds to casting directors with Shirley in tow. She tried to get baby Shirley into the *Our Gang* comedies a half dozen times. Shirley's break came with the development of a comedy series called Baby Burlesks. In these short films, children, dressed in diapers, did satires on adult movies. The production was expected to require at least twenty-five kids, age five or under. Shirley, a few months past her third birthday, became one of them.

Shirley's father was opposed to letting Shirley appear in movies, but quickly gave in to his wife's wishes. Neither parent investigated the content of the planned Baby Burlesk series, though, and as it turned out the content of these films was objectionable inasmuch as infants were required to behave in a sexually provocative manner. At one audition, for example, infants were required to strip to their underpants, stand in front of the camera, and wink and shake their shoulders. It has been suggested that the Baby Burlesk movies, of which there were four, could be viewed on two levels: Female audiences might appreciate them for the cute children they contained, while male audiences might find them titillating, in a time when movies were sexually inhibited. In one of the Baby Burlesk films, infant Shirley appeared dressed in a black lace bra and undies. Graham Greene later commented on the subtle sexuality of these films and was sued for doing so.

After winning a lead role in *War Babies*, one of the Baby Burlesk films, Shirley showed up for work with an ear infection. She was too sick to work, and the filmmakers promptly fired her. Her mother—not one to let such obstacles stand in her way—had Shirley's abscessed ear lanced and returned to the set the next morning, accompanied by the family doctor, who told the filmmakers that the child was now fine. Shirley regained the role.

Shirley's daily routine revolved around her work. The day was spent at the studio, and even as an infant, Shirley was at the studio from eight in the morning until six at night. During the drive home, Gertrude explained to Shirley what she would be doing the next day. Then came dinner, a bath, and the ritual of setting her hair in curlers. After that they reviewed the lines Shirley would have to say the next day. Then it was off to bed.

Shirley's work exposed her to a variety of hazards, some unforeseen and some intentionally created by the filmmakers. In one of the Baby Burlesk films, the script called for a bunch of black infants to chase Tarzan and Jane (played by Shirley) through the jungle. The director wanted all the black boys to fall down at once, and to accomplish this, he put (without telling them) a wire across the path they were supposed to follow. Some of the boys had their legs cut by the wire. In another Baby Burlesk film, Shirley was supposed to ride in an ostrich-drawn carriage. The ostrich bolted (as the director had hoped it would), almost throwing Shirley out of the carriage. Another time Shirley, age five, was nearly kicked by a mule while filming a scene. She ad-libbed and kicked the mule back. The filmmaker caught it all on film.

Later in her career, during the filming of *Heidi*, Shirley tripped and fell, and got cut over the eyebrow. A makeup artist was called in and filming continued. A few days after this, artificial snow caused Shirley's throat to close up. This time, filmmakers saw fit to allow Shirley two days off in which to recover.

Was Gertrude exploiting her child? To her way of thinking, she was not, and in support of this view she pointed out that the family did not rely on Shirley as their source of income. This state of affairs soon changed, though, when the studio put Gertrude on the payroll; and later her husband quit his job at the bank and became Shirley's paid financial adviser. Despite these changes, the Temples continued to deny the exploitation charge.

Gertrude argued that in pushing along Shirley's career, she had the child's best interests in mind. Thus, Gertrude defended signing Shirley up for dancing lessons by insisting that she was simply trying to give Shirley the fun that she, Gertrude, had missed. And when dancing was supplanted by acting, she asserted that acting was a form of play and that Shirley regarded it as such. Gertrude was also careful to remind listeners that her own position as mother of a child star was no bed of roses. In Gertrude's mind, then, by promoting Shirley's career, she was sacrificing in order to advance the interests of her child—her motives, in other words, were pure.

Gertrude realized that adult audiences liked to compare child stars to their own children. Thus, behavior that audiences would find astonishing in a three-year-old they might find unremarkable in a five-year-old. To make Shirley's acting, dancing, and singing skills seem more remarkable than they were, Gertrude subtracted a year from Shirley's age. She was so successful in this deception that it was only at her "twelfth" birthday party that Shirley learned she was in fact thirteen.

As Shirley approached age six, her father advised Gertrude to put Shirley's acting career on hold and enroll her in school. (Shirley's father tended to oppose Shirley's career and push for a more normal childhood whenever Shirley's career prospects looked bleak, but tended to back Gertrude's plans for Shirley whenever things started looking up.) Shirley might have given up acting for school had she not been "discovered" by songwriter Jay Gorney while standing outside a movie theater. Gorney told Shirley and her mother to pay him a visit. When the Temples showed up for the meeting, though, they were turned away by a studio guard who said that no Jay Gorney worked there. This scene was repeated on the next three days. Finally, Gertrude found Gorney's home phone number and established contact again; it turned out that the guard did not have an updated list of employees. Shirley's ultimate success, then, was in part due to luck, but the luck would have been for naught had it not been for Gertrude's determination that her child become a star.

Shirley's breakthrough movie was arguably *Little Miss Marker*, in which she played a child put up as the "marker" (i.e., collateral) for a racetrack ticket. Thus, in *Little Miss Marker*, audiences were treated to the spectacle of a child being used by adults to play the part of a child being used by adults—an irony lost on most of the audience in question. Incidentally, *Little Miss Marker* has had three remakes, evidence of the popularity of the "used child" theme; in none of the three did the child who played the "marker" go on to film stardom.

By the end of her infancy, Shirley was spending six days a week at the studio, with only Sunday off. Even when she was not shooting a film, she was expected to be at the studio for interviews, costume fittings, and photographic sessions. She was photographed an average of fifty times a day. And at that time, being photographed could be a tedious process: It might require you to stay absolutely still for a full second.

Photographers even followed Shirley on her "vacations," which meant that Shirley had to quit playing for real and pretend to play for the cameramen.

Thanks in part to the intense publicity she received, by 1935 Shirley could not venture beyond the gates of her home. Sometimes she had to crouch on the floor of her limousine to avoid being seen. She needed a bodyguard, for fear that her clothes would be torn from her by fans in search of mementos. And even at home Shirley's childhood activities had to be restricted. For example, Shirley's family had a swimming pool, but Shirley was not allowed to swim on her day off: Shirley's hair always had to spend the day in curlers.

Shirley's contract called for three movies a year, a grueling schedule for even an adult. Nevertheless, her mother in 1935 gave the studio permission to use her in a fourth movie; similar permissions followed in 1936 and 1937. Thanks to this hard work, in 1936 Shirley earned $307,000 in salary and far more in "sponsorship" deals. By way of contrast, her father, a bank officer, had earned $90 a week. Shirley's income allowed her family to live in lavish style.

As Shirley grew, normal rights of passage became minor crises. One fear was that she would lose a baby tooth during the shooting of a film. Shirley always kept false baby teeth with her as a precaution.

And as Shirley grew older, so did the danger that she would outgrow child parts but be unable to play more mature parts. Filmmakers were aware of this. Magnate Darryl Zanuck said of her, "What a shame it is that she has to grow up."[29]

A major turning point in Shirley's career came when she had a chance to play Dorothy in *The Wizard of Oz*, which was being made by another studio. Her studio would not agree to a deal. She instead starred in the eminently forgettable *Susannah of the Mounties*. She went from being the number one box-office attraction in 1938 to number thirteen in 1939. Her career had begun its long slide downward.

In fall of 1940, the demand for Shirley's acting had diminished sufficiently that she was able to attend a "real" (but nevertheless exclusive) school for the first time. Her exposure to other children meant a speedy loss of innocence. It also made her aware of what she had missed as a child. But the change was a change for the better: She became as happy as she had ever been. After 1940 her existence as a "normal" child was still interrupted periodically by making movies, but her cinema career was clearly in decline. Whatever screen presence she had as a child, she did not have as an adolescent.

By the time she was sixteen Shirley was plotting to escape from her mother's control. One way was to wait five years until she became an adult. Another, quicker, alternative was to marry, and marry she did: On September 19, 1945, at age seventeen, she became Mrs. John Agar. In the end, this attempt at freedom failed. For one thing, the couple lived next door to Shirley's parents—in Shirley's old playhouse, no less. This choice of homes meant that Gertrude's presence was still felt. Also, Shirley's husband turned out not to be her ideal mate; nor she his. The marriage ended in divorce.

Shirley Temple did go on to have what was in many respects a successful adult life. She had children of her own. Her first daughter could have been pushed into an acting career—she was talented and had her mother's famed dimples—but Shirley was strong in her desire that the child have a "normal childhood," and she fought against any attempts by others to use her daughter the way she had been used. She allowed her children to act professionally, but only once.

Shirley Temple's childhood raises a number of interesting questions. Why, in particular, did Shirley put up with it? Why didn't she rebel? The answer is simply that Gertrude controlled Shirley's environment so carefully that Shirley truly did not realize that other childhoods were possible.

The control took many forms. For one thing, Shirley's contact with other children was restricted. When other children were around, like at dance school, Shirley was expected to remain aloof. She typically wasn't allowed to play with or talk to her fellow child actors in movies. On her day off Shirley was allowed to play with children, but only those chosen by Gertrude, and always at Shirley's house. Part of Shirley's bodyguard's job was to see that Shirley did not play with other children.

Gertrude also isolated Shirley from other adults. Gertrude was always present at the studio—where, besides controlling Shirley's environment, she could sabotage the careers of potential rivals. Filmmakers gave Shirley instructions through Gertrude. To avoid spoiling Shirley, only the director was allowed to compliment her work.

Another question we might ask is this: What did governmental authorities think of Gertrude sacrificing her child's childhood for a career in the movies? It turns out that the authorities *did* monitor the careers of child actors. In particular, California required that contracts between children and studios be approved by a judge. The problem was that judges did not appear to take their oversight responsibilities very seriously. The "hearing" would be short and to the point: The judge would ask the child if he liked what he was doing. If the child answered Yes, the judge approved the contract. As a legal process, this little ceremony is disturbing for a pair of reasons: First, the child might have said Yes, not because he liked what he was doing, but because he felt that it was what adults wanted him to say; and second, even if he genuinely did like what he was doing, he might like it simply because he did not know of the existence of even more likable alternative childhoods—as was the case with Shirley Temple.

The Dionnes

When Shirley Temple's career was at its peak, she encountered competition for attention from some newcomers, the Dionnes.[30] Whereas Shirley had begun her career at age three, the Dionnes starred in their first short subject when they were under five months old. (If this seems young to be in the movies, realize that until recently, filmmakers used two-week-old premature babies to make birth scenes realistic. A California state law ended the practice in 1998: Child actors now have to be at least one month old.)[31] They made their first feature movie, *The Country Doctor*, when they were barely two years old. The Dionnes went on to appear, as children, in two other feature films. And while their acting skills were not comparable to Shirley's, this was no problem for the filmmakers: The Dionnes had been hired not to act, but simply to be themselves.

The Dionnes were five in number, and were in fact quintuplets. While the birth of quintuplets was, at that time, quite rare (such births are less rare since the development of fertility drugs), what made the Dionne quints even more special was the fact that they were *identical* quintuplets. They were probably only the third set of identical quintuplets in the previous three hundred years and were almost certainly the first identical quintuplets in the history of the world to survive for more than a few days.

The Dionne Quints—Emilie, Marie, Cécile, Annette, and Yvonne—were born at home on May 28, 1934, near North Bay, Ontario, to Oliva and Elzire Dionne, who already had five children. The quints were premature and tiny at birth. The midwives present thought they would not survive more than a few minutes, but survive they did.

After news spread about the birth of quintuplets, a promoter approached Oliva Dionne, the quints' father, and persuaded him to sign a contract allowing the quints to be exhibited at the Chicago Century of Progress Exposition. It is not clear whether Oliva understood what he was doing. The family doctor (who had helped deliver the last few quints) advised him to make what he could from the quints, since they were unlikely to live long. Oliva's priest not only urged him to sign the contract, but agreed to become Oliva's business agent for seven percent of the net proceeds the quints generated. One other factor that must have motivated Oliva in his decision to sign was his concern over whether he could afford to raise his ten children, five of whom would need extensive (and expensive) medical care.

Although the quints were never displayed in Chicago, word of the contract got out. In the eyes of the public Oliva promptly became the villain in the story. The family doctor, Dr. Allan Roy Dafoe, soon came to represent the forces of good. Subsequent events suggest that what bothered many Canadians was not that the quints would be put on display or even that Oliva would profit from the display; what bothered them was instead the fact that Oliva had sold out to the despised Americans.

The quints' precarious state of health required special care, and Dr. Dafoe not only took charge of them but did so to the exclusion of the parents. He took over the first floor of the Dionne's house and banished the family to the second floor.

The government of Ontario, in the aftermath of the contract fiasco, took the quints from the Dionnes; it felt that the quints needed to be protected from the greed of their parents. When Oliva signed the guardianship papers, he did so (he claimed) out of fear that otherwise the quints' supply of breast milk would be cut off. The government's justification for the removal could not have been that it thought the Dionnes were unfit to be parents: After all, it let the Dionnes keep their previous five children. Instead, the government argued that the quints had special needs for which the Dionnes could not provide. Furthermore, the quints needed to be sheltered from publicity, and Oliva had not shown himself up to the task of shielding the quints from the eyes of the world. Later, the Ontario legislature passed a bill that extended guardianship of the quints to age eighteen. Generally speaking, the public welcomed the removal of the quints from their parents.

Days after the guardianship was effected, the government announced that it planned to build a hospital for the quints next to the Dionne home. The road to the house was improved, and wires were run so that electric and telephone service could be provided. The hospital was named not after the quints or their parents, but after Dr. Dafoe.

With the Dionne parents out of the picture, Dr. Dafoe asserted his control over the quints and did so with apparent delight: "These children are the only ones I have ever had with whom I could do what I liked. With the ordinary baby that you look after the mother or father object, the relatives object, and you cannot do as you like with them."[32]

Dr. Dafoe's control extended into every aspect of the children's life. The quints were raised by medical personnel. Dr. Dafoe did not let the mother touch or cuddle her own children. They were not allowed to play with other children until they were two, at which time they were allowed to play briefly with two of their brothers. These restrictions were intended to prevent the quints from being exposed to germs. Germ-avoidance also led Dr. Dafoe to decree that the quints could not play with things made of cloth and could have no pets. The quints later paid a price for this early avoidance of germs: In their teens, they suffered from a series of communicable diseases that most people suffer from as infants.

The quints were more or less held captive within the hospital. They were not allowed to visit their parents' home across the road from the hospital. For the first five years of their life they left the hospital grounds only once, for a ten-minute ride in their father's car. And within the hospital compound they led a sheltered existence. They lived together and were never out of sight of one another. They never had to do chores and never handled money.

Control over the lives of the quints became even more thorough when Dr. Dafoe was joined by Dr. William Blatz, director of the Institute of Child Study at the University of Toronto, who more or less invited himself to oversee the babies' upbringing. Blatz planned the quints' daily routine down to the minute, scheduling, for example, a drink of water at 8:45 A.M. Whereas Dr. Dafoe seems to have had (as we shall see) a monetary interest in the quints, Dr. Blatz appears to have had a purely scientific interest. For Blatz, because the five girls were identical to each other and spending their lives in a carefully controlled environment, the quints were the perfect guinea pigs for psychological research.

The quints' schedule included an hour a day for picture taking. There was a huge public demand for photographs of the children, and the rights to photograph them had been sold early on. The Dionne parents, however, had sold the rights to photograph *themselves* to a different photographer. This meant that no photographs of the quints with their parents were taken between 1934 and 1941. The figure who replaced the parents in pictures was Dr. Dafoe. Furthermore, because the person who owned the rights to photograph the quints would not allow it, the quints' parents were unable to photograph their own children.

At Dr. Blatz's instructions, the quints' nurses took minute-by-minute behavioral observations of the quints and detected, for example, 1,301 instances of anger in a sixteen-month period. Dr. Blatz kept records of their vocabulary development and noted that "doctor" (not surprisingly) was one of the first words the babies learned.

Despite the doctors' attempts to control every detail of the quints' lives, some confusions were bound to arise due to the girls' identical appearance: One handler remarked, "You were always in the position of not knowing if you'd taken the same one to the toilet five times or if you'd taken them once each."[33]

Some—most notably Dr. Alfred Adler—were critical of the way the quints were being raised, but Drs. Dafoe and Blatz shrugged off these objections. Dr. Dafoe summarized his position as follows: "[The quints] can't live the normal life of ordinary individuals so there isn't any point in bringing them up as ordinary children."[34]

When the quints were four, the Dionne parents regained control of them. The government, blown by new political winds, pledged to build a new house for the Dionnes. The government later turned the quints' nursery into a school and recruited nine other girls to be their schoolmates.

The Dionne parents—in particular the father—carefully controlled most aspects of the quints' existence. The mail they received and sent was read by the father. Their parents gave them a tiny allowance, and the girls felt guilty about spending even this, in the belief that it was their father's money they were spending. Guilt appears to have been the dominant emotion felt by the quints: "We were drenched with a sense of having sinned from the hour of our birth...we were riddled with guilt."[35] As we shall see below, this sense of guilt seems to be common among child stars.

The quints finally left home at age eighteen. They were glad to get out. The grown quints later confessed that they loved their years at the hospital, but not their years with their parents.

Dr. Dafoe benefited in a number of ways from his association with the quints. Soon after their birth he became the toast of New York, making three thousand dollars for a single speech. He became known in the public mind as the archetypal country doctor, an image he carefully cultivated. He made significant sums from commercial testimonials. In 1939, near the peak of his popularity, he was asked to give a paper for the Herald-Tribune forum in New York. Other presenters included Franklin D. Roosevelt, Madame Chiang Kai-shek, Lord Halifax (the British foreign secretary), and Édouard Daladier (the premier of France). When all was said and done, Dr. Dafoe probably made as much money from the quints as the quints themselves made.

The Dionne parents also profited from their children. The quints were put on display—by the very government that had once fought to maintain the quints' privacy—with two daily showings. For these showings the quints were dressed alike, and they had their otherwise-straight hair curled daily so they would look cuter. The line of people to see the quints could be as long as half a mile. The Dionne homestead was transformed to cater to the tourist hordes. Although the showings themselves were free, people spent money at shops that sprang up near the hospital. The quints' midwives had a shop. The quints' father had two souvenir stands where you could buy, among other things, binoculars, with which to better see the quints. Tourists might also come away with stones from the quints' playground. These stones (which in fact came from a nearby lake) were referred to as fertility stones and were much sought after by barren women. Thanks to his entrepreneurial talents, Oliva Dionne was able to buy a new car every two years, no small accomplishment during the Great Depression.

The fame of the quints was exploited in other ways. The quints "endorsed" a number of products, including Lysol, Colgate's dental cream, Sanitized Mattresses, Quaker Oats, Carnation Milk (which the quints hated), and Palmolive soap. There were also Dionne quint dolls, sales of which were, in 1936, greater than those of Shirley Temple dolls. These latter dolls, by the way, were ubiquitous; even the Dionne quints had one.

But it wasn't just individuals who benefited from the quints. The whole region benefited economically from their existence, inasmuch as the quints were a hugely successful tourist draw. Between 1934 and 1943, close to three million people came to see them. By 1936 they tied with Niagara Falls as the biggest tourist attraction in Canada.

In 1940 the New York World's Fair sought the quints, but Canadian officials rebuffed the proposal. By this time the health of the quints was no longer used as a justification for prohibiting this display; instead the justification—largely left unstated—was that if the quints went to America, the Canadian tourist industry would suffer.

The quints' lives as adults were unremarkable and somewhat unsuccessful. Emilie was the first quint to die: In 1954 she suffocated during an epileptic seizure. Marie suffered a nervous breakdown; got married; was separated from her husband; spent money with abandon; became an alcoholic; and died, possibly from a blood clot in her brain. She was alone at the time of her death, and it was days before the body was discovered. Cécile married, but her husband's spendthrift ways depleted her trust fund. She was forced to go to work as a supermarket clerk. Annette married and wound up in relative poverty. Yvonne tried unsuccessfully to become a nun. She ended up financially the best off of the quints, but lived the life of a recluse.

In the 1990s the quints were still making headlines: In 1995, three of the quints announced that as children they had been sexually molested by their father.[36] And in 1998, the surviving Dionne quints accepted a $2.8 million payment from the Ontario government as compensation for their childhood exploitation.[37]

The case of the Dionnes is, by the way, instructive for the parents of "normal" children. Parents who have more than one child typically puzzle over how their children, despite being biologically similar and despite being raised by the same parents and under similar circumstances, could turn out so differently. In the Dionnes we have five *identical* children raised in nearly identical circumstances, and they turned out quite differently. (The differences, by the way, began to emerge at an early age.) It would appear, then, that relatively small differences in the upbringing of children or in their existences within the womb can have profound consequences years later.

Other Child Actors

To put the experiences of Shirley Temple and the Dionne quints into context, let us consider the fates of some other child actors.

Baby Peggy (a.k.a. Peggy Montgomery and Diana Serra Cary) became a star at age two and did quite well as a child, but as is the case with most child actors, her career went into a decline when she started to grow. She tried to make a comeback as a teenager, but her reason for doing so was not a love of acting. Rather, she said,

> I agreed because I was sixteen and very determined to make a comeback in films so that I could set my parents up in satisfactory lives of their own. I had it in my head that if I could have even ten years of success…I could earn enough to enable me to walk away, as I longed to do, and start living my own life.[38]

In short, she returned to acting in part because she felt guilty that her parents (who had depleted her childhood earnings through a series of bad investments) had nothing to show for her years of acting and in part because she thought that only more acting could help her escape from life as an actor.

Other child actors use similar terms to describe their motivations for acting. Natalie Wood said that the thing that kept her and her fellow child stars acting was a sense of guilt. Jane Powell acted because she felt it was her duty, as a child, to do so.[39] It should be noted that children who lack a sense of guilt and responsibility also probably lack the drive to succeed, and see their movie careers quickly come to an end.

Jackie Coogan earned $4 million as a child star, but his parents (at first his mother and father; then his mother and stepfather—his father had died three months before Jackie's twenty-first birthday) spent and gambled away his money. He ended up with a tiny percentage of his earnings, and even this was eaten up by legal costs and a divorce settlement with Betty Grable. As an adult, Coogan had a marginal existence as an actor, and finally made a comeback, if you can call it that, when he appeared as Uncle Fester on *The Addams Family* television series.

Two other child actors who saw their childhood earnings dissipated by relatives were Judy Garland and Freddie Bartholomew. Judy Garland's mother and stepfather lost Judy's childhood earnings in unwise investments. In Freddie Bartholomew's case, relatives could not agree on how to divide Freddie's earnings. They chose to carry on their fight in courts of law, and filed twenty-seven lawsuits in this connection. Legal costs stripped Freddie of most of what he had earned.

Reacting to such cases, California enacted the Child Actor's Bill, which required that one half of a minor's earnings be placed directly into a trust fund whose investments were subject to the court's approval. Later the law was extended to apply retroactively to contracts already in effect.

Despite these reforms, it would be a mistake to think that exploitation of child stars is a thing of the past. It is still possible for a child star to enter adulthood with his childhood earnings severely depleted, despite the fact that these earnings were "protected" in a trust fund. Gary Coleman (star of television's *Diff'rent Strokes* program) earned $18 million, but ended up broke. (And what adult career did his childhood stardom prepare him for? That of security guard.)[40] The legal system of New York allowed actor Macaulay Culkin (star of *Home Alone* and other movies) to "support" his parents—who were having trouble meeting their $8,000-a-month rent payments—with trust fund money.[41]

And what about the physical well-being of child actors? Accidents happen. In 1982, two children, a girl age six and a boy age seven, were employed in filming the movie *The Twilight Zone*.[42] The children were used in a manner clearly at odds with California law. For one thing, the scene they were to appear in was to be filmed at night, and California state law does not allow children this young to work late hours. Also, it requires that when children work on a film set, a state-certified worker be present to look out for their well-being. The absence of such a person was, in this case, particularly significant, inasmuch as the scene the children were to appear in featured special-effects explosions and a helicopter hovering nearby. One of these explosions caused the helicopter to crash, and when it fell it killed the two children (one by decapitation and the other by crushing)[43] and actor Vic Morrow.

The director of the movie and others were charged with involuntary manslaughter. They were all acquitted.[44]

Child star Paul Petersen (who played Jeff on *The Donna Reed Show*), has formed A Minor Consideration, a nonprofit foundation to speak on behalf of past and present child stars.[45] In the beginning the goal of the foundation was to try to help former child actors recover from their childhood exploitation. It soon added the function of trying to prevent such exploitation in the future by reforming the movie business and by publicizing the plight of child actors. The investigations conducted by Petersen's foundation demonstrate that these reforms have a long way to go.

Child Models

There have long been child models.[46] What has changed in the last few decades are the uses to which child models have been put. At one time they were used only in ads for products aimed at children; they now appear in ads for products aimed squarely at adults. In particular, teenage girls are used to model adult clothes.

Why the move to teens? There are a number of reasons. For one thing, our culture equates beauty with youth, so it makes perfect sense for advertisers to employ the young. And since youthful beauty is an evanescent thing, it also makes sense for models to start their careers at the earliest age possible: Each year's delay is a precious year wasted. We can also expect competition between photographers and agents to hasten the move to younger models. A photographer or agent who tells a promising young girl to come back in a few years when she can better withstand the pressures of modeling will likely find that he has lost her to another photographer or agent who has fewer scruples. *Someone* is going to put her to work; it might as well be *him*, and it might as well be *now*. And finally—though many in the industry would be reluctant to admit this—if your goal in selecting models is not just to photograph them, but to manipulate them, it makes sense to stick with teenage girls. They are much less likely than adults to realize that they have the power to say No.

Many people have a mistaken idea about how teenage girls become models. They might imagine that models start modeling as infants, attend modeling school to learn the tricks of the trade, and finally make their debut as fashion models. Some models take this path, but most do not. Instead, they are "discovered" as teenagers and immediately put to work.

Consider, by way of illustration, the discovery of model Christine Bolster. At age fourteen she was riding her bicycle through Palo Alto, California, and was pulled over by a man in a white Jaguar. He encouraged her to enter a modeling contest. She won, and five days later was by herself on a plane to Paris. Two weeks after arriving in Paris, her agent paid for an apartment for her. His intentions in doing this were less than honorable: "I was waiting for him to ask me to dinner, but I went into his office one day after work, and he just jumped on me. I was so shocked. There was no way that he was going to get turned down. It was like I had no choice!"[47] After that, she lived with the agent.

Christy Turlington was discovered by a local photographer at age fourteen while riding a horse. By age sixteen she had moved to New York for the summer to work as a model for the Ford agency. She later quit school to become a model full-time. Kate Moss was discovered as a fourteen-year-old at Kennedy Airport, where she had been waiting three days for standby seats back to England. Jane Hitchcock also started her career at age fourteen. Cindy Crawford started modeling in her junior year of high school.

One might wonder whether the parents of teen models worry about their daughters' well-being. Doubtless some do. But agents are practiced at convincing parents of the benefits of a modeling career. Reluctant parents are sometimes paid a cash "bounty" to let their child become a model.

The ascent of a model can be breathtakingly fast. A girl can go from being an unpaid teenage nobody to a highly-paid fashion star in a matter of months. What counts as highly-paid? In the early 1990s, Claudia Schiffer was making $12 million a year. And lesser models can earn $15,000 an hour at fashion shows.

Once their careers are in full swing, models tend to find themselves with abundant free time. In many "event-related" professions—for example, pro tennis—people must train hard between events in order to maintain their competitive advantage, but this is not true of modeling. Models are paid to look the way they look, and this takes no practice.

The combination of free time and easy money can mean trouble, especially for young models. In the words of model Tara Shannon, "Excuse me—you put a fourteen-year-old on Wall Street, unchaperoned, what do you think they're going to do? This is a bunch of big unchaperoned babies getting away with murder. Nobody put any boundaries up."[48] Because of the nature of modeling, a model who lacks self-discipline or is immature can get herself into lots of trouble during her time away from the camera. As one observer of the modeling business put it, "On the pages of magazines models presented images of perfection. But the real girl behind the controlled image on the page was often a total mess."[49]

Things like recreational drug use, which might, in another profession, hurt a person's performance, can actually be beneficial to a model (in the short-run, at any rate) if the drug used suppresses the appetite; as ex-model Lisa Taylor puts it, "the more weight you lose, the more they love you. It was not a healthy job."[50] The fashion industry's views on drug use? According to one *Vogue* editor, "all they wanted to know was, Would [a model] be able to work the next day."[51]

As professions go, modeling has a distinct disadvantage. Whereas doctors and teachers can practice their professions until they are ready to collect Social Security, the career of a model might end in her mid-twenties. Her principal asset is her face, and a face, unfortunately, is a wasting asset, one that will be worthless (as far as the fashion industry is concerned) in a matter of years.

Sometimes it isn't the aging process that brings a model's career to a halt; it is instead a change in "the look." The features that are desirable in a model change from year to year, and those very features that make a model a star today might make her unemployable tomorrow.

Inasmuch as modeling involves beautiful females, it is a profession that attracts what some would describe as male sexual predators. The men in question might work as photographers or agents. Such jobs give them not only access to females, but a certain amount of power over them, and they have an unfortunate tendency to use this power to make sexual conquests.

Sexual taking of adult females would be one thing, but as we have seen, many of the female models are fourteen- and fifteen-year-olds alone in the world for the first time. Those making these conquests appear not to understand or care about the concept of statutory rape. Above I described the events that led fourteen-year-old Christine Bolster to live with her agent. Other agents claim to be more discriminating about which underage models they sleep with. Agent Claude Haddad, for example, admits to having "been with" girl models, but he says he has his standards: For one thing, he manipulates the girls not with drugs (like other agents do), but with charm and power; for another thing, he refuses to have sex with girls under sixteen years of age.

Besides attracting photographers and agents, models also tend to attract rich men. This was as true in the 1940s and 1950s as it is today. Carmen Del'Orefice began modeling in 1946 at age fourteen. Men soon started dating her. When she was seventeen, Joseph P. Kennedy offered her a Park Avenue apartment. Her mother, acting on her daughter's behalf, refused the offer. In 1959, Huntington Hartford offered $1 million for the famous Ford modeling agency. The deal would allow the Fords to remain in control of the day-to-day operations of the agency, but for one thing: Hartford sought the right to go out with whatever model he wanted and to have her fired if she refused. The Fords turned down the offer.

Marginally successful models are the ones most susceptible to the advances of predatory males. These models might attempt to advance their career by sleeping with the right people, but it is a stratagem that often fails: "Wannabe models, lacking the looks, the will, and the sense to understand their precarious position, are junk food for modeling's predators and bottom feeders."[52]

There are those in the fashion industry who find other ways to exploit a girl model's sexuality. In particular, they film or photograph these models in sexually suggestive poses.

This use of models became a subject of debate in 1995 when Calvin Klein used young girls (as well as boys) in ads for his products. While child pornography is illegal, the line between pornography and art is far from clear. Some thought the Klein ads crossed the line. The models weren't nude, but they were filmed in a style reminiscent of low-budget pornography. The Justice Department investigated his use of models and in the end brought no charges. Klein responded by announcing that he would no longer use racy pictures of young or young-looking models in his United States ad campaigns—saving them instead for Europe.[53]

The fashion industry's response to the Klein episode? According to a bookings editor for *Harper's Bazaar*, "Klein went over the boundary of what ordinary people could deal with, but it won't diminish the use of these young girls in the industry."[54]

One girl model whose career was affected by the uproar over the Klein ads was Raina Hamner,[55] age fifteen. Before the uproar, it looked like she would appear in a Klein campaign. When she was subsequently passed over, her age was cited as the reason.

Hamner, who lives with her parents, has done her share of sexually suggestive modeling. She has, for example, been photographed in underwear, halter top, and shackles. She has also been photographed lying in bed, with a boy lying partly on top of her, his hand slightly lifting up her undershirt. What do her parents think of this? They take steps to protect her. For example, they don't let her see a photographer alone—unless it is someone they have dealt with before. And they get to approve of the sorts of pictures that are taken of their daughter: Thus, Hamner's mother got to meet the boy her daughter was photographed lying beneath, and this overcame her reservations about the planned photograph.

Many people in the fashion industry simply fail to see children as a class apart. Your age may affect whether you are beautiful, but it does not (as long as you *are* beautiful) affect your desirability as a model. Perhaps this attitude is best summarized by Calvin Klein who, before the incident described above, said the following: "I have to be honest. I really don't focus on age [of models]. I focus on the beauty of women."[56] This may sound insensitive, but we should keep in mind that a good many of the people who see Klein's ads also focus not on the age of the model, but on her beauty.

Child Athletes

Until the late twentieth century, the phrase "child athlete" seemed an oxymoron. The prevailing wisdom was that anything a child could do, an adult could do better (adults being, after all, bigger and stronger than children), so that in an athletic competition, the adult would invariably triumph over the child. This is not to say that child athletes haven't existed in the past. There was, for example, a thirteen-year-old tennis player named Lottie Dod who competed at Wimbledon in 1887. Such cases were exceptional, though.

All this changed when, in the late twentieth century, it was discovered that in some sports, small size can be a real advantage.

Girls' Gymnastics

Consider, by way of illustration, the transformation that has taken place in women's gymnastics since the mid-1960s.[57] According to the principles of physics, the more compact and lighter a body is, the less energy it will take to make that body spin. Children by nature are lighter and more compact than adults—and at any rate are lighter and more compact than the adults they will some-day become. In theory, then, since many gymnastics routines involve flips and spins, being a light, compact child should give you an edge.

Of course, to be able to exploit this edge, the child gymnast will have to overcome one disadvantage of childhood: relatively low muscle mass. Coaches discovered, though, that this obstacle can be overcome if the child is willing to train intensively for hours each day, nearly every day of the year.

These were discoveries that transformed women's gymnastics. In 1968 the all-around gymnastics Olympic champion was Vera Caslavska. At the time, she was 26 years old and weighed 121 pounds. This same Olympics marked the debut of Olga Korbut, who was 13 years old and weighed a mere 85 pounds. In 1972, Korbut won three gold medals, defeating another child gymnast, Cathy Rigby, to do it. In 1976 the downsizing of female gymnasts was carried one step further: Nadia Comaneci (who had started in gymnastics at age six) made her debut at age 14, weighing 83 pounds. Between 1976 and 1992 the process continued: In that time the average weight of women on the U.S. Olympic gymnastics team fell from 105 pounds to 88 pounds. And by 1995 the latest phenom in gymnastics was thirteen-year-old Dominique Moceanu, who weighed a mere 70 pounds. If we consult a standard chart showing the growth curves for girls of various ages, we find that Miss Moceanu is "off the chart"—i.e., significantly below the fifth percentile curve.

At the same time that gymnastics was downsizing, it was becoming an increasingly demanding sport. In 1972, Olga Korbut could stun audiences by performing one backflip (without using her hands) on the balance beam. Now, gymnasts routinely perform three such backflips in a row. What the world witnessed was a perilous combination: Ever-younger children doing ever-more-difficult maneuvers.

The move to child gymnasts was, as I said above, motivated by "technical" considerations, but coaches soon discovered another advantage to focusing their efforts on children. They found that children were not only willing to pay the price necessary to become accomplished gymnasts, but in some ways were more willing than older people would have been. Little girls did not understand the magnitude of the sacrifice that the coach was asking them to make; nor, in most cases, did they understand that they had the right to say No.

At one time gymnastics was a sport followed by a relative handful of people. It was not particularly popular with general audiences. The popularization of gymnastics coincided with—and no doubt was largely precipitated by—the entry of children into the sport. The same adult who wouldn't have given Vera Caslavska a second look was transfixed by little Olga and little Nadia. They were just so cute out there doing their routines. And the smarter girl gymnasts played up their youth: To accentuate her girlish appearance, Cathy Rigby wore pigtails pulled so tightly that they gave her a headache. Thanks to the presence of little girls, gymnastics went from a sport with a small following to a sport with among the highest television ratings.

Soon children came to dominate women's gymnastics—dominate it to such an extent that the term "women's gymnastics" became a misnomer. "Girls' gymnastics" would have been more appropriate.

The same thing, interestingly enough, has not happened with men's gymnastics: On the 1994 U.S. national team the youngest male gymnast was two years older than the oldest female gymnast. And while male gymnastics champions are generally in their early to mid twenties, female gymnastics champions are usually fourteen to seventeen years old. Male gymnastics apparently requires a degree of physical strength that female gymnastics does not.

Of course, for every Olga, Nadia, and Cathy, there are hundreds, if not thousands of failed girl gymnasts, children who traded five or ten years of childhood for five minutes of glory, but never got the glory. Let us now consider the life of Christie Henrich, one of these also-rans.

Inspired by Nadia Comaneci, Henrich began gymnastics at age four. At age eight she enrolled in a gymnastics school run by a former gymnast. The training at this school involved two sessions a day, a three-hour session at six in the morning and a four-hour session at five in the afternoon, with school sandwiched in between. She soon became quite good. In 1984, at age 14, she came in fifth in the national junior championship. In 1988 she finished tenth in the all-around competition at the senior nationals. She failed to make the 1988 Olympic team—by a mere 0.118 of a point. In that same year, her best friend, another gymnast, broke her neck doing a practice vault, went into a coma, and subsequently died. In 1989, Henrich herself experienced a broken neck but came back three months later to place second all around in the nationals. This, at age 17, marked the high point of her career.

When she was in training for the 1988 Olympics, a judge had commented that if she lost weight, she would improve her chances of making the team. Even though she was a mere 90 pounds at the time, she took the advice to heart. Along with her intense gymnastics training, she began a strict diet, allowing herself an apple a day (shades of Gelsey Kirkland!), gradually reducing it to a slice of apple a day. This would be a radical diet for anyone, but it was an insane diet for someone doing gymnastics seven hours a day. And Henrich worked hard during those seven hours. She ran five miles a day. At moments during practice when she could have been resting, she rode the exercise bike to burn off calories. It did not help her self-image that her coach referred to her as the Pillsbury Dough Boy.

In gymnastics, by the way, an inadequate diet can be particularly deleterious: Such a diet causes the body to steal calcium from the bones, and this increases the chances of stress fractures, which are an occupational hazard for even "healthy" gymnasts.

Why, then, would a coach encourage gymnasts to diet intensively? In part because fat is the foe of gymnasts: Each ounce of fat is another ounce of weight that must be moved. Also, by encouraging girls to go on starvation diets, coaches can delay the event that will almost certainly bring their gymnastics careers to an end: the onset of puberty. After menarche, girls turn into women and in the process typically gain body fat. Thanks to her strict dieting, the average girl gymnast menstruates at age sixteen, three years later than the average non-gymnast. Many gymnasts don't menstruate until they have retired. Kathy Johnson, who won a medal in the 1984 Olympics, didn't menstruate until she quit gymnastics at age twenty-five.

Even after her gymnastics career was in decline, Henrich's obsession with dieting continued. Christie Henrich died at age 22. She weighed 61 pounds, up from a low of 47 pounds. Before her death, she described her life as "a horrifying nightmare. It feels like there's a beast inside me, like a monster."[58] And to what cause did she attribute her unfortunate state? "If I wasn't in gymnastics, this wouldn't have happened to me. It's the constant putdowns, the constant criticisms, the constant mental and physical abuse. It pushes you over the edge."[59]

Where had her parents been during this process? They had bought into Christie's dream, it would seem. Where had her coach been? At her side, pushing her toward greatness. And as part of this push, he encouraged his gymnasts to lose weight and advised them to train despite injuries. In particular, he advised them, if they got a fracture, not to get a cast because it would cause their muscle tone to deteriorate. Where were the governing bodies of gymnastics? Busy organizing meets for future Christie Henrichs.

Anyone who thinks that Christie Henrich was alone in her suffering as a gymnast would do well to consider some of the horror stories documented by Joan Ryan in *Little Girls in Pretty Boxes*. A sampling:

Kelly Garrison made the 1988 Olympic team at the ripe old age of 21. When doctors x-rayed her in connection with an injury, they found twenty-two stress fractures in her back, fractures she had lived with in silence.

Mary Lou Retton broke a bone in her wrist during an exhibition against China. Her doctor told her to give the wrist a rest, but within the hour she was using it again. He convinced her to at least keep ice on the wrist, but when coach Bela Karolyi saw the ice bag, he kicked it off Retton's arm.

Betty Okino got a stress fracture in her right elbow and was told by doctors to stop training. "But that wasn't really an option. It was just like, either you are paralyzed and you can't move, or you train."[60] Less than a year later Okino ripped a tendon away from the bone below the knee. Doctors reattached it with screws, and Okino returned to the gym. Karolyi's response to her injury? He yelled at her for slacking off. Later, after winning a silver medal in the 1992 World Championships, Okino started feeling sharp back pains. Doctors found stress fractures in her vertebrae. Despite this discovery, she continued to train and, while dismounting from the uneven bars, fractured two vertebrae in her lower back. Doctors told her that if she continued in gymnastics, there was a two percent chance that she would suffer paralysis. Her mother urged her to quit, but Okino would not.

Another of Karolyi's charges was fourteen-year-old Chelle Stack, who broke two toes while practicing the balance beam a few hours before a competition. Karolyi insisted that she compete, so she was given a shot of Novocain. With a numb foot, she stumbled in her events. Karolyi responded by screaming at her.
Even though Chelle repeatedly said she wanted to quit, her parents kept her in elite gymnastics till she broke her knee at age eighteen. Chelle Stack's years of training left her with toes so gnarled that she can't wear high heels, eighteen hairline fractures in her knee, and—of course—a missing childhood. Nevertheless, her parents felt that the effort had been worthwhile: Their daughter, after all, "came out healthy."[61] Their only regret was that they had pushed their daughter toward stardom in gymnastics rather

than in tennis or golf, where she would have had a better chance at making some money.

Shannon Miller's training routine required her to train from 7:30 to 9:00 each morning and from 3:00 to 8:00 each evening. In eight years of this training, she missed only one workout: Her coach excused her so she could have screws inserted to hold the tendon to the bone of her broken elbow.

Kristie Phillips, the hottest gymnast in the mid-1980s, appeared in her first beauty pageant when she was a year old, started modeling classes at 18 months, and started dance school at age two. By the time she was five, she was training as a gymnast for four hours a day. Kristie's mother thought that Kristie's talents were a gift from God, and that by pushing her daughter to develop these talents she was glorifying the name of God. To say that her parents were proud of her would be an understatement: They had a picture of her painted on the side of their van.

Kristie won four gold medals at the Canadian Cup and another four at the U.S. Olympics Festival, even though she had a broken wrist at the time. In an attempt to make the 1988 Olympics team, she lost 20 pounds in three weeks, but this sudden loss of weight weakened her and she did not make the team. Kristie came away feeling that she had let down her parents, not to mention God. She became bulimic and attempted suicide.[62]

Kristie's mother, looking back on it all, has few regrets. She sees nothing wrong with a child training nine hours a day, if that's what it takes to become great. And if she had it to do over again, she says she would still send her child to Bela Karolyi for coaching.

Julissa Gomez was the gymnast, mentioned in connection with Christy Henrich, who broke her neck doing a vault. At first it looked like she would "only" be paralyzed from the neck down, but an accident in the hospital put her into a coma. She ultimately died.

Before her accident, Julissa was training with Bela Karolyi

when she sprained her knee. Her doctor told her to stay off it for a month, but Karolyi wouldn't hear of it.

Why do gymnasts put up with the pain? Because they don't know any better: Because they begin gymnastics at such an early age, they can't remember a time when they were injury-free. Why do they put up with the abuse? Because in many cases, they simply aren't allowed to quit.

Two forces keep children in gymnastics long after they have ceased to enjoy the sport.

The first is money. Elite gymnasts can expect to pay $30,000 a year for coaching and to attend competitions. To make these payments, their parents often make significant sacrifices. They might take out a second mortgage or get a second job. If their children quit, it means this money and effort was wasted. Their children's training becomes a very serious business. Said the mother of Chelle Stack, "I'll be honest with you. The more money you put into it, the more you want to see."[63]

Even if money were not an issue—even if parents could push their child toward stardom without making any financial sacrifice—there is a second force that keeps gymnasts from abandoning gymnastics despite their wish to do so. The force is the intensity with which their parents live through them and greet their accomplishments, not just with pride, but rather by claiming ownership of the accomplishments.

Thus, when Chelle Stack made the Olympic team, her mother told her, "You didn't make the Olympic team. I did."[64] And when Erica Stokes quit gymnastics nine months before the Olympics, her mother's anguish was intense: "I was grieving the loss of everything we put into this. I knew she could have walked away with medals at the Olympics. I'll tell you what it's like. It's like a death."[65]

Because parents have their finances as well as their egos invested in their child's performance, they cannot help but push their child to excel. One father put up gymnastics equipment at home so that his daughter could practice in the evening—as if the daughter's intensive daytime workouts weren't enough. Another father, if his daughter had a bad practice, spent the ride home reminding her how much her training cost him and how important it was for her to make the Olympics.

How do parents justify this sort of behavior? In some cases, they see no need for justification: Once their child reaches the elite level, they find themselves surrounded by similar-minded parents, and their own desire for success at any price does not seem out of place. In other cases, parents justify their behavior by claiming that they are acting in the interests of their child: As the mother of one driven-but-failed gymnast put it, "All we wanted was a perfect life for [our daughter]."[66] And there are parents who drive their children out of fear—fear that if they don't keep pushing their child, she will someday complain that she could have been an Olympian, if only her parents had pushed her.

What becomes of failed child gymnasts? Ironically, they often go on to become successful college gymnasts. As it turns out, less is expected (in terms of training and commitment) of gymnasts who are college seniors than is expected of elite gymnasts who are in sixth grade. Significantly, the NCAA restricts college athletes to "only" twenty hours of formal training per week, compared to, at Bela Karolyi's gym, forty-six hours a week, with only Sundays off.

The man who is arguably most responsible for the plight of girl gymnasts is Bela Karolyi. It was Karolyi who, stalking through the kindergartens of Romania, discovered Nadia Comaneci, turning cartwheels in the playground. The transformation of Nadia was brought about by means of ruthless coaching.

Karolyi later defected to the United States, but discovered that he and his wife could not find coaching jobs there: Those running the gymnastics schools thought that Americans would not tolerate the level of abuse that Karolyi employed in his coaching. In the end, though, Karolyi and his training techniques triumphed in the United States. When Karolyi-trained Mary Lou Retton won a gold medal in the Olympics, parents grew willing to entrust their children to him. The parents in question either didn't realize how much abuse their child was in for, or realized it, but reasoned that the abuse was a small price to pay for a shot at an Olympic medal.

In public, Karolyi is careful of the image he projects. When the television cameras are on him, he is a smiling bear of a man, eyes atwinkle. He gives his girls big hugs after they have competed and, when microphones are present, lavishes praise on them.

When the cameras are gone, though, the other side of Bela Karolyi emerges. What you see is a man who will do whatever it takes to produce champions. What you see, if any number of witnesses can be believed, is an evil person.

We are told, for example, that Karolyi's "track record for producing gymnasts with eating disorders is stunning."[67] We are told that he subjects his gymnasts to verbal abuse to keep their weight down, calling Erica Stokes a pregnant goat, Betty Okino a pregnant spider, Kim Zmeskal a pumpkin or a butterball, and Hilary Grivich a tank. He compared one thirteen-year-old gymnast to a cockroach on the floor. He was, author Joan Ryan tells us, an expert at exploiting a girl's insecurities.

It is Karolyi who is quoted as saying, about his gymnasts, "These girls are like little scorpions. You put them all in a bottle, and one scorpion will come out alive. That scorpion will be champion."[68] Similarly, he is quoted as saying, "The young ones are the greatest little suckers in the world. They will follow you no matter what."[69]

Karolyi would use his girl gymnasts as long as it served his purposes to do so, and then discard them like broken dolls. When Amy Jackson won the junior division of the American Classic at age 11, Karolyi called her and her parents into his office and said, "Well, you are the next one." But when Amy finished second at the U.S. Classic a short time later, Karolyi started to ignore her. Five years later, Karolyi had no recollection of her.[70]

Here is gymnast Kristie Phillips on Karolyi: "He doesn't care about the gymnasts. He doesn't care what they go through, what they suffer through, what he makes them suffer through. He cares about the fame and fortune he's getting out of it.... When we're at competitions and when we're on TV and he has a microphone on, he's a different person. He's massaging our necks, smiling and laughing and patting you on the back. This is what the public sees of Bela. But it's really the exact opposite."[71]

If the parents of Karolyi's gymnasts complain about his treatment of their daughters, they are asked to leave his training program. Many parents, realizing that no one is better than Karolyi when it comes to producing Olympic medalists, decide to grit their teeth and bear it. In order to obtain "a perfect life" for their child, they are willing to put their child through hell.

In my research on girl gymnasts, there came a troubling moment when, looking at pictures of them, I stopped seeing cute little girls who could do tricks, and started seeing "enslaved" anorexics who must spin and flip and twirl with manic intensity in order to earn their keep. Even worse, I started dwelling on the fact that for each girl good enough to be shown on television, there were hundreds who had paid the same price, if not a greater price, and who never even got to enjoy their moment of glory. For me, the illusion was shattered.

It is easy to see how someone could fall victim to the illusion that girl gymnasts were in it "for fun." We have watched our own children do cartwheels across the lawn; it is for them an act of joy. We see elite gymnasts do *their* cartwheels—and it is of course an understatement to call what they do cartwheels—and we might be led to think that this is like what our children do on the lawn, only more so, and that it is an expression, at some level, of joy. The problem is that competitive gymnasts do their routines not as an expression of joy, but as a deadly serious undertaking.

Whenever we find ourselves enjoying the performances of these girls, we have a moral obligation to stop and ask a very important question: Is the enjoyment we are experiencing really worth the suffering these children have to go through in order to entertain us? We will return to this question below.

Children on Ice

Skating has undergone a transformation much like that in gymnastics. There was a time when women's skating was dominated by women. No longer. The move to younger competitors, however, has not been as dramatic as in gymnastics. Whereas in gymnastics the champions are generally between fourteen and seventeen years old, in skating they are generally between sixteen and twenty. Of course, although the champions may be older than in gymnastics, it does not follow that they begin their training at a later age than gymnasts. To the contrary, like gymnasts they must begin their training when they are quite tiny in order to have a chance of "making it" as teenagers.

Mind you, the relatively advanced age of skaters is not the consequence of any scruples on the part of coaches or skating federations. Rather, it is a consequence of the fact that in women's skating, unlike in women's gymnastics, judges are looking for femininity. It isn't enough that a skater can do wonderful tricks: She must look like the ideal woman doing them. Wind-up twelve-year-old dolls may be able to succeed in gymnastics, but not in skating.

Curiously, this difference between skating and gymnastics has made skating more lucrative for its stars than gymnastics. Since skaters ideally resemble "the girl next door," they are likely candidates for the promotion of any number of products—soups, soaps, clothing, etc. Gymnasts, on the other hand, rarely resemble the girl next door—unless the girl next door is rather short and afflicted with anorexia. It takes willpower to imagine a gymnast sitting down to a bowl of soup. In the words of one agent, "Gymnasts don't have the sex appeal that figure skaters do. They're too young and robotic."[72]

Like girl gymnasts, girl skaters experience abuse. Some of the abuse is dispensed by coaches, who might hit skaters or pull their hair to enforce skating "discipline." Some of the abuse is dispensed by parents. Tonya Harding's mother beat her with a hairbrush for missing jumps. Skating coach and former skater Evelyn Kramer, when her own child began skating, pinched her, punched her, and screamed at her in an attempt to make her skate better.

And as is the case in gymnastics, the parents of skaters are often willing to make almost any sacrifice in their pursuit of skating glory. The parents of one skater gave her away (more precisely, they arranged for their daughter's coach to have custody of her) so she wouldn't have to give up skating.

Tennis Brats

Tracy Austin[73] was to tennis what Olga Korbut was to gymnastics: She proved not just that children could compete with adults, but that they could beat them.

Austin began tennis at age two, when her mother enrolled her in a tennis program for children age three to eight. She played in her first tournament at age seven. By age nine she won her city's ten-and-under and twelve-and-under titles on the same day. She won her first nationals at age eleven, was on the cover of *Sports Illustrated* at age thirteen, and played at Wimbledon at age fourteen, where she lost to defending champion Chris Evert. One commentator said of her appearance at Wimbledon that she looked like "a deserter from the Campfire Girls."[74] Later that year, she became the youngest quarterfinalist in U.S. Open history.

Austin became a professional on October 23, 1978, less than two months before her sixteenth birthday. As a sophomore in high school she had won $189,500, but was still getting a dollar-a-week allowance and a dollar for each *A* she got in school. Austin's explanation: "I think my parents kept this up because they wanted me to still have normal childhood goals."[75] She put her mother on salary and bought her a Rolex watch and a full-length mink. The rest of the money went into trust accounts.

Injuries started striking Austin in 1980. In 1984, at age 21, her career came to what was, by historical standards, a premature end, but what is, by the standards of the late twentieth century, a typical end.

What is interesting about Austin is not just that she experienced such success at such an early age, but that her success seems to have been more self-motivated than parentally-motivated. She preferred tennis to dolls, and rather than pushing her to play tennis, Austin's parents tried to restrain her and make her realize that there is more to life than tennis. Her mother, for example, would not allow her to play tennis seven days a week. Even when she had attained star status, her parents wouldn't allow trips that kept her out of school a week or more.

Furthermore, whereas many child athletes succeed through monumental effort, Austin seemed to have been born to play tennis. In particular, her training was quite moderate compared to that of many of her child competitors:

> Seeing some of the best players my age made me realize how non-intense my tennis background really was. When I was at the *Seventeen* magazine tournament in Washington in 1976, I watched some little girls get up at six-thirty in the morning to jump rope and run several miles. For a couple days, I tried to keep up, but I didn't think it helped my tennis, so I told myself not to worry about that, that I was doing the right thing. Then I won the tournament.[76]

In the same way as Olga Korbut's success inspired legions of little girls to take up gymnastics—not to mention inspiring legions of parents to push their little girls to become competitive gymnasts—Tracy Austin's success brought on a wave of youthful tennis players, including Jennifer Capriati and Andrea Jaeger.

Jessica Dubroff, RIP

Seven-year-old Jessica Dubroff was on her way to becoming a star. Had she completed her flight across America, she would have been the youngest person ever to do so.

America watched and either supported or was indifferent to her effort until tragedy struck: Her plane crashed while taking off in a cold rain, killing her, her father, and her flight instructor. Only then did people ask the obvious questions: What was this little girl doing in an airplane, and why did no one try to stop her?

Jessica Dubroff was not a licensed pilot at the time of her flight; you have to be sixteen to get a license. Indeed, her feet did not even reach the rudder pedals of the plane she was flying. And the record she hoped to set would arguably have been a meaningless record: Although she may have at times controlled the plane, her flight instructor was by her side to help her over any rough spots. Even the *Guinness Book of Records*, home to exotic records, regarded youngest-pilot records as bogus: It dropped the category in 1989.

What, one wonders, could Jessica's parents have been thinking? Her parents, divorced, both seemed to think that childhood was a dispensable part of life and that their job as parents was to push their child to mature quickly. Jessica was schooled at home by her mother, a self-described artist and spiritual healer. Lessons sometimes consisted of doing chores rather than more conventional studies. She was not allowed to play with dolls, but instead was encouraged to play with tools.

The cross-country trip was her father's idea. At his urging, Jessica, in the publicity campaign leading up to the flight, had handed out signed photographs to members of the local city council and had written a letter to President Clinton, asking for a visit to the White House at the end of her trip. Jessica's father spent $1,300 on special "Jessica Dubroff" baseball caps, as part of a strategy to gain media attention.

The press found the picture irresistible. There she was, in her leather jacket, a miniature Amelia Earhart. ABC even gave Jessica a video camera with which to record her journey. It was the media's attention that presumably sealed Jessica's fate: If there had been no media to pay attention to Jessica's "record," there would have been little reason to try to set it.

How did Jessica's mother react to the death of her child? According to her, she had done what any good mother would do: "I did everything so this child could have freedom and choice." She apparently felt no responsibility for the consequences of her daughter's parentally-pushed "choices." She said that if she had it to do over again, she would do nothing differently and that "I would want all my children to die in a state of joy. I would prefer it was not at the age of seven."[77] She declared that she would fight any efforts on the part of the FAA to block other children from being able to follow in her daughter's footsteps.

In the end it became apparent that America, before Jessica's crash, had done what it almost invariably does with child stars and would-be child stars: It assumed that the child in question really wanted to do what she was doing and that the child's parents had her best interests in mind in letting her do it. In this case, as in the case of many of the child stars we have discussed, both assumptions were mistaken.

Jessica's words to the *Times* of London—"I'm going to fly till I die"[78]—proved in the end to be tragically ironic.

In the cases I have described in this chapter, children traded their childhoods for the sake of money, fame, or both. Such cases leave us with a very important question: Is the trade worth it? I am inclined to think that in nearly every case, it is not.

Recently I saw a television program in which former child gymnast Mary Lou Retton handed a check to a promising young female ice-skater. The check was to help pay for the skater's training, which involved, Retton informed us, getting up before dawn each day to practice for several hours. The thought occurred to me, as I watched this scene unfold, that if Retton wanted to help the little girl, she shouldn't be handing her a check. Instead she should take the girl aside and explain that there is more to life than skating, particularly if you are a child.

It is indeed curious. If the skater's parents had, in the wee hours of the morning, taken their daughter not to a skating rink, but to a job in a factory, they would likely have been arrested. At the factory, though, their daughter would probably have worked less hard than she did during her skating workout, with much less chance of suffering an injury. Furthermore, she would have been guaranteed payment for her efforts, whereas in skating she may never get paid for her efforts—or, more likely, will end up paying far more to train as a skater than she ever gets back. So why is it that, rather than treating this girl as an abused child, we instead admire her and her parents and maybe even hold her up to our own children as a role model? This is a troubling question, and one that I will explore in the next chapter.

CHAPTER 3

WHAT PRICE CHILDHOOD?

A re child stars born? Sometimes. In a born star, the talent is undeniably there, even though no one takes steps to implant or develop it. Indeed, the child's parents might be oblivious to the talent or might even try to suppress it. A classic example of a born star was Mozart: By age seven he was a more accomplished musician, both in terms of performing and composing, than most of us could ever hope to become. In the movies, Shirley Temple was arguably a born star. It is true that her mother pushed her talents along, but she had a considerable natural gift for singing and dancing. And I suppose that I would include the Dionne quints among the born stars, although their "talent" consisted in looking alike. In the realm of sports, I would submit Tracy Austin as an example of a born star. She played tennis wonderfully well at an early age, and improved steadily despite what would, by today's standards, count as minimal coaching and training.

Most stars, however, are not *born* stars; they are *manufactured* stars. They gain stardom because their parents have gone to great lengths to push them toward stardom. Sometimes these parental efforts are triggered by early, but hardly overwhelming, signs of talent. In other cases, parents push their child toward stardom even though there is little evidence of talent; for these parents, the pursuit of stardom is a triumph of hope over reason.

It is not unusual, as we have seen, for the appearance of one born child star to stimulate the manufacture, or attempted manufacture, of many other child stars. Thus, in the realm of sports, Tracy Austin's youthful success in tennis led to a surge in the number of youthful professionals, most of them arguably manufactured child stars. And in the realm of acting, Shirley Temple's fame set many parents to work trying to turn their child into "the next Shirley Temple."

Why would parents attempt to manufacture a child star? They might have their own interests in mind: They might want a child star so they can bask in his reflected fame and glory, so they can benefit financially, or so they can vicariously live out their own dreams of being famous. On the other hand, parents might attempt to manufacture a child star because they have their child's interests in mind. They might think, for example, that their child would benefit from the wealth that typically comes with stardom, conceivably wealth enough so the child could retire before reaching adulthood. And even those parents who do not aim at this level of wealth for their child might have another, more realistic, monetary goal in mind: They might push their child toward stardom so he will ultimately win a college scholarship.

Ripe Apples

When parents find themselves with star material (either by birth or as the result of parental encouragement), they are faced with a distressing dilemma: They can either exploit the talent while the child is a child, or wait to exploit the talent and thereby possibly lose the opportunity to exploit it. When child tennis star Jennifer Capriati's father was faced with the dilemma, he resolved it with the following bit of reasoning: "Where I come from we have a proverb: 'When the apple is ripe, eat it.'"[1]

To illustrate the Ripe Apple Dilemma, consider parents who innocently enroll their daughter in gymnastics lessons, only to discover that she has a natural aptitude for gymnastics. They let their daughter compete, and she wins. Coaches from far away take an interest in the girl and invite her to come live at their training facility. The parents then have the following choice: They can keep their daughter at home, even though it makes it virtually certain that she will never become a famous gymnast, or they can send her off, which means that instead of spending the next several years doing normal "kid" stuff, she will be put on a restricted diet, have a restricted social life, be forced to practice gymnastics for hours each day, suffer the injuries that are consequent to such practice, and be away from her family for extended periods. But if she does all this, she will have a chance at becoming a famous gymnast. The decision can be postponed for months, but not years: The apple is ripe now, but soon will spoil.

In some cases the talents of a child star must be exploited immediately (if at all) because those talents are likely to fade as childhood fades. This is presumably true of girls' gymnastics. In other cases the talents of the child star must be exploited immediately (if at all) not because those talents will fade, but because what makes them valuable is their presence *in a child*. In the case of Shirley Temple, it wasn't that she could tap dance better than adults (the way that Nadia Comaneci could do gymnastics better than adults); it was that her tap-dancing ability was astonishing (or at least cute) in a child. The same level of tap dancing in an adult would in no way be noteworthy.

The Ripe Apple Dilemma is nothing new. We have seen, for example, the dilemma that confronted those Italian parents of the 1700s whose children had beautiful voices. To exploit this talent to the fullest, the parents had to decide not only whether to make their child give up his childhood for the study of music, but whether to make their child give up his manhood as well. The decision was one that could not be postponed: Unless you castrate before puberty, there is no point in castrating. And if you choose not to castrate, you might thereby be consigning your child, who could have been a famous opera star, to a life of mediocrity.

To be sure, the ripe-apple comparison can be overdone. It isn't always the case that the talents that make a child a star are perishable commodities. It may well be that girl gymnasts can do things that women gymnasts can't, but it is far from clear that in a sport like tennis, a child star who is not pushed will be passing up his chance at a career in tennis. Indeed, it may even be that if a child with tennis ability is allowed to develop mentally, emotionally, and physically, before embarking on his tennis career, his career will be more successful than it would have been if he had been pushed as a child.

Most parents—the parents of ordinary children as opposed to the parents of child stars—aren't forced to make important career decisions for their child. Rather, the ordinary child is raised in a career-neutral fashion and is given the opportunity, when he is in his late teens, of choosing a career for himself.

It hasn't always been this way. Time was when, because of the years of training it took children to master a trade, parents of even ordinary children had to make important decisions about their children's careers when their children were quite young. Thus, consider the plight of young Ben Franklin. Franklin's father, a tallow-chandler, assumed that Ben would follow in his footsteps and become a chandler. Ben made it clear, however, that he did not enjoy the work. The father, fearing that Ben would follow the example of another son and run off and go to sea, decided to allow Ben to change careers. He took Ben around to see various tradesmen at work and to see what Ben was drawn to. Finally Ben's love of reading settled the matter: Ben would become a printer.[2]

Notice that for people of Ben Franklin's era (and, more generally, people before 1850), the issue was not whether childhood would be sacrificed to a profession: It was assumed that it would be. Fortunately for today's children, parents no longer have to make this assumption; so when parents (e.g., the parents of child stars) *do* sacrifice their child's formative years to a profession, the sacrifice is one that must be justified.

Childhood Stardom: Weighing Costs and Benefits

Suppose, then, parents are confronted by the Ripe Apple Dilemma: They find themselves with a child who is potential star material. Should they pursue (or allow their child to pursue) stardom? In attempting to answer this question, they might go through a costs and benefits analysis of childhood stardom. If it turned out that the costs (to the child) of childhood stardom far outweighed the benefits (to the child), then they should forgo stardom. If, on the other hand, it looked like their child could benefit substantially from the pursuit of stardom at minimal personal cost, then a decision to pursue stardom might be justifiable.

The Benefits of Stardom

What are the benefits of childhood stardom? Three that come to mind are fame, training for an adult career, and money.

By definition, child stars enjoy a degree of fame. It must be wonderful to have complete strangers love and admire you. Having said this, we must add that fame can be a mixed blessing. After all, when complete strangers love and admire you, you lose a great deal of your privacy. We saw in the previous chapter, for example, that Shirley Temple, thanks to her fame, needed bodyguards and could not play outside her home. Furthermore, the love and admiration of complete strangers can be woefully hollow if you do not love and admire yourself. There is cruel irony in being unhappy even though you are living what many would take to be a dream life.

Some would claim that childhood stardom is beneficial to children inasmuch as it gives them a head start on their adult careers. If you have been acting since you were five, you will be a truly awesome actor, it is suggested, when you become an adult. And if you have been practicing tennis intensively since you were five, you will, as a young adult, be a much better tennis player than those who took up the game later in life. The problem with this suggestion is that, as we have seen, there is little reason to think that child stars are likely to have successful adult careers in their area of stardom. Most child actors find themselves unable to make the transition to adult roles; and even if they can make the transition, they may find that they have grown weary of acting. Likewise, many child athletes "use up" their bodies long before reaching adulthood and are unable to compete as adults.

Many child stars are thus forced to make a career change in early adulthood. The intensive training required to produce a child star, however, is likely to leave that child hopelessly one-sided, with few outside interests and with a haphazard and unfinished education. This might mean that his job prospects, once he abandons his childhood career, are bleak. Child actors may go into a profession like sales in which they can trade on their fading fame. Child athletes may go into coaching; and as ironic as it may seem, they might, as adults, make their living enticing other children to give up *their* childhoods for a chance at glory.

And no matter what career an ex-child-star has as an adult, it is likely to be much less glamorous and rewarding than the childhood career was. He won a gold medal at the Olympics; big deal if he is the top insurance salesman in his district.

Money is arguably the most important benefit of childhood stardom. And although there was a time when child stars could not count on being able to receive, as adults, the money for which they traded their childhood, things have improved considerably on this score. Even so, we can ask whether these financial benefits will translate into personal benefits. One can, after all, question the value of money.

A child who reaches age eighteen with $3,000 in the bank is clearly better off than a child who reaches age eighteen broke: The former child will be able to eat and clothe and shelter himself; the latter child will not. And you might even be able to make a case that a child who reaches age eighteen with $30,000 in the bank is better off than the eighteen-year-old with $3,000 in the bank. It will be difficult, though, to show that the child who reaches age eighteen with $3 million or $30 million in the bank will be better off than the child who reaches age eighteen with $30,000. While it is true that the youthful millionaire will be able to buy a big house and won't have to work, we are left with the question of whether the person who embarks on his adult life with a big house and no need to work will, in the long run, live a better, more satisfying life because of it. If we think there are things in life that are worth having but that cannot be bought, we will not necessarily conclude that richer is better. In particular, if we think there are many benefits to be derived from spending one's adult life earning one's keep, we might conclude that a large bank balance, rather than being an asset to someone entering adulthood, is instead an obstacle to overcome.

Considerable research has been done into the effect that money has on happiness. It turns out that in America, rich people are not that much happier than poor people, and in the world at large, people in rich countries are not that much happier than people in poor countries. Summarizing this research, psychologist Michael Argyle writes that "money does not make people happy, or at any rate it has a very small effect (much less than that of social relationships, for example)."[3]

Why is it, then, that so many people labor under the illusion that greater material wealth will bring them happiness? In part because people tend to reason along the following lines: "At present I detect in myself various unfulfilled desires (e.g., the desire for a bigger house or a more luxurious vacation), and because these desires are unfulfilled, their existence detracts from my happiness. But material wealth would enable me to satisfy these desires: I could buy a bigger house and go on a more luxurious vacation. Therefore, it follows that material wealth would make me happier."

This line of reasoning sounds plausible, and because of this, many are seduced by it. Where it fails is in assuming that once material wealth has been used to satisfy a person's currently-existing desires, new desires will not spring up to replace them. This assumption is, for most people and under most circumstances, patently false.

Unfortunately, desire—and in particular, material desire—is like the Hydra of Greek mythology: For each head you cut off, two new heads grow. Thus, when people satisfy a desire for, say, a bigger house by buying a bigger house, they soon detect in themselves a new, unfulfilled, desire—perhaps for an even bigger house than the one they just bought.[4] The process of desire fulfillment, repeated many times, can produce some bizarre consequences, like a 30,000-square-foot house being occupied by a single person.[5]

The attempt to "buy" happiness is thus doomed to fail. And for this reason, those parents who push their children to stardom so that they can become wealthy at an early age and therefore be happy throughout their adult lives are probably making a big mistake.

At this point it might be suggested that our list of the benefits of stardom is not yet complete. In particular, some might argue that aside from fame, professional training, or money, there are some valuable lessons that children learn when they pursue stardom. Thus, the child who spends years perfecting his tennis game might learn the value of hard work or sportsmanship.

The problem with this suggestion is that it is far from clear that child stars actually learn the lessons just mentioned. Child tennis stars are rarely cited as examples of good sportsmen. And as far as the value of hard work goes, it is true that a tennis star works very hard to get where he is. Having arrived, though, the concept of the value of hard work gets subverted. The child tennis star reaches his late teens thinking that it is entirely appropriate to be paid hundreds of thousands of dollars for an afternoon of tennis or to be paid millions of dollars to wear a certain brand of shoe.

Another thing to realize about the above-mentioned lessons is that children need not pursue stardom to learn them. You can learn sportsmanship by participating in Little League; you can learn the value of hard work by having a paper route.

It might also be suggested that we have neglected another benefit of stardom: the intense feeling of accomplishment that comes when a child gets a recording contract, or gets the starring role in a film, or wins a medal in the Olympics.

While stardom is doubtless capable of giving child stars a feeling of accomplishment, the "victories" these stars achieve are often hollow victories. Skater Debi Thomas traded her childhood for a chance at stardom. She went on to win a medal in the

Olympics, but because it was "only" a bronze medal, the emotion she experienced was not one of joy but rather one of "horror and shame."[6] Tiffany Chin, who was favored to win the 1985 U.S. Figure Skating Championship, was asked how she would feel if she didn't win. Her reply: "Devastated. I don't know. I'd probably die." And when she did win, what emotion did she experience? "I didn't feel happiness. I felt relief. Which was disappointing."[7] For many child stars, the prospect of success is a lose-lose proposition. If they don't succeed, they are crushed; if they do succeed, they experience, in many cases, not joy, but a grim sense of relief at not failing. It is entirely possible that a Little Leaguer experiences a greater feeling of accomplishment on hitting a home run than a child skater experiences on winning an Olympic medal.

The Costs of Stardom

Let us now continue our costs and benefits analysis of childhood stardom by considering its costs.

One big cost attendant to the pursuit of childhood stardom is paid in terms of physical health. The child tennis player might end up with a ruined shoulder or elbow. The ballet dancer might hobble through her adult life as a result of injuries sustained practicing ballet. In other cases the pursuit of childhood stardom might set the stage for an adulthood plagued by eating disorders. And finally, children have died pursuing stardom.

The health cost is not, however, the only cost incurred by child stars, for in most cases child stars are forced to sacrifice a "normal childhood" in their pursuit of stardom. Their hectic schedules simply will not allow for one. And what does the loss of a normal childhood entail? It entails, for one thing, the loss of time that would have been spent in idle play—that is, in "having fun." It isn't that child stars don't want to have fun; it's that they must spend their time taking lessons or practicing or "working."

Some will deprecate the value of this "cost." They will deride idle play as wasted time and argue that we are doing children a favor by diverting them to more serious pursuits. I would argue, however, that time spent "having fun" is intrinsically valuable: By definition, it is pleasurable to "have fun," and pleasure is intrinsically valuable. Furthermore, I would argue (and many child psychologists would agree) that idle play isn't really as idle as it looks—that it is instead a time when a child can explore his world and himself and learn many things that would be difficult or impossible to learn in a more structured environment.

But there is more to a normal childhood than idle play. There is also the time spent exploring and developing one's talents. Most children (if they have good parents) will be encouraged to try lots of different activities. They might be encouraged to try a variety of sports. They might be encouraged to take music lessons or art lessons. They might be encouraged to take science classes at a museum. And all of this is (or should be) done in an effort to help the child find himself. He might be an exceptional musician, an exceptional swimmer, or have artistic ability, but how will he know unless he tries?

Notice, however, that the time and effort child stars spend developing their one big talent typically reduces or eliminates the time left to explore the other talents they might have.

It might be suggested that it is unlikely that a child star will possess a second talent as promising as the one that brought him stardom, so there is little reason to explore the other talents child stars might possess. I agree that it would be rare to find a child who is, say, both an exceptional tennis player and an exceptional cellist. At the same time, I would like to argue that even if a child is an exceptional tennis player, it makes sense to find out whether he possesses other talents which, though not exceptional, show some promise. It might be, for example, that even though a child is a world-class tennis player, he would be happier, in the long run (i.e., in the course of a lifetime), if he pursued a career as a less-than-world-class cellist. He would, to be sure, make more money as a tennis player than as a cellist, but money, as I have suggested above, isn't everything. Better to be happy and relatively poor than rich but miserable.

Some have suggested that children do not have to *sacrifice* their childhood to become stars. To the contrary, in pursuing stardom they are merely *postponing* their childhood and can enjoy it later in life—enjoy it all the more inasmuch as they will, if their push for stardom succeeds, be financially secure young adults when they enjoy it. Thus, the coach of gymnast Shannon Miller, when asked whether Miller had given up anything to become an elite gymnast, replied that she had given up nothing: "If there were sacrifices, they were from her family to allow her to strive for an identity. She'll be done with her career at nineteen or twenty and will have the rest of her life to go to the movies with friends."[8] One will naturally wonder, though, whether a trip to the movies with friends at age twenty is the same experience or plays the same role in personal development as a trip to the movies with friends at age ten.

The child star may not realize the sacrifice that he is making in giving up a normal childhood. The daily routine of the child star might keep him out of contact with other children; and when he does come into contact with children, they might not be "normal" children, but other child stars or children who have been "screened" by his parents. As a result, the child star might not realize that there are other childhoods than the one he is living, and his parents might have an interest in keeping him in the dark about the possibility of other childhoods.

In many cases, it is only when he reaches adulthood that the child star comes to realize that other childhoods were possible and that his own childhood stardom meant that he had to give up something very special and irreplaceable. Thus, former child star Diana Serra Cary, on considering the lives of her fellow former child stars, points out that they typically experience anguish as adults: "Somehow the defense mechanism breaks down around the age of thirty. They no longer seem able to suppress their outrage at the abuse and exploitation of their childhoods."[9]

Besides paying a price in terms of health and a price in terms of a lost childhood, a child star will typically pay an important emotional price as well. Childhood stardom generally changes the relationship between parents and a child. Ideally, the love of a parent is unconditional love: Parents should make their child feel that they will love him "always and no matter what." In the case of child stars, though, it can be quite difficult for parents to communicate their unconditional love to a child. Notice, after all, that the parents of the child star might find themselves constantly putting pressure on the child to "perform"; we saw some examples of this in the previous chapter. It is only natural for the child to worry about how his parents' feelings toward him might change if he fails to perform. Notice, too, that for many child stars, the parents act as coaches, constantly pointing out the child's failings and offering advice on how the child can improve. The child might come to take this constant criticism as evidence that his parents not only don't love him, but actively disapprove of him.

I'm not saying that the parents of child stars love their child only conditionally; what I *am* saying is that the circumstances of a child star's life can make it difficult for his parents to communicate their unconditional love to him. The child star might come to feel that his parents' love is conditional, and from the child's point of view, this feeling is what counts.

Another psychological cost of childhood stardom results from the child's having too much responsibility at too early an age. It is one thing to voluntarily take on major obligations as an adult, when you have had considerable experience taking them on and have developed confidence in your ability to discharge them. It is quite another thing to have major obligations thrust on you as a child, when you have had little experience taking them on and are far from certain whether you will be able to successfully discharge them.

A normal child has little of importance riding on his shoulders. He may be expected to do his schoolwork and pick up after himself; but even these are responsibilities which, if he fails to fulfill them, will have relatively minor consequences. On the other hand, a child star will typically find that much rides on his shoulders. He will find that he has to perform on cue—and speak his lines or win his match—or a large number of adults, who are depending upon him, will be disappointed. He might even find that how well he does his "job" determines in large part his family's standard of living.

In gymnastics, for example, the pressure is uniquely intense. Because training takes such a toll and because one can easily "outgrow" gymnastics, most girl gymnasts can hope to compete "in their prime" in only one Olympics. And given the nature of Olympic competition, they generally will not, in their performances, be given a second chance: Their performances must be flawless in order for them to be in competition for a medal. And to make things even worse, the whole world will be closely watching their attempt at stardom.

In gymnastics, what count as fatal errors? Little things—indeed, things so small that the untrained eye does not even see them. For example, in the 1992 Olympics, Kim Zmeskal stepped two inches out of bounds, thereby ruining her chances at a gold medal. (Think of it: trading your childhood for a chance at fame, and then failing because of a two-inch misstep!) It is a level of pressure that most adults would find unendurable.

Or consider the fate of child tennis star Jennifer Capriati. She turned pro at age thirteen. (Women's tennis bent its minimum-age rule to let her do so.) Her father—whose "ripe apple" comment was quoted at the beginning of this chapter—acted as her manager. At age sixteen she played against Monica Seles in the semifinal of the 1991 U.S. Open—and lost. A mature tennis player might have felt pride at making it that far in such an important tournament. She might have been stung by the loss, but might have taken it as an important educational experience, and gone on to learn the lesson it had to offer. For Jennifer Capriati, however, the loss seems to have triggered a personal collapse. Tennis writer (and former tennis prodigy) Eliot Berry observed Capriati shortly after the loss. She was, he has written, "just crushed inside and outside; she was truly beaten. It was not only her toughest loss ever, it was one of the toughest losses I had ever seen any athlete take. She could barely keep from crying while she tried to answer the questions that her game could not."[10] Six years later, Capriati—now a young adult in the thick of a comeback attempt—was still sobbing.[11]

What happens when children are given significant responsibilities at an early age? Judging from the comments of the child stars quoted in the preceding chapter, one consequence is that they feel a profound sense of guilt. At first this might seem surprising. These children, after all, have accomplished a great deal; they have done things other children can only dream of. One would think that rather than feeling guilty, child stars would experience a sense of pride.

The guilt arises, perhaps, because child stars are by nature unsatisfied with anything but their best effort. If they were satisfied with less, it is unlikely that they would have risen to stardom.

Adults, on the other hand, typically realize that in this life, it isn't always necessary or possible to give your very best effort. There is, in other words, such a thing as an effort which, though not your very best, nevertheless suffices: It is a "good enough" effort. Child stars, one suspects, do not realize this: For them, a "good enough" effort simply isn't good enough. Indeed, even their very best effort is barely good enough. The child star might go to sleep at night thinking not about what he accomplished during the day, but about what he might have done if only he had worked a little harder.

For a concrete example of the "driven" behavior of child stars, consider again the case of gymnast Christie Henrich. She broke her neck, but was back in competition three months later. Obviously, what she did could be done: She did it. Most people, however, would agree with the claim that although what she did *could* be done, it *needn't* be done. Most people would not have held it against Henrich if, after recovering from her broken neck, she had gone "on vacation" for a few months before returning to training. Of course, Henrich could not see things this way. Any effort of less than 110 percent was, by her standards, unacceptable; and of course 110 percent efforts are by definition impossible.

Even as adults, child stars may continue to pay a psychological price for their childhood stardom. For as adults, such stars are faced with the difficult question, What now? The star has already enjoyed some of life's greatest successes. Whatever achievements follow will seem bland in comparison; indeed, they might even feel like failures.

Ordinary people can spend their adult lives with the dream (the illusion?) that the best is ahead of them. Child stars must, in many cases, spend their adult lives in the knowledge that the best is almost certainly behind them.

Here is how writer Eliot Berry, who himself had to deal with a childhood spent preparing for tennis stardom, explains the risks that a child takes when he embarks on the path to athletic stardom:

> When you spend the best part of the years from six to thirty-two playing tennis, a large part of you remains forever a tennis player—even when you try to go on to other pursuits. It can hurt when others never think of you as anything but a tennis player. With the label of athlete or ex-athlete comes the suspicion that you have remained a type of prodigy all your life, an 'extended child.' Eventually, even great athletes are faced with living in more conventional ways. Instead of the smiles of admiration you got as a young player, now that your tennis career is over, you may get blank looks as others watch you stumble ungracefully into their world. *That* is what makes pro tennis such a gamble for the young.[12]

The above list of the costs of childhood stardom makes it sound as if every child star reaches adulthood as a physical wreck, working at some unrewarding job, and bemoaning his lost childhood. This, of course, is not true. There are doubtless many child stars who live happy, successful adult lives. We must also keep in mind that many people, despite having lived "normal" childhoods, are not particularly happy or successful as adults. In the same way as childhood stardom does not guarantee adult misery, a "normal childhood" does not guarantee adult bliss.

We also don't know what would have become of the child stars if they had lived normal childhoods. Presumably, some would have been happier having normal childhoods. Others, however, would not. Consider, in particular, those child prodigies (e.g., Tracy Austin) who are loaded with talent and who, without any pushing from adults, feel driven to use it. Such children are probably destined to become child stars unless parents actively take steps to prevent it. It could be, though, that if parents *did* take such steps, the children would be worse off because of it: They might spend their childhood in a state of intense frustration.

The Analysis

Now that we have examined some of the costs and benefits of childhood stardom, we are in a position to return to our original question and ask whether the benefits of childhood stardom typically outweigh the costs. The above discussion raises serious questions about whether they do: The benefits of childhood stardom appear to be, in many cases, mixed blessings, while the costs of childhood stardom are not only very real, but sometimes brutal. The bargain parents make when they allow their child to become a star—or even more so, when they push their child to become a star—will, in many cases, be hard to defend.

To better understand the nature of this "bargain," consider the following somewhat fanciful story. Suppose that a girl was very talented at hopping up and down on one foot. Suppose that whenever she engaged in informal hopping competitions with her friends, she easily won, hopping away long after her friends had given up. Suppose she developed an obsession with hopping and soon was hopping most of her waking hours.

In a case like this, it is clear what the girl's parents should do: They should get her psychological counseling. An obsession with hopping is not healthy. Her parents, if they love the girl, should take whatever steps they can to make her see that there is more to life than hopping up and down on one foot. It would be tragic indeed if the girl missed out on a normal childhood because she could not stop hopping.

Now change the story slightly. Suppose some very rich and eccentric man saw the girl hopping up and down on one foot and told her parents that he would be willing to pay her millions of dollars if she would hop like this for hours each day until she turned eighteen—meaning that she would spend most of her childhood hopping. (If the thought of a shady figure going around attempting to "buy" children sounds unrealistic, realize this: In America today there are "investors" who spend their time seeking out child athletes to "own." These individuals might seek out the parents of a child who is talented at tennis and offer $200,000 in return for a contract giving the "investor" in question 30 percent of the child's future income from tennis.)[13] Suppose the parents were convinced that the offer was genuine and that steps could be taken to guarantee payment of the agreed-upon sum, as long as she met the conditions of the deal. This offer would be tempting, but still many parents would resist it. To accept the offer would be to sell their daughter's childhood. Furthermore, all that hopping could cause physical injury to their child. Still, there would be all those millions waiting for her when she reached adulthood....

Now let us add one last twist to the story. Suppose that besides making millions by hopping, the girl could become a celebrity doing it. Suppose, for instance, that a hopping craze had swept the nation and that hopping competitions had become commonplace, competitions she would win. Suppose the reason the man wants to pay her for hopping is that he thinks he can profit from being her sponsor: He sells a certain brand of shoe that is favored by hoppers. In this case, the offer he made would become irresistible to many parents. To trade their child's childhood for money *and* fame makes perfect sense, right?

What does the above story prove? Not much. It does serve to remind us, though, that children can be harmed by doing too much of one thing and that part of the job of parents is to help bring a kind of balance into their child's life. The story also helps make clear the extent to which parents, when they allow their children to pursue stardom, are allowing their children to do something they know will probably harm them, but do so because they feel the harm will be compensated for. What form will the compensation take? For the most part, money and fame.

For those who deny that it is the prospect of future money and fame that causes parents to push their children to become, say, tennis or gymnastics stars, let me pose the following question: Would these same parents push their children to pursue these sports with the same intensity if it were *impossible* to become famous and wealthy playing tennis or doing gymnastics? Not likely.

Some will protest against my use of the hopping analogy and point out that tennis and gymnastics are altogether different from hopping on one foot. Tennis and gymnastics, they will tell us, are genuine sports; hopping on one foot is not. To make this protest stick, though, they will have to provide us with criteria to distinguish between "genuine" sports and "bogus" sports, and will likely find themselves hard-pressed to provide such criteria. What counts as a "genuine" sport depends on one's culture, and even within a culture, the list of genuine sports changes with time. Snowboarding and street-luging used to be regarded as bogus sports, but this has changed.

I agree that it is unlikely that hopping on one foot will ever become a "genuine" sport in this country. (But then again, I would have said the same thing about snowboarding and street-luging a decade ago, and would have been wrong in both cases.) What I am certain of, though, is that if it ever *were* possible to become famous and wealthy hopping on one foot, hopping schools would soon appear and be filled with youthful hopping hopefuls—children prepared to trade their childhoods for a shot at hopping glory. And behind each of these children would stand parents, calmly rationalizing their decision to encourage their child's obsessive behavior.

But what if a child *wants* to spend his childhood training intensely? What if it is *the child* who is pushing the pursuit of stardom? It is clearly going to be easier to justify pursuing stardom if the child wants to be a star than if he doesn't; but even if the child does want to pursue stardom, it hardly follows that his parents should let him do so. After all, one of the most important jobs of parents is to keep a child from doing things that he wants to do, but that aren't good for him. In particular, in most cases a caring parent will respond to a childhood obsession not by encouraging the obsession, but by helping the child overcome the obsession and get some perspective on life.

Young children are incapable of giving truly informed consent, inasmuch as they typically do not comprehend the consequences of their choices. So for a child to agree to a childhood spent in gyms—or to castration, for that matter—does not somehow take his parents off the hook, ethically speaking, for allowing him to do so.

What about the Failed Stars?

Suppose that the above costs and benefits analysis is mistaken. Suppose we can convince ourselves that in many or most cases, the benefits child stars derive from their stardom significantly outweigh the costs associated with stardom. Does it follow that parents should push their children down the road to stardom?

I think not. Notice, after all, that parents who have a child with "star potential" can never be certain that their child will someday attain star status. Thus, parents who are considering allowing (or forcing) their child to pursue stardom do so in the knowledge that there is a chance that their child will fail to become a star. Indeed, there is not just a *chance* that their child will fail, but it is *highly probable* that their child will fail: For every child who actually becomes a star, there are hundreds or thousands who initially looked as promising and who worked as hard, but who never quite made it.

Consider, by way of example, the odds faced by would-be skating stars. Unless a skater makes the Olympic team, she has little chance of cashing in on her skating prowess. The problem is that in a given decade, there will be only three Olympics, and America can send at most three female singles skaters to a given Olympics. This means that in a given decade, at most nine American female singles skaters have a chance at profiting substantially from their skating.[14] And yet, in each decade, how many little girls are getting up before the crack of dawn, spending hours working out in the cold of an ice-skating rink, heading off for school, and then spending their time after school not in play, but putting in even more hours skating? Hundreds? Thousands?

It might be suggested that parents should be realistic when assessing the talents of their children, and push toward stardom only those who genuinely show talent at an early age. There are two problems with this suggestion. The first is that many parents will deceive themselves about the extent of their child's talent. But even if we could overcome this obstacle, there is one very important thing to keep in mind: *Early talent is no guarantee of future success.* Indeed, Eliot Berry, who has seen lots of tennis prodigies come and go, has suggested that when it comes to tennis, "the girls and boys who first seem destined for greatness at thirteen and fourteen, usually hit a wall by age seventeen or eighteen."[15]

Thus, even if we were convinced that the benefits of becoming a child star outweighed the costs, we must, in determining whether it makes sense for children to pursue stardom, go on to ask whether the benefits that accrue *to the failed star* outweigh the costs paid by that failed star. For most parents, *this* will be the costs and benefits analysis that counts.

What are the benefits that accrue to a failed star? Does he enjoy fame? No. To the contrary, he likely experiences a degree of ignominy: He has, after all, failed to accomplish what he set out to do. Does he gain valuable training for his adult career? We saw above that it is questionable whether successful child stars have, in their star-related activities, gained valuable career training; it is doubly questionable, then, whether a *failed* child star will have gained valuable career training. Notice, in particular, that one of the adult career benefits enjoyed by successful child stars—namely, the ability to trade on their fame in whatever career they may choose—will not be available to the failed child star.

This brings us to money. The failed child star will typically have nothing, financially speaking, to show for his efforts. And not even this statement is entirely accurate, for in many cases the failed child star will end up with *less than nothing*, financially speaking, to show for his efforts. This is because being a "star in training" can be quite expensive.

In the previous chapter we saw that elite gymnasts could spend $30,000 in their pursuit of stardom. Much the same is true in other sports. Thus, consider the case of David Kanstoroom, who in the early 1980s was a rising child star in tennis. His father spent $10,000 a year on his son's budding career, with $3,000 to $4,000 going for transportation to tournaments, another $3,000 to $4,000 going for lessons and clinics, $700 going for tennis club memberships, $1,000 going for indoor court time, and yet more money going for clothing, rackets, and strings. When friends asked David's father if his goal was to win a college scholarship for David and thereby avoid the costs of college, he replied, with much insight: "With what I will have spent on David's tennis from 8 to 19, I could buy a college."[16] By the late 1990s the cost to coach an up-and-coming tennis player was up to $80,000 a year.[17]

It is fairly clear, then, that the failed child star enjoys few or none of the benefits enjoyed by the successful child star. What about the costs of failed child stardom?

How much of a price the failed child star pays depends on how quickly he fails. If he begins down the road to stardom at age five and gives up at age ten, much of his childhood can still be salvaged. On the other hand, there are failed child stars whose failure does not become apparent until they are in their late teens. In these cases their loss of childhood is likely complete.

Another thing to keep in mind is that a failed child star might have failed because he lacked natural talent, and that because of this lack of talent he might have had to work even harder in attempting to attain star status than successful child stars did.

(Along these lines, remember Tracy Austin beating her fellow competitors who, unlike Austin, got up at six-thirty in the morning to jump rope and run several miles.) In this sense, a failed child star might have paid a *bigger* price than a successful child star.

In terms of physical injuries too, failed child stars might pay a bigger price than successful child stars. Notice, after all, that one reason would-be stars remain would-be stars is that they suffer career-ending injuries that successful stars manage to avoid.

Finally, it is clear that failed child stars will usually pay a price in terms of psychological harm experienced. The failed star, after all, will have experienced a major failure, and experienced it as a child. There is, to be sure, nothing wrong with failure. Indeed, failure is one of life's great teachers, and to some extent parents should be perfectly willing to allow their child to fail if they think that the child can profit from the experience. But the failure involved in missed stardom is colossal compared to the failures normal children experience. It is one thing to get a bad grade because you did not do your homework; it is quite another to spend years of effort and thousands of dollars trying to become a tennis star only to find out that you lack what it takes.

Again, failure can loom much larger in the life of a child than in the life of an adult. An adult typically has experienced a mix of success and failure and will be able to put his periodic failures into a larger context. He will know that to be a functional adult, one must learn to live with one's failures and press on despite them. A child, however, will lack the perspective of an adult on these matters. He might be crushed, psychologically speaking, by the collapse of his dream of childhood stardom. His sense of personal failure might follow him into adulthood and indeed to his grave.

It should be clear, then, that in most cases the failed child star comes out a loser: He pays a big price—in some ways a bigger price than the successful child star paid—and comes out with nothing or less than nothing to show for it. Most parents, if they *knew* that their child would not succeed, would never push him down the road to stardom. The problem, of course, is that parents cannot *know* that their child will not succeed; and many parents, blinded by parental pride, press on in the belief that their child will be the one who beats the odds.

When a parent is deciding whether to allow his child to attempt stardom, he should weigh, on the one hand, the slim chance that his child will succeed, in which case the child will pay a very real price in exchange for benefits that have a "dark side," against, on the other hand, the likelihood that his child will fail, in which case the child will pay a similar very real price in exchange for nothing, if not less than nothing. These odds, needless to say, are not particularly attractive. It would be difficult for an adult to justify taking such a chance with his own life. (But then again, he is an adult, and it is his life.) How, one wonders, can anyone justify taking such a chance with someone else's life—which is what the parents of the would-be child star typically do?

Stanford women's tennis coach Frank Brennan sums up the lot of the failed child tennis star in the following terms: "A lot of the girls who didn't make it [in pro tennis] are bag girls at the Shop-Rite right now.... I sometimes think we should have a record book and just start printing in it all the names of the kids who passed up college and passed up having a life, names nobody ever heard of. We know about Gabriela Sabatini and Michael Chang. But for every Michael Chang and Jennifer Capriati who actually make it for a while, there are fifty kids out there who pursued that dream and gave up everything else and came up *way* short."[18]

Children who pursue athletic stardom typically put all their eggs into one basket. The problem is that the basket is likely to be dropped: Odds are, after all, that they will end up not stars, but failed stars.

The Climbing Boys of the Twentieth Century

I would like to suggest, at the risk of slight exaggeration, that the lot of today's girl gymnasts bears an uncanny resemblance to that of the apprentice chimney sweepers of two centuries ago.

Consider, to begin with, the issue of age. The "climbing boys" began their careers, as we have seen, at an early age: The younger you are, the smaller you are, and the easier it will be to climb a chimney. The careers of the climbing boys typically ended when they reached their teens; they were too big to fit into most chimneys, and their health had typically been ruined by years of climbing. In gymnastics, too, girls begin their careers at an early age. In gymnastics, as in chimney sweeping, small size is desirable: The smaller you are, the easier it is, all other things being equal, to do gymnastic routines. And like climbing boys, most gymnasts end their careers in their teens: They become too big to compete successfully, and their bodies have been "used up" by years of training.

When the climbing boys' climbing days were over, some of them, knowing no other means of employment, became master chimney sweeps themselves and acquired climbing boys of their own. Similarly, when their gymnastics careers end at an early age, some gymnasts become coaches and make their living enticing other children to swap their childhoods for a chance at gymnastics stardom.

The climbing boys were typically under the care not of their parents but of a master sweeper. This master was in theory supposed to make sure that the needs of the boys were met; more often, he used the boys to meet his own needs. In much the same way a world-class gymnast will typically be under the care not of her parents, but of a coach. Indeed, she may move away from her family to train with the coach.[19] In theory this coach is supposed to look after the gymnast's physical and emotional needs; in reality he may suppress these needs in his bid to create a star. He may advise her (as we have seen) not to take proper care of her injuries or advise her to go on a starvation diet; and rather than offering her unconditional acceptance, he will make it clear that his acceptance of her is highly conditional and tied directly to her chances of success.

The existence of the climbing boys was not a deep, dark secret. You could see them daily on the streets of London. Indeed, you were likely to invite them into your house a few times a year so that they could clean your chimney. The master sweeper did his best to maintain the illusion that his boys were cared for; the boys were not to complain to customers and were expected to act cheerful.

Didn't people suspect that all was not well with these children? Some people not only suspected but raised public protests against their treatment. Most people, however, apparently worked hard to retain their ignorance concerning the situation of the climbing boys: Ask too many questions, find out the truth, and then how are you going to get your chimney swept?

In much the same way the existence of girl gymnasts is hardly a secret. Indeed, most Americans invite them into their homes (via television) several times a year. We assume that someone, somewhere is taking care of them. And when we see them, they look happy: They smile hugely at the ends of their routines, and we take that as a sign of the joy they experience doing gymnastics. (Actually, this smile is something that they are taught from their earliest days of gymnastics training: At the end of a routine, you give the judges a beaming smile, even though you are in misery at the time.) We may wonder whether they are indeed as happy as they look, but we try not to ask too many questions. What, after all, would we do if we found out they were miserable? What would we watch then?

Having said all this, I readily admit that there are some important differences between the climbing boys and girl gymnasts. For one thing, the average climbing boy doubtless suffered worse than the average girl gymnast. (Girl gymnasts suffer significantly, climbing boys suffered horribly.) Furthermore, while the life of the climbing boy was utterly without glamor, the lives of most girl gymnasts typically have passing moments of glamor—for example, when they place at a significant meet; I hasten to add, though, that even these moments may not, as I suggested above, be as glamorous as they seem. Another difference is that whereas the climbing boys typically did not want to be doing what they were doing but were not allowed to quit, the girl gymnasts do in some sense want to be doing what they are doing and can, in theory, quit. Of course, it is easy to make too much of this difference: Girl gymnasts, one imagines, are under an incredible amount of pressure, both self-generated and imposed by others. As a result of this pressure, their decision to continue in gymnastics probably isn't, in many cases, entirely free.

A Radical Proposal

I would now like to offer what many would consider to be a radical proposal: We should treat girls' gymnastics as a form of child labor and regulate it accordingly.[20]

We should, for example, place limits on the amount of time children of various ages can spend in gymnastics training. We should place health-motivated restrictions on the sort of training they can receive. We should likewise place health-motivated restrictions on the routines they can do in competition. We might, for example, want to ban "stuck" dismounts, in which a gymnast lands on two feet, with legs straight. Such dismounts are jarring to a gymnast's body and arguably lead to a significant number of injuries. We should also regulate the behavior of gymnastics coaches and perhaps license them, the way we license schoolteachers.[21]

The proposal just described, it should be noted, would not ban gymnastics or prohibit girls from taking gymnastics lessons, engaging in gymnastics training, or participating in gymnastics competitions. (Indeed, the purely recreational girl gymnast would be largely unaffected by enactment of the proposal.) It would affect primarily girl gymnasts who hope to compete at the elite level, and affect them in a way that will keep their pursuit of gymnastic excellence from becoming the obsessive core of their existence and will prevent them from ruining their health to attain gymnastic excellence.

Why treat girl gymnasts as if they were child laborers? Bluntly stated, because they *are* child laborers.

Across America there are laws that regulate child labor. It would be illegal for, say, a thirteen-year-old to work forty hours a week in a factory. We have such laws because we feel that there are more profitable ways a thirteen-year-old can spend his time than working in a factory. For one thing, he should be going to school. And even if he goes to school full-time and works in a factory in his spare time, many would argue that his job will have a negative impact on his performance in school. And even if he turns out to be a straight-*A* student in school, many will still argue that it is wrong for a thirteen-year-old to spend this much time at work: His will be an unbalanced childhood, with too much work and too little time for play and personal development.

It is all too easy to think that elite girl gymnasts, when they are training or competing, are not working, but are playing games and having fun. As we have seen, though, there would appear to be relatively little game-playing in the life of the competitive gymnast, and workouts and meets do not appear to be particularly conducive to having fun. What girl gymnasts do is better thought of as not just a job, but an extremely difficult and rather monotonous job, and a job that has a variety of hazards. It is a job that in many respects is less desirable than working in a factory. *There is, in short, more reason to regulate the labor of girl gymnasts than there is to regulate the labor of a child who works in a factory*. Yet, we choose to apply child-labor laws to factory workers but not to girl gymnasts. We would appear to be caught up in a cultural inconsistency.

But, fans of girls' gymnastics will object, surely there is a difference between elite gymnasts and factory workers. Look at how much money an elite gymnast can make, whereas many factory workers earn minimum wage.

An interesting point. The problem is that most elite gymnasts would be far better off, financially speaking, if they worked for minimum wage in a factory. Remember, after all, that most elite gymnasts pay relatively large sums to participate in gymnastics; for them, gymnastics is a losing proposition, financially speaking. They aren't *un*paid child laborers; they are *negatively* paid child laborers. Only perhaps one in a hundred elite gymnasts ends up making money in the sport. Factory workers, on the other hand, are certain of getting a monetary return for their efforts.

While we are on the topic of child labor laws, some history is in order. It is worth noting that those who campaigned against child labor were divided on the issue of child actors. Some were as ready to abolish child labor on the stage as they were to abolish child labor in cotton mills; others, though opposed to most forms of child labor, thought that child actors did not stand in need of government protection. Indeed, some of the most prominent child labor reformers were simultaneously leading advocates of child labor on stage.[22]

Thus, some opponents of child labor were outraged when, in 1881, ten-year-old singer Corinne was not allowed to appear on stage. The debate concerning child actors intensified in 1887 with the success of eight-year-old Elsie Leslie in *Editha's Burglar* and *Little Lord Fauntleroy*. Much as Shirley Temple's success did decades later, Elsie Leslie's success triggered a surge of interest in child actors. The public that wanted to watch child stars and the parents who wanted their children to become child stars chafed at the restrictions on child acting.

In subsequent decades the forces favoring less restrictive laws on child acting won some important battles. In 1911 Louisiana, which had some of the most restrictive child labor laws in the nation, amended these laws to allow children of all ages to work in the theater. By 1932 only seventeen states had a minimum age (of fourteen or sixteen) at which children could appear in theatrical performances.[23]

Why did opponents of child labor wish to exempt child actors from the child labor laws? Lots of arguments were advanced, including the argument that child actors (unlike child factory workers) liked their work, that child actors made more money than child factory workers, that acting as a child was good training for people who wish to act as adults, and that acting in theater had educational value. Those who wished to keep children off the stage offered replies to each of these arguments. In particular, they pointed out that the mere fact that a child liked something didn't mean he should be allowed to do it; that even though child actors were making significant amounts of money, they were still being exploited by adults; that by far the majority of success-ful adult actors did not begin their careers as children; and that the educational value of acting could, in the first place, be ob-tained without embarking on a stage career and was, in the sec-ond place, counteracted by the "risk of moral perversion" that children were exposed to when they embarked on stage careers.[24]

By the way, most of those who were opposed to children being paid to act on stage were by no means opposed to children acting on stage. They saw nothing wrong, for example, with chil-dren participating as singers or musicians in churches or schools. It would be hard to make a case that such children were being exploited.

Within the debate over child stage labor was a sub-debate concerning the various things that children might do on stage. There were those, for example, who wanted to distinguish be-tween those children who appeared in stage dramas and those who sang, danced, or did gymnastics on stage. They argued that while the latter children were "unfortunate laborers" whose ap-pearance on stage should be prohibited or at least restricted, child thespians should be regarded as a privileged exception to the child labor laws.[25]

It is, of course, relevant to our argument that the generation that wrote the child labor laws concerned itself with gymnastics. If the generation in question felt that the gymnasts of their day, by being paid to perform in public, were exploited, what would they think about today's gymnasts? There can, after all, be little doubt that the job of today's girl gymnasts is *much* more demand-ing, both in terms of training and in terms of what is expected during a "performance," than was the job of girl gymnasts in the early 1900s.

Where was the public during the debate over whether chil-dren should be allowed to embark on stage careers? Many people were busy attending plays in which child actors—who were them-selves child laborers—portrayed children who had been freed from the burdens of child labor; they apparently did not see anything ironic about their enjoyment of such plays.

If we ask what would happen to gymnastics in the absence of girl gymnasts, the answer is simple: Gymnastics would be like it was before the debut of Olga Korbut in 1968. It is, in other words, entirely possible to have gymnastics without the participation of little girls. Given that this is so, why don't we restrict the participation of children in "professional" gymnastics? Arguably, because there are adults who benefit from their participation.

Which adults? To begin with, the parents of many girl gymnasts benefit. In some cases they hope to have a better, more comfortable life because of their child's exploits. In other cases, they don't seek to benefit in any material way from their child's exploits, but hope instead to bask in the reflected glory of their child's fame. Or they might enjoy vicariously living out their own failed dreams through their child.

Adults who make their living in "the gymnastics business"—and this would include both gymnastics coaches and officials in the gymnastics hierarchy—benefit from the presence of children in gymnastics. It is true, they will tell us, that you can have gymnastics without little girls, but it would not be as popular as it now is. Meets would no longer draw big crowds, and sponsors would no longer be interested. The diminished popularity would mean fewer children in training and hence less income for coaches, and it would mean that the various gymnastics organizations would experience a reduction in power and income.

The last group of adults who benefit from the presence of children in gymnastics is the adult fans of the sport. These fans might complain that older gymnasts are not physically capable of doing the incredible tricks that little girls can do, and hence a gymnastics meet populated by older gymnasts would be a boring affair. And in any case, the older gymnasts are not "cute" in the same way that the girl gymnasts are, and this cuteness is one of the things that makes the girl gymnasts so much fun to watch.

For the role of girls in gymnastics to change for the better, these various "special interest" groups would have to be taken on. They would doubtless fight against changes to the status quo.

Save Tennis!

In my research on the steps that might be taken to curb children's participation in sports, I found that although I was not alone in holding such a view, some of those who agreed with me had reasons somewhat different from my own for favoring such curbs.

Tennis is an old and noble game. For the longest time it was a game of the gentry, a game in which tradition and good sportsmanship reigned supreme. The game began to change in the late 1970s, though, and by the end of the 1980s it was clear that tradition and good sportsmanship were taking a back seat to the egos of the current crop of stars. The stars started acting like spoiled children, both on and off the court. On the court they threw tantrums when calls didn't go their way. After losing a game, they might let any pretense of good sportsmanship fall by the wayside and instead hurl an obscenity at the player who beat them.[26] Off the court they might expect the tournament sponsor to provide them with their own personal concierge. They might expect use of a luxury car during a tournament, and might, when the tournament was over, ask if they could keep the car in question. They might refuse to acknowledge the fans on winning a game. They might agree to play in a tournament in return for a six-figure guarantee, but play half-heartedly in the first round, pocket the money, and then head off for the next tournament. They might accept payments from a sponsor but refuse to show up at the sponsor's promotional events.[27]

What caused the change in tennis? Arguably, it was the appearance of the tennis wunderkind. By the 1980s players had a perfectly good reason for behaving in a childish fashion: Many of them *were* children.

All this prompted Sally Jenkins, in 1994, to write a piece on the sorry state of tennis. Her conclusion: "If you are wondering exactly when a wonderful game [viz., tennis] became such a lousy sport, the answer is, the first time a corporate executive gave a 14-year-old a stretch limo to play with."[28]

In her piece, Jenkins is obviously concerned with the damage children do to themselves when they take tennis too seriously at too early an age. She is also concerned, though, with the damage that child players do *to tennis*. They damage tennis by behaving childishly on and off court; and they damage tennis when, rather than having long careers, they ruin themselves (either physically or psychologically) by playing too much tennis too soon and joining what Jenkins calls the "teenage Hall of Flameout." Jenkins proposes that tennis be saved by limiting the extent to which child tennis players can participate in tournaments.

Jenkins and I agree that steps should be taken to protect child tennis players. Where we disagree is in our motives for calling for such protection. My primary motive is to save the children; hers is apparently to save tennis. Hers is a motive, I think, that would be more understandable to many fans of tennis than my motive.

Conclusions

I am not so naive as to think that America will any time soon pass laws to regulate the labor of girl gymnasts or, more generally, prevent people from becoming sports professionals (or professional ballet dancers, actors, or models) while still children. I present the above discussion not so much as a call to arms, but simply to point out one of the apparent contradictions that exists in America's thinking about childhood. In subsequent chapters I will reveal many more such contradictions.

As far as child athletics is concerned, there are some hopeful signs. In the 1996 Olympics, gymnasts had to be fifteen (more precisely, had to turn fifteen sometime during the year) to compete. Partly as a result of this, the girls America sent to the Olympics in 1996 were older than previously—although in some cases they did not look older, thanks, no doubt, to the growth-stunting effects of intensive training and dieting. In the 2000 Olympics they had to be sixteen.

At the same time, there are some dark clouds on the horizon of child athletics. The year 1997 saw the ascension to the top of the tennis rankings of Martina Hingis, the child tennis player.

Ms. Hingis was named after tennis great Martina Navratilova, and has been playing tennis since age two. In the 1997 women's finals match of the U.S. Open, Ms. Hingis played against (and defeated) an even younger Venus Williams.

The year 1997 also saw an outbreak of Tiger-mania in golf, as former child prodigy Tiger Woods began his professional career.

And in 1997, 14-year-old Tara Lipinski became the youngest person to win the world women's figure-skating championships. Lipinski went on to a gold medal in the 1998 Olympics. The success of Lipinski is particularly significant, inasmuch as she looked more like a gymnast (at 4 feet, 8 inches and 75 pounds) than a skater. Could it be that skating is about to abandon its "ideal women" for emaciated wind-up dolls?

Thanks to the attention devoted to Hingis, Woods, and Lipinski, it is likely that around the world there will be thousands of children who will spend their childhoods not in play, but practicing their tennis backhands, golf swings, and toe loops in deadly earnest.

CHAPTER 4

THE INVENTION
OF CHILDHOOD

What is involved in being "a child"? According to the concept of childhood held by Americans in the middle of the twentieth century, children should be sheltered from many of the cruel realities of life, and should be kept in a state of innocence for as long as possible. This meant that children were not allowed to witness acts of violence; it meant that parents tried to hide from their children any marital or financial problems they might be having; it meant that adults were careful not to swear or tell risqué jokes in the presence of children; it meant that parents expected their children to be not just sexually inexperienced, but sexually ignorant; and it meant that rather than being expected to contribute to the family's resources, children were expected to be a drain on them. Furthermore, it was expected that children would remain "children" for nearly two decades.

Go back four hundred years, though, and a strikingly different concept of childhood emerges—indeed, what you will find is children who never really experienced "childhood." In Europe in 1600, seven-year-olds were not treated much differently than adults; and in America it was only in the late nineteenth century that childhood, in its modern sense, became commonplace, at least for lower- and middle-class Americans.

This is a particularly good time to think about the concept of childhood and its rise in the western world, for there is every reason to think that this concept is undergoing a profound change.

A case can be made—and in the next chapter I will make it—that the concept of childhood reached its zenith (in America, at least) in the 1950s, and that since then the status of children has been eroding, and with astonishing speed. It could be that in another few decades childhood will be a thing of the past, and our treatment of children will be remarkably like that in Europe in the year 1600.

Let us, then, take a look at the invention of childhood. In this chapter I will be interested not in extreme uses of children—documented in the first two chapters of this book—but in the lives of "average" children. My goal is to show how, for the average child, the quality of life improved dramatically between 1700 and 1950, and to reveal some of the factors behind this change.

Childhood in Europe

One of the first people to examine the history of childhood was social historian Philippe Ariès. Ariès looked at France of the 1950s and found it wanting in the way that children were treated. He assumed that there had been, in the recent past, a Golden Age of Childhood from which society had fallen. He started doing research on the history of childhood and found, to his surprise, that the children of France in the 1950s were treated remarkably well by any historical measure—he found, in other words, that *this* was the Golden Age of Childhood. He set about trying to document the invention of childhood, an invention that transformed children from beings who, though cared for, were relatively unimportant, into beings who assumed a central and very special role in their families and cultures.[1]

Ariès faced a difficult task. There is, after all, relatively little evidence about what it was like to be a child in, say, France in 1600. Children certainly did not write accounts about what it was like to be a child, and with but a few exceptions adults did not record facts about the children in their care.

To uncover the history of childhood, Ariès turned first to art. Art provides us with pictures of children, and from these pictures we can draw a variety of conclusions about the way children were raised. Ariès discovered that before the seventeenth century, children were dressed in roughly the same sorts of clothes that adults wore. In the seventeenth century, children—boys in particular—began to wear clothes different from those of adults; and the "boy's uniform" (which might have included, for example, knee pants) remained more or less fixed until after WWI, at which point boys started to dress more like men. Art also tells us what sorts of games children played. Ariès found that before the seventeenth century they played the same games adults played; after that, children—in the upper and aristocratic classes, at any rate—started playing their own games. And art gives us an idea of how children fit into the family setting. Only in the fifteenth and sixteenth centuries do we find children depicted with family or playmates, and we have to wait until the seventeenth century before we find family portraits that are planned around children. Finally, art provides us with clues about how society thought of children. Until the twelfth century, Ariès found that the children in pictures looked like little adults. Ariès took this as evidence that the people of the time thought of children as being little men and women, not as belonging to a special and different stage of life.

Turning from art to written accounts, Ariès found that until the seventeenth century children in fact *were* treated like little adults. Little effort was made to shield them from the worldly realities of life, such as sex. In particular, there was no assumption that children were "innocent," and since they weren't innocent, there was no need to take steps to keep them innocent. They could mix and mingle with adults and fully inhabit their world, instead of inhabiting a separate-but-parallel world designed with the needs of children in mind.

Ariès summarizes his findings as follows: "In medieval society the idea of childhood did not exist; this is not to suggest that children were neglected, forsaken or despised. The idea of childhood is not to be confused with affection for children."[2] The concept of the family—and correspondingly, the concept of childhood—had to wait until the sixteenth and seventeenth centuries to emerge.[3]

Barbara Tuchman, another historian who has looked carefully at medieval society, argues not only that the concept of childhood was different in medieval times than it was in the middle of the twentieth century, but that of all the ways in which these two periods differ—and there are many—this difference is the most striking.[4]

Ariès's studies of childhood were groundbreaking, but are in many respects wanting. For one thing, his reliance on art as evidence for past views on childhood raises a variety of concerns. It might be, for example, that children of the past were dressed for portraits (as they often are today), in which case the clothing they wear in portraits would have little to do with their everyday clothing. Also, in Renaissance art we find pictures of babies who were not just well-fed, but fat, and babies who were held by and gently interacted with loving mothers. Subsequent research has shown that the children in these pictures bear little resemblance to the flesh-and-blood children of the time.

Although the methodology of Ariès's studies of childhood was flawed in certain respects, subsequent research has reinforced his view that the nature of childhood has changed dramatically in the last few centuries.

Consider, then, the plight of the typical child in Europe before the invention of childhood.[5] When his parents had him, they probably did not do so because they were in love. His father would have routinely beaten his mother and would not have let her share the table at mealtime. The absence of love became particularly apparent when a wife died. The thinking of the time:

> The loss of a stable animal grieves a peasant more than the loss of his wife. The first may only be recuperated with money; the second is repaired with another woman, who will bring with her some money and furniture and who, instead of impoverishing the household, will increase its wealth.[6]

Along these same lines, consider the following saying from Brittany: "Rich is the man whose wife is dead and horse alive."[7] No, when the typical European child was born, he was not a product of parental love; rather he probably came into existence because his father wanted sex and because of "considerations of property and lineage."[8]

Not only did his parents not love each other, but when he came along, they probably didn't love him either. After his birth, his parents might or might not have kept him. The alternative to keeping him was depositing him at a foundling hospital. In such hospitals mortality rates were so high that to place a child there was "tantamount to infanticide."[9] If, on the other hand, they chose to keep him, there is a good chance that this meant not raising him themselves, but sending him off to a wet nurse in the country to spend the first two years of life. (In Paris at the end of the eighteenth century, of the 21,000 children born annually, between 16,000 and 17,000 lived with wet nurses in remote villages.)[10] These wet nurses were purely mercenary in their motives. They might have gotten pregnant simply so that they would produce milk, and their own babies might themselves have been put out to nurse so that the mother could take in a higher-paying nursling.

Wet nurses typically took in children because they were poor, and because they were poor, they could not afford to provide adequate care for the children they took in. The wet nurse and her charges often lived together in a single room, possibly sharing the quarters with farm animals. Rather than checking a baby to see if it needed changing, a wet nurse might instead ignore the baby's needs until the stench became overpowering;[11] and since the wet nurse's room might not be heated in winter, a baby might freeze in its soaked clothing.[12] The nurse and her nurslings might share a single bed; and as a result, she might, either accidentally or on purpose, "overlay" a baby and thereby suffocate it.[13] The dirt floor might be alive with filth. And if these living conditions made babies cry, the nurses had an answer: The babies might be given alcohol or laudanum to quiet them. Parents were unlikely to learn of these living conditions, simply because they were unlikely to visit their children.

Parents who hired wet nurses may have thought they were getting mother's milk for their money, but this wasn't necessarily the case: Many of the wet nurses were in fact dry. Or if not dry, they might have so many children to feed that only some got milk. Those who didn't get milk might be fed bits of food that their nurse had softened by chewing.

As might be expected, many babies did not survive wet nursing. In some areas there was a 90 percent mortality rate among nursed babies. And when a baby died, what did the wet nurse do? She got another baby to nurse. Suppose a foundling, turned over to the care of a wet nurse, beat the odds and reached the ripe old age of seven. The wet nurse might celebrate by "trading the child in" for a new baby. Why not keep a child that she had raised for seven years? Because caring for newborns paid better.

Suppose a child was lucky enough not to be sent to a wet nurse. Did he fare better raised at home? Somewhat better, but it was far short of what we today would consider an adequate upbringing. For example, when he was a baby, his mother probably would have immobilized him by wrapping him in swaddling clothes. For modern readers who may associate swaddling with maternal affection, here is a description of the swaddling process:

> [The swaddler] stretches the baby out on a board or straw mattress and dresses it in a little gown or a coarse, crumpled diaper, on top of which she begins to apply the swaddling bands. She pins the infant's arms against its chest, then passes the band under the armpits, which presses the arms firmly into place. Around and around she winds the band down to the buttocks, tighter and tighter, pushing the diaper in between the infant's thighs, then enveloping all these little pits and parts with the wide swaddling cloth. She takes it clear down to the feet, and after this neat work, covers the baby's head with a bonnet; a kerchief atop of this hangs down to the shoulders and is fastened with pins.[14]

Thus wrapped, the child might have been hung on a nail so his mother could do her work.

If the reader wonders how a mother could interact with a child so wrapped, the answer is simple: The mother *didn't* interact with the child. Indeed, she barely related to it at all. She might have referred to the child as "it," might not know the child's age, or how many children she had given birth to, and might give a new baby the same name as a dead baby. Displays of affection were uncommon.

When a child outgrew his swaddling clothes but was still in his infancy, his mother might not have thought twice about going out and leaving him under the care of an older sibling—or leaving him alone, for that matter. This parental inattention might result in his being attacked and eaten by barnyard hogs or having some other unfortunate accident. And if he was upset and could not sleep, his mother might have dealt with the situation with a bit of "forceful shaking"; such shaking may not have calmed children and certainly wasn't good for them, but it appears to have been successful in making them sleep.

If a child did not survive this harsh treatment, his parents were not likely to have mourned his death. His mother might have left him, dead or dying, in the gutter or on a dung heap.[15] If, on the other hand, he did survive his infancy, he would not necessarily be welcomed into the bosom of his family. To the contrary, he might have been sent off to work for another family. Thus, in rural France the children of cottagers would go off at age seven or eight to work for a farmer or as apprentices for an artisan. Alternatively, a child's parents might "trade" him for the child of a neighbor: He would work for the neighbor's family, and the neighbor's child would work for his family.

And whether a child stayed with his family or lived with his neighbors, his living conditions were likely to be a far cry from what we today think of as acceptable. For one thing, he would probably have to share one room with all the members of the family he lived with as well as the people in their employ. He might also share a bed with someone else. Rather than being hidden behind closed doors, all the "secrets" of adult life (the fighting, the swearing, the lovemaking) would be there for him to observe.

This is not to say that parents never provided their children with separate sleeping arrangements. In Scandinavia, for example, farmers' daughters were sometimes asked to sleep in the barn in the summer. The reasoning behind this move was simple: It was expected that young men would come to court in the night, and parents didn't want their sleep disturbed by the young lovers' carryings-on.

Throughout his childhood, a child would have experienced corporal punishment—from his parents, from his teachers, from his master[16]—that by today's standards would count as extreme. Religious fanatic John Hersey advised parents to "beat the devil" out of their children and "break their wills." He also advised them to get an early start on their child discipline: "Let a child from a year old be taught to fear the rod and cry softly."[17] Bartholomew Batty advised Renaissance parents to "keep the golden mean" in their punishment of their children; more precisely, he advised parents not to "strike and buffet their children about the face and head, and to lace upon them like malt sacks with cudgels, staves, fork, or fire shovel," but instead to "hit [their child] upon the sides...with the rod, [since] he shall not die thereof."[18]

Ariès argued that among the upper classes, a change in parental attitudes from indifference to lovingness took place in the sixteenth and seventeenth centuries. Others—most prominently, social historian Edward Shorter—have argued that lower- and middle-class European parents only started to love their children—or at least display their love—in the second half of the nineteenth century and that it took until the beginning of the twentieth century to complete this transformation in parental attitudes.

Not everyone would accept the above account of the evolution of the concept of childhood. Some have argued—contrary to Ariès—that a concept of childhood *did* exist in the Middle Ages.[19] Others have argued that modern minds have misconstrued some of the child-rearing practices of the past and because of this have drawn the conclusion that parents of days gone by cared little for their children. It has been suggested, for example, that parents swaddled babies not because they were malicious or indifferent to their well-being, but because it was what generally-accepted child-rearing standards of the time required. It has also been argued that swaddling was not as detrimental to children as modern minds might think.[20]

Indeed, while I read historical accounts of childhood, I kept thinking about Shakespeare's *Romeo and Juliet*. In this play, we find parents who love their children and grieve for them when they die. We find children who, in deciding to couple, do so not out of "considerations of property and lineage," but because they experience romantic love. We find a wet nurse who appears to dote on her former charge. We find, in short, a world unlike the world described above. *Romeo and Juliet* is, of course, just a play, but one that audiences could relate to in the late sixteenth century. This suggests that childhood in Europe in centuries gone by, although bleak, was perhaps not quite as unremittingly bleak as some historians of childhood would have us believe. At the same time, there is every reason to think that what would have counted as typical European parents in the year 1600 would today count as woefully inadequate or even criminally bad parents.

Childhood in America

Edward Shorter has argued that childhood in America was never quite as bad as childhood in Europe. This is in part because much of America was settled after the transformation of childhood had begun; but more importantly, he claims that "the American family was probably 'born modern' because the colonial settlers seem to have seized privacy and intimacy for themselves as soon as they stepped off the boat."[21] Nevertheless, we can trace a change in the nature of childhood even in America, and if we compare the typical American childhood of the mid-nineteenth century with that of the mid-twentieth century, we find some remarkable differences.[22]

One important change between the nineteenth and twentieth centuries involved child labor. American children are (for the most part) no longer expected to earn their keep. In the mid-nineteenth century, however, it was not at all unusual for children to get jobs at an early age. And the jobs in question did not, in many cases, involve chores around the home, but were real jobs, with demanding employers. Children were expected to work long hours for what was often minimal pay, which they dutifully turned over to their parents. And even when children worked "around the home," it was not at all the sort of thing modern Americans would expect, particularly if home was a farm. Chores were difficult and often dangerous. All in all, the contribution children made to the family's economic well-being was significant. In Philadelphia in 1880, for example, Irish children in two-parent families contributed somewhere between 38 and 46 percent of total family income.

By the end of the nineteenth century, a movement was under way to abolish child labor—or, as some referred to it, "child slavery." Leaders of the movement were critical of those "fathers and mothers, who coin shameful dollars from the bodies and souls of their own flesh and blood."[23] By 1899 more than half the states had some level of legal protection for child workers, but the regulations were not strictly enforced. In 1916 the federal government tried to curb child labor by passing a law banning the products of child labor from interstate commerce. The law in question was found to be unconstitutional (dramatic evidence of the extent to which the notion of constitutionality has changed during the twentieth century). Effective federal regulation of child labor finally became a reality in 1938.

In the late nineteenth century the typical American child was increasingly expected to spend his childhood not at a job but at school, and the rise of public education made the schooling of their children all that much more attractive to parents. In the first half of the twentieth century, high school was typically taken to be the end of a child's education. By the second half of the twentieth century, the "child's" education was, in many cases, extended to include college. And when, in this century, American children were asked to work, it typically was not because parents wanted to profit from their labor, but because they thought their children would profit from laboring: In particular, minor jobs in and out of the home were thought to build character or be a valuable educational experience. And when children did work outside the home they were typically allowed to keep and spend the money they earned.

Another striking change between the nineteenth and twentieth century involved the monetary value of children. There are those, to be sure, who would claim that it is impossible to assign a monetary value to people. The courts, however, are frequently asked to do it, and by looking at the values they assign to children's lives we can gain some insight into a society's values.

In the mid-nineteenth century, if your infant child died in an accident, it is unlikely that you would get much in a wrongful death suit. The monetary value of your child was taken to be equal to the value of his labor and services. Thus, if a child was very young and lacked a job, he wasn't worth much in the eyes of the law. It was only later that children, in the eyes of the law, began to acquire a worth other than for their labor. Courts began to care, for example, about the mental anguish and pain of parents who lost a child. The awards given in wrongful death cases rose dramatically. And since, as we have seen, the value of a child's labor has declined dramatically in this century, the emotional value of the child must therefore have increased substantially for these larger awards to be "justified."

The changes just described in the court's views on the monetary value of children were no doubt due in part to changes in the American legal system, and in particular to the increasing craziness of tort law. Nevertheless, a case can be made that the change in the monetary value of children reflects, more than anything, the fact that between the nineteenth and twentieth centuries, parents became more emotionally involved with their children—began to see them not so much as a source of labor, but as a source of joy.

At the same time that the court's views on the accidental death of children were changing, the public's views were changing as well. One area in which this change became apparent was in the public's reaction to traffic accidents involving children.

Around the turn of the century, there was a dramatic rise in the number of children killed or injured in traffic accidents. More and more children were living in cities, in which their only playground was the street. When traffic in these cities increased and the car made its appearance as well, the stage was set for disaster. By 1910 traffic accidents were the leading cause of death of children between five and fourteen years of age.

At one time, the death of a child in a traffic accident might have been shrugged off as merely unfortunate. By the early 1920s, the accidental death of a child was no longer treated as an isolated neighborhood tragedy; instead, it was viewed as part of a national problem.

In response to the plague of traffic accidents, parents started taking steps to get children off the streets. This meant making homes more child-friendly by doing things like converting parlors into playrooms. It also meant starting campaigns to build playgrounds in cities. In short, adults found children sufficiently valuable to alter the environment to suit the needs of children, and in doing this they took an important step in creating the separate world for children that is required by the modern concept of childhood.

With the change in the public's views concerning children came a variety of governmental measures undertaken on children's behalf. Government began to take an interest in the health of children. In 1908 New York City opened the world's first children's health bureau; by 1926, forty-seven states had such bureaus. In 1912 the United States Children's Bureau was established.

By the mid-1870s, child abusers, rather than being tolerated, were prosecuted.[24] In subsequent decades the role of government in the fight against child abuse broadened considerably.

For another example of the change that took place in America's views on childhood between the nineteenth and twentieth centuries, consider the fate of "unwanted" children.

In the nineteenth century it was not uncommon for an unwanted baby to be abandoned in a public place or in a foundling asylum. In either case the future well-being of the baby was hardly assured. Some enterprising people—who became known as baby farmers—got into the baby-disposal business. For a fee, they would take the baby of a woman who did not want it, with a promise to find a good home for the child. All too often, the baby died before such a home could be found. Indeed, some baby farmers even took out life-insurance policies on children they acquired in an attempt to profit doubly from a child's death.

Out of this chaos arose a movement to see that abandoned and orphaned children, if not exactly well-cared for, at least made it through childhood intact. In the 1850s, for example, the New York Children's Aid Society, organized by Charles Loring Brace, began sending needy city children to rural homes in the famed "orphan trains." Farmers were particularly fond of this setup, inasmuch as it meant a cheap source of labor for their farms.

By the middle of the twentieth century, people adopting children did not see them as a source of labor, and did not expect to be given a child "for free." Instead, couples competed intensely for the available adoptable children, often spending significant amounts of money in the process.

Why Different Concepts of Childhood?

I have suggested above that different cultures have different concepts of childhood, and that a particular culture's concept of childhood can change dramatically with the passage of time. Climbing boys were once a common sight on the streets of London; now the existence of such a boy would be scandalous—in London, at any rate, but perhaps not in other corners of the world. Why is this? More precisely, can we isolate the factors that determine what concept of childhood a culture will adopt?

This question is difficult to answer. Nevertheless, a case can be made that three of the most important factors are the extent to which parents love their children, infant mortality rates, and the level of affluence of the culture in question. Let us examine these factors one at a time.

Parental Love

One reason cultures might treat their children differently is that they love their children to differing degrees. Thus, if in one culture children were cherished, while in another they were reviled, one would expect to find different concepts of childhood: In the former culture, children might spend their days at play and in school, and in the latter culture children might spend their days harnessed to a plow.

Edward Shorter has pointed to a difference in the intensity of parental love to explain why modern mothers treat their children differently than medieval mothers did. More precisely, Shorter claims that whereas modern mothers are quite loving, medieval mothers felt almost no love for their children. Indeed, Shorter argues that the high mortality rate of children in medieval times (which subject we shall soon revisit) was due in large part to the fact that mothers did not love their children enough to take adequate care of them.[25]

Some will be dismayed by this suggestion. They will protest that parents at all times and in all places have loved their children. In reply to such a protest, one can only point out that *within* a culture (ours, for instance), there are interpersonal differences in how intensely parents love their children, with some parents being indifferent, if not hostile, to their children, while other parents cherish their children and make great sacrifices on their behalf. If such differences in parental attitudes are possible *within* a culture, similar differences should be possible *between* cultures. It would not be surprising, then, to find cultures in which parental love was the exception rather than the rule. Parents in such a culture might be capable of love, but not deem children to be a proper object of love; or they might, because of their upbringing, be incapable of loving children or anything else.

Infant Mortality

In the animal world some species survive by making lots of off-spring and taking little or no interest in them after they are born. Frogs take this approach to reproduction: They make lots of eggs and then abandon them. This is what has been called a *bearing* strategy. The other common reproductive strategy is to make very few offspring, but to invest time, effort, and resources in those you do produce in an attempt to increase the odds that they will survive. Cows take this approach to reproduction: They typically have one calf (at a time), and rather than abandoning it at birth, they feed and care for it for a period of time. This is what has been called a *caring* strategy.[26]

Which reproductive strategy is best, caring or bearing? As it turns out, both are successful strategies, inasmuch as we can find many examples of species that have used one or the other of these strategies successfully. And either of these strategies is clearly preferable to a "mixed" strategy that involves trying to have a large number of offspring and investing a considerable amount of time, energy, and resources into each offspring, or that involves having one or two offspring that are subsequently ignored. The first of these strategies is a recipe for exhaustion; the second is a recipe for extinction.

Human beings use what is basically a caring strategy in their own reproductive activities. Nature leaves us little choice in the matter: Our children cannot be abandoned at birth without disastrous consequences, not only for them but for our chances of surviving as a species.

It is possible, of course, for different human beings to differ in the degree to which they care for their children. At the one extreme we find couples that engage in a pure caring strategy: Such couples have but one child and devote all their resources thereafter to fulfillment of its needs. At the other extreme we find couples who produce many children, but give each child the minimum amount of attention necessary for its survival.

If you, as a parent, had the reasonable belief that any children you made had little chance of reaching adulthood alive, you would be foolish to engage in a pure caring strategy. Instead, it would make sense for you to move as far as biology would let you toward the bearing end of the continuum of reproductive strategies: You should make lots of children and invest relatively few resources in any particular child.

Among the resources you might withhold from the children you create is your love: If the infant mortality rate is high, parents who become emotionally attached to their children will likely end up paying an emotional toll so great as to jeopardize their ability to provide for the needs of their children.

Notice, too, that when parents have bigger families, even though they may *want* to shower their children with resources, there will be relatively fewer resources per child: A child in a family of thirteen children, for example, will surely receive less parental attention (and in particular, fewer demonstrations of parental affection) than he would have received as an only child. A case can be made, then, that high infant mortality rates diminish the amount of parental love available to children in two ways: Parents suppress their love as a form of emotional protection; and what love *is* expressed is, thanks to larger family size, divided among more children, with each child getting proportionately less.

If parental indifference toward children were caused by high infant mortality rates, we would expect parental indifference to decline as infant mortality rates declined, and this is exactly what happened. In Europe, the decline in infant mortality rates that took place in the eighteenth century was accompanied by a significant improvement in parental attitudes toward their children. And in the centuries after this, as the standard of living rose, as medical breakthroughs were made, and as child-care practices improved, child mortality rates fell further and children became ever more cherished.

Likewise, if parental indifference toward children were caused by high infant mortality rates, we would expect parents in countries that today have low infant mortality rates to be more concerned with the well-being and happiness of their children than parents in countries with high infant mortality rates. This, to a large extent, is true, although as we shall see in the next chapter, things may be changing.

A few last comments are in order with respect to infant mortality. We have seen that when infant mortality rates are high, parents tend to be indifferent to the death of their child. I have argued that this indifference can be a perfectly understandable "protection mechanism" for parents to use in a time of high infant mortality. We should keep in mind, though, that if parents practice a religion that teaches that children who die go to heaven, the indifference of these parents might in part be due to their sense that the death of a child isn't really such a bad thing: Better paradise now than a childhood spent suffering. In such cases, the "indifference" of parents should not be taken as a sign that the parents do not love their children.

We should also keep in mind that not everyone accepts the notion that high infant mortality rates caused the indifference of parents. Shorter argues, as we have seen, that it was the indifference of mothers that caused high infant mortality rates. As is usually true in such cases, cause and effect can be difficult to tease apart.

The Influence of Affluence

Besides being affected by infant mortality rates, the quality of parenting can also be affected by parents' level of affluence. More precisely, inasmuch as it "costs" parents to treat childhood as a special time, impoverished parents might simply be unable to afford to offer their offspring what we today would think of as childhood.

Notice, to begin with, that if you are dirt poor, you might be unable to afford to keep the children you have; and if they are cast off, their chances of experiencing "childhood" will be minimal. According to Shorter, it was in part the desperate poverty of European mothers that led them to abandon their children in the centuries before childhood was invented.[27] And if you are affluent enough to be able to keep your children, you might not be able to afford to educate them or give them adequate food, clothing, or shelter. Indeed, rather than devoting the family's resources to your children, you might be forced to exploit their labor: You might send them off to work at an early age. Finally, even though you are sufficiently affluent that your children don't have to be sent off to work, you might not be affluent enough to be able to give your children their own room. They might instead be forced to share a room with the whole family, and this will make it virtually impossible for you to maintain their childhood innocence. How, for example, are you going to keep them in the dark about sex if they share the parental bed?

Shorter argues that the rise of capitalism helped trigger the invention of childhood, inasmuch as it raised the standard of living of average people.[28] With more resources at hand, parents could afford to keep their children instead of casting them off; they could devote more resources to the children they kept, introducing to them a number of childhood pleasures; and they could afford the multiroom houses which are arguably necessary if one is to maintain a child's innocence.

As we have seen, the rise of capitalism was at first a mixed blessing for children. In the early stages of the industrial revolution, factory owners discovered that children made wonderful tenders for many of the machines being installed. Of course, a childhood spent tending machinery is a childhood deprived of "childhood." It was only after the industrial revolution was well under way that the lot of children improved. Four things in particular helped take children out of the factories and enabled them to spend their childhoods in homes and schools: The increasing sophistication of the economy led to an increased demand for a skilled, educated labor force, so children were sent to school; rising real incomes reduced families' need for their children's wages; an influx of immigrants displaced children; and, finally, technological breakthroughs allowed child workers to be replaced by machines.[29]

Shorter also argues that the rise of capitalism brought about a change in the thinking of parents: Instead of thinking of themselves as merely a cog in the machine that was their community, they started thinking of themselves as individuals with needs that came before the needs of the community. Instead of having children in order to do their duty to hand down the family name and the family property, people started having children simply because they wanted to.[30] Shorter also suggests, by the way, that this change in thinking from a community orientation to individualism encouraged the rise of romantic love.

If the American concept of childhood changed between 1850 and 1950, it changed again between 1950 and 2000. The "child" of 2000, if he could be transported back to the 1950s, would be singularly out of place. He would have a full vocabulary of swear-words; he would be sexually experienced, or at least very well informed about sexual matters; he would have been witness to any number of acts of gruesome violence (some witnessed in real life, and many more on television and in movie theaters), and he might even have committed some acts of violence himself; and he would have little respect for authority.

In the next chapter I will document the extent of this change. I will argue that when it comes to our concept of childhood, our society is, for better or worse, hurtling back into the Middle Ages.

CHAPTER 5

CHILDHOOD'S END?

Many writers have suggested that childhood is disappearing. I am quite inclined to agree with this claim, but at the same time I realize that it is a dangerous claim to make. For one thing, it is a tradition, within our species, for each generation to bemoan the fate of the succeeding generation and complain about the disappearance of values, the loss of innocence, and the decline of their civilization. So if we want a claim about the disappearance of childhood to stick, we will have to prove that this time it's different—that this time, there really is a significant change in the nature of childhood.

In what follows, I will try to document the change that has taken place in the concept of childhood between 1950 and 2000. In particular I will be interested in changes that have taken place in our views on childhood innocence. At one time the adult world worked diligently to keep children in a state of innocence. No longer. I shall argue, among other things, that the child of 2000 is in lots of respects less "innocent" than many adults were back in 1950.

Childhood Then and Now

In the early 1980s books began to appear that argued, timidly at first and then more boldly, that the concept of childhood had undergone a profound change in America. These books were able to defend their claims by invoking statistics which, though perhaps debatable, were persuasive.

Consider first crime statistics. In 1950, only 170 Americans under the age of fifteen were arrested for serious crimes—that is, murder, forcible rape, robbery, and aggravated assault—and they were 215 times less likely to commit such crimes than people age fifteen and older. By 1960 they were 8 times less likely to be arrested for such crimes than people age fifteen and older, and by 1979 they were only 5.5 times less likely. This decline in the adult-to-child crime ratio could have been caused by a decline in the adult crime rate while the child crime rate remained constant—could have been, but in fact wasn't, since adult crime increased threefold between 1950 and 1979.[1]

And since 1979 child crime has taken a distinct turn for the worse. Many children now not only carry guns (which would in itself have been startling in 1979), but use them with little provocation. By 1990 individuals ten to seventeen years old made up 11 percent of the population, and accounted for 12 percent of the arrests made that year—meaning that they got arrested at about the same rate as adults. More strikingly, they accounted for 17 percent of all violent crime arrests, meaning that they were more likely to be arrested for violent crimes than adults. Some crimes in which juveniles were overachievers included arson (being involved in 38 percent of the cases solved), larceny-theft (being involved in 30 percent of arrests), burglary (33 percent of arrests), robbery (24 percent of arrests), and forcible rape (15 percent of arrests). While juveniles do not appear to be committing murder at the adult rate, they *are* killing others and at an early age. In 1990 in the United States, five children under the age of ten and 279 juveniles age ten to fourteen were arrested for murder or nonnegligent manslaughter.[2]

If "innocent" children don't commit crimes, then the children of the 1990s were demonstrably less innocent than the children of 1950.

The legal system has changed to reflect the surge in child crime. In the 1950s the law was careful to treat children differently than adults. An action that would result in a jail sentence for an adult might result in a reprimand for a child. The legal differences were significant enough that adults and children had separate court systems, with different rules. The courts still distinguish between crimes committed by adults and crimes committed by children, but much less than in the 1950s. It is now commonplace for minors to be tried as adults. As a result, the number of people under 18 admitted to state prisons more than doubled between 1985 and 1997.[3]

Indeed, in America it is not uncommon for youthful murderers to receive the death sentence. Twenty-four states allow the death penalty for crimes committed by a juvenile, and about seventy people are on death row for crimes committed as minors. Our willingness to execute children makes us a bit of an anomaly: According to Amnesty International, America is one of only six countries in the 1990s to execute people for crimes they committed when they were under 18. The other five are Iran, Nigeria, Pakistan, Saudi Arabia, and Yemen.[4]

Turning from crime to sex, we find that today's child not only knows much more about sex than the child of the 1950s (including "deviant" sexual practices), but is much more likely to be sexually active than the child of the 1950s. Statistics on virginity are notoriously unreliable, but there is good reason to think not just that people are much more likely to lose their virginity before leaving high school than was true in the past, but that the age at which they are losing it has declined significantly. There is even evidence that an increasing number of girls are having their first sexual activity before menarche. There is also evidence to suggest that in some parts of America, sexual activity is to the teenagers of the 1990s what going bowling or going to the movies was to teenagers of the 1950s.[5]

While we may dispute the statistics on virginity, the statistics on teenage motherhood are beyond questioning. Interestingly, the rate at which teens become mothers has *fallen* substantially since 1950; what has risen is the rate at which *unmarried* teens become mothers.[6]

Also, because they become sexually active at an early age,

teens acquire sexually transmitted diseases at an early age. In America today, adolescents are more likely to have sexually transmitted diseases than any other age group. One disease that has hit adolescents particularly hard is human papilloma virus. It is estimated that between 38 and 46 percent of adolescent females are infected with it.[7]

The attitude of children toward drugs has changed since the 1950s. Back then, drug experimentation by juveniles would likely have involved alcohol or tobacco, both of which were legal substances that could not legally be purchased by minors. Now juveniles who experiment with drugs often use a wide variety of illegal substances.

The attitude of children toward authority has also changed dramatically in the last forty years. In the 1950s children were expected to obey, even when the authority in question was mistaken. Parents had ultimate say over how their children lived their lives; teachers had ultimate say over how they behaved in school. If a child of the 1950s did not like the use of authority by adults, he was expected to keep his dislike to himself: Even if he didn't respect his elders, he was expected to act as if he did. Adults insisted on being addressed not by their first names, but as Mr. Smith or Mrs. Jones, one more indication of the level of deference expected from children.

In present times, authority no longer goes unquestioned. In many cases, when children don't respect an adult, they don't keep their feelings to themselves, but describe in graphic terms the extent of their disrespect for the adult in question.

Some of the most important changes between 1950 and 2000 took place in schools. The traditional subjects are still taught, but along with them are classes on sex education, which would have been unthinkable in the 1950s. Indeed, many schools today not only explain to students what condoms are, but also dispense them, on the assumption that today's students will be sexually active.

What schools expect of children in the classroom has also changed. Behavior that in the 1950s would not have been tolerated—that would have been beyond imagining—has become the accepted norm. When watching documentaries about education in America, I am often amazed to see teachers try to lecture while their students, oblivious to them, are engaged in countless separate conversations among themselves. (You would think that the students would at least behave themselves while cameras were present, wouldn't you?) And of course, the students who are talking among themselves instead of listening to the teacher are quite possibly the school's *good* students: At least they bothered to come to school.

In some schools the change in our attitude toward children becomes apparent at the front entrance: Many schools now make you pass through a metal detector, which, thanks to the rise in child crime, is a sensible precaution. In the hallways you will notice patrols of policemen—not "school monitors," but armed policemen, trained in assault tactics.[8] Some commentators have even gone so far as to suggest that time has come to start arming teachers.[9]

If the relationship between teachers and students has changed, so has the relationship between teachers and parents. Rather than being supportive of teachers and doing their best to present a "united front" alongside the teachers, many parents now feel that what goes on in the classroom is the teacher's business, not the parents'. Indeed, in many cases teachers are expected to assume a significant part of the role of parent, teaching children social skills that the parents of the 1950s probably would have taught their children, but that today's parents are either unable or unwilling to teach. Of course, when teachers have to spend a significant amount of time trying to teach students things parents used to teach children, there is that much less time for the regular curriculum.

Because of these changes in parents, children, and the school environment, teaching has become, for many, a frustrating profession. Teachers who have witnessed the transformation tend to be particularly frustrated. One longtime teacher I know recently told me about an occurence in her classroom that made her start thinking long and hard about whether she wanted to remain a teacher. She had for years described to me the extent to which her job in the classroom had changed from being a teacher to being a disciplinarian, how just getting the children to stay in their seats was a victory, and how unsupportive the parents were. What, I wondered, was the straw that in her case broke the camel's back? Had she been physically assaulted?

As it turned out, the incident in question was hardly life-threatening: A student had made an obscene gesture at her. What made the incident significant is that the student in question was only five years old and appeared to understand perfectly the meaning of the gesture. As she put it, she did not go into teaching so she could spend her days dealing with students like this. She has since resigned.

If the picture presented by today's schools is bleak, think about what will happen when those teachers who view teaching as the molding of innocent youth have abandoned the classroom, only to be replaced by teachers who view teaching as the successful confinement of miniature adults, having most of the adult vices and all the adult reluctance to being told how to live their lives. Schools staffed by such teachers will cease to be educational institutions in the normal sense of the word. They will instead resemble penal and/or psychiatric institutions.

Because of these and other changes in schools, the typical American schoolchild of 2000 arguably learns less—leaves school less well educated—than the typical American schoolchild of 1950. There are a variety of statistics one could use to demonstrate this, but I will instead point to my own experience.

I teach at a state university in Ohio. My university is not particularly stringent in its entrance requirements: It is delighted to admit essentially anyone who has graduated from high school. This would be a defensible admissions policy if one could safely assume that people who graduated from high school were in some meaningful sense ready for college. The problem is that this is by no means a safe assumption. It is entirely possible to graduate from high school not having learned much at all since eighth grade.

In order to guarantee that high-school educations be "meaningful," the state of Ohio some years back began using proficiency tests. This had seemed like a sensible move until I became aware that at my local public school, students almost always pass these "high-school" proficiency tests while still in the eighth grade. Admittedly the school in question is—however they measure these things—one of the better schools in the state, and the community in which I live is populated largely by professional people who have high expectations for their children. Still, the fact that our eighth-graders easily pass these tests speaks volumes about what is now expected from high-school graduates: Before they are allowed to graduate, they must be as "proficient" as one might reasonably expect an eighth grader to be!

Here is a different way to make the same point. At the beginning of each quarter, the university at which I teach distributes to faculty members a profile of the students in their classes. Recently, I was startled to discover that one-fifth of the students in my logic course could, at the time they entered the university, do math at only the sixth- to seventh-grade level. This raises a number of interesting questions. Can one teach symbolic logic—which is really abstract math—to someone who has a limited ability to do applied math? More generally, does it make sense to offer a college education to someone who apparently had trouble mastering (or at least retaining)[10] the material taught him in high school? And most relevant to the present discussion, is it possible, in today's educational environment, to graduate from high school having learned no math since seventh grade? Sadly, the answer to this last question is probably Yes.

Education is still an important part of childhood, but in America today the education children receive is in many cases a watered-down version of the educations their parents received. Indeed, in a recent survey, 63 percent of employers and 76 percent of college professors said that getting a high-school diploma from a public school was not a guarantee that a student had received a "basic" education. In particular, it did not mean that they had mastered basic math skills or could write clearly.[11]

When compared to students in other countries, American high-school students also fail to measure up. In 1995, twelfth-grade students in 21 countries participated in the math and science components of the Third International Mathematics and Science Study. In math, American twelfth-graders came in nineteenth, beating the students in Cyprus and South Africa. In science, American twelfth-graders came in sixteenth, trailing such countries as Iceland and Slovenia.[12]

If the children who attend school are having a different experience than the children of decades past, so are those children who drop out of school. If we go back in time, not to the 1950s but to the 1850s, we find that there would have been a fairly high level of expectations with respect to a child who was not in school (as most children were not). In particular, he would have been expected to work, probably as an apprentice in some trade. The apprentice system is a shadow of what it used to be, though, and much employment requires a high-school diploma. Therefore, while it would be nice if the school dropout went to work, he often doesn't. In many cases he instead goes on welfare, a move that allows him to extend his "childhood" by years or even decades.

As one final indication of the change that has taken place in the nature of "childhood" in recent decades, consider this: In 1992 children between 5 and 14 years of age were three times more likely to commit suicide than in 1960.[13] Suicide had become the fifth leading cause of death among children in this age group.[14] If one assumes that happy, carefree children do not commit suicide, one can only conclude that, in recent decades, there has been a marked decline in the number of happy, carefree children.

The End of Innocence

As the focal point of our discussion of the change in the nature of childhood, let us take an extended look at childhood innocence. Innocence used to be a key feature of childhood, and arguably the biggest single change in the concept of childhood between

1950 and 2000 was the withering away of the idea that children should be innocent.

Innocence as Ignorance

What is innocence? The defining feature of innocence, in the sense I have in mind, is a kind of selective ignorance. Thus, in the 1950s those same parents who worked hard to make sure that their children knew a lot about some things (e.g., reading, writing, and arithmetic) worked equally hard to make sure that their children remained ignorant about other things. High on the list of desirable ignorance was an ignorance of sex—this is, of sexual anatomy and physiology, as well as sexual techniques and deviant sexuality. Children were also expected to be ignorant of the violence of which the world was capable. They were expected to be ignorant of the existence of various obscenities. They were expected to be ignorant of many of the problems of adult life, including financial problems, marital problems, and problems involving chemical dependencies.

Besides not knowing some things that were true, innocent children were also expected to believe some things that were false. They might, for example, have been expected to believe in Santa Claus. Thus, their enforced ignorance can best be described as a blend of misinformation and missing information.

It might be suggested that innocence requires more than ignorance: It also requires inexperience. According to this line of thinking, to count as innocent, a child must not have had sexual relations, must not have committed crimes, must not have disobeyed authority, must not have used swearwords. I would like to suggest that although we commonly *do* count experienced children as "corrupt," a child's level of ignorance is much more important than his level of experience in determining whether he is innocent. Notice, after all, that being experienced is neither a necessary nor a sufficient condition for being corrupt. To begin with, it is possible for a child to be inexperienced and nevertheless be corrupt: Consider, for example, the child who has not yet had sex (for lack of a willing partner) but who knows all there is to know about sexual reproduction, sexual techniques, and "deviant" sexual practices. Such a child would be sexually inexperienced, but would not count as sexually innocent. Conversely, a child might be "experienced" and nevertheless retain his innocence. Suppose, for example, that a child commits some "adult act" out of sheer ignorance. Such a child might touch the private parts of a member of the opposite sex, not out of lust, but simply because he has been kept so thoroughly in the dark about sex that he doesn't understand that some body parts are private. (Thus, the grope was an innocent grope.) Such a child would arguably count as "experienced," but would nevertheless count as innocent. Thus, while it is true that being inexperienced is part of the notion of innocence, being selectively ignorant lies at the very heart of the notion. It is for this reason that I will, in my discussion of childhood innocence, focus my attention on ignorance rather than inexperience.

The loss of innocence is, for most individuals, a one-way process: When you lose it, you aren't likely to get it back. This is because the acquisition of knowledge is generally a one-way process: When you learn something interesting, you aren't likely to forget it. It was in large part their realization that the loss of innocence is irreversible that led the parents of the 1950s to fight long and hard to protect the bits and pieces of their child's innocence—to protect them from the onset of knowledge.

The thing to keep in mind about the pleasures we associate with a traditional childhood is that they are, for the most part, pleasures that can only be enjoyed if one is innocent in the sense I have described. Writer Marie Winn likens the situation of innocent children to that of Adam and Eve in the Garden of Eden.[15] The Garden of Eden was doubtless a wonderful place to live, but to remain there, you had to be innocent—more precisely, you had to be ignorant of good and evil. So it is with children: The bliss of childhood is in part the bliss of ignorance. When they cease to be ignorant, they can no longer be carefree children.

Childhood Innocence in the 1950s

Children haven't always been innocent. Go back before 1800 and you find children who were simply too knowing to be innocent.

Why was this? Was it because the parents of the time did not value innocence? Perhaps, but notice that even if they did, they could not, in many cases, afford to raise their children in innocence. For as we have seen, when the whole family and its hirelings inhabit one room, it is very difficult to keep secrets from the children; and keeping secrets from children is part and parcel of keeping them in a state of ignorance.

By the 1950s, of course, parents no longer had to live in the same room with their children. Changes in the housing situation meant increased privacy and a reduction in the "cost" of maintaining childhood innocence. This is not to say, however, that parents of the 1950s paid no price at all for keeping their children in a state of innocence. To the contrary, maintaining the selective ignorance of childhood innocence required considerable effort on their part. It required, for example, that parents remain sexually aloof whenever their children were present. It required that parents remain married even when they had stopped loving each other. It required that parents mind their language, else their children might become aware of the existence of certain swearwords. It required that parents stay up late on Christmas eve, wrapping presents and putting up a tree, so they could maintain the mythology of Christmas.

And it wasn't just parents who had to pay a price for children to remain innocent: It was the whole adult world. Adults everywhere had to enter into a conspiracy to keep children in the dark about some things and maintain their false beliefs about other things. Thus, books, magazines, and newspapers typically used to be written so that children would not, if they read them, become corrupt—i.e., learn things they were not supposed to know. Television programs were designed so that even if a six-year-old were watching television at ten at night (an unlikely event in the 1950s, I might add), his innocence would remain unblemished. Movies, too, engaged in self-censorship with the innocence of children in mind. The violence and sex they depicted were largely implied. Swearwords (even mild ones, like "damn") were used sparingly, and only when it was clear that circumstances called for them. Most adults of the 1950s did not mind such sacrifices, since to them, childhood innocence was a precious thing.

Some aspects of 1950s parenting are understandable only when we keep in mind how important childhood innocence was to the parents of the time. Consider, for example, the insistence by parents that children accept their authority. To many modern minds, this insistence is taken as evidence of the pomposity of the parents of that time. A case can be made, though, that their insistence on parental authority was part of their strategy for preserving the innocence of children. Allow me to explain.

Children are naturally curious and ask questions. If you answer a child's every question, though, you run a danger of undoing his ignorance and thereby diminishing his innocence. Thus, the parent who cares about the innocence of his child might want to discourage the child from challenging authority—might, for example, want to raise a child to accept answers like "Just because" or "Because I say so, that's why." The alternative to giving such answers would be, in many cases, to provide the child with information that would jeopardize his innocence.

Thus, suppose a seven-year-old girl asked her parents why she wasn't allowed to walk to the store alone. The parents could either tell her the truth—that they were afraid she would be abducted on the way to the store and raped—and thereby destroy some of her innocence, or they could tell her not to ask such questions, that these were the rules. (There was, to be sure, a third route open to parents: They could make up a reason for their daughter's not being allowed to walk—for example, because it looked like it was going to rain. Of course, if the child persisted in asking the same question on other occasions, they would ultimately face the dilemma just described.) Parents who took the authoritarian route in many cases did so not because they valued authority, but because they valued childhood innocence.

Weren't the parents of the 1950s guilty of hypocrisy in the way they raised their children? Isn't it hypocritical, after all, for parents and children to go around pretending they are something that they are not? Indeed it is, but advocates of childhood innocence will be quick to point out that a certain measure of parental hypocrisy is necessary if one is to keep children selectively ignorant.[16] Of course, we live in a time in which people have—or at least claim to have—little tolerance for hypocrisy, and this spells trouble for childhood innocence.

It is worth noting, in passing, that although the parents of the 1950s did a lot to keep their children in a state of innocence, earlier generations of parents were in some respects even more zealous on the subject. There was a time, for example, when parents took steps not just to keep their children ignorant of sex, but took steps to retard sexual maturation. Thus, we are told that "Many of the puzzling child-rearing practices of the past begin to make sense when we understand that their hidden purpose was to delay the child's sexual development."[17] One of these "puzzling practices" involved keeping children in a state of malnourishment even though food was available; by doing this, parents hoped to delay the onset of puberty.

The Decline of Childhood Innocence

As far as childhood innocence is concerned, things changed dramatically between 1950 and 2000. Television provides us with a nice way to track our changing standards on what we think is appropriate for children to see and hear. Regular network broadcasts were begun (to very limited audiences) in 1939. It took eleven years for the first swearwords, "damn" and "hell," to be uttered on national TV. The following year, 1951, saw the first pregnant character in a prime-time television program: Lucille Ball was shown pregnant on *I Love Lucy*, but the word "pregnant" was not uttered. In 1952, Ozzie and Harriet Nelson became the first married couple to be shown sleeping in the same bed. But even ten years later, twin beds were still common for married TV couples: Witness the Petries on *The Dick Van Dyke Show*. The female navel made its first appearance on TV in 1961, with female breasts making their first intentional appearance in 1977—there had been unintentional appearances before that. Abortion was first mentioned in 1962. The first divorced lead character would have been Mary Richards in *The Mary Tyler Moore Show* in 1970, but the topic was regarded as too controversial, so the Mary Richards character was rewritten to have recently ended a long engagement. The honor of first divorced lead characters instead went to *The Odd Couple* in that same year. *All in the Family* was the source of several "firsts" in the early 1970s, including the first homosexual characters in prime time, and the first show dealing with rape and its aftermath. The first prime-time beheading was in 1980 on the miniseries *Shogun*. The first locker room full of naked men was in 1983 on *The Bay City Blues*. The first lesbian kiss was in 1991 on *L.A. Law*. And the first episode devoted to the topic of masturbation was in 1992 on *Seinfeld*.[18]

As the 1990s progressed, so did the rate at which television's taboos were discarded. By 1998 it was possible to watch—on one of the major networks, no less—as a transsexual bodybuilder exposed her vagina.[19]

In the 1990s it was possible to switch from channel to channel and witness a wide range of acts of violence and a wide variety of sexual situations. Daytime talk shows—of which there were 21 by 1996—started devoting themselves to letting utterly shameless people describe their depraved existences to all America—including any child viewers who might be watching. According to one study of daytime television, by the mid-1990s the *typical* talk show had "four sexual-activity disclosures, one sexual-orientation disclosure, three abuse disclosures, two embarrassing-situation disclosures, two criminal-activity disclosures and four personal-attribute disclosures."[20] To keep his share of the daytime audience, Geraldo Rivera was presenting shows with titles like "Men in Lace Panties and the Women Who Love Them." It was no longer enough to have shows featuring teen prostitutes; instead, you needed to have shows with titles like "Watch Teenagers Tell Their Parents: Mom and Dad, I'm a Hooker."[21] Jerry Springer became famous not just for the lurid content of his talk show, but for the fistfights that almost inevitably broke out among his guests. When television station WDIV-TV moved the show from the 10 A.M. time slot to the 4 P.M. time slot, ratings soared, as the show became children's after-school favorite.[22] And evening television fare came to include "snuff TV"—shows featuring not actors pretending to die, but people actually dying or narrowly escaping death. You could see, for example, what happens when a bungee-cord jumper's cord breaks, a pipe bomb explodes in the face of a policeman, or animals attack humans.[23]

By the late 1990s steps were taken to "clean up" television: A television-show ratings system was initiated. Of course, the system in question can work only if parents are around to make sure that their children tune in only those shows with an appropriate rating. Plans were also made to introduce television sets containing so-called V-chips. This technological fix would avoid the just-mentioned defect of the ratings system, but it has defects of its own. For one thing, while V-chips might make it easier for parents to prevent their teenagers from being exposed to adult material, it will do nothing to prevent their infants from being exposed to material which, although suitable for teenagers, is hardly suitable for infants. (Such fare would not be blocked by a V-chip.) Also, the presence of a V-chip in a television set will accomplish nothing if parents "disable" it by giving their children access to the "forbidden" shows. Is there reason to think that a parent who lets his child play with a graphically violent video game or go to a graphically violent movie will deny his child access to graphically violent television shows?

There has been a backlash against attempts to "clean up" television. By way of illustration, consider the debate concerning the fate of New York City's channel 35. This channel, which, in the mid-1990s, featured "a nightly diet of straight and gay stripping and sex,"[24] came as part of the basic cable package. Its signal was not scrambled, meaning that anyone—old and young alike—

who had cable had access to the channel. There was a time, of course, when such a channel would have been unthinkable: Adults would have recoiled at the thought of exposing (or even possibly exposing) children to such fare, and they would not have minded going out of their way to view pornographic material—by going to an X-rated theater, for example, from which children were banned—if taking these steps "protected" children. Such is no longer the case, though. Channel 35 became the subject of a court battle over whether cable operators can restrict the content of its shows: A significant number of adults felt that the benefits of receiving an unscrambled sex-oriented channel outweighed any harm that might be done to children by viewing it.

The content of movies has also changed over the decades. In the 1950s almost every movie was rated G—or would have been rated G if a rating system had been necessary. In the 1960s filmmakers in ever-increasing numbers made movies that were unfit for consumption by children. The movie industry—still at some level concerned about the preservation of innocence—adopted a rating system so that parents could select for their children movies that were appropriate to their level of innocence. The three things that most determined the rating a movie would get were its sexual content, its level of violence, and its use of profane language.

With the passage of time, movies experienced a sort of ratings inflation. Movies rated R in the late 1960s would have been rated merely PG-13 in the 1980s. Furthermore, the ratings system, which was supposed to prevent children below certain ages from attending unsuitable movies, stopped being enforced. Thus, at one theater I recently visited, someone had taped up a handwritten sign that read, "No children under five at R-rated films."

Of course, even if theaters saw fit to enforce the ratings system, it might accomplish little. Children could view those same R-rated movies a few months later on cable television, by renting them from a local video store, or in many communities by checking them out of the local public library.

Why did television and the movies abandon their role in preserving the innocence of children? The motivation was, no doubt, largely financial. Filmmakers found, for instance, that teenagers were reluctant to attend movies rated merely G; they found that they could obtain a PG-13 rating for a G movie by the simple expedient of adding a few swearwords, and by doing so increase their profits.

Similarly, by making the sexual content of movies more graphic, filmmakers found they could draw a larger audience. In movies of the 1950s, when characters in a movie were about to have sex, they might be shown leaving the room. It was clear to the knowing viewer why they had left the room. The innocent viewer, on the other hand, might assume that they had gone out for a walk, and this mistaken assumption would in no way lessen his enjoyment of the movie. By the 1990s, when characters in a movie decided to have sex, little was left to the imagination.

Along with television and movies, the content of magazines and newspapers has changed over the decades. It used to be that when a magazine or newspaper felt compelled to mention an obscenity, it used the device of giving the first and last letters of the word, with an appropriate number of dashes in between. People who already knew the obscenity could meaningfully read the sentence, and people who did not know the obscenity would not learn it by being exposed to the sentence.

These days, books, magazines, and newspapers are significantly less concerned about keeping children in the dark. Grisly crimes are described in detail. (Thus, in a newspaper story we are told not merely that someone was murdered or even that he was murdered with a railroad spike; instead we are treated to information on exactly which body parts the spike penetrated.) Feature articles on sexual practices appear alongside stories on presidential politics. Four-letter words are often spelled out.[25]

Children's books have become increasingly lurid. In "young-adult" literature—that is, books published with children fourteen and under in mind—one can now find a variety of themes that at one time would have been saved for adult literature. In the 1970s and 1980s, books dealt with "adult" problems like alcoholism or prostitution, but dealt with them in an uplifting way: The alcoholic child gets help, and the girl-turned-prostitute turns over a new leaf. By the 1990s uplifting was out, and bleak was in. One could find books about a teenage girl who falls in love with a serial killer; about a thirteen-year-old who, for no apparent reason, murders a liquor store owner; or about a thirteen-year-old girl whose lover, the middle-aged father of a friend, is shot by her mother's ex-boyfriend, who thereupon takes his own life.[26]

In 1998 newsmagazines and newspapers were presented with a dilemma: How many details of the Starr Report—which described President Clinton's sexual activities in the White House— should they reveal to their readers? Several papers chose to reveal everything: They printed the entire text of the report. America's parents were also faced with a dilemma: Should they shield their children from current events? Should they explain what the stain on Monica Lewinsky's dress was? And what did it say about our society if their preteen children already knew what the stain was and how it got there?

The coming of the Internet age will likely have dire consequences for childhood innocence. It is now possible for any computer-savvy child to access, with a few clicks of the mouse (and in his very own living room), material that by 1950s standards would have counted as radically obscene. He can take part in on-line discussions with individuals whose sexual practices count, even by today's standards, as bizarre.

Even a perfectly innocent child might find his innocence undermined by the Internet. Suppose, for example, that this child, while attempting to access the popular Alta Vista search engine, accidentally types in "www.alta-vista.com" rather than "www.altavista.com"; he will find that he has accessed a pornographic site. And suppose that having finally found the Alta Vista search engine, he enters an apparently nonsexual word like "thumb" or "donkey." In doing so, he will unintentionally unleash a flood of pornographic sites which, because of the manner in which he accessed them, might not even go through the formality of asking him to affirm that he is over eighteen before displaying profoundly pornographic images to him.

I know a high-school student who, in the process of writing a paper on W. Somerset Maugham, entered "of human bondage" on a search engine. The sites uncovered were startling, to say the least.

Thanks to the Internet, the line between public library and X-rated theater has largely vanished in many localities. At the public library of Selah, Washington, for example, a bunch of preteens were watching, on an Internet terminal, a naked lady perform fellatio. When an adult patron told the librarian what the children were doing, the librarian informed her that to kick the children off the terminal would violate their free-speech rights and that to inform the children's parents would violate the children's privacy rights.[27]

It is possible for libraries to give their patrons access to the Internet while at the same time blocking access to pornographic sites: They can install "filtering" software on their computers. But even then, problems can arise. The Baltimore County Public Library, for example, used such software until it started getting complaints from patrons who wanted to do Internet research on Super Bowl XXX. The antismut software saw the "XXX" and cut off access. The library's solution was to turn off the filtering software.[28] This meant that children again had access to pornographic sites. Apparently, the price to maintain childhood innocence—namely, irritating a few football fans—was, in the judgment of this library, too great to pay.

Attempts to "clean up" the Internet have met with stiff resistance from those adults who regard such efforts as an infringement on their freedom of speech—or, less grandly, as an irksome impediment to their access to pornographic material. In 1997 the Supreme Court supported their claims and struck down a federal law whose intent was to keep smut off the Internet.[29]

If what children watch has changed since the 1950s, so have the toys children play with. In the 1950s "violent toys," such as toy guns, were popular with little boys. By the 1990s many little boys put down their toy guns in favor of the virtual guns of video games. In the games in question, they no longer had to pretend that they were shooting someone; to the contrary, they could view the effects of their marksmanship and watch their victim suffer the pangs of death.

Picture, then, the modern American living room. The mother is quietly working on her cross-stitching. The father (if he is still part of the household) is reading the newspaper. Their child, having bludgeoned his video-game opponent into unconsciousness, is in the process of pulling off his head, which comes up with part of his spinal column still attached. This is what, these days, passes for a scene of quiet domesticity.[30]

I mentioned above some of the changes that have taken place in the juvenile justice system. In particular, I commented that we have grown less willing to treat juvenile criminals as mere children than we would have been in the 1950s. These changes are in part a reflection of the decline of childhood innocence.

Despite the maxim to the contrary, ignorance *is* an acceptable excuse in the law. It was largely with this thinking in mind that Americans of the 1950s favored a separate legal standard for children. The children of that period had purposely been raised to be ignorant of many things and because of this could much more easily appeal to ignorance to excuse themselves from what looked like criminal behavior. Thus, if one child shot another, the natural assumption was that the act was an "innocent mistake." Perhaps the child did not know what a gun was, or if he did, perhaps he didn't realize that the gun was loaded or that the other child was in the line of fire. What would have been difficult to imagine was that a child would have pulled the trigger with murderous intent: A child raised in innocence would be incapable of such a thing.

Of course, with the decline of childhood innocence came

the sneaking suspicion that many of the children who were committing crimes *did* have the requisite capacity for evil thoughts and *did* know full well what they were doing; and as their crimes grew ever more horrible, this suspicion led to calls that we return to the old days, in which children were judged by the same standards as adults.

No Secrets

Suppose an adult of the 1950s had done something that, at that time, would have been regarded as shameful. A man, for instance, might have cheated on his wife or engaged in sex with another man. A woman might have become pregnant out of wedlock or had sex with her brother. In the 1950s the standard procedure was for a person to take knowledge of such shameful acts to the grave with him; or, if a person felt compelled to share his secret, he might have shared it with his minister or psychiatrist. Alternatively, if he had secretly wronged a certain person, he might have shared his secret with that person and asked his forgiveness. Under no circumstances would he have shared it with his neighbors, his children, or the world at large. To the contrary, he would have gone to great lengths—and might even have submitted to blackmail—to keep his secrets out of the public eye.

By the 1990s things had changed. Americans found it increasingly difficult to keep secrets. Rather than taking their secrets to the grave or sharing them with a trusted few individuals, they felt compelled to reveal them to anyone who would listen. If they could tell their secrets to a national television audience, so much the better. As a result, several television shows came into existence to act as forums for the revelation of secrets.

What caused the change? Quite simply, many Americans had lost their sense of shame. The sorts of acts that would have shamed their parents and mortified their grandparents didn't shame them. It was no longer shameful to cheat on one's spouse or to have sex with one's siblings; to the contrary, this was merely an act of sexual self-expression. It was no longer shameful to be an alcoholic; alcoholism, after all, is a disease, and it is inappropriate to feel ashamed because you have a disease. It was no longer shameful to be pregnant out of wedlock: Unwed mothers and fathers were as proud of their procreative activities as their married counterparts.

How did Americans come to lose their sense of shame? It was a consequence, I think, of their adopting the view (which I will develop shortly) that nothing—not their family, not their country, not their culture, not God—was "bigger than" they were. What mattered, in the last analysis, is what was good *for them* and what felt good *to them*. Shame is the voice within you that tells you that you have wronged something bigger than you— that you have failed to make your own interests subservient to the larger interest. But if nothing is bigger than you, it is impossible for you to wrong something bigger than you; hence, no matter what you do, you need not feel shame.

Actually, it is an overstatement to say that Americans have *lost* their sense of shame. If a person felt absolutely no shame in doing something, he would feel no need to tell others what he did: It is precisely because I feel absolutely no shame in the daily act of brushing my teeth that it wouldn't occur to me (once this sentence has ended) to go around telling people about it. People who feel compelled to share their "secrets" with the world in many cases do so because they feel a lingering sense of shame about their activities. By declaring their secrets openly, they are attempting to expunge their diminished sense of shame. Their logic goes something like this: If I were ashamed of what I did, I would keep it a secret; I am not keeping it a secret; therefore, I must not be ashamed of what I did.

And when they reveal their secrets, Americans want their neighbors not only to *know* what they have done, but to *accept* what they have done. It is, after all, hard to overcome a lingering sense of shame if your neighbors regard your actions as shameful. Eliminate their feelings of shame *for you*, and you go a long way to eliminating the lingering feelings of shame *within you*. And if a neighbor will not go along with this plan—if he insists on being disgusted by your behavior—you can always label him "intolerant"; in doing so, you shift the character flaw from yourself to him, and you are freed from the burden of his disapproval.

Americans' inability to keep secrets has unfortunate consequences for childhood innocence; the preservation of childhood innocence, after all, requires adults to be meticulous about keeping a variety of secrets.

Maintaining Childhood Innocence in Modern America

Suppose a parent of today wanted his children to be innocent in the sense that the children of the 1950s were innocent. It would be possible to accomplish this objective, but only with considerable effort.

It would require, for one thing, that the parent act as censor. This, of course, is a role that parents who wanted to maintain the innocence of their children have always had to play, but in the 1950s it meant blocking your child from obtaining, say, a "forbidden" magazine. These days, acting as censor means that a parent will probably have to scan newspapers and magazines before letting his child see them—or not subscribe to any but a select few newspapers or magazines. It means carefully investigating the contents of movies (and not merely trusting the ratings) before allowing a child to watch them. It means carefully monitoring a child's television viewing—or, more realistically, living without television.

In order to keep his children innocent, a parent must also be quite careful about which other kids his children associate with. One prime source of childhood "corruption" is contact with children who have already lost their innocence—or who never really had it to begin with. They are likely to share innocence-robbing secrets with other children, who in turn will become corrupt. Corruption spreads among children like a particularly contagious virus.

And it is not only other children about whom the modern parent has to worry, but other adults as well. In the 1950s parents could count on the world at large to share their goal of preserving childhood innocence; modern parents cannot. Many adults no longer assume that children should be kept in a state of innocence. Indeed, some adults appear not even to understand the concept of childhood innocence.

Such adults might (without even realizing it) do things that undermine the innocence of someone else's child. Thus, a fourth-grader I know reported that she saw her first R-rated movie during a sleepover at a friend's house. It did not occur to the friend's parents that anyone would object to letting a fourth grader watch a movie that, because of its sexual content, had earned an R-rating. Indeed, even schoolteachers, if they don't value innocence, can act to undermine it: A fifth-grader I know reported that he saw his first R-rated movie during a school party. Again, the teacher did not have malicious intent in allowing such a movie to be shown; it had simply never occurred to her that some parents would worry about a "mere" R-rating.

Most schools, rather than expecting schoolchildren to be innocent, expect them to have lost their innocence. Consider, by way of illustration, the following incident. In the part of the country in which I live, when children order soda pop they sometimes ask for what is called a Suicide. To make a Suicide, the counter person moves the glass from spigot to spigot on the pop dispenser, pouring in a mix of all the available kinds of pop. A precocious and (thanks to the efforts of his parents) relatively innocent boy I know was doodling in school and designed a machine that would save the counter person from having to move the glass from spigot to spigot; instead, all the spigots were joined by tubes, which fed into one final tube. His teacher saw the doodle, and asked what it was a picture of. The boy answered that it was a Suicide machine. This set into motion a somewhat comical chain of events. The picture was turned over to the school psychologist, who called the mother, who, like the teacher and psychologist, had never heard of a culinary Suicide. Prompted by the psychologist, the mother asked her son if he was feeling sad and whether he had perhaps been reading about the activities of Dr. Kevorkian, the suicide doctor. The boy denied any knowledge of Dr.

Kevorkian, said he was feeling fine, and went on to explain his invention.

In the 1950s, one suspects that the case just described would have been handled differently. The child would have been presumed innocent until proven knowing. Adults have become quite ready to presume, when a child "crosses the line," that he did so not because he is innocent (so that "crossing the line" was an innocent mistake), but because he has been corrupted. And of course by presuming this, adults make it all that much easier for a child to lose the ignorance requisite to a state of innocence. The young inventor of the "Suicide machine," for example, lost some of his innocence as a result of the chain of events just described. He found out that people sometimes commit suicide and that there is even a doctor who helps them do so.

Perhaps, then, it isn't enough for parents who value innocence to keep their children away from other children and other adults. Perhaps they even have to keep them away from schools—which might be part of the reason 1.5 million American children are schooled at home.[31]

Why the Change?

Granted, then, that our concept of childhood and in particular our views on the importance of childhood innocence changed dramatically between 1950 and 2000. What is the reason for the change?

The most important thing to realize is that the change was not the result of a conscious choice on our part. We did not sit down in the 1950s and ask whether we were better off with childhood innocence or without it. We did not take a vote. The change just happened, as a by-product of other social changes—but then again, this can be said of most interesting cultural changes that take place. Furthermore, it is clear that any attempt to specify these "other changes" will involve a high degree of speculation. Let us, nevertheless, press on and try to determine what changes in the last forty years helped precipitate the decline of childhood and in particular the decline of childhood innocence.

The Changing Role of Women

One important change in America between the 1950s and the 1990s involved the role of women in society. Above I suggested that in the 1950s women wanted to be at home with their children rather than at work. This was doubtless true in some cases, but in other cases the reason that a woman was at home with her children was the realization that society did not want mothers in the workforce. Many a woman was doubtless deprived of what might have been a wonderfully fulfilling career by society's intolerance for working mothers.

The women's movement changed all this. Mothers were freed to decide how they wanted to spend their adult lives. Some chose to remain at home with their children. Others decided to have a career and enjoy motherhood at the same time. Thanks in part to their newfound freedom, an ever-increasing number of mothers entered the workforce. In 1950 only one in ten married women with children under six years of age worked; in 1993, six in ten did. Not only that, but most married women did not even wait a year after giving birth before returning to the labor force.

The fact that mothers chose to have careers changed the lives of their children in many important respects.

In the first place, having a working mother affects the environment in which a child develops. In the 1950s a child spent his days at home, with his mother as his principal caregiver. As mothers started entering the workforce, their children were increasingly sent off to day care; and by the 1990s it was not unusual for a child to enter day care when only a few weeks old.

Day-care centers are almost always less conducive to the maintenance of childhood innocence than a mother's lap. In a day-care setting, a child's principal caregiver will be a day-care worker—or, more likely, a series of day-care workers, since turnover rates tend to be high at day-care facilities[32]—who might not be particularly interested in preserving childhood innocence. The child raised in day care will also experience prolonged exposure to other children, which will likely make it quite difficult for the child to remain in that state of ignorance necessary for innocence. Unless a day-care setting is strictly controlled, the group of children cared for will quickly become as innocent as its *least* innocent member.

Much has been written about the effects of day care on children. Researchers have examined whether day care makes children more violent, more aggressive, more antisocial, or more resistant to discipline; whether children raised in day care are more likely to develop schizophrenia or other mental disorders; whether day care affects a child's cognitive and linguistic development, and so on. Social scientists still debate the proper interpretation of these studies.

What is interesting to me, in the present context, is the dearth of studies to determine the effect of day care on children's levels of *innocence*. Perhaps this is because innocence is a hard thing for researchers to quantify. Or perhaps it is because researchers do not regard the loss of innocence as a particularly noteworthy event; for them, the fact that day care undermines a child's innocence would not count as a defect of day care, inasmuch as innocence isn't particularly worth preserving.

But if day care is indeed hazardous to a child's innocence (as there is every reason to think it is), and if preserving a child's innocence is an important goal of parenting (a claim I shall defend in the next chapter), it follows that parents should be reluctant to put their children in day care.

Having a working mother will also affect the quality of the child's environment when he is not in day care. To maintain childhood innocence requires time and energy; a working mother is typically lacking in both. At the end of a workday, a working mother might find herself tempted to take the path of least resistance with respect to her child. Rather than trying to research the content of a movie, it is so much easier simply to give her child the necessary money and be done with him; rather than playing with her child, it is so much easier to let him watch television; and rather than "screening" the programs he watches, it is so much easier to let him watch whatever he wants on the patently false assumption that if a show weren't fit for children, it wouldn't be on television.

It is arguable, then, that the women's movement, in smashing down the 1950s role model for mothers, simultaneously struck a blow against the concept of childhood innocence. This is not to say that the advocates of women's liberation were opposed to childhood innocence. More likely, they simply did not stop to consider the ramifications that women's liberation would have for childhood in general and childhood innocence in particular.

In the above remarks I have talked about mothers who chose careers over their traditional role as principal caregivers for their children. Am I assuming, then, that only women can play this role?

No. It is entirely possible for a father to play the role of principal caregiver. And if, when women had started going off to work, their husbands had stayed at home and played this role, then perhaps childhood innocence would not have been undermined to the extent that it has. The problem is that husbands did not, in many cases, stay home to play this role. For like their wives, the husbands in question found themselves unwilling to sacrifice their careers for the sake of the innocence of their children.

Making Ends Meet

Someone might respond to my discussion of the women's movement and its effect on childhood by arguing that I am mistaken if I think mothers returned to the workplace simply because they wanted to enjoy a fulfilling career. To the contrary, many mothers were *driven* back to the workplace by financial considerations: They had to go to work in order to "make ends meet." In short, these days it isn't a selfish personal desire (namely, the desire for career fulfillment) that makes mothers work; rather, it's the unselfish desire to provide for one's children.

This line of argument has as a premise that today's Americans are financially worse off than Americans of the 1950s. Although this is a premise many Americans will unhesitatingly accept, it is demonstrably false. By almost any measure, Americans are much better off today, materially speaking, than they were in the 1950s. Allow me to explain.

It is true that prices have risen dramatically in this century.[33] Thus, in 1897 a nine-inch pair of steel scissors cost seventy-five cents; by 1997 that same pair of scissors cost five dollars, a 567 percent increase. But among the prices that have risen this century is the price of labor, and this has meant a dramatic increase in the average wage of American workers. In 1897 the average wage was 14.8 cents per hour. By 1997 the average wage was $13.18, an 8,800 percent increase. And this increase in wages means that although the "dollar-cost" of scissors may have risen during this century, their "labor-cost"—that is, the number of hours the average worker must work in order to pay for them—has fallen dramatically: In 1897 the average worker had to work 5.1 hours to pay for the above scissors; by 1997 he had to work only 0.38 hours to pay for the scissors, a 93 percent decline in the labor-cost of the scissors.

For present purposes, what is of most interest to us is not the dollar-cost of goods and services, but their labor-cost. After all, from a child's point of view, the true cost of an item is not the number of dollars being charged for the item; rather, it is the number of hours he must be separated from a parent in order for that parent to earn the money necessary to buy the item.[34]

Consider, then, the cost of shelter. Some two-income parents might argue that although *their* parents could afford to buy a home on a single income, they cannot. Thus, the "second" parent's decision to enter the workforce (and consequently put their child in day care) was not entirely voluntary: It was the price she (or, less commonly, he) had to pay to keep a roof over their child's head.

Did the cost of shelter in fact increase in recent decades? In terms of dollar-cost, it most certainly did: Between 1956 and 1996, the average dollar-cost of a new home rose from $14,500 to $140,000, an 865 percent increase. And what about the labor-cost of a new house—which cost, as we have seen, is the relevant cost for purposes of this discussion? Interestingly, it also rose. Between 1956 and 1996, the average hourly wage rose from $1.95 to $12.78, meaning that the labor-cost of the average house rose from 7,435 hours in 1956 to 10,955 hours in 1996, a 47 percent increase.

This makes it sound like two-income couples are justified when they claim that the high cost of housing forces them to work, but the numbers cited above are misleading. For not only did the *cost* (both in dollar terms and in labor terms) of the average house get bigger between 1956 and 1996, but *the average house itself* also got bigger during that period: The average new home in 1956 was 1,150 square feet in size; by 1996 it was 1,950 square feet in size—a 75 percent increase. If we examine the labor-cost of a house not in terms of hours-worked-per-house, but hours-worked-per-square-foot-of-house, we find that the cost of housing *fell* from 6.5 hours per square foot in 1956 to 5.6 hours per square foot in 1996—a 13 percent decline. By this measure, housing got cheaper between 1956 and 1996.

Another thing that changed in recent decades is the quality of the average new home. In 1956 only 28 percent of new homes had more than one bathroom; in 1996, 91 percent did. In 1956 only 35 percent of new homes had fireplaces; in 1996, 62 percent did. In 1956 only 6 percent of new homes had central heat and air conditioning; in 1996, 81 percent did. In 1956, new homes rarely came with garage door openers and never came with microwave ovens; in 1996, 78 percent of new homes came with garage door openers and 85 percent came with microwave ovens. In 1956 only 11 percent of new homes came with dishwashers; in 1996, 93 percent did.

Suppose, then, that a couple in the year 1996, instead of buying a house that was average by current standards, found and bought a new home that was average by 1956 standards: a smallish house that had only one bathroom, no microwave, no air-conditioner, no dishwasher, and so on. Such a house could be purchased for a fraction of the $140,000 price tag of the average

1996 new home. Consequently, it might be possible for them to buy such a home on a single income.

The problem, of course, is that although their parents (in the year 1956) probably would have been delighted to own a home such as this, the 1996 couple would likely find it unacceptable. Indeed, to avoid living in a home like this, they will both go to work, even if it means consigning their children to day care.

I became painfully aware of this change in housing standards when, in 1992, I bought a house and, a few months after that, visited, for the first time in decades, the house my family occupied in 1960. I was astonished by how small, how "primitive" my childhood home had been. It would have easily fit into the first floor of the two-story home I had just bought. There was only one bathroom; my new house had three. The garage would accommodate only one car; my new garage housed two. In my childhood home there was only one "common area," a living room that blended into a dining room that in turn blended into the kitchen. In my new home the "common area" was much more extensive: There was a (seldom used) living room, a dining room, a family room, a breakfast room, and an office. In my childhood home, to leave your bedroom was to be in the presence of other family members; in my new home all four family members could be out of their bedrooms but be nowhere near one another.

If, when I had been home hunting in 1992, a real estate agent had shown me a house like the one I occupied in 1960, I would have been insulted. And yet, my parents had not minded living in such a home. And when I was a child, living in such a home had seemed neither demeaning nor confining. The house was small, but it was plenty big enough to sustain family life.

Housing isn't the only "cost of living" that has declined (in labor-cost terms) in modern times. The labor-cost of food has also fallen dramatically. In 1901, 14.7 percent of the average worker's wages went for food. By 1995 this number had fallen to 5.3 percent. It is therefore unlikely that modern Americans are driven to become two-paycheck couples in order to feed their children.

Likewise, the labor-cost of transportation has declined. Cars cost more today in dollar terms than they did forty years ago, but significantly less in terms of the hours someone must work to pay for them. And of course today's car is luxurious compared to the cars of the 1950s: It is likely to have power steering, air-conditioning, cruise control, a remote-control side-view mirror, a stereo system, and power brakes. The average American is driving what would have been a dream car in the 1950s, a fact that few modern Americans appreciate.

When we start examining the labor-cost of various goods and services, what we find is that, with but a few exceptions,[35] the labor-cost-of-living has fallen throughout the century. The above statistics give lie to the claim, made by many modern couples, that they must abandon their children for the workplace (i.e., must put their child in day care so that both parents can work) *in order to make ends meet*. It is altogether likely that the couples in question are far more affluent (in terms of what their labor can buy them) than their parents were; where they differ from their parents is in their definition of what counts as "making ends meet." Their definition goes far beyond providing adequate food, clothing, and shelter. It includes "necessities" that their parents would have regarded as luxuries, and that their grandparents would have regarded as the stuff of fantasy.

In other words, a case can be made that many modern American parents become two-income families not so they can make ends meet, but so they can buy neat stuff, take neat vacations, and keep up with the Joneses. And to fund their materialistic life style, they are willing to "sell" to an employer the time that they might otherwise have spent with their children.

The Rise of No-Fault Divorce

Another major change between 1950 and 2000 that damaged childhood innocence was liberalization of divorce laws. The divorce rate soared between 1950 and 1990. Divorce typically involves a shattering of many of the illusions that protective parents create to keep their children in a state of innocence. During a divorce, children might find out that their parents are splitting up because of unmet sexual needs—or, more correctly, unmet sexual desires. And after the divorce, sex again comes to the foreground as parents start to date. There was a time when parents (especially mothers) would have refrained from dating, or would have dated but done their best to maintain the illusion that they were sexless creatures, but this is no longer felt to be necessary. And of course it is difficult to keep children ignorant of sex when there is a new man sleeping with mommy (or a new woman sleeping with daddy) each month.

Besides being exposed to sex, children of divorce are exposed to a variety of adult problems they would normally be sheltered from. Money problems top the list, since divorce often causes a steep decline in the standard of living of children.

Children of divorce spend their days worrying about why daddy yells at mommy, about who that man is that mommy keeps going off with, about whether the child-support payment will come this month, and about a hundred other things that would never have crossed the mind of the typical child of the 1950s. With the rise of divorce, the family, rather than offering children shelter from the problems of the adult world, has become a source of some of the most serious problems many children are likely to face. Rather than being a source of psychic energy for children, the family has become a sink for whatever psychic energy they possess.

If it were only the children of divorce whose innocence was affected by divorce, it would be bad enough. But the harm done by divorce spreads to the children of stable families as well. These children watch their friends' formerly-stable families vanish in a flash and start to worry that the same thing might happen to their family. They experience their friends' parents' divorces at a distance.

The Rise of "Individualism"

Finally, between 1950 and 2000 there has been an enormous change in the values of adult Americans. It used to be that people felt that many things in life were bigger than they were: God was bigger than you, your country was bigger than you, your family was bigger than you. And because there were things bigger than you, many times in life you could not do what you wanted to do but instead had to serve the larger interest. Thus, if your country called you to go and fight in a war, you did, possibly at the cost of your life.

In the 1960s people increasingly came to doubt that there was something bigger than they were; and because of these doubts, they felt freed from the obligation to serve the larger interest.

The magnitude of this change in values becomes abundantly clear when one talks to senior citizens. Thus, consider an elderly acquaintance of mine who attended a high-school football game for the first time in years. When I asked how she had liked it, she replied that she had been utterly shocked when, during the playing of the national anthem, people had not stood in silence, with hands over hearts, but had instead carried on with whatever they had been doing. To her way of thinking such behavior was deplorable. This is a woman, after all, who had been raised to think that lots of things were bigger than she and that one of them was her country.

There are those who, on reading of this woman's reaction, will dismiss her as hopelessly old-fashioned, but such a dismissal only reinforces my point that our country has undergone a profound change in values. She is not alone, in her generation, in thinking that God, your country, and your family come first.

Whether we think that individualistic values are good or bad, one thing most of us can agree on is that adoption of these values has had a considerable impact on our concept of childhood. In the value system of the 1950s, your family was one of the things that was bigger than you, and this in turn meant that children were at or near the top of the list of things for which parents would sacrifice. For many modern Americans, your family is no longer bigger than you, and as a consequence, children are, in many cases, well down on the list of things for which parents will sacrifice.

Thus, in the 1950s, many parents sacrificed sexual fulfillment to the well-being of their children: They stayed in loveless marriages "for the sake of the children." (How often these days do you hear of couples staying together for the sake of the children?) On the other hand, many of today's Americans are content to tear apart a family and uproot the very existence of their children so that they can change sexual partners.

Likewise many Americans today see nothing wrong with putting their career goals ahead of their children's interests. Such thinking would again have been foreign to many mothers of the 1950s who, whatever their own career ambitions might have been, thought it essential to put the needs of their children ahead of their own.

And many Americans today see nothing wrong with spending at the workplace the time they could have spent with their children. They may convince themselves that they make this choice with the interests of their children in mind, and in some cases they clearly do. But in other cases parents go off to work in order to satisfy a variety of material desires: They are willing to give up time with their children in order to afford "more stuff."

In believing that their family was bigger than they were, parents of the 1950s believed in what has come to be called—sneeringly, in many instances—"family values." As we shall see in a subsequent chapter, the striking thing about family values is that they involve a value system built around the needs and interests of children. We shall also see that the alternative to family values is what might be called "parental values"—a value system that puts the wants and needs of parents ahead of the wants and needs of their children.

It is, by the way, a bit misleading to list the rise of individualism as just one of many factors behind the decline of childhood innocence; for as the last few paragraphs show, it is arguably *the key factor*—the factor responsible for the other factors. Why did women enter the workforce? In part because they put career satisfaction or material desires ahead of their children. Why did people clamor for more liberal divorce laws? In part because they no longer put the integrity of their family ahead of their sexual desires. Thus, if one wanted to point to the single factor most responsible for the change in the nature of childhood that took place in the last half of the twentieth century, a prime candidate for this dubious honor would be the rise of individualism.

Whether today's parents love their children less than parents of the 1950s did is debatable; one thing that is beyond debate, though, is that many of today's parents love *themselves* more than parents of the 1950s did. The rise of individualism is one manifestation of the rise of parental self-love.

In the above remarks, am I arguing against individualism? By no means. Am I suggesting that the sexual fulfillment or career goals of parents don't matter? Not at all. I am a firm believer in individualism. People who want sexual fulfillment should have it (if they can find a consenting partner); women who want to be fully committed to their careers should do so. What I find troubling—and this will be a central topic of discussion in Part Two of this book—are those cases in which people, *after having children*, seek sexual fulfillment or pursue career goals *at the expense of their children*.

We live in a world in which no one has to have children. This hasn't always been the case. Until quite recently, the only sure way to avoid having children was to live a life of celibacy, which for most people would be an impossible sacrifice. Thanks to modern methods of birth control, one can be sexually active beyond the wildest imaginings of our ancestors with little or no chance of creating children.

This means, though, that when previous generations neglected their children, they had an excuse for doing so: "I didn't really want the kid; the kid was just a by-product of my getting the things I did want." Medical technology has deprived the current generation of this excuse. For almost all of us, children are a *choice* (or at least the result of conscious choices), not a *by-product*. We can, without much difficulty and without significant sacrifice, avoid having children; and this means that when the typical modern American has a child, it is because at some level he or she *wanted* to have a child.

Now, if we think that when a person chooses to have children, he or she is voluntarily assuming an obligation to provide the children in question with a rather high level of care, what are we to think of parents who turn their back on this obligation because, for example, they desire a change of sexual partners? We can only conclude that they are acting rather shabbily, morally speaking. Such people, rather than being described as individualists, can better be described as selfish egoists.

It is, of course, possible for those people who want to put sexual fulfillment or their career ahead of everything to do so without being accused of selfishness: All they have to do is take steps to avoid having children—which steps, we have seen, are easy to take. With no children, there will be no obligations to children; and with no obligations to children, they can do pretty much what they want with their lives without incurring moral censure.

The problem is that many people, besides wanting sexual or career satisfaction, also long for reproductive satisfaction: They have an urge to make children, even if they do not feel driven to put themselves out raising the children they have made. What we find in America today is people who have selectively adopted the values of the 1950s: They share the common 1950s belief that starting a family is an important step toward self-fulfillment, but they lack the common 1950s belief that the family you create is, in some sense, larger than you are, so that once you have created it, your own wants and needs must take a back seat to those of the family you have created.

One author, on considering the choices that modern Americans face, offers the following piece of advice:

> If their objectives are primarily self-fulfillment, sexual excitement, a deeply gratifying adult relationship, then it might be advisable for them to think twice about embarking on a family in the first place. The thought of a family mainly as a source of fulfillment and gratification for the marriage part-

ners does not bode well for children's future. Parents need to understand that the successful raising of a family requires a greater focus on the well-being of the children and that they must sacrifice some of their own ambitions, desires, and strivings for personal happiness if the children are to grow up well.[36]

It is unlikely, one suspects, that many of the selfish egoists around us will take this advice to heart. People are likely to continue wanting it all: A variety of sexual partners, an all-consuming career, *and* children by the fireside. So much the worse for children.

In Part Two of this book I will return to the topic of what, exactly, parents owe their children. In the remaining chapter of Part One, though, I would like to inquire into whether childhood, in the 1950s sense of the word, can be resurrected, and if it can, whether we should seek to resurrect it.

CHAPTER 6

THE RESURRECTION OF CHILDHOOD?

A case can be made, then, that the 1950s were the zenith of the concept of childhood in America. And if we project the trends of the last fifty years, we are left with an image of an America in the not-too-distant future in which the notion of childhood has essentially been abandoned. We can imagine seven-year-old children being sentenced to death for their crimes, as was the case in England in the late 1700s. We can imagine parents sharing drugs with their children (although, to be sure, this sort of thing is happening even today). We can imagine parents having sex in the presence of their children, or children having sex in the presence of their parents. We can imagine children having access to every form of entertainment known to adults. We can, in short, imagine a world like that of the sixteenth century, in which children, rather than being sheltered from the adult world, are full participants in it.

Can Childhood Be Resurrected?

It took centuries of slow but steady change to form the modern concept of childhood; it has taken only decades to undo much of this transformation. Is it, one wonders, possible to resurrect childhood? My guess is that it probably isn't; at any rate childhood will be a long time coming back, if it comes back at all.

Consider first the social forces that are undermining childhood innocence. In the preceding chapter we focused on three of them: the movement of women into the workforce, the increase in the divorce rate made possible by liberal divorce laws, and the rise of "individualism." Is it likely that women (or men) will give up their careers to stay home and raise children? No. Is it likely that divorce laws will be made more stringent so that people with children will find it difficult to divorce? Again, no. Is there reason to think that people are going to grow less selfish and more altruistic in the coming years? One can of course hope, but the more realistic answer is that they will not. What this means is that the forces that helped bring about the decline of childhood innocence look like they will be with us in the foreseeable future.

And even if these forces were somehow curbed, it wouldn't necessarily result in a restoration of childhood innocence. For remember that maintaining childhood innocence requires more than that *parents* find it worth preserving; it requires that *the vast majority of adults* find it worth preserving. So we must also ask, Is it likely that television, the movies, magazines, and newspapers will engage in the sort of self-censorship necessary to maintain childhood innocence? Again, probably not.

A case can be made that in America today, we have reached the point of no return with respect to childhood innocence. To see why I say this, consider the dilemma faced by the parent who values childhood innocence. This parent, on regarding the world around him, might come to the conclusion that he would be doing his child a grave disservice to raise him to be innocent. To the contrary, he might conclude that in today's world it is the duty of a loving parent to systematically undermine his child's innocence. After all, if your child is going to be exposed to children who are likely to experiment with sex at an early age, he would do well to have a full understanding of sex and its possible consequences. If your child is going to attend a school at which obscenities are going to be used regularly on the playground, he should be taken aside and told which words are publicly acceptable and which are not, or he might make the mistake of thinking that since all his friends are using these words, they are acceptable in all social contexts. If your child is going to be surrounded by people prone to acts of violence, he would do well to learn about violence and about how to commit acts of violence himself, in order to protect himself from such acts.

In short, as far as childhood innocence is concerned, we appear to be in a vicious circle: Because childhood innocence has eroded as far as it has, caring parents will take steps to undermine their children's innocence; and because parents take such steps, childhood innocence will erode further.

Here is another thing to realize about the long-term outlook for childhood innocence. Parents are likely to raise their children the way they themselves were raised. If you were raised to be an innocent child, it will be natural for you, as an adult, to raise your children to be innocent. (My generation, of course, turned out to be the exception to this rule.) If, on the other hand, you were not raised an innocent child, it might not be obvious to you that innocence is worth fostering in your own children; indeed, the thought that children can be kept in a state of innocence might not even occur to you. It is therefore unlikely, one suspects, that the parents of the next generation, who did not themselves have the benefit of being raised in innocence, will raise their own children in innocence.

Indeed, when I talk to college students—the parents of tomorrow—about childhood innocence, they often get that blank look in their eyes, the look that says, "What's he talking about?" For many of them the concept of childhood innocence is something new. When I explain the concept to them and ask whether childhood innocence is worth preserving, in many cases they argue that it is not: "They're going to lose their innocence eventually anyway, so why bother preserving it."

The chances, then, of a comeback of childhood innocence are slim. But before we give up hope altogether, we should keep in mind that social changes are very difficult to predict, so that the future prospects of childhood innocence and more generally the concept of childhood may be less bleak than I have made them out to be. To put the issue into perspective, how many people in 1950 would have been able to predict the decline of childhood that would take place in the next forty years? So perhaps childhood will, in the coming decades, stage an unexpected comeback.

Should Childhood Be Resurrected?

There are those who will respond to the above commentary on the decline of childhood innocence with a shrug of the shoulders. These individuals will *greet* the changes that have taken place between 1950 and 2000. The loss of childhood innocence is a loss, they will tell us, to be celebrated, not mourned. It is good that today's children grow up faster than children did in the past; it is good that children have a thorough understanding of the world in which they live rather than being allowed to live in a fantasy world for the first decade or two of their lives; it is good that children aren't deprived of the pleasures of sex; and it is good that children question authority.

The question we must now address is this: Are these people correct? Should we mourn the end of childhood or celebrate it?

We have reached the stage in our inquiry at which we must attempt something that the adults of the 1950s would never have dreamed of doing: We must attempt to defend childhood innocence. The adults of the 1950s took it for granted that childhood innocence was valuable and well worth preserving. We, of course, live in a different world.

Women and Children

Why would anyone wish to disparage childhood innocence? One way to answer this question is to consider not children, but women and their status before the women's movement.

Not long ago, many people, both men and women, felt that not just children should be kept in a state of innocence, but that women should as well. Indeed, look back to the 1950s, and we find that many of the "innocence-preserving" measures used on children were also used on women. Men did not, for example, swear or tell risqué jokes in the presence of women. Women were shielded from acts of violence. Women were kept in the dark about their husband's (or father's) finances, lest they worry "their pretty little heads."

Why keep women innocent? Because (people of the time thought) it was best for them: They were not psychologically capable of dealing with the ugliness of the world.

Feminists have attacked this mind-set by arguing, in the first place, that men's motives in keeping women innocent were not entirely "pure." In particular, by keeping women in a state of ignorance (about, for example, family finances), men could keep women in a state of artificial helplessness and thus keep them under their control. Feminists have also argued that women were fully capable, psychologically speaking, of dealing with the ugliness of the world—or at any rate that they would be capable if they were raised properly. Finally, feminists have argued that even if a case could be made that women benefited from being kept in a state of innocence, the costs of being kept in such a state far outweighed the benefits. What costs were these? Women had to give up much of their freedom and control over their destinies. They had to give up many opportunities for personal growth. It is better, many feminists would argue, to be a relatively miserable but autonomous being than to be carefree but under the domination of another.

In much the same way as feminists have argued against keeping women in a state of innocence, we might develop an argument against keeping children in a state of innocence. In the argument in question, we might point out that parents have mixed motives in keeping their children innocent, that children are perfectly capable of dealing with the harsh realities of adult life, and that it is unclear that children benefit from being kept in a state of innocence. Let us now examine the extent to which such an argument can be developed.

A Question of Motives

Some would argue against childhood innocence by maintaining that it involves an unjustifiable deception of people. Remember that in order to keep our children innocent, we adults must engage in a concerted program of misinforming them about some things and withholding information about other things. Thus, to the extent that deception is wrong, keeping our children innocent is wrong.

In reply to this claim, the advocate of childhood innocence might admit that parents must deceive their children to keep them innocent, but argue that there is nothing wrong with the sort of deception involved. Notice, after all, that there are times when it is perfectly permissible to deceive another human being. Suppose, for example, that your aunt is dying of some illness and that she has asked you to care for her pet cat. Suppose that as she nears death her cat suffers an unfortunate accident. Suppose, finally, that after burying the cat, you go and visit the aunt in the hospital. It would not be wrong for you, under the circumstances, to refrain from volunteering information about the fate of her cat. It would likewise not be wrong for you, if she asked about the cat, to misinform her and tell her that the cat was doing fine. Under the circumstances described, the aunt stands to gain little from knowing what happened to her cat and stands to lose a lot from finding out.

This is not to say that deception is *always* morally permissible. Suppose, for example, you go to a used-car salesman to buy a car. He does not volunteer the information that the car you have picked out has a bad transmission. And when you ask him whether the car in question was ever in an accident, he lies and says No. The salesman has deceived you, and I think we can agree that he has wronged you in the process. (Some might forgive him for not volunteering information about the transmission, but lying about the previous history of the car seems clearly wrong.)

How can we determine whether a particular instance of deception is morally permissible? We must inquire into the motives the person had in deceiving someone and into the consequences of the deception. In particular, if his motive was to benefit the person being deceived, and if there is reason to think that the deception in question *will* benefit that person, then he has probably done nothing wrong in deceiving that person. When you deceived your aunt, it was because you wanted her to be happy in her few remaining days, and there is good reason to think that if you failed to deceive her about the fate of her cat, she would have died in misery. On the other hand, the used-car salesman not only did not have your interests in mind when he deceived you about the car, but was out to sabotage your interests.

The advocates of childhood innocence will claim that when they deceive their children in order to keep them innocent, their motives in doing so are pure, and the deception in question is beneficial to the children deceived—they will claim, in other words, that the above conditions are met by their deception of their children.

The opponent of childhood innocence might at this point call into question the motives of parents who keep their children innocent. While it may well be that parents who keep their children innocent have their children's interests in mind, they have their own interests in mind as well. Consider, by way of illustration, two children. One is breathtakingly innocent; he is likely to walk up to you and tell you, with a smile, how wonderful are the clouds in the sky and how he can hardly wait for Santa to visit. The second child is anything but innocent; he is likely to walk up to you and, after using an obscenity to get your attention, tell you of his plan to sleep over at his girlfriend's house. The typical parent will find the former child much more agreeable to be around than the latter child.

Innocent children are like kittens, and nearly everyone loves a kitten. Children who have lost their innocence are like old cats—jaded, indifferent to the world, and ornery.

One should also note that by keeping their children in a state of ignorance, parents augment the power they have over them. Their children simply will not know enough to rebel effectively. Thus, a child in the 1950s may have threatened to run away, but his parents could be fairly confident that the child wouldn't get very far before realizing his own helplessness, at which point he would return home, vanquished in the struggle for control. These days, on the other hand, when a child threatens to run away, the threat must be taken seriously: Children are no longer helpless. Indeed, there are parents who, out of fear that their child will run away, have given up attempts to put limits on his activities. Along these same lines, in the 1950s a parent could dramatically restrict a child's freedom by the simple expedient of cutting off the child's allowance; today, a child might compensate for a lost allowance by dealing drugs.

As we have seen, in the process of keeping their children innocent, parents not only withhold information from them but misinform them; and in many instances the process of misinforming them also contains elements designed to increase the power parents have over their children. Thus, a parent might tell his credulous child about the boogie man—who will get the child if the child misbehaves. Or a parent might tell his child about a benevolent character like Santa Claus, but remind the child that only good children get presents. (This parent might add that Santa knows if you've been bad or good, so don't try to pull a fast one.)

In conclusion, a case can be made that parents keep their children innocent in part because innocent children are more pleasant to be around and easier to control than children who have been corrupted: Their motives in keeping their children innocent, then, are not "pure," but are at best "mixed." This in turn seems to undermine the justification of parental deception offered above: The deception involved in keeping children innocent isn't merely for the sake of the child, it is for the sake of the parents as well.

In reply to this claim, let me point out that while "pure" motives are admirable, "mixed" motives are not necessarily contemptible. There is nothing wrong with my doing something that benefits both myself and someone else. Indeed, most voluntary transactions between people are entered into simply because both parties to the transaction benefit from it. And more to the point, there is nothing wrong with my benefiting from deceiving someone else as long as the deceived person benefits from the deception. Thus, from the fact that you benefit personally from your sick aunt's tranquil state of mind in her last days (the result of your deceiving her about her cat), it does not follow that it was wrong to deceive her: In the case in question, she benefited from your deception even more than you did. Parents who keep their children in a state of ignorance might make the same claim with respect to their deception of their children: "Yes, I benefited, but my child benefited even more."

A Question of Psychology

Opponents of childhood innocence might at this point shift their attack away from the issue of motives and instead focus on the issue of whether children in fact benefit from being kept in a state of innocence. If they don't benefit, then their parents' mixed motives for keeping them in such a state will deserve condemnation.

Thus, some opponents of childhood innocence will argue that we *harm* children by keeping them in a state of innocence. In particular, by keeping children in the dark about the problems they will face as adults, we prevent them from developing the ability to deal with these problems and therefore make it less likely that they will successfully deal with them when they grow up.

In reply to this claim, it might be pointed out that children who are exposed to adult problems don't necessarily develop the ability to deal with these problems. In the words of one psychoanalyst: "Children who are pushed into adult experience do not become precociously mature. On the contrary, they cling to childhood longer, perhaps all their lives."[1] Thus, those who claim that children benefit from being kept innocent might defend their views along the following lines: Children simply aren't ready, emotionally or intellectually, for certain information; to force it on them would likely prove harmful to them.

Consider, for example, the obvious truth that everyone dies, including children and their parents. This is information which, if provided to a very young child, would increase his level of anxiety substantially without providing any obvious benefit.

Or consider acts of violence. Parents typically want to shelter their children from witnessing such acts—this is one of the things traditionally involved in keeping children innocent. A case can be made that children exposed to such acts—either in the real world or in movies and television—are given something to worry about, once again without any counterbalancing benefit.

Indeed, a case can be made that not just children, but society as a whole benefits when children are sheltered from witnessing acts of violence. It can be argued, for instance, that constant exposure to acts of violence desensitizes children to violence, and that a child who has been desensitized to violence is more likely to commit violent acts against others; and even if he does not commit such acts himself, he might be more tolerant of their commission by others.

Many will deny that children are influenced by, say, the violence depicted in movies. In particular, filmmakers are fond of arguing that the violence they show in PG-13 movies cannot undo a proper upbringing, that all they are doing is depicting the world around them, and that society is ultimately to blame for the evils that these days plague childhood. These same filmmakers will turn around and sell "product placements" in their movies: They will, in other words, charge the manufacturer of a product a fee for arranging to have the product briefly appear in a movie.

Thus, a brewer might pay thousands of dollars for the privilege of having a character in a movie shown drinking his brand of beer. To the brewer, the price is worth paying since the brief appearance of his product in the movie will plant an unconscious idea in the heads of moviegoers, who in turn will buy that brand of beer. Can it be that we adult moviegoers are highly susceptible to a seconds-long exposure to a particular brand of beer, but children are psychologically unscathed by the gratuitous violence that makes up the rest of the movie?

The question of whether exposing children to movie violence desensitizes them to violence and thereby increases the chance that they will either commit acts of violence themselves or tolerate the commission of such acts by others is difficult to answer. Indeed, it is a question that society has been attempting to answer for as long as there have been movies. Both sides of the debate have their favorite evidence to bring forth; both sides ignore or explain away the evidence brought forth by the other side.

That this question remains unanswered is not surprising. Many of the most interesting questions regarding social behavior (e.g., Does capital punishment deter crime? Would decriminalization of drugs result in an increase in drug abuse? Do welfare programs make it less likely that people will become financially independent?) fall into the same category. And the reason they remain unanswered is that we are unwilling to do the experiments required to conclusively answer them. The experiments in question would be controlled experiments. Thus, to learn conclusively whether exposure to violence makes children more violent, we would need to take two similar groups of children at birth and as we raised them, we would need to treat them alike but for one thing: The children in one group would be exposed to a wide variety of acts of violence, whereas the children in the other group would not. As we raised them, we would look for signs of violent behavior and would record it as it happens. Finally, when the experimental subjects were, say, forty years old, we would examine our records and draw appropriate conclusions: We would at last "know" the answer to our question.

Such an experiment, although it would teach us much about the effects of violence on children, has two obvious drawbacks. First, as long as we value the rights of individuals, it would be wrong for us to undertake the experiment in question; the experiment would, after all, involve a serious infringement of the rights of the experimental subjects. Second, even if we decided to go ahead with the experiment, its results would not be available for decades. The problem, of course, is that we don't have the luxury of waiting several decades before deciding how to raise our children. We need to decide here and now how much violence to expose them to, even though we cannot be certain of the effects of such exposure.

In this state of affairs, there is an argument for *restricting* our children's exposure to, say, violence in movies. After all, consider the mistakes we might make because of our ignorance about the effects of violence on children. If we expose children to movie violence and it turns out that such exposure *is* harmful to them (and/or to society), we will have made a very big mistake in exposing them. Suppose, on the other hand, we strictly limit the amount of movie violence to which our children are exposed, and later research shows that such exposure is *not* harmful. We will have made a mistake: We will have needlessly deprived our children of the amusement that can be derived from watching people suffer and die. In the cosmic scheme of things, this is not a very significant mistake to have made, particularly since there are other things children can do for entertainment than watch people suffer and die. Given this choice of possible mistakes, there is every reason, in our ignorance of the effects that exposure to violence has on children, to restrict such exposure.

So much for keeping children innocent with respect to violence. What about innocence with respect to sex?

Parents of the 1950s, as we have seen, took great care to keep their children in the dark about sex. In my own case, the innocence of childhood meant being astonishingly ignorant about sex until I was a teenager. It was only in junior high (or was it high school?), after reading an article on insect reproduction in *Scientific American*, that I finally came to understand the exact mechanics of sexual reproduction. (Before that, people not only didn't tell me about the facts of life, but they discouraged me from asking questions.) Although I think a convincing case can be made for limiting the exposure of children to acts of violence, I am much less confident that one can defend the view that children should be kept ignorant about sexual reproduction.

Why did parents of the 1950s keep their children in the dark about sex? For one thing, in much the same way as they wished to spare their children the ugliness of violence, they wished to spare them the ugliness of sexual reproduction. This reason will not seem particularly compelling to those who, like myself, don't find acts of sexual reproduction to be ugly in the way that acts of violence are ugly, and in fact don't find them to be ugly at all.

Another reason parents of the 1950s kept their children in the dark about sex is that they thought it would lessen the chance that their children would engage in sexual activities. This reason, however, is arguably obsolete. If we lived in a world in which almost all children were in the dark about sex, keeping one's own child in the dark about sex might make it less likely that he would have sex. The problem, of course, is that we live in a world in which most children have a rather extensive knowledge of sex. This means that any child who is in the dark about sex is in trouble in two ways. First, he is likely to be sexually exploited by those children who *do* know about sex; and second, if he *does* engage in sex, the consequences are likely to be more serious because he has been kept in the dark. A sexually ignorant boy would not be likely to use a condom, and would therefore run a risk of contracting a sexually-transmitted disease; and a sexually ignorant girl would not be likely to use birth control, and would therefore run a considerable risk of pregnancy.

I would advocate, in short, that parents be frank with children about the basic facts of sexual reproduction. At what age should they begin telling their child the facts of life? In many cases parents can safely let the child set the pace and simply answer the sexual questions the child asks. Should a child be told about sexual reproduction at age three? If the child asks about it, why not?

At the same time, I should add that there is little upside to forcing sexual information on a child who is not psychologically ready for it. Furthermore, the manner in which a parent answers a child's sexual questions should obviously depend on a child's age. The reply to a three-year-old's question about how babies are made should be much more basic and much less graphic than the reply to a thirteen-year-old's question.

While parents are supplying all this information about reproduction, I think they should also do what they can to discourage their children from engaging in sexual acts. Why discourage them? For much the same reason as parents should discourage their children from experimenting with drugs.

Children who use drugs are harmed in a number of ways. First, using drugs can harm their health. Second, using drugs can damage their childhood: Time and energy that might have been spent in self-exploration and self-development is instead spent trying to acquire illegal drugs, recovering from using them, and worrying about the consequences of such use. Third, using drugs can dramatically affect the quality of one's future life: If you develop an addiction, it may make it nearly impossible for you to live the life you otherwise would have chosen to live.

Children run similar risks when they engage in sexual activities. First, by becoming sexually active they run health risks, for example, the risk of contracting sexually-transmitted disease or—in the case of girls—the risk of becoming pregnant. (Remember that a thirteen-year-old girl who becomes pregnant has a significantly higher chance of complications than, say, a twenty-year-old.) Second, by becoming sexually active they can damage their childhood. Being sexually active makes life complicated. You have to worry about whether you have contracted some disease. You have to worry about whether you are (or the girl you had sex with is) pregnant. And if you *are* pregnant, you are faced with what would for most children be a very difficult choice: You can either have an abortion, carry the baby to term and give it up for adoption, or carry the baby to term and raise it. The first two options will, for most children, be psychically scarring. The third option, on the other hand, will mean the abandonment of childhood. Finally, by becoming sexually active, children can forfeit much of their future freedom. This is particularly true if they contract a sexually-transmitted disease like AIDS, if they become pregnant and choose to keep their baby, or if they impregnate someone and are forced to shoulder some of the responsibility (financial or otherwise) for their reproductive act.

Besides counseling their children against sexual activity, parents should take steps to shield their children from the pervasive view that casual sex affords a person lots of pleasure with minimal negative consequences. Hollywood would have us believe that sexual intercourse is on a par, socially and psychologically speaking, with a handshake. This may be true for adults (although I am inclined to doubt it), but it certainly isn't true for children.

Childhood Innocence: Some Last Thoughts

Someone might, at this point, attempt to defend childhood innocence, not by endorsing its various components, as I have been trying to do, but by pointing to the risks we run when we abandon childhood innocence. It might be suggested, in particular, that as far as its children are concerned, America today has embarked on an experiment of monumental proportions. It is an experiment to find out, for better or worse, what happens to children when you dispense with what were, until quite recently, the defining features of childhood. In coming years we will learn the outcome of this experiment.

Those taking this line will argue that we are foolish to undertake such an experiment. Even if we think that the concept of childhood favored in the 1950s was flawed, the flaws were not so great as to justify resorting to untested and radical measures to eliminate them. What we are doing, in abandoning a "tested" concept of childhood, is like drinking a bottle of untested and possibly poisonous liquid to cure a few pimples.

Although I am sympathetic to those offering this line of argument, I think it is unsound. Notice, after all, that America's experiment with the concept of childhood is hardly an "untested" measure. To the contrary, it has been thoroughly tested—during most of man's history, in fact. Can children survive a life without childhood? Not only can they, but they did, up until the last few centuries. The lesson of history makes it clear that by discarding childhood we are neither dooming our species to extinction nor signing a death warrant for our civilization.

Although the "dangerous experiment" defense of childhood fails, it contains the seeds of what I think is a far more promising argument for the preservation of childhood.

Earlier in this chapter we considered the argument for women being kept innocent. The argument in question was based on the premise that women could not withstand the psychological pressures of dealing with the ugliness of the world. There is, however, a second, less sexist, way this argument for female innocence can be developed. In particular, there were (and to a lesser extent still are) people who argue that women are perfectly capable of dealing with the ugliness of the world, *but who see no reason why they should have to*—particularly if men are willing to shoulder a double-load of ugliness on behalf of the women in their lives.

What I am talking about here is an old and largely outmoded notion, that of chivalrousness. The chivalrous male besmirches himself, both physically and in other ways, so women will not have to besmirch themselves. It is one form that male altruism commonly used to take.[2]

My point in raising this issue is not to resurrect old sex-roles, but to point out that the defender of childhood innocence can construct an argument along similar lines. He can, to begin with, admit that children can survive being raised without innocence; but after making this admission, he can go on to argue that our goal as parents should not be simply that our children "survive" childhood but that they live delightful childhoods, free from most of the cares and worries that they will encounter as adults. In short, from the mere fact that children *can* live lives devoid of innocence, it does not follow that they *should* live lives devoid of innocence.

In order to clarify the logic of this argument, consider life in the workaday world. People *can* work 14-hour days, as the history of labor clearly shows. From this does it follow that we *should* return to 14-hour workdays? Of course not. People *can* work 52 weeks a year and never take vacations; they will be very tired, but will "survive." From this does it follow that we *should* eliminate vacations? Again, clearly not. A fourteen-hour workday or a vacationless job are things that people can survive, but it is truly wonderful that we live in an economy that can "afford" for us to work only eight hours a day and take vacations.

Back to children. We saw, in our discussion of the history of childhood, that in this century a rising level of affluence made it much easier—much less "costly"—for parents to keep their children in a state of innocence. With increased affluence, families could make decent livings without relying on the wages of their children. With increased affluence, multiroom houses became affordable to the masses, and with multiroom houses, as we have seen, it became much easier for people to keep their children ignorant of certain facts of adult life.

So why should we keep children innocent? According to the present line of argument, we should do it not because they won't survive if we don't, but because they will flourish if we do. Children will eventually be confronted with the problems of the world. Why not give them a carefree period before they join the fray? Why not show them how wonderful life can be when one is surrounded by loving individuals, and thereby furnish them with an ideal they can carry into their adult lives? As Rousseau put it, "Why rob these innocents of the joys which pass so quickly?"[3]

Today's children have typically lost their innocence at an early age—or, lamentably, never had it to begin with. They are "knowing," and as a result have lost their sense of wonderment. In all too many cases they are cynical, jaded, bored, and find the world to be not beautiful but sad, ugly, and unfair. I pity them. Deprived of a wonderful time in life, they never even had the chance to live in a world that all of us would love to inhabit.

Even if a traditional childhood were nothing more than a vacation at the beginning of life, an extended carefree period, it would be defensible. But I think that childhood is more than a vacation in life. I will argue in Part Two of this book that a primary goal of parenting—construed in one way—should be to make your children maximally free (in a sense to be described) when they reach adulthood. I will suggest that in order to attain this level of freedom, children need to spend their childhood exploring themselves and discovering and developing their talents. Arguably, children can best conduct this exploration if they are relatively free of worries. Ideally a child should spend her days worrying not about whether she is pregnant, whether mommy and daddy will still be living together in a week's time, whether someone is going to blow up her car the way they blow up cars in the movies, or how her getting sick will mess up her single parent's day-care arrangements, but about whether she should try out for basketball or volleyball, about whether she wants to take art classes, and about which of her many friends is her best friend.

This, I think, is our best argument for preserving childhood in the 1950s sense of the word. The argument is not that children perish if deprived of childhood, but that they thrive if bestowed with it. Of course, for our children to be able to experience childhood, we adults, and in particular we parents, will have to shoulder a double-burden of worries—much the same as chivalrous men used to shoulder a double-burden of the ugliness of the world so that women could be spared it. To the extent that our generation fails to shoulder the burden, it is not because of a lack of resources—our ancestors had fewer resources than we do and gladly shouldered the burden—but because there is something else we would rather expend the resources upon—namely, ourselves.

PART TWO

THE OBLIGATIONS
OF PARENTHOOD

CHAPTER 7

MODELS OF PARENTING

Let us now shift our attention from the concept and decline of childhood to the goals of parenting. As it turns out, the conclusions we draw concerning these goals are likely to depend in large part on which of two competing models of parenting we adopt. The models in question describe the moral nature of the relationship between parents and children. In particular, they describe the duties and rights parents have with respect to their children.

I will devote most of the remainder of this chapter to a description of the two models in question, the *ownership model* and the *stewardship model*. In the next chapter, I will present an argument in favor of the stewardship model of parenting, and in the chapter after that I will return to the question of the goals of parenting. More precisely, I will ask what parents who advocate the stewardship model should be trying to accomplish in raising their children.

Parents as Owners

Why do people make and raise children? According to the ownership model of parenting, for much the same reason as they buy and own cars. Children are useful to have around. And according to the ownership model, children, like cars, are there to be used or exploited; they are there so that the owner's life can be made easier, or so that the owner can accomplish various self-interested goals. The children are not an end in themselves, but are instead means to an end, that end being the well-being of the owner-parent.

If we asked someone who favored the ownership model of parenting why he had children, he might answer that he needed them to work on the farm, that the family benefited from the wages his children brought home, that having children increased his welfare payments, or that he wanted someone to comfort and provide for him in his old age. These answers would demonstrate a willingness to engage in a "materialistic exploitation" of children.

Besides materialistic exploitation, there is also what might be called "psychic exploitation" of children. An owner-parent might thus have children because as a child, certain dreams had never been fulfilled; his hope is that by carefully arranging his child's life, he will get a second chance to live out these dreams, albeit vicariously. Or an owner-parent might have children as an act of narcissism: In the same way as a narcissistic person might be inordinately fond of hanging photographs of himself, an owner-parent might likewise be fond of making physical copies of himself—namely, children.

It would be a mistake to think that owner-parents will care nothing about the interests of their children. To the contrary, the owner-parent *will* care—more precisely, he will care *to the extent that caring enables him to further his own interests*. If his goal in having a child is so he can benefit from the child's wages, it would be foolish for him to let the child become too hungry or too sick to work, for then the wages will stop. Likewise, if his goal in having a child is so the child can care and provide for him in his old age, he might see to it that the child gets a proper education, for then the child can that much better afford to care and provide for him. And of course, laws in effect might place limits on the manner in which he can exploit his child: It will not be in his interests to exploit his children in ways prohibited by law, since that could result in a jail sentence. And even where there are no such laws, he might behave nicely to his child, not for the sake of the child, but so his neighbors will think well of him.

According to the ownership model of parenting, then, the rights parents have with respect to their children are property rights—that is, the right to use their possessions as they see fit, as long as they don't harm anyone else's property rights in doing so. And of course, when the advocate of the ownership model of parenting talks about "anyone else," he does not include his children as being "someone else." Thus, while it would be wrong for him to use his children in a way that harms his neighbor, there would be nothing wrong with him using his children in a way that harms *them*: They are, after all, his property.

In summary, an owner-parent is someone who is quite willing, when questioned about some aspect of his behavior toward his child, to reply, "It hurts the child, but it helps me." He is an egoist with respect to his children: His interests first, their interests second. In the owner-parent's view of things, he has many rights with respect to his children, but few duties.

Parents as Stewards

By way of contrast, someone holding the stewardship model of parenting—call him a steward-parent—will be an altruist with respect to his children: Their interests first, his interests second. And when questioned about some aspect of his behavior toward his child, he is likely to reply: "It hurts me, but it helps the child." Finally, unlike the owner-parent, he would regard himself as having lots of duties with respect to his child, but few rights.[1]

What Is Stewardship?

The notion of stewardship is a bit murkier than the notion of ownership, but the idea is this: A steward in the conventional sense is someone who manages the property of someone else on behalf of that other person. Thus, if your neighbor were going away on a trip, he might ask you to act as steward for his lands. If you accepted, your job would be to manage his lands in a way that would benefit him. As steward, you should look out for opportunities to improve his lands and do your best to prevent them from being harmed. Thus, you might plant trees on his lands so he will be able to benefit from their lumber when he returns. Or you might cut currently-existing trees, sell the lumber, and reinvest the proceeds if you thought doing so would improve his lands. As his steward, you would be remiss if you failed to prevent the spread of a noxious weed across his meadows if it was in your power to do so.

In your activities as steward, you must be careful not to profit at your neighbor's expense. You are not, after all, the owner of the lands; you are only the steward. There may be times, however, when both you and the owner can profit from your activities as steward. Thus, suppose that in your efforts to halt the spread of the noxious weed just mentioned, you purchase (with the landowner's money) herbicide from a store you happen to own. There would be nothing wrong with such a transaction if the price you charged for the herbicide was the going price.

One very important thing to realize about stewardship is that your activities as steward should depend to a large extent upon the values of the owner of the lands. If, for example, the owner's primary interest in holding the lands is to sell them at a profit, then your goal in stewardship should be to enhance the market value of the lands. If, on the other hand, the owner's primary interest in holding the lands is as a place of residence, then enhancing the market value of the lands would not be your primary concern; indeed, you might even, under these circumstances, do things that would reduce the market value of the lands, if you had reason to think the changes would make the lands more desirable as a residence. Thus, if you knew that the owner's dream was to have a vineyard, then you might want to cut his trees and plant grapes, even though doing so would make the lands less salable.

The nature of your activities as steward will also depend upon the owner's expected date of return. If, for example, your neighbor told you that he was going to be back in twenty years, then the object of your stewardship should be to bring the lands to their maximal value (in the owner's eyes) twenty years hence, and this could mean undertaking any number of long-term projects. If, on the other hand, he told you that he would be back in a month, then your job would not be to start new projects or even to make any dramatic changes in his lands, but merely to preserve the status quo.

In the preceding comments, I have assumed that the owner either left you instructions for the stewardship of his lands or that you knew him well enough to be able to infer his values with respect to his lands. Suppose, however, that this is not the case. Suppose that the owner, a neighbor whom you know hardly at all, extracts a promise from you to look after his lands if anything happens to him, and suppose that the next day he is spirited away by terrorists, who announce that he will not be seen again for twenty years. (Suppose, too, that the activities of these terrorists are well known and that there is every reason to think that, despite the best efforts of the police, your neighbor will not be seen again for twenty years.) What should you do in the absence of specific instructions about how to manage the lands and in the absence of information about the values of the owner? Your best bet would be to rely upon what is sometimes called a "reasonable-man standard": You should assume that the owner is a reasonable man with fairly typical values and should manage his lands accordingly. You should, in other words, manage his lands in such a way that on his return he would probably, if he was a reasonable man with fairly typical values, be satisfied with your efforts. The goal, then, is not that you do *exactly* what he would have done, for that, under the circumstances, is impossible. (You cannot read his mind.) Furthermore, it is entirely possible for you to have been an excellent steward, as judged by the reasonable-man standard, and for the owner nevertheless to berate your efforts as steward and to complain that if he had been in charge, things would have been done differently. Such criticisms, of course, will be utterly unfair.

In keeping with the reasonable-man standard, the land steward will employ a conservative management style. He will be unwilling to "take chances" with the lands entrusted to his care. He will be unwilling, for example, to plant an experimental crop which, if it flourishes, will make the owner of the lands vastly wealthy, but which, if it fails, will ruin him. It is one thing to take extravagant chances with your own property; it is quite another thing to take such chances with someone else's property.

Besides trying to maximize your neighbor's values in your stewardship of his lands, you should also, to the extent possible, manage his lands in a way that will give him, on his return, a considerable amount of freedom in determining what is done with them. Thus, one measure of your success as a steward will be the number of significant choices that the owner has on his return. Ideally, the owner will find, not that all the important decisions about the future of his lands have been made for him, but that their fate is in his hands.

Thus, out of respect for the owner's future freedom of choice, the land steward will be careful not to take steps that "lock in" the owner to one particular use of his lands. A good steward, for example, would probably not let a coal company strip-mine the lands, even if a good income could be had by doing so. Notice, to begin with, that strip mining will render the lands useless for any other purpose to which the owner might wish to put them on his return. Also, coal not strip-mined today will presumably still be strip-minable in twenty years time. Better, then, to hold off on mining and let the owner decide if that is what he wants to do when he gets back.

Furthermore the land steward will, out of respect for the owner's future freedom of choice, take steps to broaden the number of attractive choices the owner will have on his return. Suppose, then, that a patch of weeds on his lands can be replanted with grapes. There would be an argument for going ahead and planting them (assuming it was cost-effective to do so). If the owner likes the idea, the steward's actions will have benefited him; if he doesn't like the idea, it will cost him nothing to let the weeds grow back. Consider, after all, that the "price" of turning the vineyard back into a weedy field is mere neglect.

What's in stewardship for the steward? It depends on the promise he made to the owner of the lands. In particular, if he promised to take care of the lands at no charge (as one relative might do for another), then there is *nothing* in it for him; indeed, materially speaking there might be *less than nothing* in it for him, since he will have to expend time and energy and most likely will not be compensated materially for having done so. If this state of affairs had been unacceptable to him, he should not have promised to act as steward.

Although unpaid stewards might get less than nothing, materially speaking, for their efforts, they might enjoy certain psychic rewards. They might enjoy working the land. They might enjoy helping others. They might enjoy the compliments they get from neighbors on how well they are taking care of the lands. And of course, they can hope someday to get a warm "thank you" from the owner of the lands when he returns, but there are no guarantees.

Suppose that someone promises to act as steward for a land-owner, knowing at the time that he cannot do so effectively. He might lack the knowledge and time to act as steward; or he himself might be about to take a trip, in which case he won't be around to act as steward. In such a case, the promise to act as steward would be fraudulent: It would be a promise made in the knowledge that there is little chance that it will be kept. And the person making the promise is clearly wronging the landowner in making it; the landowner would be better off if, rather than making the promise, the person in question had simply said that he was in no position to act as steward. A good steward is not only *willing* to shoulder the obligations of stewardship, but *able* to shoulder them as well.

The notion of stewardship, by the way, involves not only people who go away on a trip, but also people who are "here but not all here." Consider, for instance, someone who is incapacitated by illness. We might act as steward for that person's property until he "comes back"—that is, until the illness ends. Likewise, when someone falls victim to a drug addiction, we might reason that the situation is as if the person were "away" and would return when the addiction was conquered. We might try to act in the "away" person's best interests, even though the person's body (which is what we must deal with until he "comes back") protests.

Let me make one last point before ending my discussion of stewardship: It would be unfair to judge land stewards in an absolute fashion; instead, we should judge them relative to the lands they were given to manage. Thus, we should have far lower expectations for a steward who is managing desert land than we would have for a steward who is managing prime farmland.

The Role of Steward-Parents

Now that we have cleared up the concept of stewardship, let us turn our attention back to the stewardship model of parenting. The steward-parent acts as if the person who is his child is away on a trip, a trip from which he will return at (say) age eighteen.[2] Instead of leaving behind lands to be managed, this person "leaves behind" the body and mind of a child to be "managed." The steward-parent's job is to take care of this body and mind until the person "returns."

In the same way as the land steward will try to seek out opportunities to develop the lands in his care, steward-parents will seek out opportunities to develop their child: They will explore the interests and talents of the child and take steps to develop them when they find them. In the same way as the land steward will prevent harm from coming to the lands in his care, steward-parents will prevent harm from coming to either the mind or the body of their child: Thus, they will do what they can to prevent him from playing on the freeway or experimenting with drugs. In the same way as the land steward might plant a vineyard even though the owner might ultimately choose not to take advantage of it, steward-parents will educate their child: It is far better, as a young adult, to have an education that you choose not to use than to lack an education that you wish you had.

Steward-parents will be relativistic in the sense that they

will not apply a one-size-fits-all approach to their children, but will vary their approach to parenting depending on the needs of each child, much the same as a good land steward would tailor his stewardship activities to the piece of land under his care, treating desert land differently than he would treat prime farmland. One child might need a lot of attention and guidelines to flourish; another child might need a lot of freedom. One child might profit from advanced music lessons; another child, because of a birth defect, might profit from extensive physical therapy.

Since parents do not have the benefit of knowing the person who is their child before he "departs," they cannot be expected to know what this person would want them to do with the body and mind that will be in their care. As a result, parents must rely on a "reasonable-man standard" in their parenting: They should raise their child in such a way that he would, if he were a reasonable man with fairly typical values, be satisfied with their efforts. They should raise him "conservatively": They should not jeopardize their child's well-being in a long-shot attempt to gain him future fame or fortune, as the parents of many would-be child stars have done. They should also respect his freedom and try to arrange things so that when he "comes back" at age eighteen, he will find not that all the important decisions about his future have been made for him, but that he has before him a nice range of choices about what he can do with the rest of his life.

Ideally, the steward-parent's child, on reaching age eighteen, will view the world as his oyster. Much effort will have been spent by the steward-parent in opening doors of opportunity for the child. The child will spend the next decade of his life closing those doors, as the choices he makes and the very passage of time narrow the range of things he can do with his life. By the time he reaches his middle years he may find that, what with mortgage payments to make, a family to support, and a pension plan to fund, very few doors remain open: He will, for better or worse, be living his chosen life.

The land steward, as I've said, has an obligation to look out for the owner's lands because of a promise he made. Steward-parents, of course, make no such promise—at least not explicitly. According to the stewardship model of parenting, in having a child they make an *implied* promise to act as steward for the child. If this promise is unacceptable to a couple, they should not have had the child in the first place; or, on having it, they should have given it up for adoption to someone willing to shoulder the burdens of stewardship.

Furthermore, according to the stewardship model of parenting we should be critical of parents who want what's best for the children they create, but lack the ability to deliver the goods. Wanting what's best is simply not enough, particularly if it is clear at the outset that there is little chance that the child's needs will be met. Consider, by way of example, an unwed thirteen-year-old mother. She may tell us that she wants what's best for her child, but in most such cases, she will lack the characteristics necessary in a good steward-parent. What are these characteristics? Presumably they include a certain level of emotional maturity, a certain level of financial wherewithal, a certain level of education, and so forth. A case can be made, after all, that if you lack these characteristics, you will not only have a difficult time helping your child develop his talents, but will have a difficult time meeting your child's basic needs. If, despite all this, the girl in question attempts to raise her child anyway, she is like the person who agrees to manage someone's lands but who lacks the ability to do so: She has, in effect, made a fraudulent promise to the child.

The steward-parent, then, acts as if he had made a promise to his children to act in their best interests (as determined by the reasonable-man standard) until they reach adulthood. This duty, it should be understood, will not mean that the parent should do whatever *the child believes* to be in his best interests, since children may have very little understanding of what is or isn't in their best interests. Instead, it might involve using coercion to make the child do something that, although unpleasant, is arguably in the child's best interests, for example, getting vaccinated against some illness. By way of analogy, the good land steward won't let the land "do as it pleases"; he won't, for example, let nature take its course and turn cultivated fields into weed patches. Instead he will use "coercion" to enhance the value of the lands for which he is steward.

This is not to say that steward-parents will take *no* interest in the wishes of their children. They will, in part because they realize that it would not be in the long-term best interests of their children to have their wishes always ignored, and in part because they realize that by paying attention to their children's wishes, they can uncover potential talents or tastes in their children that they, as stewards, can then attempt to develop. And when parents refuse to act on their children's wishes, they will be careful to justify the refusal, for one of their goals as steward-parents is the transformation of their child from a willful creature into a rational being who, rather than simply acting on whims, stops to consider the consequences of his actions.

What's in stewardship for the steward-parent? The rewards are at best psychic: the pleasure derived from the relationship with the child, a feeling of a job well done, the admiration of other parents, and—although this is by no means assured—the thankfulness of the child as an adult.

The deal entered into by the steward-parent, then, is largely one-sided. It involves considerable sacrifice on his part, and all for the good of a child who may or may not appreciate the sacrifice. Why anyone would voluntarily enter into such a deal is a bit of a mystery—but then again, the same can be said of many altruistic acts people undertake.

Actually, it would be a mistake to assume that steward-parents will think *nothing* of their own well-being. After all, even if they were completely committed to the well-being of their children, it would be a mistake for them to try to "give their all" to their children. Such an effort would lead to a state of exhaustion, and in such a state they would be of little use to their children. So even in the purest form of the stewardship model, a parent *can* be concerned with his own interests.

There will also be instances in which the interests of the child and the parents can simultaneously be served. It may be argued, for example, that children benefit from doing routine chores: It teaches them various housekeeping skills and a sense of family responsibility. But parents also benefit from children doing chores, since it means fewer chores for the parents to do. It would be easy for parents to cross the line that separates chores done for the sake of both the children and the parents from chores done solely for the sake of the parents; steward-parents will be careful not to cross this line.

In the same way as we should judge the success of a land steward relative to the lands he was given to manage, we should judge the success of steward-parents relative to the child they raised. Some children are more stubborn and willful than others. Some children have more talents than others. Some children are quicker learners than others. The steward-parents of a particularly difficult child may be judged successful if the child makes it to adulthood with no limbs missing. For most steward-parents, though, the standard of success will be considerably higher than this.

In summary, then, for the owner-parent, his child is a means to an end, while for the steward-parent, his child is an end in himself. If the owner-parent's goal with respect to his child is exploitation, the steward-parent's goal is benefaction. The owner-parent will be notable for his selfishness with respect to his child, whereas the steward-parent will be notable for his selflessness with respect to his child.

Deceptive Appearances

Before ending my discussion of the stewardship and ownership models of parenting, let me clarify a few things. It might not be possible, simply by looking at how parents relate to their child, to tell whether they favor the stewardship or the ownership model. Suppose, for example, we are told that Child A spends his days doing chores around the family farm, while Child B spends his days in school. We might be willing, on the basis of this evidence alone, to conclude that the parents of Child A are owner-parents, while the parents of Child B are steward-parents, but this conclusion would be premature. While it is *probably* the correct conclusion to draw, we can imagine cases in which it would be incorrect.

In particular, suppose that the farm child was on the farm because, after repeated efforts to educate him, his parents had found that he was, perhaps because of birth defects, unteachable, but suppose that these same parents found that the child loved doing farm chores. Imagine, finally, that in the society in question, it looked like the child's best chance at becoming a self-supporting, independent adult was as a competent farmhand. These parents, in putting their child to work around the farm, would arguably be acting as steward-parents. On the other hand, suppose that the parents of Child *B* (the child in school) had purely self-interested motives in sending him there. Suppose, for example, they were sending their child to school not because they cared about education or about his well-being, but because it was the law that they do so: They sent him because it was less trouble than getting arrested for not sending him. Such parents, in sending their child to school, would arguably be acting as owner-parents, despite appearances to the contrary.

Along these same lines, realize that the fact that a person has lots of children does not necessarily mean that he favors the stewardship model of parenting. One reason for having lots of children is that you love children and want what's best for them. Another reason for having lots of children, though, is that you seek to exploit them, and having multiple children creates multiple opportunities for exploitation. A parent with this latter motivation certainly would not count as a steward-parent.

And even a parent who has lots of children because he loves them will not necessarily count as a steward-parent. Suppose, in particular, that his love of children causes him to father so many offspring that he is incapable of meeting their needs. He would be like the person who, because he has agreed to act as steward for so many of his neighbors, cannot adequately act as steward for any of them.

Furthermore, the fact that a person decides not to have any children at all does not necessarily mean that he is opposed to the stewardship model of parenting. To the contrary, it might be that a person does not have children because he feels incapable of shouldering the burdens of parenthood. His reasoning, then, is as follows: "Parents should act as stewards for their children; I am incapable of acting as steward; therefore, it would be wrong for me to have children." This person, though childless, would clearly be an advocate of the stewardship model of parenting.

Is the fact that a child, on reaching adulthood, "turns out well" evidence that his parents were good steward-parents? Not necessarily. What makes someone a steward-parent are his intentions in parenting and his ability to act on these intentions: He will always put the interests of his child first and foremost. There is no guarantee, however, that his efforts will translate into a child who turns out well. It is possible for the child of exceptional steward-parents to turn out poorly. One tragic example of this is the child who, despite an excellent upbringing, develops schizophrenia as a young adult. It is also possible for a child whose parents were selfish and abusive to survive the experience and turn out well. I will have more to say on this matter in my discussion of easy and difficult children in Chapter 11.

One last thing to realize is that just because someone says he favors the stewardship model of parenting, we can by no means be certain that he does. In our day and age few parents will be willing to admit that they regard and treat their children as a form of property. It sounds so much nicer to say that they act as stewards for their children's interests. The real test of steward-parenthood, however, is not a parent's declarations with respect to parenthood but his actions with respect to his children.

Other Ownership/Stewardship Debates

Let me also point out, before moving on to other topics, that parenting is not the only activity in which the ownership/stewardship debate arises.

Consider, for example, the debate about how to treat the environment. Those taking an ownership attitude toward the environment favor exploiting it, using it to meet the needs of man. People, they argue, own the land and trees, and it is up to them to decide what is done with it all. The other side of the debate rejects this view and declares that we do not "own" the environment. Our job is not to exploit it but to preserve it, to act as stewards for the environment.

In our stewardship of the environment we act with the interests of future generations in mind. It is as if they are away on a trip and we have been left in charge of the environment until they return—several generations from now. In the meantime we must not exploit the environment or, at the bare minimum, must take their interests into account when we do. We must act so that the environment will serve them well when they finally "arrive."

The ownership/stewardship debate also arises in connection with animal rights. Those who take an ownership attitude toward animals argue that animals are here for our pleasure and that we may exploit them as we see fit. We may, for example, kill and eat them so our lunch will have a bit more variety than would otherwise be the case. Others argue that it is wrong for us to exploit animals, that we do not own them, and that instead we have a moral obligation to look out for their interests—to act, that is, as their stewards. According to this line of reasoning, animals are like severely retarded humans. Such people might be very easy to exploit, but it would be wrong for us to do so. Instead, we must—it is argued—look out for their interests.

Another area in which the ownership/stewardship debate arises is in the ongoing battle over abortion. In the same way as there are two models for how parents can relate to a child—either as an owner or as a steward—there are two models for how pregnant women can relate to the fetus within them: either as its owner or as its steward.

Those who hold that a pregnant woman is the owner of her fetus are likely to look kindly on abortion. They will argue that a fetus is just a part of a pregnant woman's body, the same as her hair, fingernails, and tonsils are; and since she has clear ownership rights over her hair, fingernails, and internal organs, she has parallel ownership rights over any fetus within her; and in the same way as her body-ownership rights include the right to cut her fingernails or hair, or have her tonsils removed, her body-ownership rights include the right to remove any fetus growing within her—that is, to have an abortion. Here is the argument in a nutshell: A pregnant woman owns her body; the fetus is part of her body; therefore she owns the fetus and can do with it as she pleases.

Those who favor the stewardship model of pregnancy, on the other hand, will reject this line of reasoning and instead argue that as steward for a fetus, a pregnant woman must put the interests of the fetus first. And since it would obviously not be in the best interests of the fetus to be aborted (at least not in most cases), she would be forsaking her responsibilities as steward if she had an abortion.

Which view on abortion is correct? It is difficult to say. Some observations are in order, though.

Relatively few people would push for a "pure" ownership model of pregnancy that would allow a pregnant woman to do *whatever she wants* with the fetus.

Suppose, for example, that a woman decides, on a whim, to have an abortion very late in her pregnancy, late enough that the fetus can be removed (via caesarian section) and kept alive. Suppose that when her doctor informs her of this option, she replies that she doesn't want to have to raise a child. Suppose that when her doctor reminds her that she needn't raise the child, but can instead give it up for adoption, the woman rejects even this option, telling her doctor that she doesn't want anyone else raising her baby. She wants, in effect, to "throw away" the fetus. She instructs her doctor to remove the fetus in such a way that it will die. There aren't many people who will hold that a woman's ownership rights with respect to the fetus extend *this* far.

Or suppose a pregnant woman agrees, in return for a small payment, to let doctors test the teratogenic effects of a certain drug by injecting it into her womb. (Her goal in doing this is to make a little extra spending money at the expense of the fetus.)

Suppose that because she takes part in this experiment, her baby is born horribly defective and lives a life of misery. Few of those who say that a woman owns the fetus when it is in her body would condone this sort of treatment of the fetus. Most would agree that even if the woman "owns" the fetus, there will be restrictions on what she can do with her property; and perhaps one of these restrictions is a restriction on her ability to "abuse" it.

Those who favor a "pure" stewardship model of pregnancy, on the other hand, will also find that the abortion issue isn't as cut-and-dried as they had imagined, for even under the stewardship model there will arguably be times when it is morally permissible for a pregnant woman to have an abortion.

The most striking such case is probably an ectopic pregnancy in which doctors determine that if the pregnant woman aborts, the fetus will die (of course) but the woman will live, and that if the woman does not abort, both she and the fetus will die. The fetus, in other words, is doomed no matter what the woman does. Her choice amounts to a choice of whether or not to save her own life.

As we have seen, the duties of stewardship do not require stewards to completely ignore their own interests. They allow them, for example, to advance their own interests when doing so does not harm the interests of the people for whom they are acting as steward. In the ectopic pregnancy described, the pregnant woman is indeed acting in her own interests by getting an abortion: She is saving her own life. In doing so, though, she is not acting against the interests of the fetus, for in the case we are considering, it is assumed that the fetus is going to die no matter what she does. The stewardship model of pregnancy, in other words, sometimes allows abortions.

Other Models of Parenting

Although I have focused my attention on the ownership and stewardship models of parenting, it is clear that these are not the only two models of parenting.

For one thing, there exist "mixed models" of parenting: Someone could view the role of parent as being part owner and part steward. Thus, we could view the ownership and stewardship models not as alternative choices but as the endpoints on a continuum of parental behavior. Indeed, most parents probably favor mixed models, with parents favoring a "pure" ownership model or favoring a "pure" stewardship model being relatively rare.

It should also be noted that there are choices with respect to parenting that lie off the continuum just described. In particular, one model of parenting—we shall call it the *liberation model*—rejects both the notion that parents own their children and the notion that parents should act as stewards for their children.[3] According to this view, children should be treated by their parents as equals—that is, they should be treated more or less the way you would treat your (adult) next-door neighbor. Thus, it would be wrong for parents to act as if they owned their children, since it is wrong for one adult to own another; but it would likewise be wrong for parents to act as stewards for their children, since it is wrong for one adult to paternalistically control another adult's life.

According to certain other models of parenting that are off the continuum described above, you should raise your child not in *your* best interests (as the ownership model would have you do) and not in *your child's* best interests (as the stewardship model would have you do), but *in the interests of something or someone else*. By way of illustration, consider political regimes that convince parents to raise their children with the good of the country in mind—we might call this the *political model* of parenting. Such children might be raised to be superior soldiers, which would arguably be in neither their best interests nor in their parents' best interests, but in the interests of their nation. Or consider religions that convince parents to raise their children with God's interests in mind—we might call this the *religious model* of parenting. Such parents may feel that a sacrifice of both their interests and those of their children is entirely appropriate as long as God's plan for the world is advanced by the sacrifice.

In the remainder of Part Two of this book, we shall ignore these other models of parenting and focus our attention on what for most parents is the relevant choice: Which to be, an owner-parent or a steward-parent? And in dealing with this choice, we will spend most of our time thinking about the two endpoints of the continuum of parental roles—namely, a fairly pure version of the ownership model and a fairly pure version of the stewardship model. I do this primarily to simplify the discussion: Ethical analysis of a "pure" theory will generally present fewer complications than ethical analysis of a "mixed" theory.

CHAPTER 8

CHOOSING A MODEL
OF PARENTING

In the preceding chapter I was content simply to *describe* the two competing models of parenting, the ownership model and the stewardship model. I will now address the process of *selecting* a model of parenting. I will break my discussion into two sections.

In the first section I will be concerned with the history of the "debate" over the two models of parenting. I will describe how, at one time, the ownership model was dominant and how, during the late nineteenth and early twentieth centuries, the stewardship model rose in popularity. I will then describe the reemergence of the ownership model in the last half of the twentieth century. In telling this history I will try to explain some of the factors that led people to favor one model of parenting over the other.

In the second section I will be concerned not with what model of parenting people *have in fact chosen* over the centuries, but with what model of parenting people *should choose*: I will shift, in other words, from a historical and sociological question to an ethical question. I will present an argument against the ownership model of parenting. Why is it wrong to treat a child as property? For much the same reason, I will suggest, as it is wrong to treat an adult as property. I will also present a thought experiment to help the reader better appreciate the moral superiority of the stewardship model of parenting.

The Rise and Fall of the Stewardship Model

Earlier in this book I described the rise of the concept of childhood. I would now like to suggest that this rise corresponded with the rise of the stewardship model of parenting. Parents who saw their children as a form of property had little reason to treat childhood as a special time of life. The modern (i.e., 1950s) concept of childhood is intimately bound up with the notion that parents should act as stewards for their children rather than as owners of their children, and it was only when parents started putting the interests of their children ahead of their own interests that it made sense to treat childhood as a special and protected stage of life.

If we go back a few centuries, we find a time in which there was little that parents were willing to do for their children. If, after having them, you found them to be inconvenient, you simply disposed of them: You might have exposed them to the elements or you might have "sold" them. And if you kept them, you might have made them pay for their keep: At the earliest possible date you might have found them a job which, though arduous, paid wages that the child obediently turned over to you. And if the child was damaged in the process? No problem, since property exists to be exploited by its owner. Along these lines, it will be remembered that in our discussion of the history of childhood we came across some nice encapsulations of the ownership model of parenting, as when a chimney sweep defended his mistreatment of his climbing-boy son by pointing out that "the boy was his own child, and he could do with him as he pleased."

In the middle of the nineteenth century, the stewardship model of parenting began to gain ground—in the developed world, at any rate—as parents not only became aware that children had interests, but started taking these interests into account when making their decisions as parents. Earlier I suggested that the concept of childhood reached its zenith in the 1950s. By then, parental exploitation of children, when it existed, was a pale shadow of the exploitation witnessed three hundred years earlier. Indeed, rather than exploiting their children, parents made considerable sacrifices on their children's behalf. Parents sent their children off to school, not to factories. And parents expected their children to spend a fair amount of their free time playing.

Since the 1950s the stewardship model has gone into decline, and parents (perhaps without realizing it) have begun reverting to—or at least gravitating toward—the ownership model of parenting. In saying this, I don't mean to suggest that today's parents have stopped caring about the interests of their children. They do care. It's just that they typically are significantly less willing to put the interests of their children ahead of their own interests than were parents of the 1950s.

Stewardship and the Law

Shifts in the popularity of the various models of parenting are often reflected in changes in laws concerning children. Thus, in England before 1850 (and even for some time after), the ownership model of parenting was built into the law. The law saw nothing particularly wrong with beating children, with drugging them, with forcing them not just to work from an early age but to risk their lives in doing their jobs, or even with blinding them so that they would be more effective at begging. (It will be remembered that the woman mentioned in an earlier chapter who put out the eyes of children got in trouble only because the children she blinded were not her own.)

Having made these claims about the incorporation of the ownership model of parenting into British law, two qualifications are in order. First, it is inaccurate to say that British law regarded children as the property of their *parents*; they were instead the property of their *fathers*. If parents separated, the courts would not hesitate to award the children to the father, even if the mother was clearly the better parent. Second, although British law regarded children as a form of property, it did not regard them as a particularly valuable form of property. For as we have seen, there was a time when to steal a child's clothing was, in the eyes of the law, worse than to steal a child—the latter offense not being a crime at all.

One would like to say that British law treated children like animals, but that would not be correct, since at one time British law treated animals *better* than children: At the time in question there were laws against cruelty to animals, but not laws against cruelty to children. The same was true in America. Indeed, it was not until 1874 that an American, Henry Bergh, reasoning that children are animals, used the laws prohibiting cruelty to animals to prosecute child-abusing parents. The British soon followed suit.[1] This represented an important shift in favor of the stewardship model of parenting.

British laws concerning child labor also changed between 1750 and 1950. As we saw in an earlier chapter, it was once regarded as a radical reform for the government to forbid children *under ten* from working in mines or children *under nine* from working in factories. By the twentieth century, British law took it for granted that even teenagers should be in school, not at a job.

Like British law, American law has evolved to reflect changing views on the role of parents. American law at present seems to be based on a mixed model of parenting: Parents are in some respects regarded as owners of their children and are in other respects regarded as stewards for their children.

Consider, by way of illustration, American divorce laws. American courts care not the least how a divorce will affect a couple's children, which suggests that the law embodies the ownership model: No problem if in divorcing you hurt your children; they are, after all, your property. On the other hand, once the divorce has been granted, American courts typically use the best interests of the children as their basis for determining who will get custody, which suggests that the law also embodies the notion of parental stewardship: As parents, you have a duty to do what is best for your child.

For another example of the way a mixed model of parenting is built into American law, consider "divorces" between parents and children. Parents are allowed to cast off their children at will, even though their children will be harmed by their doing so. (They cannot, of course, simply desert their children, particularly if doing so would endanger them. They can, however, relinquish their parental rights and turn their children over to other responsible adults.) This suggests the ownership model of parenting: Part of what is involved in owning something is the right to throw or give it away. Children, on the other hand, cannot likewise get rid of their parents, even though they may long to do so. Again, the ownership model comes to mind: Property lacks the freedom to determine its destiny. At the same time, the law calls for removal of children from their parents if the parents do an inadequate job of stewardship.

Actually, it probably would take more than an *inadequate* job of stewardship for the state to take your children; if your biggest shortcoming is that you fail to do good things for them, the children will remain yours. For the state to get involved, you would probably have to act as an "anti-steward"—that is, you would have to take steps to harm them.

How bad do parents have to be before the state will take their children? In some cases, incredibly bad.

Latrena Pixley smothered her six-week-old daughter, put her in the trash, and went out for barbecue with her boyfriend.[2] The state did not think this crime merited jail time, but instead placed Ms. Pixley in a halfway house. Ms. Pixley got in trouble again, was sent to jail, and her latest baby was turned over to foster care.

When the foster mother attempted to adopt the baby, the state denied her, pointing out that in Maryland the law does not take the fact that parents murder their children as grounds for severing parental ties. Family ties, after all, are sacred.

As far as education is concerned, the state requires that parents act as stewards. It requires, for example, that parents send their children to school or make other arrangements for them to receive a K-12 education. It does not, however, require parents to get music lessons for their child, even though there is evidence that the child would benefit from such lessons. Nor does it, in most cases, require parents to send their children to college. The state expects, in other words, a fairly low level of stewardship with respect to education.

Thus, in America the law would appear to be of two minds with regards to parenting: Parents own their children, but cannot simply ignore the interests of their children. It favors, in other words, a mixed model of parenting, with arguably less emphasis on stewardship than was the case fifty years ago.

Of course, laws do not always reflect public attitudes, so changes in the laws concerning children do not necessarily reflect changes in popular thinking about the role of parents. I would like to suggest, though, that as far as models of parenting are concerned, it is for the most part the law that has been following the lead of public attitudes. When, for example, no-fault divorce laws were enacted in America in the 1970s, opposition to them was minute. It was clearly a case of politicians giving the voters what they wanted. And once easy divorce became the law and divorce became commonplace, public views on the importance of married couples staying together "for the sake of the children" weakened. What we have in many such cases is a "feedback loop," with changes in public attitudes bringing about changes in the law, which in turn bring about changes in public attitudes.

Which Model of Parenting Is Correct?

So far I have tried to be value-neutral in my discussion of the models of parenting. There are, I have said, two primary models that compete for our favor. One holds children to be property of their parents, and the other says it is the duty of parents to act as stewards for their children. I have said nothing to suggest that one of these models is morally preferable to the other. I will now tackle the moral issues raised by the ownership/stewardship debate.

Of the two models of parenting, the stewardship model is presumably the easier to defend. Stewardship, as I have explained it, involves performing selflessly altruistic acts; such acts rarely need ethical justification. If anything needs defending, it is the ownership model of parenting.

Then again, ownership has its place in our world: Looking out for the interests of others is important, but so is looking out for our own interests. Perhaps, then, it will turn out that taking an ownership attitude toward your children will be no more offensive, morally speaking, than taking an ownership attitude toward your automobile.

Let us begin by inquiring into a rather obvious argument that might be given *against* the ownership model of parenting. As we shall see from the discussion that follows, the ownership model is not as easy to attack as some advocates of childhood might hope.

Children as Slaves

Some would suggest, at the outset, that the ownership model of parenting is morally objectionable inasmuch as it calls for one person to act as the owner of another: Owned people are slaves, and slavery is wrong.

There are at least two ways that the owner-parent can defend himself against the charge of treating his children as slaves.

He might, to begin with, argue that since children are not ready to use their freedom, by not letting them use it he is not harming them. Indeed, he may even be helping them by preventing them from misusing their freedom. By way of contrast, when you take an adult as a slave, you are harming him because you are depriving him of the freedom that he is not only ready to use, but is in the habit of using. And of course, as a parent, you will not keep your children under your domination forever. You will release them the moment they are ready to handle freedom—say, at age eighteen.

An owner-parent might also defend himself by arguing that there is an important difference between his relationship with his children and the relationship between, say, a plantation owner and his slaves: The plantation owner didn't make his slaves; the parent *did* make his children. Since it is appropriate to claim ownership of things that you make, it is appropriate for parents to claim ownership of their children; but it was not likewise appropriate for plantation owners to claim ownership of their slaves.

The theory of property that this view is based upon—namely, that if I make something, it's mine—was initially propounded by British philosopher John Locke. According to him, we come to own something previously unowned by "mixing our labor with it."[3] Stated in more commonplace terms, if I dig up some clay, shape it into a vase, and fire it, the resulting vase is clearly mine. And the reason it is mine is *because I made it.* In general, things that I bring into existence "owe" their existence to me, and it is because of this "debt" that I own them. But mothers, and to a lesser extent fathers, mix their labor (no pun intended) with their children. Thus, an owner-parent might argue along the following lines: "My children owe their existence to me: If I did not make them, they would not exist. But if they *owe* their lives to me, then does it not follow that I *own* their lives—meaning that I own *them*?"

Each of these justifications of children-as-slaves has its problems.

To begin with, realize that from the mere fact that someone is not ready to function as a free being, it does not follow that it is morally permissible to enslave that person. If it did follow, you would be justified not only in the enslavement of your own children, but the children of others (if you could successfully kidnap them), or even the enslavement of mentally incapacitated adults. Few would morally condone such enslavement.

And when it comes to the claim that my children are mine because I made them, the most obvious response is to point out that children, unlike vases, have feelings, have hopes and ambitions, can make plans and have them frustrated, and so forth. And this means that children, unlike vases, have interests. It is one thing to claim ownership of something that has no interests, for if something has no interests, then you are in no way harming it if you treat it as a means to an end. You in no way harm the vase by owning it. On the other hand, if something *has* interests—as children do—and you subordinate these interests to your own, you might well be harming the thing in question.

It is significant that Locke, who propounded the theory that what I make is mine, did not (as we shall see in the next chapter) favor the ownership model of parenting. To the contrary, he thought that parents should play the role of steward so as to prepare their children for life as autonomous individuals.

The owner-parent might at this point dig in his heels, admit that he treats his children like slaves, and challenge us to explain exactly why slavery is wrong.

He might point out, to begin with, that for most of the history of mankind in most places on earth, slavery has been an accepted institution, and that there are places on earth today where the institution of slavery still exists. Furthermore, we are mistaken if we think, as many modern Americans do, that only an unenlightened individual would advocate slavery. The Greek philosopher Aristotle is widely admired for the level of enlightenment he attained, but he is unapologetic in his defense of the institution of slavery.[4] Along these same lines, we admire the wisdom embodied in the United States Constitution, and yet in its unamended form, it was a document that treated slavery as a morally justifiable institution; indeed, many of its framers were themselves slave owners. Slavery is apparently an issue about which reasonable people can differ; after all, it is an issue about which reasonable people *have* differed.

The defender of slavery might also remind us that most Americans are woefully inconsistent in their views on the subordination of interests. Surely cows have interests,[5] but most of us do not hesitate to subordinate their interests to our own: We do this whenever we eat a cow for lunch. And what are our interests when we eat the cow in question? Are they compelling interests? In particular, will we die if we don't eat the cow? Usually not. Usually, we eat the cow for the simple reason that we prefer his taste to the taste of, say, carrots and tofu.

If the reader finds the forgoing claims about cows to be implausible—if it seems obvious that animals are different from people—he or she should call to mind that in every culture that has allowed slavery, those who engaged in slavery viewed their slaves as a "breed apart," and used this viewpoint as a basis for downplaying or ignoring the interests of their slaves.

I will not attempt to develop this argument any further,[6] inasmuch as doing so would carry us astray from our present project—namely, to explain why the ownership model of parenting is morally objectionable. I developed it to the extent I did, not because I think that slavery is morally justifiable—indeed, I don't even think that "slavery" of animals is morally justifiable—but simply to remind the reader that it would be naive to think that one could talk an owner-parent out of his ownership views simply by telling him that his children had interests and that it was therefore wrong for him to treat them as property. Such an owner-parent would likely scoff at any such assertion. We might be able to get him to admit that his child had interests, but even then he would likely follow this admission by reminding us, first, that *he* had interests, and second, that his interests were far more important to him than those of his child. Along these same lines, it would in most cases be impossible to talk a plantation owner out of slavery simply by pointing out to him that his slaves have interests.

Suppose, then, that we encountered a "hard-core owner-parent"—someone who responded to the argument that the ownership model is wrong because it treats children as slaves by simply denying that slavery is morally wrong. Is there any way to convince such a person of the error of his ways? Perhaps there is. We could ask him to do the following ethical thought experiment.

An Ethical Thought Experiment: Reincarnation

Suppose that you learn, in some mysterious fashion, that you will die one year from today. Suppose you also discover that the theory of reincarnation is true, that when you die you will come back to life as a human child, and—most importantly for our purposes—that you will be allowed to pick the parents to whom you are reborn. Suppose, too, that you cannot choose to be reborn to your actual parents—they have retired from the baby-making business. And suppose, finally, that you cannot assume that when you are reborn, you will be a clone of you: You will genetically resemble your new parents, and this means that you will likely have a different body than you now do and might be of a different sex than you now are. There is also a good chance that no matter which parents you pick, you will have different talents and a different personality than those you possess in this life.

This, I realize, is a lot to suppose, and the reader will naturally ask whether there isn't some way you can avoid dying, or how you could possibly know that the theory of reincarnation is correct and, if it is correct, how you could pick your parents. Furthermore, there are logical questions that might be raised about whether it makes sense to say that the reborn child is really *you*.[7] The reader is asked to push these and similar questions out of mind and instead focus on the basic issue: If you, knowing what you know as an adult, could choose parents to be born to, what sort of parents would you pick?

Notice that the above scenario, although implausible, does have a "real world" correlate: There are, after all, flesh-and-blood people who are faced with questions rather like the one raised above. Suppose, for example, that a woman who has just given birth to a baby is told by doctors that she has only one year to live. Suppose there is no father around—he died eight months back—and that neither the mother nor father has any relatives. In the year the woman has available to her, she could consider just the sort of questions raised by the reincarnation scenario: Given that she cannot raise her baby and her relatives cannot raise her baby, who shall raise her baby? What are the characteristics one would seek in a parent? What does the ideal parent look like?

Likewise, parents who write wills find that they must contemplate what is involved in good parenting. For one of the questions they typically must answer in their will is, Who shall raise our children if we die? Of course, in answering this question, parents are somewhat more limited than in the reincarnation scenario. This is because parents designating guardians are restricted to those few people who would be willing to raise their child, whereas in the reincarnation scenario, you can be reborn to any of billions of people and don't need their consent.[8] Another difference is that when parents designate a guardian for their child, they themselves do not suffer the consequences of their choice; it is their children who suffer. In the reincarnation scenario, on the other hand, they will be personally affected by their choice.

So, what kind of parents will you pick? Indeed, will you choose to have plural parents, or just a father? Or maybe you want two mothers? Do you want young parents or old parents? Do you want rich parents or poor parents? Do you want to be an only child, one of a handful of children, or one of, say, thirteen children?

These are interesting questions, and we will return to them in a moment. First, though, let us deal with a more basic question: Which model would you want your future parents to raise you in accordance with, the ownership model or the stewardship model? Would you, in other words, want to be owned as a child and possibly have your labor and life exploited, or would you want parents who looked after your best interests when you were a child? My guess is that the overwhelming majority of people would prefer to have parents who would raise them in accordance with the stewardship model. Most people are, after all, averse to being exploited, and to ask for owner-parents is to ask to be exploited.

It is clear that as childhoods go, you would almost certainly have a better childhood under steward-parents than under owner-parents. It may not be fun to take piano lessons—and this is what steward-parents might make you do "for your own good"—but it is not nearly so bad (one hopes) as having to work in a factory at an early age. And a case can be made that you will also have a better adulthood if you were raised by steward-parents than you would have if you were raised by owner-parents. Remember that steward-parents will attempt to discover what your talents are and will take steps to develop what talents you have—which is why they might force you to take piano lessons. They will educate you so that you will have many choices when you become an adult. The child raised by owner-parents, on the other hand, will not have these advantages. He will have lived a hard childhood and will likely find himself with limited choices when he reaches adulthood.

Indeed, let us try to fathom the reasoning of someone who, when faced with the reincarnation scenario described above, chooses owner-parents.

Someone might, to begin with, choose owner-parents because he thinks that it is not good for children to have their every wish granted. Children are better off if many of their wishes are ignored, and of course owner-parents will be quite adept at ignoring the wishes of their children. Someone taking this line, however, can be fairly accused of misunderstanding the stewardship model of parenting. This model does not say that parents should accede to every wish of their children. It says instead that parents should put the well-being of their children first, and of course sometimes it will be best for a child *not* to be allowed to do the thing he wishes to do.

Alternatively, someone might choose owner-parents because his own upbringing has corrupted him. It might be, for example, that because he was so severely abused as a child, he has lost all sense of self-worth and consequently feels that he doesn't deserve parents who love him and will care for him. We will return to this case below.

Yet another reason for choosing owner-parents is the following: Someone might argue that you will have, all things considered, a better life if you choose owner-parents than if you choose steward-parents. It may be true that if you choose owner-parents, you will be exploited as a child. But then you can relax as an adult, have lots of children, and live off their labor. On the other hand, if you choose steward-parents, it may be true that your childhood is more pleasant, but your adulthood will be miserable, as you spend your time putting your children's interests ahead of your own, as the stewardship model will have you do.

This is, to be sure, an interesting argument, but it ignores three factors.

First, the person raised by steward-parents will probably be better-educated than the person raised by owner-parents. Because of this, he probably will have an easier time finding employment and be able to live a comfortable lifestyle without having to exploit children. Indeed, looking around the world, one is tempted to conclude that those parents who rely on the labor of children to maintain their lifestyle generally have far less attractive lifestyles than those parents who don't.

Second, the burdens of becoming a steward-parent, though very real, have their own rewards: Steward-parents often find considerable satisfaction in doing a good job of raising their children.

And third, a person raised by steward-parents can easily avoid the burdens of steward-parenthood himself. One way to accomplish this would be, after having enjoyed the benefits of being raised by steward-parents, to act as an owner-parent when it came time for *him* to have children. Or, if the moral inconsistency involved in this course of action bothers him, there is a second way he can enjoy the benefits of being raised by steward-parents without having to shoulder the burdens of steward-parenthood himself: He can simply avoid having children when he is an adult. No children, no burden.

In summary, it would be difficult to justify choosing owner-parents in the reincarnation scenario described. As far as your childhood is concerned, a strong case can be made that you are better off being raised by steward-parents than by owner-parents; and probably as an adult, you will be better off having been raised by steward-parents than by owner-parents. It is therefore unclear why anyone with a say in the matter would choose owner-parents.

Now let us turn our attention to some of the other aspects of the choice presented by the reincarnation scenario. I have tried this scenario on a large number of people, most of them college students. I have been struck, over the years, by the extent to which people agree on their choice of parents to be born to. Not only do students favor the stewardship model—for the sorts of reasons just described—but they fill in the details of that model by describing parents who come close to what is (or, at any rate, what used to be) the middle-class American ideal.

They want both a mother and a father and want them to be happily married. They are averse to parents who are too young; in particular, they find teenage mothers unappealing. They are equally averse to parents who are too old. Technology has made it possible for women to have children when they are 63;[9] but how many people would want a mother who was 81 when they graduated from high school? And even without technology, men can father children when they are in their eighties: Writer Saul Bellow became a father when he was 84. In his case, the question isn't whether his daughter will want a 101-year-old father at her high-school graduation; it is whether he will be alive to attend.

My students want their future parents to be free of addictions, to be financially secure (although not necessarily rich), and to meet certain educational minimums. They seek parents who are free of genetic defects, particularly after I remind them that the way the reincarnation scenario is set up, they would run a risk of inheriting any such defects. Likewise, they sometimes favor attractive parents over ugly parents, reasoning that, because our culture cares about physical beauty, your chance at a good life is improved if you are attractive. Along similar lines, they sometimes favor parents of one race over parents of another race, reasoning that they could avoid the hardships imposed by racism by choosing to become a member of the majority race. My students (predictably, perhaps) overwhelmingly favor the United States as the country in which to be born. And finally, they seek parents who are well-adjusted, loving, and patient.

There are issues about which my students tend to disagree. For example, although my students are similar in wanting parents who are talented, they differ over which talents their ideal parents would possess. Some would favor parents who are musical, while others would favor athletic parents.

Of course, when students make such choices, I remind them that they must not assume that they will have the same talents and interests in the next life as they do in this life—indeed, the odds are that they won't. They may favor musical parents because they are musical and have long resented the fact that their parents in this life did not start them on piano lessons at an early age, and their choice of musical parents for their next life might be an attempt to get a head start on their musical career. But once I remind them that in the next life they may not have musical talent, but might instead wish to spend every waking hour engaged in athletic endeavors, these students come to realize that the choice of musical parents could be a big mistake: Imagine having to practice piano when what you really want is to be outside playing baseball.

A less risky choice, then, is to select not parents who have one particular talent, but parents who are multitalented, or at least parents who, though not particularly talented in any area, will devote their resources and energy to allowing their child to try different things (both baseball and piano, both ballet and karate) in an attempt to find out what the child enjoys doing and is good at.

Along these same lines, my students sometimes differ with respect to the sexual orientation of their future parents. Thus, a radical feminist might announce that she would like to be born not to a man and a woman, but to two women (with the aid, one supposes, of artificial insemination), her rationale being that two women could better help her handle the challenges of becoming a woman. In such cases, though, I have to remind the student that there is no guarantee that in the next life she will be born a woman; indeed, there is a 50 percent chance that she won't. Would she really want to be a boy raised by two women? Or would she rather "play it safe" and pick a man and a woman for her future parents, thereby guaranteeing that at least one of her parents can play the role of "gender mentor"?

It is also worth noting that people considering the reincarnation scenario might make different choices at different times in their lives. Try the reincarnation scenario on a ten-year-old, and he is likely to choose parents who would spoil him rotten. A few years later this same child might seek parents who would not so much spoil him as stay out of his life altogether. As a young adult he might shift his views again, and choose parents who would neither spoil him nor give him complete freedom, but give him what he should have, even though he doesn't want it at the time.

In describing student reactions to the reincarnation scenario, I am not suggesting that people everywhere share an ideal of parenthood. My students, after all, are not a good cross-section of humanity. They are, for the most part, middle-class Midwesterners and have (judging from their choices) what some would call hopelessly middle-class Midwestern values. And it is entirely possible that their responses to the reincarnation scenario weren't sincere, but that they were merely telling me what they thought I wanted to hear. (Such things have been known to happen in the classroom.) My purpose in describing their reactions is simply to help readers think about their own response to the reincarnation scenario.

Suppose that someone's choice of parents differs radically from the "mainstream" choice of my students. Suppose he tells us that he would like to be reborn to an abusive unmarried teenage mother who is a drug addict and carries multiple genetic defects. How might we deal with such a response?

In the first place we might wonder whether such a person really understands the "rules" of the thought experiment. And if he shows that he does understand them, we might wonder whether the choice is in fact sincere. We might test his sincerity by asking *why* he would prefer to run the risk of genetic defects when it is possible to avoid them, or *why* he would want to be born to a drug addict when it is possible to be born to parents who are free of addictions. Such questions, to be sure, would be difficult to answer.

Suppose that someone defended his choice of abusive parents by pointing out that there are lots of people who are abused as children but who recover from the abuse and become productive, happy adults. This, of course, is true, but it misses the point. It is like someone who chooses to become infected with pneumonia, defending his choice by pointing out that most people recover from the disease. When given a choice between an unpleasant experience from which you will probably recover and a pleasant experience from which you won't need to recover, the latter choice is obviously preferable.

If we become convinced that a person's choice of an abusive parent is sincere, we might then wonder whether the person has been in some way "corrupted" by his own upbringing. For example, an adult who knew only abuse as a child might not know there is any other way to be brought up, and when offered a choice of parents, he might without hesitation choose abusive parents. Or, the abuse he experienced as a child might have been severe enough that even as an adult, he does not feel like a worthy person. He might, in particular, feel that he deserves bad parents, and so might choose abusive parents. Such a person would not really be picking the parents he thought were best, but rather the parents he thought he deserved.[10]

Finally, consider someone who picks parents as much like his own (actual) parents as possible—remember that according to the "rules" of our thought experiment, you are not allowed to choose your own parents—and picks them because he feels that any other choice would amount to a betrayal of his (actual) parents—would be tantamount to accusing them of not raising him properly. Again, such a person, in his response to the reincarnation thought experiment, would not be choosing the parents he thought were best, but the parents he thought should be chosen. He would not be following the rules of our experiment.

The Golden Rule

Once the reader has reacted to the reincarnation scenario, he or she will be in a position to draw conclusions about his or her own notion of good parenting. One assumes, after all, that in choosing parents to be born to, the reader is picking what is pretty close to his or her notion of ideal parents. (And if the reader chooses less-than-ideal parents, why? Why not ask for the best when there is no cost to doing so?) They will be the parents who, in the reader's own view, will not only have the right goals, as parents, but will be in a position (in terms of resources, education, and personality) to accomplish the goals in question.

Suppose that a reader who either has or intends to have children of her own performs the reincarnation thought experiment and comes up with certain ideal parents. This reader will then be in a position to compare the sort of mother she is (or someday will be) with her self-selected ideal mother, and this comparison may yield some unpleasant conclusions.

Suppose, for example, that the reader falls far short of her own ideal. Suppose that although the reader is, say, an unemployed, unmarried teenage mother, her own ideal parent would be a gainfully employed, married adult, so that there is, by her own admission, a huge gulf between her qualifications as a parent and those of her ideal parent. Such a case raises an interesting question of moral consistency. After all, a basic ethical principle that many people accept is the Golden Rule: Do unto others as you would have them do unto you. But in the case described, we have a woman doing unto her own children something she would not want done unto herself—or at any rate, something far inferior to what she would want done unto herself. We could point out to such a woman that *according to her own standards of parenting* (as revealed by the reincarnation thought experiment), she does not count as a good parent. What business, we might ask, does she have inflicting herself (as a parent) on some innocent child?

Here is the issue in a nutshell. What the reincarnation thought experiment might reveal to someone is that she would not want herself as a parent, if she had any say in the matter. Surely it would be wrong for this person to foist herself, as a parent, upon some child.

Many parents or potential parents would find, on undertaking the reincarnation thought experiment, that although they fall short of their own parental ideal, they don't fall hopelessly short, as was the case with the teenage mother just described: They have not quite as much money as their ideal parents would have, not quite as much education, not quite as much patience, and so on. Would such people be involved in a moral self-contradiction in having children? Not necessarily.

For consider the following variation on the reincarnation thought experiment. Suppose that after describing the reincarnation scenario, we ask a person not to choose his *ideal* parents, but instead to divide people into those who would be *acceptable* parents and those who would not. We instruct him to place a person into the unacceptable category only if he would rather *not be born at all* than to be born to (and raised by) that person.

Different people will "draw the line" with respect to parental acceptability in different places. Most people will want to exclude from their group of acceptable parents those individuals who would be truly abusive parents: Better not to exist at all than to exist as the child of abusive parents. Yet other people will be quite exclusive in their choice, including only (say) five percent of prospective parents in their group of acceptable parents. For these individuals, nonexistence will be preferable to a second-rate childhood.

Wherever a person "draws the line" with respect to acceptable parents, he is faced with the following question: By his own standards of acceptable parenting, would he himself count as an acceptable parent? If he would, then it is not morally inconsistent for him to become a parent, even though he is a less-than-ideal parent; but if he would not include himself (or rather, someone like him) in his group of acceptable parents, then it is indeed difficult to see how he could morally justify becoming a parent. If he became a parent, he would be guilty of doing unto another (and a perfectly innocent other, at that) something he would not want done to himself: He is consigning someone else to a fate so terrible that he would rather not exist than experience it himself. Such an individual has absolutely no business, morally speaking, becoming a parent.

CHAPTER 9

THE GOALS OF
THE STEWARD-PARENT

Suppose someone favors the stewardship model of parenting. A question that now arises is, What are the goals of the steward-parent? More precisely, what should the steward-parent be trying to accomplish in raising a child? And how can the steward-parent tell if he or she has done an effective job of stewardship?

In previous chapters I have described some of the things that a steward-parent will try to accomplish. In this chapter I will expand on these goals, but I will also be interested in picking out the "central goals" of the steward-parent. In particular, I will argue that one of the most important goals of the steward-parent will be that his child, on reaching adulthood, be "free."

Child Psychology

Before we begin our exploration of the goals of steward-parenting, it is important that we distinguish between what *science* can tell us about our goals and what *value theory* can tell us. Science can tell us how to attain whatever goals we might have, but it cannot tell us what goals are worth attaining. Value theory, on the other hand, has much to say about what our goals should be, but has precious little to say about how to attain them.

Consider, by way of illustration, the goal of building an atom bomb. Physics (as a science) has much to say about how to attain this goal. The study of physics will tell us how much fissionable material we will need, how to trigger a chain reaction, and so forth. There is nothing in physics, however, that tells us whether the goal of building an atom bomb is an appropriate one. It may be true that if we build atom bombs we run the risk of annihilating our species, but the laws of physics have nothing to say about the merits or demerits of this possible fate. As far as the laws of physics are concerned, human beings are just another form of matter, as are carrots, chairs, and rocks.

On the other hand, an ethicist (i.e., one skilled in value theory) will have a lot to say about the moral appropriateness of our building an atom bomb, but probably won't have a clue about how one is actually built.

Or consider the goal of reducing unemployment. An economist, in his role as a scientist, should be able to tell us what steps to take if we wish to reduce unemployment. The science of economics, however, tells him nothing about whether these steps should be taken. Thus, when an economist tells us that we *ought* to help the unemployed gain employment, he has temporarily abandoned science in favor of value theory. There is nothing wrong in this abandonment, but we should realize that there is nothing in his scientific training that qualifies him to make such a claim, and that although he might be a superb economist, he might be woefully inadequate when it comes to reasoning his way through an issue in value theory. (Similarly, we should think twice before accepting an ethicist's recommendations on how to increase employment.)

Consider, finally, medicine. Medical science has much to say about what steps we should take if our goal is to commit suicide, but it has nothing to say about whether the goal of death by suicide is an appropriate one. This is not to say that medical scientists lack opinions on the issue of suicide. We need to keep in mind, however, that when they offer such opinions, they are no longer playing the role of medical scientist, but have slipped (perhaps successfully, perhaps not) into the role of ethicist.

When it comes to discussing the goals of the steward-parent, there are two ways we can proceed. We might, to begin with, try to determine what goals are appropriate for steward-parents and what goals are not. In proceeding in this fashion, we are doing value theory. Alternatively, we might take certain goals for granted and talk about what parents should do to attain these goals. In proceeding in this fashion, we are doing science—more precisely, we are doing child psychology.

In my discussion of the goals of the steward-parent, my primary interest is in value theory: I am out to argue for the appropriateness of certain goals and for the inappropriateness of others. There will be moments, however, when I cross the line into child psychology. Each time I do so, I put myself at risk, for my professional training is in ethics, not in psychology. Nevertheless, I think that most of the psychological claims I make (that, for example, if you want your child to feel that he is a worthy individual as an adult, you should love him unconditionally as a child) are fairly commonsensical. Should the reader disagree, however, with my comments with respect to child psychology, he or she should keep in mind that even if I am wrong about how to *attain* the goals I describe, I might nevertheless be perfectly correct in my *identification* of the goals of steward-parents.

Having said all this, I should add that the typical steward-parent will take an active interest in child psychology. He will spend a fair amount of time observing his child and studying his child's reactions to various situations. He will do this so he can better judge what steps should be taken to shape his child's behavior. He will be a consumer of advice on child rearing, but a thoughtful one: He will realize that much of what is written about child psychology is nonsense. He will understand that as his child goes through the various stages of childhood, what is expected of him as a parent will change; he will do his best to adapt. He will also realize that when it comes to child psychology, there is no such thing as one-size-fits-all. Techniques that might work wonderfully on one child might not work at all on another.

To better understand this point, it is useful to compare the act of parenting with various sports.

Consider first the sport of curling, which resembles shuffleboard played on ice. A curler slides a large stone toward a target. Once the stone has been released, it cannot be touched, but other curlers are allowed to slide ahead of the stone and sweep the ice; by their sweeping, they can ever-so-slightly influence the course of the stone. In some cases, being a parent is like curling: The best way to influence the behavior of a child is with an almost subliminally-placed suggestion. This sort of child won't need to have things spelled out to him and will resent it if you try.

In the case of other children, being a parent is more like playing golf. In golf, you hit the ball, take a long, relaxing walk, then hit the ball again. (In saying this, I do not, of course, mean to suggest that a parent should strike his children the way a golfer strikes the ball. What I *am* suggesting is that the parent periodically has to "vigorously interact" with a child, say, by grounding him.) If a parent tried to influence a "golf child" by means of a subliminal suggestion, it would have zero effect.

In the case of yet other children, being a parent is like playing tennis: You hit the ball over the net only to have it hit right back at you a few seconds later. You have to wait a long time before you can relax at the end of a set. And then the next set begins. A "tennis child" will require constant monitoring and repeated disciplinary measures. The parent of such a child will find himself in an ongoing game of wits against a skilled and seemingly tireless opponent.

The steward-parent will hope that his job as parent will resemble curling; but if the child he ends up with makes his job as parent more like tennis, he will do his best to play and win the game.

Generally speaking, the steward-parent will be an experimentalist in his approach to parenting. He will constantly be trying to improve his parental skills. He will try new parenting techniques to see if they are an improvement on the old—that is, to see whether they are a better, easier way to achieve the goals of steward-parenting. He will discard those techniques that don't work. By the time his children are nearly adults, he may have gone far toward perfecting his parental skills. The ironic thing, of course, is that by this time, his days as a parent (in the full-fledged sense of the word) will be drawing to an end.

Success as a Goal

Why not simply state, at the outset, that the goal of the steward-parent should be for his child to grow into a successful adult? If, for example, he grows up to be a doctor or lawyer, isn't that evidence enough that his parents were successful stewards?

The problem with identifying adult success as the goal of steward-parents is that it is far from clear what counts as a successful adult. In particular, there are those who would take it as a sign of parental failure, rather than success, if their child became a doctor or a lawyer; they might argue that successful steward-parents turn out poets and musicians, not doctors and lawyers. Others would find nothing objectionable about their child becoming a doctor or a lawyer, but would scoff at the idea of declaring him to be a successful adult simply because he had become a doctor or lawyer. Suppose, for example, that the doctor their child became was both medically incompetent and miserable in the practice of medicine; or suppose that the lawyer their child became, though highly successful in the practice of law, had a dysfunctional personal life. Despite their professional credentials, such individuals would not be prime examples of successful adulthood.

Any attempt to define successful steward-parenting in terms of success as an adult, then, is likely to degenerate into a debate over what counts as adult success. For this reason, for us to propose "adult success" as the goal of steward-parents is not terribly useful.

Happiness as a Goal

If not success, then what about happiness? Shouldn't the goal of steward-parents be for their children to be happy both when they are children and when they are adults? Won't steward-parents' goal be to maximize their child's lifetime happiness?

A recent survey reveals considerable popular support for the notion that happiness should be the goal of parenting: When parents were asked which is more important for their children to have, wealth, high intelligence, a successful job or career, or an overall happy life, more people chose happiness than the other three choices combined.[1]

While I don't for a moment want to suggest that steward-parents shouldn't be concerned with the happiness of their child, either as a child or as an adult, I have qualms about picking out happiness as a goal of steward-parents, for reasons that I will describe below.

Before we go any further in this discussion, let us take a moment to reflect on the nature of happiness.

It is important, first of all, to distinguish between happiness and what philosophers would call "mere pleasure." Whereas pleasure is a physical thing, happiness is a mental thing; and in part because of this, happiness tends to last longer than pleasure. It is possible (but difficult) to be happy while one is in physical misery; consider, for example, a woman the moment after giving birth to a child. It is also possible to be unhappy but be in a state of physical bliss: Many drug addicts, one assumes, understand this only too well.

It is also important to realize that many common views about happiness and what one must do to attain it are mistaken. This, at least, is the conclusion of those psychologists who have studied happiness and its causes. It is not at all difficult, they tell us, to come up with examples of people who should, according to conventional wisdom, be happy, but who are not, and of people who should not be happy, but who nevertheless are.

Consider, to begin with, the alleged connection between material well-being and happiness. Many people in developed countries operate on the assumption that material possessions (i.e., "things") will make them happy—more precisely, that the reason they are unhappy is because they lack things, and that on acquiring the things in question, they will become happy. In reply to this, it is worth mentioning that if we look to other lands in which people are conspicuous in their material poverty, the people in question are about as happy as those of us who live lives of material abundance.[2] Similarly, even within the borders of one country, the materially rich are typically only a bit happier than the poor.[3]

Or compare today's Americans with those of previous generations. Our great-great-grandparents had almost none of the "good things" that we take for granted. They lacked televisions, electric lights, indoor plumbing, antibiotics, automobiles, jet planes, air-conditioning, exotic fruit in winter, and so on. Yet, judging from their writings, they were not unhappy. Indeed, in many cases, they seem to have been happier than we are.

Just as we look back on our ancestors and say, "The poor souls, they didn't know what they were missing," our descendants will look back *on us* and say much the same thing. Of course, if you don't know what you're missing—as we don't—it won't affect your happiness.

Take a poor person and make him rich. Does he become happier? For a while, but his happiness tends not to last. This claim is based on studies of people who won the lottery.[4] The same person who at one time thought that the only thing standing between him and happiness was gobs of money will often, after winning the lottery, take steps that are likely to decrease his happiness. He might quit his job, and thereby sacrifice the social relationships connected with his place of work. In quitting his job he also sacrifices an important part of his sense of identity: Before, when asked what he did, he could answer that he was, say, a welder; now he must answer that he doesn't really do anything, he won the lottery. His next mistake might be to move to a bigger house in a better neighborhood. He soon finds that his neighbors, who worked to get their houses, don't accept him as a social equal. He will also find that his old dreams about what he could do if only he had more money remain: He used to long for a new Ford, but now he longs for a new Rolls Royce. Typically, it will be only a matter of time before he finds himself not much happier than he was before he gained his sudden wealth, but with considerably bigger bills to pay.

But back to happiness as a goal. My reluctance to identify happiness (of a child) as a goal of steward-parenting stems from the fact that happiness is, in an important sense, unpursuable as a goal.

It does not appear to be possible to attain happiness by taking aim squarely at it and endeavoring to attain it. In almost every case, happiness is best attained if you spend your time pursuing not it, but various other goals. Happiness, when it comes, comes as a by-product of these other pursuits. Thus, a person who sets out to be happy this afternoon will almost certainly fail. Indeed, he may, thanks to his efforts to attain happiness "head on," end up less happy than he would have been if his goal this afternoon had been not to become happy, but to plant a garden or take a walk.

Attaining happiness, then, is not at all like going to the store and obtaining a quart of milk or like going to college and obtaining an education. It isn't as if there is a certain process which, if you go through it carefully, will automatically bring you happiness. Instead, there are lifestyles which, if lived, will tend to produce happiness as a by-product—but there are no guarantees. The Founding Fathers realized as much: Thomas Jefferson speaks of the *pursuit of* happiness, not happiness itself, as a basic right of man. Thus, while government can do things that enable you to *pursue* happiness, happiness itself it cannot provide.

Happiness often arises out of activities that are not in themselves particularly pleasant. An athlete may spend years training for a marathon. The training is boring and painful. Yet the athlete may discover happiness when, as the culmination of years of training, he wins an important race—or comes in last place, but sets a personal record doing so.

Happiness can't be faked. Suppose the above marathoner wins a race by cheating. His happiness at winning—assuming that he experiences any—will likely be pale in comparison to the happiness he would have experienced had he won the race fair and square. Likewise, if other people "let" him win the race and he realizes as much, his happiness—if he experiences any—will not be nearly as great as if he had won the race "for real."

One last thing to realize about happiness is that it can't be given as a gift. You can't "make" someone happy, and in particular, parents can't "make" their child happy. The best anyone can do is to remove obstacles to happiness. If, for example, a person is sick or starving to death, it is difficult (but not impossible) to be happy. If you cure a sick person or feed a starving person, you are therefore removing an important obstacle to his happiness, but there is no guarantee that he will thereby become happy; the world is full of unhappy people who are both healthy and well-fed.

Thus, steward-parents will want to take steps to remove various obstacles to happiness from their child's life. In particular, they will have as a top priority that their child is healthy and well-nourished. They might also take steps to see that their child understands how it is that happiness comes about and that certain lifestyles are more likely to lead to happiness than other lifestyles. I will have more to say about this below.

Freedom as a Goal

When I discussed the stewardship model of parenting in Chapter 7, I mentioned freedom (for their children) as a goal of steward-parents. I would now like to argue that freedom is not merely *a* goal, but is a *central* goal (and maybe even *the* central goal) of steward-parents. In what follows I will argue that one very important way to judge the success of steward-parents is in terms of how free their children are on reaching adulthood.

Before I embark on the argument in question, it will perhaps be useful to briefly examine the concept of freedom.

Freedom clearly involves choices. If there is but one thing a person can do, and he does it, he is not acting freely, since he doesn't have a choice in the matter—unless, of course, the thing in question is the one thing the person most wants to do—that is, the thing he would have wanted to do, even if other actions had been possible. Generally speaking, the more choices you have, the freer you are. A person who can choose either *A*, *B*, or *C* is obviously freer than a person who is limited to choosing either *A* or *B*.

Of course, even when a person has many possible choices open to him, he might not be free if the choices in question have been "artificially" restricted. Suppose, for instance, that we abduct a person and take him to prison. When we arrive there, we give him a choice of 999 different prison cells in which to live. Our captive, it is clear, has lots of choices. But his choice of, say, cell number 977 will not be a free choice, inasmuch as what he would have chosen, had we not restricted his freedom, is not to live in any cell at all. So, when talking about freedom, we must keep in mind that how free a person is depends not just on the quantity of choices available to him, but also on the "quality" of those choices.

And finally, it can be argued that even if a person has lots of choices and picks something for which he has a deeply-felt desire, his choice may not have been free. For it may be that his ability to make choices has been corrupted. Suppose, for example, he has been brainwashed: Suppose that since he was a child, he has been told by parents, teachers, and the culture in which he lived that the honorable thing to do on reaching age thirty is to commit suicide. Approaching age thirty, this person might have a wide range of options open to him, one of which is suicide, but the rest of which involve life-affirming choices that most people would find rather pleasant. On reviewing these options, this poor soul might conclude that suicide is the thing he most wants to do. In such a case, he will have chosen the thing he wants from a meaningful list of possible choices, but most would be reluctant to call his choice a free one.

Now that we have a better idea of what freedom is, we can ask whether it is worth having. And if it is, *why* is it worth having? Notice that unless freedom *is* worth having, steward-parents will not be acting in the best interests of their children in raising them to be free. Allow me, then, to present the case for freedom.

Perhaps the best way to show why freedom is valuable is to ask whether there would ever be circumstances under which a person would desire less freedom. Suppose, for example, that a person had, at present, three things he could choose to do, A, B, and C. Would it ever make sense for him to desire less freedom— and in the present case that would mean wanting to have his choices limited to, say, only A and B, with choice C being rendered unchoosable? Arguably not. For either C is the choice he prefers (given choices A, B, and C), or C is not the choice he prefers. If C *is* the choice he prefers, then it makes no sense for him to desire that it be removed as a choice: He would be desiring that he not be allowed to choose what he prefers, which seems inconsistent. On the other hand, if C *is not* the choice he prefers (from among A, B, and C), then there is little reason for him to desire not to be able to choose it; since there is something else he prefers more, he will not choose C even if it is an option.

On the other hand, it would be natural for someone presented with choices A, B, and C to take steps to expand his choices to include, say, D and E as well. Having more choices cannot hurt him. If they turn out to be *less* desirable than A, B, or C, he has the option of not choosing them, in which case their addition as choices has done him no harm; and if they turn out to be *more* desirable than A, B, or C, their addition as choices will prove beneficial to him.

The only time it would make sense for a person to argue that his freedom be restricted is if the person in question suffered from weakness of the will. Such a person might complain that if we offered him A, B, and C as choices, he would, because of a weak will, choose C, all the time knowing that this choice would have terrible consequences for him. Such a person might plead with us to remove C as a choice—that is, to reduce his freedom.

Consider, for example, a person who has a choice this weekend of watching television, doing his taxes, or getting hopelessly drunk. If the person were an alcoholic, he might, presented with this array of choices, choose to get drunk, even though he knew that drunkenness would have undesirable consequences for him. He might beg his relatives to keep him away from alcohol for the weekend—beg them, that is, to restrict his freedom.

Of course, our question is whether a *fully rational* person would ever argue for less freedom, and the weak-willed person just described is arguably irrational, at least in this aspect of his life.

Freedom, then, appears to be intrinsically valuable. It would be difficult to fault parents who spend considerable effort trying to increase the amount of freedom their child will have on coming of age.

There is another important reason for steward-parents to value the freedom of their children: It is probably the single best way they can demonstrate their respect for their child as a person. In raising a child to be free, they are raising him not to play some role in *their* grand design; they are raising him to make his own grand design and live his life in accordance with this design. They are acting, in other words, not as if they owned the child, but as if they were merely temporary stewards acting on behalf of the child.

Freedom and the Steward-Parent

At this point it might be suggested that if steward-parents want their child to be free, they can best accomplish this goal by simply setting their child free—that is, by letting him do whatever he wants. (This, by the way, would be the recommendation of those favoring the liberation model of parenting discussed in Chapter 7.)

Steward-parents will quickly reject this suggestion. In wanting their child to be free, after all, steward-parents want not just to maximize their child's *childhood* freedom, but to maximize their child's *lifetime* freedom. Steward-parents will point out that by placing some strategic limitations on their child's freedom when he is a child, they can produce enormous gains in his freedom when he is an adult. These latter gains, the argument goes, far outweigh the decrease in his childhood freedom.

Consider, for example, the child who finds in himself a desire to experiment with blasting caps. Parents who favored the most extreme form of the liberation model would let him experiment with them; parents who favored the stewardship model would not. The child would thus, in the short run, have less freedom under the stewardship model of parenting than under the liberation model. Then again, the child could be maimed or blinded experimenting with blasting caps, in which case his future choices would be very much limited. Better, then, to curb the freedom of the child with respect to blasting caps, if what we are interested in is the child's total lifetime freedom.

Along these same lines, the steward-parent will take steps to prevent his child from experimenting with drugs. (Reasonable people may differ concerning exactly what steps a parent should take.) After all, a drug addict typically has fewer choices than a sober person does, and many of the choices he makes are not genuine—not a true reflection of himself—but are instead driven by an "artificial" craving for drugs. In an important sense the drug addict is not free.

A steward-parent's interference with his child's freedom will not end with preventing the child from doing things the child wants to do; the steward-parent might also force the child to do things that he doesn't want to do. In particular, if the steward-parent thinks that engaging in a certain activity will open up meaningful choices for the child in the future—will increase his future freedom—he might "force" his child to engage in the activity in question. Schooling, presumably, would be one such activity.

One big thing that steward-parents know that their children don't know is that a life consists of several life-stages, and that as a result, over the course of a lifetime, one person will be many different persons. The toddler will obviously be a different person than the teen, but the teen at age 14 will also be a different person than the teen at age 16. Thus, steward-parents will realize that the high school freshman who has little interest in college—and consequently, little interest in academic achievement—might someday be the high-school junior who is deadly serious about his college prospects. They will therefore do what they can to encourage the freshman to take school seriously. They will work hard to block their child from "burning any bridges" that he might someday, as a substantially different person, wish to cross.

When his child is sick, a steward-parent will be intent on getting medical help for him. Why this concern? Because the steward-parent recognizes that physical well-being is essential not only to happiness, as was mentioned above, but to freedom as well. A healthy child can typically accomplish all he could have accomplished if he were sick or physically defective, and more.

A steward-parent will also be concerned that he transmit to his children what might be called "freedom-preserving" values— values which, if held, increase one's chances of living in freedom. I will have more to say about these values later in this chapter.

Unlike steward-parents, owner-parents will not place a high value on the future freedom of their child. Indeed, they might even take steps to sabotage their child's future freedom. They might, for example, raise him so that he will never be able to walk out of their lives and take on the world as an autonomous being.

Why would an owner-parent sabotage his child's future freedom? For one thing, the owner-parent (as we have seen) might be interested in exploiting the child—exploiting, perhaps, his labor. Indeed, for some owner-parents, the goal is not simply to exploit their child's labor when he is a child, but to exploit it until the day the parent dies. The parent may seek to arrange things so that even when the child is an adult, his days will be spent providing for and caring for his parent. Were the child to become independent, the days of exploitation would end: The child would no longer be slave to the parent. The plans of the owner-parent would be ruined.

Other owner-parents might seek not to exploit a child's labor, but to use the child to satisfy their own emotional needs.

They might recognize in themselves, for example, a strong need to be needed. To fulfill this need, they might bring a child into existence, and then raise the child so his need for them, rather than diminishing with time as the child comes into his own, will remain constant. Thanks to the efforts of these parents, their child, on becoming an adult, might find himself unable or unwilling to walk into the world as an independent person.

Owner-parents who have and raise children to fulfill their own need to be needed are treating their children rather like pets. One of the most attractive things about having a pet is that it will never "grow up." It will never not need its owner. Steward-parents, on the other hand, will be careful not to mistake their children for "pets."

Notice that in having the freedom of their child as a goal, steward-parents are promoting their own future obsolescence as parents: If they do their job well, there will come a day when their child no longer needs them, but is ready to take on the world as an independent being. The ultimate "loss" of one's child (to a life of independence) is just one of the sacrifices that the steward-parent must be willing to make.

At the same time, if steward-parents have done their job well, there is an excellent chance that although their child no longer *needs* them, he will nevertheless still view them as friends and seek their companionship. Notice, too, that because their child has achieved independence, the friendship will be a friendship of equals. Such a friendship is arguably both healthier and more satisfying than would be a continuation of the old parent-child friendship.

Educating for Freedom

The costs of educating a child can be quite high. Even "free" public education is not entirely free. And of course if you go on to send your child to college—as many steward-parents will—the costs of educating your child can be exorbitant. But this isn't the only price parents pay when they send their child to school. They also pay a price in terms of the income the child could have earned (and duly turned over to them) if the child, rather than spending his days in school, had spent them working at some occupation that did not require schooling.

If we ask owner-parents whether it makes sense to educate children, they might answer that it does not: Educating children imposes high costs on parents but provides them (the parents) with few or no benefits, so it would be, for many owner-parents, foolish to educate their children.[5] If, on the other hand, we ask steward-parents whether it makes sense to educate children, they would almost certainly answer that it does. In particular, they will likely point out that education is one of the best ways for them to accomplish the goal of raising their children to be free. Education increases one's choices in life, and an educated child is likely to experience greater freedom as an adult than an uneducated child.

When I talk about educating children for freedom, I have two sorts of education in mind, one formal and the other informal. Formal education, in the sense I have in mind, takes place inside a classroom and typically involves books and tests. Informal education, on the other hand, takes place outside the classroom. There are no (assigned) books, and all the "tests" are unwritten. The parents themselves are often the primary informal educators. Despite its unstructured nature, informal education can do as much to educate children for freedom as formal education.

Formal Education

In formally educating children, we teach them reading, writing, arithmetic, and related subjects. Although children have to give up a significant amount of freedom as children in order to be educated in these subjects, most people would agree that in the course of a lifetime, it is an investment that pays huge dividends in terms of freedom. Notice, to begin with, that an extensive formal education as a child substantially increases the number and quality of choices a person has on becoming an adult. First, it gives him the option of attending college. And the more extensive his education is, the greater will be his range of choices of which college to attend. And by enhancing his choices with respect to his postsecondary education, his childhood formal education can substantially increase the number and quality of careers from which he can choose. Of course, the career a person embarks upon as an adult can determine to a significant extent the amount of freedom that person has to live his life the way he chooses.

This makes it sound as if formal education is merely job training, but nothing could be further from the truth. Even if a child never works a day in his life, his formal education would still serve him well in helping him get whatever it is he wants in life. Knowledge, said Bacon, is power. And the most interesting power conferred by knowledge is the power, once you have decided you want to be at Point *B*, to get there from Point *A*. A person who is capable of fulfilling his desires is in an important sense freer than a person who is not, and an educated person is likely to be more capable of fulfilling his desires than a person who is not.

A formal education can also increase one's recreational choices. A person who can't read, for example, will be cut off from the world of literature. So once again, even if a child never worked a day in his life, a formal education might expand his choices of what to do during his days of unemployment.

Notice, more generally, that a person with a formal education can do all the things he could have done without an education, and several other things as well. Stated differently, a person with a formal education can easily act as if he weren't educated, but it can be difficult if not impossible for a person without a formal education to act as if he were educated.

Informal Education

If all they did was provide a formal education for their children, steward-parents would be remiss in their duties; for just as important as a formal education is the informal education they provide.

We have already discussed one aspect of informal education: Steward-parents will take steps to discover and develop their child's talents. After all, the more talents a child has discovered and developed, the more choices he will have open to him. Thus, a person who has developed his musical talents has opportunities open to him that he would otherwise lack.

A second aspect of a child's informal education will involve a cultural education. Among other things he will learn the language of his culture; how to greet people, ask for things, dress properly, and behave in crowds; when it is appropriate to touch another person; and what activities must be done in private. As a result of this cultural education the child will be easily able to "fit in" to his culture.[6]

In making this last claim, am I pushing for a kind of cultural conformity? Indeed I am. I am suggesting that for most steward-parents, the sensible thing to do is to "indoctrinate" their children in the ways of their culture. In defense of this conformity, I can only point out that the alternatives to raising a child "in one's culture" can have disastrous consequences for the child.

Suppose, for example, that certain American parents decided to fight against cultural conformity by teaching their child—who they had every reason to believe would spend his life in America—Icelandic rather than English.[7] Or suppose that rather than teaching their child English they teach it a dead language or—even worse—a language they made up. The child, on growing up, would find his choices in life severely restricted by his linguistic limitations.

Or, to take another example, suppose that American parents, again to fight against cultural conformity, teach their child not the standard American customs and manners, but a radically different set of customs and manners: Suppose, for example, that they raise a child who customarily greets people with profanity; who, rather than asking for things, simply takes what he wants; who goes around naked; who shouts whenever in a crowd; who routinely hugs complete strangers; and so forth. Such a person would again find his choices in life severely restricted, inasmuch as he would probably end up behind bars.

Cultural nonconformity, it should be clear, comes at a price. And notice that in the cases I described, the person who pays the greater part of the price is not the parent who has chosen to strike a blow against cultural conformity, but rather his child, who had no say in the matter.

For most parents, to teach their child the customs, manners, and language of the dominant culture will not only seem the sensible thing to do, it will be the path of least resistance. If an American is going to teach his child Icelandic rather than English, he must first know Icelandic; and for most Americans, the cost of learning Icelandic will be high. Similarly, if a parent is going to teach his child to greet people with profanity, he himself will have to put up with two decades of being greeted with profanity, which presumably won't be much fun.

Although steward-parents will appreciate the value of cultural conformity, they might not opt for *complete* conformity. They might, for example, teach their child not only the customs and manners of their culture, but those of some subculture as well— for example, a religious or ethnic subculture. They also might want to teach their children that each set of customs has its appropriate place. It is unlikely that they would diminish their child's future freedom by providing such a multicultural education; to the contrary, they might even increase their child's future freedom by doing so.

A third part of a child's informal education will involve teaching him "the way the world works." What I have in mind here are lessons not in the way the world works in chemical or physical terms, but the way the world works in social terms. A child needs to learn how people are likely to react to various actions on his part, even though the reactions in question are not necessarily reasonable.

Suppose, then, that a child is caught telling a lie. The child might feel, quite reasonably, that telling one lie does not make him a habitual liar. He might defend himself by pointing out that this particular lie was a special case, and that he intends not to tell any more. What the child needs explained to him is how serious the world's reaction to lying can be. The child needs to be taught that the price you pay in telling a lie is not so much the punishment for getting caught, but the loss of people's trust. Life can be difficult when people refuse to take you at your word. It can take years of truth-telling to regain the trust of those around you.

Or suppose that a child, because of his poor attitude at the beginning of the Little League season, finds himself warming the bench. The natural reaction of many children in such a situation will be to complain that it isn't fair that they are warming the bench and then start playing the role of victim. Such experiences, though distressing to the child, provide his parents with an opportunity to teach him several important lessons about the way the world works. The first lesson is the importance of first impressions. (It is unreasonable for people to judge you by first impressions, but they do.) The second lesson is that the world *isn't* fair, and that as a result he must make a choice about whether he wants to react to the world's unfairness by playing the role of victim or by taking positive steps to overcome the unfairness he encounters. The third lesson (which relates to the second), is about the possibility of redemption—about how a person can, with perseverance, prove to the world that its judgment of him is wrong. For the steward-parent, Little League is a little about baseball and a lot about life. The same can be said of many of the other activities of childhood.

A fourth part of a child's informal education will involve teaching children what Laura Purdy has called the "enabling virtues" (and could just as well have called the enabling *traits*). She defines these as "habits that help us get what we want."[8] Some examples of enabling virtues are rationality, self-control, a capacity for hard work, and the desire for excellence. The idea is that a person who possesses these enabling virtues, when he decides he wants something, will be more likely to get it than a person who does not possess enabling virtues. Thus, a person who possesses these virtues will in an important sense be freer than a person who lacks them.

Notice that the enabling virtues—despite being given a name that suggests otherwise—are value-neutral, by which I mean that people with wildly-differing values will likely agree on the importance of a person's possessing these "virtues." Conservative Republicans thoroughly entrenched in middle-class values will obviously recognize the importance of such things as a capacity for hard work or a desire for excellence. But so will anarchists of the bomb-throwing sort. Such anarchists will realize that an anarchist with a capacity for hard work will in many respects be a better anarchist—will accomplish more of his anarchistic goals—than an anarchist who is lazy. Although anarchists and conservative Republicans will differ in many respects, they will probably agree on the importance of indoctrinating their children in the enabling virtues.

Of course, when steward-parents indoctrinate their children in the enabling virtues, they will be careful not to overdo it. It is true, for example, that a capacity for hard work can enable a person to get what he wants in life. But if we teach our children that hard work is *everything*, they might end up less free than they would otherwise have been: They might feel that they have no choice but to work hard, and that work is done not to achieve goals, but as an end in itself. Such feelings would obviously diminish their freedom.

How will steward-parents informally educate their child? Probably not by means of "lectures." The truth of the matter is that most children are not particularly receptive to being lectured.

If you don't lecture your children, then how can you teach them? In a number of ways.

For one thing, a parent can informally educate a child by answering the child's questions. When a child asks a parent a question, it is because he realizes that there is something he doesn't know, and because he suspects that the parent can supply the missing information. Thus, when a child asks a parent a question, it is evidence that the child is in an unusually receptive state of mind, and the steward-parent will want to take full advantage of such opportunities to "plant seeds" in the child's mind—seeds that, when they grow, will round out the child's informal education.

Even when a child is not asking his parents questions, he is learning from them. A parent informally educates his child every time he reacts, in the child's presence, to situations that arise. When, after tasting some ice cream, the parent says, "Mmmm!" he is informally educating his child: He is letting him know how desirable ice cream is. When, after hearing of someone falling ill, a parent says, "I'll have to pray for him," he is fostering certain religious views in his child. When, upon seeing a child strike a cat, a parent comments on what an awful thing this is to do, the parent is making a contribution to his child's moral education. It is difficult to overstate the importance that parental "reactions" play in a child's informal education.

Sometimes parents are frustrated because their children seem to ignore the values they express. Suppose, for instance, that parents (in keeping with the argument offered back in Chapter 6) decide that they don't want their child playing excessively violent video games and tell him that they disapprove of such games. This will probably make it unlikely that the child will play these games at home, but what if he is at a friend's house? Or at a movie theater? Or at a toy store? Unless you keep him under 24-hour guard there is no way to stop him from playing them. Does it follow from this that parents are wasting their breath if they express their disapproval of violent video games? Not at all. It is far better that their child understand, and possibly ignore, his parents' disapproval than mistakenly take his parents' silence on the subject as a sign of their approval.

Children will, almost without exception, sample whatever fruits their parents forbid. What is important is that when they sample such fruits, they feel the need to "sneak" to do so, and feel a bit ashamed for having done so. Even though a child seems to dismiss out of hand the things his parents tell him, it is likely (in all but exceptional cases) that the parental values in question, despite the child's best efforts to block them, will make it into his moral conscience. Parents, in short, should not underestimate their power to shape their child's moral outlook.

If I am right about how children are informally educated—not by being lectured but by having their questions answered, by watching adults' reactions to situations, and by being exposed to adult role models—it follows that parents who care about their child's informal education will want to spend plenty of time around their child.

It is, after all, impossible to answer a child's questions if you aren't around when those questions are asked. Even if you have someone else write down your child's questions so that you can answer them later in the day, the effect will not be the same: Later in the day the child might no longer be interested in the answers to these questions, and the opportunity to "plant a seed" will have been lost. Likewise, a child cannot learn from his parent's reactions to situations if the parent is not around to react. And finally, it is unlikely that a child will take his parent to be a role model if, because of parental absences, the child hardly knows the parent.

A steward-parent will instinctively realize that it is impossible to provide a child with a proper informal education if his exposure to his parent is a half-hour of "quality time" each day. Steward-parents will be advocates not of "quality time," but of "quantity time."

This isn't the only reason that steward-parents will want to spend time with their children. Unless you spend time with a child, it is unlikely that you will develop a complete understanding of who he is, what he wants, and how he works; and without this understanding, it will be difficult for you to properly guide his development. By way of analogy, unless a land steward spends a considerable amount of time observing the lands under his care, he will have a hard time managing them.

Also, steward-parents will want to spend time with their child because (one hopes) they enjoy his company. Having said this I should add that even if steward-parents do not enjoy the company of their child—a possibility we will explore further in Chapter 11—they will nevertheless feel obligated to spend significant amounts of time with him, since this is essential if they are to properly perform the job of steward-parent.

The steward-parent will also be quite careful about what adults his children are exposed to. He will realize that the hand that rocks the cradle (and wipes the nose and serves the meal and distributes the allowance) will, like it or not, play a significant role in a child's informal education. The steward-parent will think long and hard before turning his child over to strangers paid minimum wage (e.g., workers in a day-care center) for hours each day. He will fear that these strangers, although they might do an excellent job of taking care of a child's physical needs and keeping a child entertained, might not provide a child with a proper informal education.

There is, to be sure, more to a child's informal education than the elements described above. The forgoing discussion should, however, give the reader a good idea of what sort of thing I have in mind when I talk about a child's informal education.

Autonomy

Besides wanting to provide a child with the tools to get what he wants—which is what steward-parents do when they give their child the formal and informal educations described above—steward-parents will want to raise their child so that he will have the capacity to make meaningful choices. They will want to raise their child, in other words, to be an autonomous being. To get a better handle on the concept of autonomy, let us consider some of the ways in which a person might lack it.

In the first place, consider a person who, though having been given the capacity to get what he wants, wants nothing (or, at any rate, wants nothing worth having) because he feels that he isn't worthy of having anything. Such a person would lack autonomy.

In the second place, consider a person who simply does not

know what he wants. It isn't that the person doesn't want any of the options open to him; he does want one, but hasn't a clue which it is that he wants.

In the third place, consider a person who wants things, but wants them not as the result of a rational decision-making process; instead, he wants them as the result of impulse. Such a person might, at one moment want intensely to become a doctor, might at the next moment want to join the army, and might the moment after that want to become a rock star—all without much thought about why he has these ambitions and what he must do to fulfill them. And such a person, we might suspect, is no more making genuine choices than a coin makes a choice of whether to come up heads or tails when you flip it.

Along similar lines, consider a person who wants things, but in wanting them isn't expressing his "true self." Thus, an alcoholic might want intensely to get drunk, but we would be reluctant to call this desire one that emanates from his "true self"; rather, it comes from his self as clouded by alcohol addiction. Similarly, a zealot might tell us that what he truly wants is to die committing an act of terrorism. We might once again suspect that this desire, rather than arising "from within," was imposed "from without," and therefore that this person lacks autonomy.

Steward-parents will want to keep all this in mind in raising their child. They will, to begin with, want to do what they can to make their child feel that he is somebody, that he is a worthy individual, and that his choices do matter. The obvious way to accomplish this is to raise their child in an environment in which it should be unquestionably clear to the child that he is a valued member of the family, and what better way to communicate to someone their value than by making them the object of unconditional love? Ideally, a child will reason as follows: "If my parents, who I think are the most important people in the world, think I'm the most important person in the world, I must be someone." A child who is ignored by his parents—or worse, abused by them—will likely have a hard time emerging from childhood with his self-esteem intact. He will reason—quite logically, and in most cases correctly—that there are many things in his parents' lives that are more important to them than he is. A child without self-esteem might find it hard, as an adult, to make "genuine choices."

Steward-parents will also want to take steps to develop their child's self-control. What this means, in practice, is engaging in a conscious effort to help a child think through his actions, consider their consequences, and think about what alternative actions lie open to him. Only then will the choices he makes be "genuine choices," rather than transient urges.

There are those who badmouth self-control and claim that spontaneity is preferable. People who act spontaneously, they might argue, are more free than people who possess self-control. Those who possess self-control are, after all, "controlled" in a way that spontaneous people are not, and with control comes a diminution of freedom.

In reply to this claim, two comments are in order.

In the first place, the goal of steward-parents is not to produce a child who is incapable of acting spontaneously or on a whim. Often in life, spontaneity is perfectly acceptable. What steward-parents will want is to implant in their child a sense of when spontaneity is appropriate and when it is not. It is okay to be spontaneous, for example, in deciding what to wear or what to order for dinner, but not in deciding whom to marry or what career to embark upon.

In the second place, gaining self-control does not necessarily entail a diminution of freedom. It may be true that those individuals who possess self-control are "controlled" individuals, but they are controlled *by themselves*. It is those individuals who *lack* self-control whose freedom is limited, for those individuals, rather than being controlled by themselves, are controlled by "external forces."

To possess self-control is to possess the ability to carry through your plans and get what *you* want. To lack self-control is to lack this ability and therefore run the risk of not getting what you want, instead having to settle for what the world wants to give you. It is hard to see how someone who lacks the ability to get what he wants could count as more free than someone who possesses this ability.

To develop a child's autonomy, steward-parents will want to give their children plenty of chances to make decisions and experience the consequences of their decision-making. They will, in other words, give their children plenty of chances to make mistakes, realizing that mistakes are a wonderful teacher. The mistakes in question, however, will be small ones: A steward-parent might, for example, let a child experiment with not studying for spelling tests, inasmuch as the downside risk—a bad grade in spelling—is relatively small. A steward-parent will be quite unwilling, however, to let a child experiment with drugs, inasmuch as the downside risk—a life-afflicting addiction—is huge. A motto of the steward-parent will be, Lots of mistakes, but all of them little.

A steward-parent might also want to share his own decision-making activities with his child, explaining how in a certain choice he has to make, certain trade-offs are involved and certain consequences are likely. He might also seek out the opinions of the child when it comes to decisions that affect the whole family, as when a vacation is being planned. He might ask the child what he wants to do on the vacation and why he wants to do it, and he might explain the trade-offs involved in making that choice.

Other Advocates of Freedom

I am not, to be sure, the first person to suggest that a central goal of parenting is to raise children to be free. Philosophers John Locke and Jean Jacques Rousseau both agreed with this goal, but had differing interpretations of what it meant to be free.

Locke on Childhood Freedom

John Locke is best known today for his work in philosophy, but he played a prominent role in the evolution of the concept of childhood. In 1693 he wrote *Some Thoughts Concerning Education*, which enjoyed considerable popularity.

Locke was a bachelor, but one with wide experience of children. He was a lecturer at Christ Church, Oxford, and there spent his time acting *in loco parentis* for up to ten pupils ages thirteen to eighteen. Since Locke had a good reputation as both teacher and doctor, Anthony Ashley Cooper—Lord Ashley and later the first Earl of Shaftesbury—asked Locke to raise his sickly fifteen-year-old son. Since this boy was Lord Ashley's sole heir, and since it was not clear that the boy would make it into adulthood, Lord Ashley decided that the boy should get married (and make some sons) as soon as possible. He left it to Locke to choose the wife. Apparently, Locke chose wisely: The couple went on to have seven children. Lord Ashley's son asked Locke to raise these children, and again Locke appears to have done the job well: One of the seven children later wrote that Locke had raised them "with such success that we all of us came to full years with strong and healthy constitutions."[9]

In *Some Thoughts Concerning Education*, Locke offers advice on how to raise children. He advises, for example, that shoes should be "so thin that they might leak and let in water, whenever [a child] comes near it"[10] and that the clothes of children should be light, even during inclement weather; that parents should not feed a child at the same time every day; and that the beds of children should be hard and varied.[11] This advice might sound a bit strange to modern ears, but it becomes less strange when we realize that Locke's goal in giving it was to raise children to be free. Thus, when Locke instructs us to vary the feeding time of children, his reasoning is that a child who is fed on a set schedule will become a slave to his stomach, and will hence become less free. And when he instructs us to make children sleep on hard beds, wear light clothing in winter, and wear leaky shoes, his reasoning is that a child who always sleeps on a soft bed and who is always kept warm and dry will become a slave to comfort, and will again become less free.

In Locke's view, a child is a willful creature—that is, one whose will is not guided by reason. The job of the child's parents is to battle the willfulness. According to philosopher Edmund Leites, who has written about Locke's educational philosophy, it is a battle that "the parents must win, for if they do not, they will not only end up his slave but make him a slave to his own willfulness." The goal of parenting, then, is to produce a child who will not be a slave—a slave, that is, to his own willful nature. The goal of parenting, in Leites's words, is to "prepare...children for the freedom to which they have a right as adults" and to make it "likely that children will become adults who will be self-reliant in judgment and masters of their own will."[12]

By forcing a child to obey them, parents accustom the child to obeying something other than his own will: They accustom him to obeying the reason of his parents. Then, when the child's own ability to reason finally develops, the child will have little trouble obeying it. As Locke puts it, "He that is not used to submit his will to the reason of others when he is young, will scarce hearken to submit to his own reason when he is of an age to make use of it."[13]

Do you tame the will of a child through corporal punishment? Locke thinks not—or at any rate, he thinks that corporal punishment should be used as a last resort.[14] He thinks, to the contrary, that parents should create—again in the words of Leites—"a sense of awe in their children which will lead them willingly to conduct themselves as their parents wish."[15] This sense of awe is, presumably, a complex mix of love, respect, and fear; and to maintain this sense of awe, a certain distance must be kept between the parents and the child.

Won't parenting in accordance with Locke's theories require parents to act paternalistically? Indeed it will, but Locke is not bothered by this. It is one thing to use authority simply to keep another person in a state of subjugation; it is quite another to use authority so that person can become free. Locke would remind us that parental authority can be used to a good end, and that failure to exercise parental authority can have disastrous consequences: "To turn him loose to an unrestrain'd Liberty, before he has Reason to guide him, is not the allowing him the privilege of his Nature, to be free; but to thrust him out amongst Brutes, and abandon him to a state as wretched, and as much beneath that of a Man, as theirs."[16]

Won't Locke's plan for parenting require that parents be strict? Indeed it will, but probably less so than might appear to be the case. Locke tells us, after all, that "the true secret of education" is to know "how to keep up a child's spirit easy, active, and free, and yet at the same time to restrain him from many things he has a mind to, and to draw him to things that are uneasy to him."[17] Locke would have parents raise their children strictly, but not oppressively. Lockean parents would be masters of gentle persuasion.

Locke also tells us that as a child grows older and begins to gain possession of himself, his parents will take steps to transform their relationship with him. For one thing, they will take steps to lessen the "distance" between themselves and their children:

> If you would have [your son] stand in awe of you, imprint it in his infancy; and as he approaches more to a man, admit him nearer to your familiarity; so shall you have him your obedient subject (as is fit) whilst he is a child, and your affectionate friend, when he is a man.[18]

In Locke's plan for raising children, as a child grows to adulthood, his relationship with his parents evolves into a friendship between equals.

Furthermore, as children grow and develop a capacity for reasoning, Locke advises parents to gradually relinquish their "rule" over them. Indeed, rather than advising his child, a parent might start asking for his child's advice on matters within the child's scope of understanding.[19] To Locke's way of thinking, a child's freedom should come not all at once, but by degrees, as the child is ready for it; and one of the best ways to prepare a child for his future freedom is to grant him freedom in measured doses while he is still a child.

Rousseau on Childhood Freedom

Nearly seven decades after Locke's *Some Thoughts Concerning Education*, Rousseau described his plan for raising children in his *Emile*.[20] You might think that anyone who writes a book containing advice on how to raise children would either have considerable experience raising them or would at least love them. Rousseau appears to have had neither of these characteristics. Although Rousseau fathered at least five illegitimate children, he acted as father to none of them; instead, he left them at the door of a foundling hospital.[21] Indeed, by his own admission, Rousseau felt unfit to raise children.[22] It is therefore somewhat odd that Rousseau would have thought himself qualified to write a book on how to raise children, and even more odd that anyone would have paid attention to his advice. Nevertheless, we are told that Rousseau's *Emile* was "probably the most widely read child-rearing manual of its age."[23]

In *Emile*, Rousseau declares that it is best if parents—more precisely, fathers—educate their own children.[24] He is critical of fathers who, rather than raising their own child, turn him over to a hired teacher.[25]

If it is impossible for a father to raise his son, he must find a tutor who will take on the task for love and not for money. Why the aversion to a paid teacher? "There are callings so great that they cannot be undertaken for money without showing our unfitness for them; such callings are those of the soldier and the teacher."[26] Where are parents to find such a tutor? They might, Rousseau suggests, try asking a friend to undertake the task.

Rousseau believes that childhood should be treated as a special time of life: "Mankind has its place in the sequence of things; childhood has its place in the sequence of human life; the man must be treated as a man and the child as a child."[27] Expanding on this thought, he tells us that,

Nature would have them children before they are men. If we try to invert this order we shall produce a forced fruit immature and flavourless, fruit which will be rotten before it is ripe; we shall have young doctors and old children. Childhood has its own ways of seeing, thinking, and feeling; nothing is more foolish than to try and substitute our ways....[28]

Rousseau also makes it clear that the goal of parents should not merely be that their children survive, but that they thrive.[29] This suggests that Rousseau was not an advocate of the ownership model of parenting.

Much of Rousseau's practical advice on child rearing sounds eminently sensible to modern ears. He counsels, for example, that children should be breast-fed, preferably by their mother. He suggests that many children are weaned too soon. Rousseau also opposed swaddling babies. Rousseau's advice on breast-feeding and swaddling doubtless contributed to a significant improvement in the standards for child care in the late eighteenth century.

Rousseau's advice on certain other issues will seem odd to modern ears. He is in favor of bathing older children in ice water, in both winter and summer. He counsels parents to wait until a child has stopped crying before they come to him.[30] And curiously, Rousseau plays down the importance of books in childhood: "When I thus get rid of children's lessons, I get rid of the chief cause of their sorrows, namely their books. Reading is the curse of childhood, yet it is almost the only occupation you can find for children. Emile, at twelve years old, will hardly know what a book is."[31] Rousseau explains his dislike of books in the following terms: "I hate books; they only teach us to talk about things we know nothing about."[32] For Rousseau, there is no better teacher than experience.

In the process of learning from experience, children will invariably have accidents and suffer as a result; suffering, Rousseau tells us, should be a child's first lesson. At the same time he makes it clear that parents should take steps to make sure that the accidents in question are small ones.[33]

Rousseau agrees with Locke on the importance of raising children to be free. He rejects Locke's idea, though, that we can foster their future freedom by reasoning with them when they are children. "'Reason with children' was Locke's chief maxim; it is in the height of fashion at present, and I hardly think it is justified by its results; those children who have been constantly reasoned with strike me as exceedingly silly."[34] Instead, he advises parents to "be reasonable, and do not reason with your pupil."[35]

Rather than reasoning with children, Rousseau tells us, you should let experience teach them life's important lessons: "Give your scholar no verbal lessons; he should be taught by experience alone."[36] Nature, not man, Rousseau tells us, should be his schoolmaster.[37] Enlarging on this theme, Rousseau offers the following advice for parents:

> Give him no orders at all, absolutely none. Do not even let him think that you claim any authority over him. Let him only know that he is weak and you are strong, that his condition and yours puts him at your mercy; let this be perceived, learned, and felt.... If there is something he should not do, do not forbid him, but prevent him without explanation or reasoning....[38]

The goal of this training is to produce an individual who would, as an adult, be free: "Freedom, not power," Rousseau tells us, "is the greatest good."[39] Free of what? Free, primarily, of the pernicious influences of society. For Rousseau, a child, raised successfully, will become a Natural Man. "God makes all things good; man meddles with them and they become evil."[40] Thus, the proper education of a child "should be merely negative. It consists, not in teaching virtue or truth, but in preserving the heart from vice and from the spirit of error."[41]

Thus, Locke and Rousseau agree that a central goal of parenting is to raise children to be free. Where they differ is in their views on what constitutes freedom and on what steps should be taken to foster freedom in a child. Locke thinks that a free individual is one whose will is guided by reason and that we teach children to be reasonable by making them submit to our will. Rousseau, on the other hand, thinks that a free individual is one who has not been corrupted by society; and he argues that nature will teach our children to be free, if only we will let it.

Although Locke and Rousseau both oppose the ownership model of parenting, it is clear that Locke's approach to raising children requires far more of parents than Rousseau's. Indeed, in Rousseau's plan, parents ideally won't need to do anything at all, since a tutor will raise their child—and for free! And even if no tutor appears, it will presumably require less effort for parents to allow nature to instruct their children (as Rousseau would have them do) than to exercise constant parental authority (as Locke would have them do).

A Question of Values

Notice that as goals go, freedom is relatively value-neutral. People with widely differing values might agree on the importance of raising a child to be free and providing a child with both the formal and informal educations described above.

Some, however, will be troubled by this value-neutrality. They might argue that it would be a mistake for parents simply to raise their children to be free, for it raises the question, Free to do what? A case can be made, in other words, that besides providing their child with the tools required for freedom (a formal education, the ability to make meaningful choices, etc.), steward-parents should also provide their child with a sense of what to do with those tools. Or, to change the analogy, in raising a child to be free, steward-parents provide him with a ship and a set of maps that will enable him to sail to almost any destination he chooses. Shouldn't they also, as parents, provide him with a sense of which destinations are worth sailing to and which aren't?

This sounds plausible, but the steward-parent, when he transmits values to his children, will keep two very important things in mind.

First, he will realize that reasonable people can value different things in life. In many cases it will be difficult, if not impossible, to "prove" that one value system is better than another.[42] Furthermore, part of the reason that different people value different things in life is because different people have different personalities. If a parent's personality is different from that of his child, his values might differ from those of the adult his child will become.

Second, he will keep in mind that in his attempts to transmit values to his children he runs a danger of "brainwashing" them, and thereby negating many of his efforts to increase their freedom. Consider, by way of example, a child who, thanks to his parents' efforts, could do any number of things with his life, but who has been told from his earliest days that there is only one thing worth doing in life—say, running the family business. Such a child would not be free.

The desire to live vicariously through one's children is common in parents. You know the mistakes you made in your own life. When you have children, you get a second chance at life—or as close as you can come to it in this world. It is very tempting to guide your child's personal, educational, and career choices, helping him avoid the mistakes you made and seize the opportunities you missed, and thereby providing him the life you wish you had had. Of course, in doing so you deprive him of the life he might have wanted. What would have been the perfect life for you might be a life of perfect misery for him.

A fine line separates giving a child helpful advice on life and engaging in a low-grade form of brainwashing. For a steward-parent, production of a child who thinks like and lives like his parents might not be a sign of success, particularly if the child in question feels he has no choice but to be that way.

Should the goal of the steward-parent, then, be to *avoid* the transmission of values altogether? Clearly not, for it is a goal that is unattainable. Parents cannot help but transmit values to a child. In the way they treat him, relate to him, behave when he is present, and react to situations that arise, they educate their child about what they think is valuable in life. The choice that steward-parents have, then, is not *whether* to transmit values to their child, but *what* values to transmit.

And when it comes to transmitting values, parents have a variety of choices. To begin with, they can simply transmit whatever values they happen to possess. For most parents this is easiest and most natural. Alternatively, they might choose to transmit certain of their values to their child but withhold others—they might, for example, keep hidden from him the extent to which they value recreational use of a certain drug. Or they might try to transmit to their child values that are at odds with their own, telling him, say, how wonderful opera is, when in fact they hate opera.

In talking about the values of "the parents," we are assuming that a child's two parents share the same values, which often is not the case. Suppose, for example, that the mother thinks it is important for children to learn the values of one religion while the father favors the values of another religion. (With such differing values, is it likely that the parents would marry and have a child? It happens.) The parents in question could choose to indoctrinate the child in the values of one of the two religions (i.e., one parent could "sacrifice" his values); or they could indoctrinate their child in the values of both religions, even though the values in question were in many senses incompatible; or they could raise their child without religious values.

Parents might also have conflicting political values (e.g., one parent is conservative and the other is liberal), conflicting aesthetic values (e.g., one parent likes opera and the other likes baseball), or conflicting moral values (e.g., one parent likes barbecued ribs and the other refuses to eat them on moral grounds). Or the parents might have conflicting views on "the meaning of life," with one parent feeling it important to have lots of friends, and the other parent feeling it important to have lots of money even if you have to lose friends to make it.

Notice, finally, that regardless of what values parents attempt to transmit to their children, they also have a choice concerning what alternative value-systems to expose their children to and what form the exposure should take. If, for example, both parents are practicing Catholics, should they expose their child to other religions? And if they do, should they bad-mouth other religions or treat them as reasonable alternatives to their own? Likewise, if both parents are political liberals or baseball-lovers, to what extent and in what manner should they make their child aware of those who hold differing views?

The discussion of values that follows will be limited in scope and restrained in the conclusions it draws. I will proceed by considering various categories of values. Within each category I will comment on the choices involved for steward-parents. My goal is not so much to declare a certain set of values to be the official value-set of steward-parents, but rather to discuss some of the things that steward-parents will take into account when deciding what values to transmit to their children.

Recreational Values

Parents will typically value some recreational activities more than others. Some parents might favor watching baseball over watching opera, and others might favor knitting over watching either baseball or opera. The question thus arises, To what extent should parents attempt to transmit their recreational values to their children?

If some recreational activities were demonstrably superior to others, we could argue that it was the duty of steward-parents to transmit to their children a preference for the former activities. Of course, it will be difficult for us to "rank" recreational activities. Consider, by way of example, the question of which is recreationally better, watching opera or watching baseball. Each activity has ardent supporters who will be more than willing to point out the redeeming features of their favored activity. The argument will not soon be settled.

When it comes to recreational activities, it is important that we keep two things in mind. First, recreational activities are generally acquired tastes: It requires an "investment" of time and effort before a recreational activity becomes pleasurable. Second, how easy a taste a recreational activity is to acquire depends to a considerable extent on the personality of the person in question. This suggests that steward-parents would do well, rather than trying to force their own recreational values on their children, to expose their children to a wide variety of recreational activities. This might mean that opera-loving parents expose their child to baseball, or conversely, that baseball-loving parents expose their child to opera. This will increase the chance that their child will find recreational activities suited to his personality. It is also possible that by being exposed to a wide variety of recreational activities, their child will be better able to acquire new recreational tastes as an adult, as his personality evolves.

In the final analysis, what matters most is not so much *what* recreational activities (within broad limits) children have as *that* they have recreational activities. It is, after all, better to go through life with some acquired tastes than with none at all, better to go through life with a passion for something (even if that passion might be difficult to defend rationally) than to go through life utterly passionless.

Occupational Values

One of the most important decisions a child can make, on reaching adulthood, is his choice of an occupation. It is not uncommon for parents to long for their children to follow, occupationally speaking, in their footsteps. If the father or mother was a lawyer, then the children should be lawyers—or, if not lawyers, at least highly-paid professionals.

I myself am no stranger to this longing. I happen to be a philosopher by profession, and there is a side of me that would love nothing more than for my children to follow in my footsteps. And I confess that I have used whatever opportunities arose to inform them of the advantages of the profession. At the same time I realize that what is important is not so much that my children follow in my footsteps, vocationally speaking, as that they find something as rewarding for them as philosophy is for me. It is entirely possible that they are not well suited, in terms of personality, to a life of professional philosophizing, and it would be a grave mistake for them to choose a career just to make me happy or in the misguided belief that it is the only career worth having.

Which is the better vocation, being a high-paid lawyer or being a low-paid cook at a fast-food restaurant? The question will be answered in different ways by different people. In this respect, it's like the question, Who would make a better wife, Madonna or Eleanor Roosevelt? The question immediately gives rise to a second question: Better wife for whom?

There are people who, by virtue of their personalities and talents, are far better suited to life as a cook than as a lawyer; if these people tried to become lawyers they would not only feel unfulfilled, but probably wouldn't be very successful. It is hard to be good at something you hate doing.

Many would respond to these claims by pointing out that lawyers make more money than fast-food cooks, the implication being that this alone makes it a better vocation. There are some obvious problems with this response.

In the first place, money isn't everything. Parents should keep in mind that job satisfaction is not only important, but is arguably more important than money. Does it make sense, after all, to spend a third of your adult life doing something you hate simply in order to have more money, money you might spend trying to heal the psychic wounds brought on by your dissatisfaction with your career?

Thoreau wrote that the mass of men lead lives of quiet desperation, and in my working life I have seen more than enough to convince me that—at least in terms of people's occupational choices—he was right. It is far better to be low-paid but happy in your work than highly-paid and miserable.

In the second place, even if the above comments are mistaken and money *is* everything, it is far from obvious that parents will be maximizing their children's financial prospects by pushing them into a career they dislike. Consider, by way of illustration, the person who loves cooking but who, simply in order to fulfill his parents' wishes, embarks on a law career. There is a reasonable chance that this person won't complete his law training or that he will complete it but will abandon the practice of law after a short period. Such a person might end up financially worse off, after a decade, than he would have been if he had started out doing something that, although less lucrative than the practice of law, was something he loved doing. In particular, if he had started out as a cook in a fast-food restaurant, he might (driven by his passion for things culinary) have gone on to become a highly-paid chef in a fancy restaurant. The idea here is that in the long run you are far more likely to succeed (financially speaking) in a career you love than in one you hate. Thus, if parents were (somewhat misguidedly) interested solely in their children's financial well-being, they might be making a big mistake by trying to force their children into careers they're indifferent to or—even worse—that they despise.

While I am on the subject of jobs, let me offer a few thoughts on "ideal jobs." In the ideal job it will be difficult for a person to tell, at any given moment, whether he is at work or at play. In the ideal job someone pays you to do the thing you would most want to do if you were independently wealthy and didn't need to work for a living. The ideal job will therefore be different things to different people.

For me, teaching philosophy is the ideal job, or something very close to it; but for someone else who didn't like spending his days alternately nurturing and arguing with college students—which is what, basically, I do for a living—it might be hell on earth.

How does one find the ideal job? It is difficult to say. Let me describe, though, how I came to have what is for me the ideal job, and then try to generalize from the particulars of my case.

My journey toward an ideal job began in sixth grade. The teacher instructed us to give a two-minute talk on a topic of our own choosing. I was fascinated by meteorology at the time and decided to do a talk on the weather. My two-minute talk went on for fifteen minutes before being terminated by the end-of-period bell. I discovered that I liked explaining things I had figured out to groups of people. I discovered, in other words, that I liked to teach.

Although this sixth-grade experience might have predisposed me toward a career in teaching, the question remained, Teach what? The thought of teaching philosophy did not spring to mind, largely because I didn't realize that philosophy existed. I became aware of its existence by accident: When I was in high school I happened to watch a public-television biography of Bertrand Russell, the British philosopher. As a senior in high school, I read Bertrand Russell's autobiography. I found myself captivated by his uniquely philosophical approach to life.

In college I set out on a math/physics double-major, but dabbled in philosophy. I soon discovered that philosophy was more to my liking than physics, and decided to look into the possibility of switching to a math/philosophy double-major. I went to the office of one of my philosophy professors and knocked on his door. He yelled to come in, and when I did, I found him lying on his office couch, reading. In most professions his behavior would have been frowned upon; but as a philosophy professor, he was doing exactly what his employers were paying him to do: He was thinking.

In that moment my occupational fate was sealed. It dawned on me that the prospect of being paid to read books that I wanted to read anyway was rather attractive. And the prospect of getting paid to share my discoveries with groups of students was not in the least disturbing.

There was, it should be clear, a fair degree of luck involved in my obtaining an ideal job. Suppose, for instance, I had never seen the television show on Bertrand Russell. Or suppose that my quest for employment after getting a Ph.D. in philosophy had failed—as it very nearly did. At the same time, my own life illustrates the importance of childhood experiences in helping one discover an ideal career. It suggests that steward-parents are doing their children a favor when they "push" them to try new things, and if, when their children develop new interests, they help their children explore these new interests.

Although steward-parents are generally making a serious mistake if they attempt to pick their child's career, they can nevertheless offer their child important advice in choosing a career. The child might, for instance, be blind to the realities of a particular career path; steward-parents can make their child aware of these realities.

In the end, the best piece of advice steward-parents can provide their career-seeking children is probably this: Find out what it is that you love to do, and then figure out a way to get paid to do it.

Religious Values

Many parents take one of their most important duties to be the transmission of their religious values to their children. These parents spend a fair amount of time and energy "indoctrinating" their children in the ways of their religion and have as a goal that their children retain their religious faith throughout their life.

In what follows, I will downplay the importance of transmitting religious values to one's children. Indeed, I will argue that if parents want their child to be truly religious, it is perhaps best that they give their child no religious training at all.

It is not necessarily a tragedy if children end up with different religious values than their parents. To see why I say this, let us consider a pair of parents—call them Mr. and Mrs. Smith. The Smiths have religious values that are either different from those of their parents or the same.

If the Smiths' religious values are *different* from those of their parents, then they should realize that in the same way as *they* found it personally rewarding to abandon their parents' religious beliefs and develop beliefs of their own, *their children* might find it personally rewarding to do the same.

If, on the other hand, the Smiths' religious values are *the same as* those of their parents, they should realize that although *they* stayed true to their parents' religion, they have ancestors who did not. We may have to go back many generations to find these dissenting ancestors, but they are there. The ancestors in question abandoned *their* parents' religious values in favor of others they found more personally rewarding; it is because they did so and because succeeding generations of Smiths stayed true to their parents' religion that Mr. and Mrs. Smith (in the case we are considering) have the religious beliefs they do.

To better understand this last branch of the argument, suppose that Mr. and Mrs. Smith favor, say, Lutheranism because it was the religion of their parents, who favored it because it was the religion of *their* parents, and so on. Not all of the Smiths' ancestors can have been Lutherans: It has been possible to be a Lutheran only for a few hundred years. Thus, if we look back in Mr. and Mrs. Smith's family trees, we must of necessity find ancestors who abandoned, say, their parents' Catholicism to adopt Lutheranism. For this reason, it seems inconsistent at best (and hypocritical at worst) for the Smiths to declare that children should stay true to their parents' religion: The Smiths are Lutherans today precisely because their ancestors ignored this advice.

A variant of this argument, by the way, could have been used back in our discussion of occupational values. Suppose that a business has been in the family for generations and the current owners are pressuring their children to take it over. It is clearly inconsistent for these parents to argue that children should follow in their parents' occupational footsteps; for if these parents' ancestors— and in particular, the ancestor who started the family business— had followed this advice, the very business that the parents so value wouldn't exist. If parents are thankful for the occupational freedom of this ancestor, doesn't consistency require them to respect the occupational freedom of their children?

Someone might, at this point, try to defend the transmission of religious values by arguing that children who lack religious values will also lack ethical values—that they won't know the difference between right and wrong.

In reply to this, let me point out that it is entirely possible to teach ethics without appealing to religion. Consider, after all, the manner in which Christians commonly teach ethics. First they extract various ethical principles from the Bible. One central ethical principle, for most Christians, would be the Golden Rule (discussed back in Chapter 8). Other ethical principles would be commandments like, "You shall not kill" and "You shall not steal." They then teach these principles to their children.

The thing to realize about this process is that most of the ethical principles extracted and taught by Christians are nonreligious principles. The Golden Rule can as easily be espoused by a Hindu or an atheist as by a Christian. Likewise for the "commandments" prohibiting murder and theft. And since the principles that lie at the heart of Christian ethics are not themselves religious, it is possible to teach not just ethics, but "Christian ethics" in a nonreligious manner.

A Christian might reply to this suggestion by saying that without Christianity, the principles of Christian ethics will have no force. Suppose your child asks *why* it is wrong to steal. The Christian parent can answer that God punishes those who steal—perhaps with hellfire and damnation, perhaps with some lesser punishment. The atheist, on the other hand, can offer no such sanction. Won't his children therefore be disinclined to take ethics seriously?

It is true that those who teach children ethics outside of a religious framework cannot invoke hellfire to get their children to toe the ethical line. They can, however, appeal to their child's reason in support of various ethical principles: "How do you like it when people steal from you?" They can also teach their child that one should do the right thing, not out of fear of getting caught and punished, but *because it is the right thing to do*.

A person who does the right thing out of fear of getting punished will be tempted to do the wrong thing as soon as he thinks he can avoid punishment. A person who does the right thing because it is the right thing to do will not likewise be tempted: For him, the point is not to avoid punishment but to do right. A case can be made, then, that not only is it *possible* to teach children right and wrong outside of a religious framework, but that in some ways it is *preferable* to do so.

Someone might also defend the transmission of religious values to children by arguing that unless you introduce your children to religion when they are young, you make it unlikely that religion will ever play an important part in their life. According to this argument, religion is like ballet: Unless a person starts his training at an early age, it is unlikely that he will be able to dance successfully as an adult.

This argument is less than persuasive, though, when we realize that the world is full of people who successfully acquired religion as adults. Indeed, not only is it possible for people to acquire religion as adults, but a case can be made that if what parents want is for their children not merely to possess religion, but to possess it ardently, they would do well not to try to indoctrinate their child with religion, but to wait until he is an adult and then do their best to precipitate in him a "religious crisis." People who have been raised in a religion have a tendency to take their religion for granted. People who discover a religion as adults—for example, "born again" Christians—tend not to take their religion for granted, but to *live* their religion.

Of course, most parents, while wanting their children to be religious, want them not to be *too* religious. One wonders, then, whether some parents indoctrinate their children in a religion from their earliest days to avoid the "danger" of having them discover religion as adults—that is, to avoid the danger of their taking religion "too seriously."

Finally, someone might argue that if parents fail to pass on their religious values to their child, their child's soul is doomed; and what parent who cares about his child would allow his soul to be doomed?

The problem with this line of argument is that many competing religions claim to be the one true religion—that is, the one that, if you follow it, will save your soul from damnation. And to the unbiased outsider, the evidence that these religions adduce in support of this claim is of comparable quality. (To "insiders," of course, it does not seem this way. *Their* holy writings are undeniably authentic, while those of competing religions are fraudulent.) This makes it hard to tell which, if any, of the competing "true religions" is in fact true; and this in turn means that parents, in choosing a religion for their children, might well be choosing the wrong one and thereby dooming their child's soul. Better, perhaps, to let the child size up the odds for himself as an adult.

Having said all this, I don't mean to suggest that religious parents should hide their religious values from their children. If parents take solace in a religion, if it gives their life meaning, then they are probably doing their child a favor by introducing him to the religion. The child might, after all, find as much solace in it as they do. At the same time, though, they should let the child understand not only that other religious beliefs are possible, but that many thoughtful people feel about these other religions the way they feel about their chosen religion; and that although their religion happens to suit their spiritual needs better than alternative religions do, it might not be best-suited to the spiritual needs of the child.

Most American parents would not dream of choosing their child's future spouse. They might justify this "hands off" stance in three ways. First, they might reason that unless a spouse is the child's choice, it is unlikely that the child will be truly devoted to the spouse; and if the child is not truly devoted, it makes it much less likely that the marriage will succeed. Second, they might reason that their child has a much better understanding of what it is that he or she needs in a spouse than they do. Third, they might reason that the choice of a spouse is such an important life-choice with such serious consequences for one's future happiness that it would be presumptuous for one individual to undertake to make this choice for another.

In much the same way, it is not unreasonable for parents to take a "hands off" stance as far as the religion of their children is concerned. First, they might reason that unless their child comes to a religion of his own free will, it is not likely to fulfill his spiritual needs. Second, they might reason that their child (when he is grown) has a much better understanding of his spiritual needs than they have. And third, they might reason that the choice of a religion has such serious consequences for one's future happiness (particularly if we believe that those who choose the "wrong" religion will go to hell) that it would be presumptuous for them to make this choice for their child.

In a way, religious values are like clothing. An article of clothing that fits one person wonderfully well might not fit another. An article of clothing that fits the father or mother might not fit the son or daughter. Parents should keep this in mind when considering the issue of whether and how to pass on religious values to their children. The religion that is right for the parents—that satisfies *their* spiritual needs—might not be right for their children.

When a parent feels compelled to raise his child in a certain faith and then do what he can to "force" his adult child to remain in that faith, he may be serving the interests of his religion in doing so, but it is far from clear that he is serving his child's interests. Parents who put the interests of their church (or any other organization) above the interests of their children in most cases are not acting as steward-parents.

Goal-Related Values

If a steward-parent has as goals that his children be happy and free during their lives, there are certain values he will want to instill in them—namely, those values which, if held, will make it more likely that his children will remain happy and free as adults.

Consider, to begin with, what might be called *freedom-preserving values*. These are values which, if someone possesses them, increase the chance that he will live his life in freedom. Some obvious freedom-preserving values that steward-parents might want to instill in their children are a healthy fear of recreational drugs (since addictions deprive one of freedom) and respect for the law (since jails deprive one of freedom). Steward-parents might also want to impress on their children the importance of attaining financial independence (since those who are financially dependent on someone else are not free).

Likewise, steward-parents will want to instill *happiness-preserving values* in their children. These are values which, if someone possesses them, increase the chance that he will experience happiness.

What are some happiness-preserving values? Any answers that one might offer to this question will likely give rise to dispute, but let me suggest two values which, if parents instill them in their children, will likely increase their children's chances at happiness in life: the importance of maintaining one's self-respect and the importance of taking responsibility for one's actions and choices.

How does maintaining one's self-respect contribute to personal happiness? Before I try to answer this question, let me explain what I mean by self-respect.

The difference between self-respect and self-esteem is subtle. Indeed, the dictionary offers them as synonyms. Yet it is possible to tease apart two different concepts, both involving our opinion of ourselves. A person with self-esteem thinks that *the world* should hold him in high regard. A person with self-respect, on the other hand, holds *himself* in high regard.

Thus, a person who fully expects the world to despise him might nevertheless hold himself in high regard. Presumably, the early Christians who were fed to the lions were in this situation. The persecution they were subjected to may have stripped them of their self-esteem, but not of their self-respect. Conversely, a person who fully expects the world to admire him might nevertheless despise himself. Consider, by way of example, a bank president who is embezzling from his bank so that he may engage in a lavish lifestyle. This individual might bask in the world's admiration of him, and yet his knowledge that he is living a lie might cause him to have a very low opinion of himself.

Following in the footsteps of political philosopher Charles Murray, it is possible to observe certain distinguishing differences between self-esteem and self-respect. First, notice that whereas self-esteem can be "faked," self-respect cannot. It is one thing to trick others into admiring and respecting you; it is quite another thing to convince yourself that you are worthy of respect when you know, in your heart of hearts, that you are not.[43] Second, while it is easy to imagine ourselves criticizing a person for having too much self-esteem (i.e., for being too self-important), it is hard to imagine a situation in which we would criticize a person for having too much self-respect.[44] Third, notice that although it is possible for others to do things that boost your self-esteem, it is not likewise possible for others to do things that boost your self-respect. Thus, although you might boost someone's self-esteem by praising him (whether he deserved your praise or not), you cannot likewise boost his self-respect by praising him. To the contrary, it would appear that the only one who can boost a person's self-respect is that person himself, and that the best way for him to boost it is by living in accordance with his values—by consistently doing what he takes to be "the right thing." And what enhances a person's self-respect the most is when he does the right thing even though it causes him pain to do so.

It should be clear that both self-esteem and self-respect are connected with a person's happiness. If a person is lacking in self-esteem—in particular, if he feels that the world despises him—it is unlikely that he will be happy. Similarly, if a person is lacking in self-respect—if he finds himself to be loathsome—it is unlikely that he will have a happy existence, even if the whole world admires him.

It follows that steward-parents who want their child to be happy should be concerned both with their child's level of self-esteem and level of self-respect. Notice, however, that parents will take different steps to deal with these concerns. To build their child's self-esteem, they will offer him their unconditional love. They will behave toward their child in a positive fashion, praising him when he deserves praise. And to build their child's self-respect? Well, as was explained above, there is an important sense in which *they* cannot build their child's self-respect; only *he* can. And he must do it by doing "the right thing," especially when doing the right thing is painful. What steward-parents *can* do, though, is to teach their child the importance of doing "the right thing" and thereby maintaining his self-respect. Steward-parents will, in other words, be quite interested in the old-fashioned concept of character, and they will do what they can to "build character" in their children.

Sometimes a parent's goal of maintaining his child's self-esteem will come into conflict with his goal of helping his child maintain his self-respect. Suppose, for example, that his child does something wrong: Say he steals something from a store. In such a case, a parent has a choice. On the one hand he can tell his child that what he did wasn't really so bad, that lots of people steal, and so on. In doing so he will preserve his child's self-esteem, but undermine his child's self-respect. On the other hand he can shame his child for his behavior. In doing so, he might crush (for the time-being, at least) his child's self-esteem, but he will make it more likely that his child will, in the long run, maintain his self-respect. Or consider a parent who, in his efforts to boost his child's self-esteem, carefully arranges things so that his child wins any competition he enters. (The parent might accomplish this by bribing his child's competitors.) This maneuver might do wonders for the child's self-esteem, but it would undermine his self-respect if he became aware of the reason for his victories.

Thus, parents will sometimes find that in their relations with their child, they must choose, at a given moment, between taking steps that boost his self-esteem but deal his self-respect a blow, and taking steps that will help him maintain his self-respect but deal his self-esteem a blow. When faced with such choices, I think that most steward-parents will choose self-respect over self-esteem: Self-esteem is easier to restore when it is lost than is self-respect. Furthermore, consistently maintaining one's self-respect can by itself generate a certain amount of self-esteem.

The other happiness-preserving value that a steward-parent might want to transmit to his children is the importance of taking responsibility for their actions and for the choices they make.

At first this advice might sound counterproductive: Someone who takes responsibility for what he does will have to admit his mistakes, his failures, his shortcomings. Surely such admissions will cause him not happiness, but its opposite. Why, then, am I suggesting that taking responsibility for one's life will induce happiness?

Research has shown, curiously enough, that people who believe that events are under their own control—who believe that what happens to them is a consequence of the choices they make rather than being attributable to fate, luck, or "external forces"—are more likely to be happy than people who do not.[45] Although taking responsibility for one's life may cause moments of unhappiness—as happens when a person admits his mistakes and failings—it also makes possible periods of happiness, and the happiness of these periods would appear to more than compensate for the moments of unhappiness.

Why should this be? One possibility is that a person who takes responsibility for his life is more likely to take steps to shape his future—and shape it for the better—than a person who does not take responsibility for his life. Indeed, if you thought that what happened to you was entirely a matter of luck or fate, there would be little reason to spend your days working toward some goal, since—according to your worldview—whether you attained the goal in question would have nothing to do with how hard you worked toward it, but would instead be due to factors outside your control. But if taking responsibility for your life makes it more likely that you will take steps to shape your future, and if taking such steps makes it more likely that your future will be an agreeable one, then it follows that a person who takes responsibility for his life is likely to have a future that is more agreeable, and more conducive to personal happiness, than a person who does not take responsibility for his life.[46]

Let me end this section with some final thoughts about ethical values. That a steward-parent will want to teach his children ethical values is, I think, clear. For one thing, these values are freedom-preserving values: Children who lack these values are much more likely to have their liberty curtailed by the legal system than children who possess them. A case can be made, though, that they are also happiness-preserving values. A child who is convinced of the importance of doing "the right thing" is more likely to maintain his self-respect than a child who is not; and since, as we have seen, a person's level of self-respect is linked to his level of happiness, it follows that a child who is convinced of the importance of doing the right thing is more likely (all other things being equal) to be happy than a child who is not.

This last point also reinforces my view that steward-parents, when they teach their children ethical values, will not want to tell them they should do the right thing because they will be punished if they don't; rather, they should teach them to do the right thing *simply because it is the right thing to do.* The child who does the right thing only out of fear of being punished will likely do the wrong thing as soon as he thinks he can get away with it. The problem is that such transgressions, although they may go unpunished, are likely to be ruinous to his self-respect. The child who does the right thing simply because it is the right thing to do will be less likely to undermine his own self-respect. He will realize that even though you might fool others in your transgression, you won't fool yourself.

Valuing Love

Some will read what I have said so far and complain that I have neglected a very important ingredient in the parent/child relationship—love. Parents typically love their children, and they typically hope that their children will love them in return. When their children grow up, parents long at first for their companionship and later for their emotional support. And when parents are on their deathbed, the faces of their children are among those they will most want to see. So, along with educating children to be free, doesn't it also make sense to educate children to love? And more generally, doesn't it make sense to educate children to value love and understand its importance as a motivating factor in human affairs—to understand that love may very well be what makes the world go 'round?

There is much to be said for this suggestion, but some comments are in order.

First, if you want your children to genuinely love you, it is important that you raise them to be free. For love to be genuine, after all, it must be given freely. If you "force" someone to love you, the "love" you receive will be a pale and pathetic imitation of the real thing; and it is arguable that only a mentally unbalanced individual would seek or value "forced love."

An owner-parent might, out of a desire for his children's love, take a number of steps to "make" them love him. When, for example, they are little, he might punish them for showing a fondness for other people; and when they are adults, he might threaten to withhold an inheritance from them unless they shower him with their love.

Steward-parents, on the other hand, wouldn't dream of forcing their children to love them, and as a result, they run the risk that their children will use the freedom that—thanks to the efforts of their parents—they possess as adults to direct their love elsewhere. When faced with this risk, the proper response of the steward-parent is clear: It is true that the love of his children is not guaranteed, but then again, who would want "guaranteed love"? Unless it is freely given, love is not particularly worth having. And because a steward-parent raises his children to be free, any love they *do* choose to bestow as adults will be genuine love, not the ersatz love that owner-parents must settle for.

Another thing that steward-parents should keep in mind is that perhaps the best way to win the love of your children is by showering them with unconditional love as they grow. If a child is incapable of responding to this level of devotion, there are serious questions about whether the child is capable of love at all.

Notice, finally, that a wonderful way to teach a child about the power of love is to let the child watch love work. The child can witness the loving bonds between parents, between siblings, and between parents and children. He can see for himself how love benefits both the person who gives it and the person who receives it. He will come to understand that his parents go to such great lengths to do what's right for him because they love him and genuinely care about his well-being. It may take a child years or decades to put this parental love into perspective, but as he grows up and experiences the world firsthand—as he witnesses its indifference and its cruelty—he will (it is hoped) come to understand what a remarkable thing his parents' love was.

Other Values

The above discussion of the transmission of parental values only begins to scratch the surface. In the process of parenting, a number of questions will naturally arise concerning what values parents should transmit to their children. Which should they tell their children is the better strategy in life, playing it safe or taking (sensible) risks? Which is better, having an abundance of money to buy things with, or having an abundance of time for personal development? Which is better, having lots of casual acquaintances, or a handful of true friends? Which is better, the liberal political viewpoint, or the conservative political viewpoint?

The questions just listed are, obviously, questions about which reasonable people can differ. Indeed, they are questions that a given person might, after years of trying, remain unable to answer for himself. Perhaps the sensible thing for the steward-parent to do with regard to these questions is not to try to implant certain answers in his children, but to help his child explore the issues involved and come up with his own answers. He should keep in mind the reaction of Cronshaw, a character in W. Somerset Maugham's *Of Human Bondage*, when asked to explain the meaning of life: Cronshaw refuses to answer the question on the grounds that any answer is "worthless unless you yourself discover it."[47]

CHAPTER 10

REINVENTING THE FAMILY

Are some family structures better than others, if what we are interested in is a child's well-being? In this chapter I will answer this question in the affirmative. More precisely, I will argue that if we had at heart the needs and interests of children (as opposed to the needs and interests of their parents), we would structure families in a way that is quite different from how many families in America are now structured.

My discussion of family structure will proceed in four stages. In the first stage, I ask whether there are reasons for favoring a certain number of parents per family. Generally speaking, can one parent do as effective a job of stewardship as two? And would three or more parents do an even more effective job than two? In the second stage, I ask whether we should, in designing our "Model Family," care about the sexes of the parents. Would a family with two parents, one male and one female, be preferable to a family with two female parents or two male parents? In the third stage, I ask what the relationship between parents should be. Should they be merely friends? Should they be lovers? Should they be married? And in the fourth and final stage, I examine the issue of family size. More precisely, I ask whether, if our primary interest is the well-being of children, we will be concerned with the number of children parents have.

It is important to keep two things firmly in mind as you read this chapter. The first is that all my comments are based on the stewardship model of parenting. If you reject this model of parenting, you will find yourself unsympathetic to my suggestions about how the family might be redesigned. The second is that the family structure I end up advocating is a "model" family structure in the sense that it is the structure that steward-parents should, to the extent possible, strive to obtain. My claim is not that families that fail to conform to this model should not be allowed to exist; nor is my claim that families that fail to conform to this model are invariably worse for children than families that do conform. My only claim is that the family structure I advocate is the structure that, *by and large*, will do the best job of catering to the needs and interests of children.

How Many Parents?

How many parents should there be in the "Model Family"? The traditional answer to this question was that there should be two parents per family, and two-parent families were in fact the norm. This is no longer the case. Indeed, among certain segments of the population, the two-parent family is the exception: Demographer Larry L. Bumpass has estimated that a black child born today has only a one-in-five chance of living with two parents until age sixteen.[1] And there are those who would argue not just that one-parent families are as good as two-parent families, but that one-parent families are in fact preferable to two-parent families, if what we are interested in is the well-being of children. Let me, then, begin my discussion by arguing that as far as our Model Family is concerned, two parents are better than one.

The Case for Two Parents

I can think of at least five reasons why a two-parent family would be preferable to a one-parent family.

First, in most cases it will be quite difficult for one person to shoulder the burdens of steward-parenthood. Being a steward-parent is a demanding twenty-four-hour-a-day job. While it is no doubt true that many single parents can meet the physical needs of a child, it is only the exceptional single parent who can go beyond this to meet the emotional and intellectual needs of a child as well; and if we are talking about more than one child, the burdens of parenthood become that much heavier, and the argument for parent-pairs becomes that much stronger.

In earlier chapters I suggested that many steward-parents will want their children to be raised by a stay-at-home parent. In almost every case, though, it will be easier for one parent of a parent-pair to act as stay-at-home parent than it will be for a single parent. The single parent, after all, will probably have to work for a living, and this will preclude a stay-at-home existence. With parent-pairs, one parent can earn the family's daily bread while the other acts as full-time parent.

Second, it is advantageous for a child to be raised by two parents inasmuch as two parents, particularly if they have diverse interests and talents, are more likely to do a thorough job of discovering and developing the talents and interests of their child than one parent would. (It will be remembered that this process of discovery and development is one of the more important tasks of the steward-parent.) The realm of potential talents and interests is, of course, enormous: It includes art, science, athletics, music, mathematics, and literature, for starters. It will be far easier for two people to "cover" (or at least attempt to cover) this realm than it would be for one person to do so.

Third, a two-parent family will typically be more "secure" than a one-parent family: A child with two parents will suffer less from disruptions caused by parental health problems or parental death than would a child with a single parent. It is much less likely that two parents be simultaneously laid up in a hospital than that one parent be laid up, or that two parents die simultaneously than that a single parent die.

A fourth advantage of being raised by two parents is that it makes it more likely that the parenting a child receives will be "balanced." In most two-parent situations, one parent will periodically lose perspective with regard to his parental role. It is helpful to have another parent around to help him regain his perspective. Consider, for example, the parent who mistakenly thinks that his child is talented at piano and keeps pushing him to take lessons, in the sincere belief that he is acting in the child's best interests. If there is a second parent around, it improves the odds that the piano-pushing parent will be shown the error of his ways sooner rather than later. Or consider the parent who, in a moment of exasperation, gives a stiff punishment to a child, much stiffer than the child deserves. A second parent could act, in such a case, as the child's court of appeals. In the absence of a second parent, the child has little choice but to take the punishment.

A parent-pair will typically offer a child two different personality types and two alternative worldviews. A child might benefit from having one parent who is risk-averse and a second parent who is more of a risk-taker, one parent who nurtures children and a second parent who challenges them, one parent who is politically conservative and a second parent who is politically liberal, one parent who is vivacious and a second parent who is taciturn. As the child develops, and as his own personality changes and his worldview takes form, having two parents makes it more likely that he will have, at the various stages of his development, someone he can relate to—and, perhaps just as important, someone he can "relate against." There are times when a child needs a parent who is gentle and understanding and times when he needs a parent who is unyielding, times when he needs a parent who will engage in a no-holds-barred tickling session and times when he needs a parent who will just lie still with him, times when he needs to be pushed to take chances and times when he needs to be restrained from taking them. It may be possible for a single person to shift from role to role—or from personality to personality—depending on the child's needs; one suspects, however, that it is far more likely that the child of a single parent will be expected to conform to whatever his parent's personality type happens to be. Also, a child with "diverse" parents will be more likely to emerge from childhood realizing that the world is a complex place, in which reasonable people can differ on basic issues.

A fifth reason it is advantageous for a child to be raised by two parents is that by having two parents, a child learns about adult relationships. As he observes the give-and-take between his parents, the support and encouragement they offer each other, the way they keep each other "in line," he will gain insight into human relationships. As the result of spending years observing what is (one hopes) a functioning relationship, the child has a better chance of entering into such a relationship as an adult. He is less likely, at any rate, to enter into a relationship full of unrealistic expectations, or to think that relationships are a one-way street, with all take and no give.

Some Replies

Above I have laid out the case for two parents in our Model Family. There are a number of ways in which the defender of single-parent families might respond to the points I raise.

To begin with, someone might admit that single-parents cannot effectively meet the needs of their children, but follow this admission with a defiant, "And so what? Parents are under no moral obligation to meet the needs of their children."

This criticism is misguided inasmuch as it ignores the fact that my arguments in this section are based on the assumption that the stewardship model of parenting is correct. I freely admit that if we "own" our children, it will be difficult to argue that they should have two parents, or any parents at all, for that matter.

A defender of single-parent families might also reply to my argument by pointing out that it is absurd to think, as I apparently do, that two-parent couples invariably will do a better job of parenting than single parents will. There are obviously lots of cases in which a family has two parents who either ignore or abuse their children; and likewise there are cases in which a single parent, through diligent effort, does a commendable job of raising his or her children.

I can't quarrel with this claim: It is undeniably true that some single parents do a better job of parenting than some parent-pairs. I would like to point out, however, that these claims in no way undermine my argument. My goal, as I laid it out above, is not to argue that two parents will *always* do a better job than one parent; instead, my goal is to design the Model Family—that is, the family that will, all things being equal, tend to do the best job of raising children. Thus, our goal as a society should be to encourage two-parent families—if, at any rate, the well-being of children is what our society is interested in. We should view single-parent families as (generally speaking) a second-best alternative.

What my argument for two-parent families shows, at best, is that parent-pairs will typically be somewhat more effective as steward-parents than single parents. And this "somewhat more effective" can be counterbalanced by other factors.

Thus, suppose that a committed parent-pair has children and that while they are still little, one of the parents, let's say the father, dies. According to the argument for parent pairs, the surviving mother will be a less effective steward-parent than she and the father were together. Indeed, the surviving mother will probably be the first to realize this. She might have to go to work and put her children in day care. She might not be able to pursue certain of her children's interests that, while he was alive, had been the father's "specialties." She might find it much harder to keep a balanced perspective as a parent: In particular, she might become somewhat depressed and, rather than being the cheerful mother she used to be, develop a quick temper with her children.

Should we, under these circumstances, declare this mother to be unfit to continue acting as steward for her children? Certainly not. It seems clear that her children will be better off, in the long run, remaining with her despite her diminished ability to act as steward than they would be if they were removed from her and turned over to a parent-pair whose stewardship abilities were unexcelled. In other words, the gain in quality of stewardship would be more than offset by the trauma the children would experience in being removed from the mother they love. The conclusion: While it may be *desirable* for children to have two parents, it is not *essential* that they have two parents.

In response to my claim that two parents are better than one because two can better shoulder the responsibilities of steward-parenthood, the defender of single-parent families might raise the following criticism: Although it is true that it would be arduous for one person to raise a child, the task can be made more manageable if the single parent hires help or gets help from relatives—much as the land steward might hire help or ask relatives for help if he felt overburdened by the job of stewardship he had taken on. It can likewise be argued that a single parent who has a limited range of interests or talents can make up for this by paying people who have other interests and talents to teach his children. He might, for example, sign his child up for classes at a museum, for music lessons, or for gymnastics training, where paid individuals will help him explore his interests and develop his talents.

I am willing to admit that if high-quality help is available, it will be possible for a single parent to effectively shoulder the burdens of parenthood. Of course, the "if" in the preceding sentence is a big one. Notice, for example, that quality day care is hard to come by. And a single parent who turns his child over to an unfit day-care provider is the moral equivalent of a land steward who turns over management of lands to an unskilled worker: He will have abandoned his role as steward. Notice, too, that even though it is possible for a single parent to pay people to help develop his child's talents, if that parent is sufficiently limited in the scope of his own interests and talents, it might not even occur to him, for example, to get oboe lessons for the child who had so enjoyed using a toy flute. The presence of a second parent, particularly one whose interests and talents complement those of the first parent, makes such an omission less likely.

Another problem with the suggestion that single parents hire help to make the burden of stewardship more bearable is that it takes money to hire help. Even if qualified steward-helpers are available, many single parents would find themselves unable to afford such helpers. They might instead be forced to settle for a diminished level of stewardship.

In reply to my claim that two parents provide better "security" for a child than one parent would, the advocate of single-parenthood might counter that having two parents creates a source of considerable insecurity that is avoided by single-parenthood—namely, the possibility of divorce or, if the two parents are unmarried, a breakup. The children of single parents, on the other hand, need never experience parental divorce or breakup.

This reply is curious, for in admitting that a divorce or breakup is a devastating event for a child, the advocate of single-parenthood seems to be admitting that children regard the change from a two-parent family to a one-parent family as a change for the worse. In short, he appears to be in agreement with my claim that two-parent families are, by and large, preferable to one-parent families.

Why Stop at Two?

It is worth noting that the above argument for two-parent families can easily be turned into an argument for more-than-two-parent families. If parent-pairs make the stewardship workload more manageable, think of what parent-triplets (consisting, perhaps, of two women and a man) could accomplish. Each parent in a parent-pair has 50 percent less work than a single parent would, but each parent in a parent-triplet has 33 percent less work than a parent in a parent-pair would. Similarly, if we are worried about parents "covering the bases" as far as their children's talents and interests are concerned, having more than two parents would make it that much easier to ensure that the child would be exposed to a wide variety of activities and subjects. And if we are interested in parents keeping a balanced perspective, having three or more parents would bring more voices—and correspondingly more balance—into the picture. Thus, if our goal is to show that as far as the stewardship model is concerned, the ideal number of parents is two, we will have to do more than argue that two parents are better than one; we will also have to argue that two parents are better than three or four or a dozen.

How might such an argument go? It would presumably have to point to problems that arise as the number of parents increases. Let us, in order to better focus our discussion, consider polygamous marriages.[2]

Picture, then, a family consisting of one man, his various wives, and their children. Knowing only this, is there any reason to think that in such a family the quality of stewardship would be lower than in a monogamous family consisting of a man, a woman, and their children?

It might be suggested, at the outset, that the quality of stewardship in the polygamous arrangement will be lower, inasmuch as the parent-to-child ratio will be worse. Consider, in particular, a polygamous family in which the man has ten wives, each of whom has one child. There will be a parent-to-child ratio of eleven-to-ten, much lower than the two-to-one parent-to-child ratio that exists when a monogamous man and woman have one child. At any rate, if we think that the quality of stewardship is proportional (all other things being equal) to the ratio of parents to children, then the quality of stewardship is likely to be higher in monogamous families than in polygamous families.

This argument is, however, misleading. In the example just considered, the parent-to-child ratio is indeed worse in the polygamous family. But consider another case: Compare the polygamous family just described with a monogamous couple that has *two* children. For this couple, the parent-to-child ratio will be one-to-one, slightly worse than the polygamous family's ratio of eleven-to-ten. Or compare a polygamous family consisting of a man, ten wives, and only three children with a monogamous family consisting of a man, his wife, and their ten children. The parent-to-child ratio in the former family will be eleven-to-three, and in the latter will be one-to-five: In this case, the polygamous family wins the ratio game hands down.

We might modify our argument to focus not on the parents-to-children ratio, but on the fathers-to-children ratio. More precisely, it might be suggested that in polygamous families, many children are forced to share the same father and that this robs them of the paternal attention they need and deserve.[3] This line of reasoning also fails, though. In a polygamous family with ten wives and ten children, each child gets one-tenth of a father; in a monogamous family with ten children, each child also gets one-tenth of a father. (And of course, in the monogamous family just described, each child gets only one-tenth of a mother, whereas in the polygamous family just described, each child gets a full mother; if we assume that mothers count for something, the polygamous family again wins the numbers game.)

Another way we might argue for limiting the number of parents to two is as follows. One problem that will arise in polygamous families but not monogamous families is rivalries between wives. In a monogamous family, the mother—ideally, at any rate—loves all the children equally: They are, after all, *her* children. (Well, not always. Let us, for the sake of argument, ignore "blended" families.) In a polygamous family, on the other hand, it might be difficult for the wives to love all the children equally. There might be a tendency to favor one's own children. This could get in the way of parental stewardship of children.

Suppose, in particular, that a wife is willing to subvert the interests of the children of the other wives in order to advance the interests of her own children. If this sort of thing were common, it would, on the stewardship model, count against polygamous parenting. Whether such rivalries are common, though, is unclear. Also, even if such rivalries exist, it is possible that there are counterbalancing goods that come from having "multiple mothers."

Above I have provided a number of reasons for thinking that, by and large, two parents are better than one if what we are concerned with is the well-being of children. The interesting—and for me, unexpected—thing about the argument for parent-pairs is how difficult it is to "turn off" the argument in question: The same reasoning that shows that two parents are better than one seems to show that three parents are better than two, and so on. Indeed, a case can be made that two parents with ten children will typically be worse stewards than ten parents with two children.

A Man and a Woman?

Suppose we accept that, generally speaking, two parents are better than one; and suppose we ignore, for the sake of argument, the advantages that might result from having more than two parents. There remains the issue of the sex of the two parents.

Many readers, on hearing me talk about the reasons to favor two-parent families over one-parent families, might have assumed that the two parents in question were a man and a woman. Strictly speaking, though, the reasons given above for favoring two-parent families do not directly imply anything about the sex of the two parents. They allow for the two parents to both be men or both be women.

Thus, consider my claim that two-parent families are preferable to single-parent families inasmuch as two parents can share the burdens of parenting better than a single parent. Notice that two men can as easily share the burdens of parenting as can a man and a woman. Or consider my claim that two-parent families are preferable to single-parent families inasmuch as two parents can do a better job of discovering and developing the talents of a child than a single parent can. Two women, one of whom is athletically inclined and the other of whom is musically inclined, might do a far better job of discovering and developing the talents of a child than might a man and woman whose interests are narrow and overlapping.

If we wish to show that the two parents in our Model Family should be a man and a woman, it will be incumbent upon us to come up with reasons why a man and a woman will generally do a better job of parenting than two men or two women will.

Some might argue for opposite-sex parents by appealing to parental love. Biological parents, they will tell us, love their children "by nature." Hence, a man and a woman, as biological parents of their children, will find it easier to love them and therefore do a better job of stewardship than would a man and a man or a woman and a woman, since these obviously could not both be the biological parents of their children; at least one member of each same-sex couple would be an adoptive parent.

The problem with this line of reasoning is that it is not at all difficult to find biological parents who do not love their children, but instead ignore or abuse them. Likewise, it is not at all difficult to find adoptive parents who are devoted to their adopted children. A case can be made, in other words, that adoptive parents can be every bit as loving as biological parents; and if this is true, then it should be possible for a man and a man, or a woman and a woman not just to love their children, but to love them as much as any parent can.

A more promising argument to show that parents should be a man and a woman is based on the notion that men and women tend to differ in certain ways and that because of these differences, each has something unique and valuable to bring to his or her role as parent. If men and women were really interchangeable, then two men or two women would parent as effectively as a man and a woman; but if there are gender differences between the sexes, and if the differences typically complement each other and thus bring "balance" to parenting, then there is reason to think that in our Model Family a child's parents should be of the opposite sex.

Are there significant gender differences between males and females? Only a radical feminist would deny it. To most people it is clear that little boys behave differently from little girls, that teenage boys behave differently from teenage girls, and that men behave differently from women. In making these claims I am not suggesting that it is good that gender differences exist, that these differences are the result of nature rather than nurture, or that these differences have to exist. I am simply suggesting that at present there are significant gender differences between males and females. And because these differences exist, we should take them into account when we design our Model Family.

Because of gender differences, there is reason to think that a child benefits from having at least one parent of the same sex as the child. This same-sex parent can play an important role as "gender-mentor."

The gender-mentor has two functions. The first is to help the child through the rites of passage involved in growing up and maturing sexually. The rites of passage of a boy will typically be significantly different from those of a girl; and the rites of passage in question will not only involve physical changes in the child but emotional changes as well. It can be quite valuable to a child, in going through the process of changing from a boy into a man or from a girl into a woman, to have a trusted figure nearby who is able to say, in essence, "I've been where you are, this is how it works, and if I lived through it, so can you." The second function of the gender-mentor is to provide a gender role model for the child. When, for example, a boy goes through puberty and its accompanying flood of hormones, there are a number of ways he can express his new sense of self. He can, for example, express his feelings of masculinity in a predatory fashion by joining a gang; alternatively he can express them by shouldering various responsibilities. What the gender-mentor can do is guide the boy through the maze of possible expressions of masculinity to find the one that will be best for the child.

To better understand the gender-mentoring process, suppose a woman tries to raise a boy. Although she might work hard at understanding the male experience—she might have read whatever books there are on the subject and talked to experts—there are many respects in which she would be a poor substitute for a male parent.

Consider first her responses to "rites of passage" crises. However much she might have learned about the male experience, she could never say to her son, as the ideal gender-mentor could, that "I've been where you are." Notice, too, that one of the typical (and unfortunate) male rites of passage involves attempts to dominate others through physical intimidation. A father will typically be bigger and stronger than (or approximately as big and strong as) his teenage son; the same generally cannot be said of the mother of a teenage son. But if a mother cannot win battles of physical domination with her son, her effectiveness as a parent might be diminished.

Because the experience of being a boy is so different from that of being a girl, there will likely be aspects of her son's behavior which, though well within boyish norms, will seem foreign to the single mother: Not only did she probably not engage in that behavior when she was a little girl, but most likely despised those who did. Thus, she might be shocked on hearing that her son has been throwing snowballs at passing vehicles. A man, on the other hand, probably wouldn't be all that dismayed by this behavior, especially when he reflected on his own boyish indiscretions.

A woman's attempts to guide her son's expression of his masculinity could easily backfire. When a woman casually mentions to her teenage son that she admires men who are thus-and-such, her son might make a mental note that the men in question are not men's men, but women's men, and are therefore anti-role models.

Like it or not, there is powerful chemistry between fathers and sons. A father is (or can be, if he accepts the role) an almost magical figure in a boy's life. When a father is absent from the scene—or physically present but not really functional—a boy's life is impoverished in a number of respects and he may suffer serious psychological damage. Numerous statistics indicate the harm done when boys are raised without fathers, but the following are particularly telling: In America, boys without fathers are far more likely to commit rape, commit adolescent murder, or become long-term prison inmates than boys with fathers.[4]

My father died twenty years ago, and nevertheless his memory haunts me. I am astonished by the intensity of my feelings both about the things he did for me and about what I perceive to have been his shortcomings. Powerful chemistry indeed. Had I not been raised under the influence of a father, I would clearly have been a different person—not that I would have understood or appreciated the magnitude of my loss.

Many of the above comments about mothers single-handedly raising sons apply equally well to a man attempting to raise a girl. Try as he will, he might not be able to understand, say, her sulkiness or her obsession with appearance.

I don't mean to suggest that a woman can't successfully raise a boy or that a man can't successfully raise a girl. If the woman or man is a sensitive individual who is willing to listen and learn, she or he can take various steps in an attempt to deal with the problems of opposite-sex parenting. A woman might, for example, try to offer her son as much contact with his uncles as possible, or a man might talk to his own mother for explanations of the unaccountable (from a male perspective) things his daughter does. What I am suggesting is that it is, all other things being equal, desirable for a child to be raised in part by a person of the same sex.[5]

At this point, someone could take my gender-mentor argument and turn it on its head. In particular, someone could argue that if a boy benefits from having one male parent, he could benefit even more from having two male parents—for example, a gay couple. Two fathers could do a better job than one in helping their son get through the crises involved in growing up male; two fathers would offer their son a double-helping of male role models; two fathers could easily subdue any of their son's attempts at physical domination; and so forth. And of course the same holds true for girls: If a girl benefits from having one female parent, she could benefit even more from having two female parents—for example, a lesbian couple.

In reply to this suggestion I must point out that although it is true that there are some things of importance that a child can best get from a parent of the same sex, there are other things of importance that a child can best get from a parent of the opposite sex. And one of these other things is what we might call gender balance. Because of gender differences (some of which I have described above), a man typically brings something different to parenting than a woman does: "Women," we are told, "tend to be *nurturers*, seeking to connect, be intimate with, and respond to their children. Men tend to be...*encouragers*, stressing the development of the children's independence."[6] Sometimes children need to be nurtured, particularly when they are infants. Sometimes they need to be encouraged, particularly when they are adolescents. And much of the time, what a child needs is a mix of nurturing and encouragement. Thus, when a child falls and hurts himself, he needs someone to sympathize with him and kiss the hurt, but he also benefits from having someone who, after the initial nurturing, says, basically, "Shake it off, and let's get back to play." A child will arguably lose out if he is overly nurtured, as might be the case if both his parents were nurture-oriented females; and would likewise lose out if he is overly encouraged, as might be the case if both his parents were encouragement-oriented males.

A child with a (typical) man and woman for parents will quickly discover the differences between the two. If he is in the mood for rough play or a tickling session, he will (in most families) head for the father, who will probably be an expert in both activities. If he is in the mood for a quiet interaction, perhaps as a prelude to a nap, he will head for the mother, who (if he is lucky) has been happy to engage in these quiet interactions for as long as he can remember.

In response to these comments, someone might suggest that I am mistaken if I think that only men can tickle or that only women can engage in a quiet interaction. And more to the present point, it could be that in a given family, the man is the quiet nurturer while the woman is the encourager who specializes in rough play. It could also be that two homosexual males exhibit the gender differences I describe: One of them might be a nurturing sort while the other might be an encouraging sort. If a homosexual couple was so constituted, they would arguably do as well at providing "gender balance" to their child as a heterosexual couple would.

These points are well taken. As long as a couple, regardless of their sex, provides gender balance, the above comments will not apply to them. Having said this, let me add that I think it would be the exceptional female who can successfully embody the full range of "masculine traits," and likewise it will be the exceptional male who can successfully embody the full range of "feminine traits." But if this is true, then *most* children will indeed benefit from being raised by a man and a woman, as opposed to two men or two women; and in describing my Model Family, I am of course interested in "most children."

Parental Relations

Suppose we are in general agreement, at this point, that in our Model Family, there will be two parents and that the two parents in question will be a man and a woman. This leaves open the nature of the relationship between this man and woman. In particular, it says nothing about whether the opposite-sex parents should be married. Let us, then, turn our attention to the issue of parental relations in the Model Family.

The first thing I think we can agree on is that in the Model Family, the parents will live full-time with their children. In much the same way as you cannot effectively act as steward for your neighbor's lands if you are not present, you cannot effectively act as steward for your children if you are not present. When one parent is always away, the other parent becomes, in effect, a single parent, and I have described above the disadvantages of single-parenthood.

If the two parents are to live full-time with their children, it follows that they will live full-time with each other. When the two parents are together under one roof, the child has unlimited access to both and will seek out one or the other depending on his needs of the moment. If he awakens from a nightmare at 3 A.M. and calls for one parent, that parent will be there; if at 3 P.M. he feels like a tickling session, the appropriate parent will be there; and if, when the tickling session has come to an end, he feels like cuddling, the appropriate parent will also be there. Even if one parent lives in the house next door to the house where his children live, it will to some extent impede his ability to act as steward-parent.

Of course, for children to have *unlimited* access to both parents is, for all but the independently wealthy, an impossibility. In most cases, even when a child's parents live together under one roof, they cannot both be accessible to the child all the time. Typically, one parent (or maybe both parents) must go away for hours at a time to make a living. Even allowing for this, though, it is clearly better for the child to have as much access as possible to both parents, and this is clearly best accomplished when both parents live together under one roof.

Above I have argued for the importance of children being in daily contact with an opposite-sex parent-pair. This leaves open the possibility of children having, over the years, a succession of opposite-sex parent-pairs. One parent might remain constant, while the second parent might change periodically (as the one parent's love life progresses); or both parents might change periodically as the couple who had the child hands him off to another opposite-sex parent-pair who might pass him along to yet another parent-pair. Nothing said above specifies the "stability" of parenthood.

I think that there will be general agreement that children benefit greatly from continuity in parenting—that is, from having the same two parents throughout childhood. When the same parents act as steward for a child over the course of his childhood, they can make long-term plans with respect to him and bring these plans to fruition. When the parents change every few years, so, typically, do the plans they have with respect to the child, and this change is typically detrimental to the child. Indeed, if parents' plans with respect to a child change often enough, they come to resemble no plan at all.

Furthermore, notice that children care very much about who parents them. They do not (or, ideally, should not) regard adults as interchangeable beings. Instead, they become attached to the adults who care for them and typically mourn the "loss" of one of these adults. (They may even mourn the loss of a bad parent.) A child's parents are his tour guides to what is, in many respects, a very frightening place—our world. When children "lose" a parent, they typically lose a trusted tour guide, and the trip becomes that much scarier.

The child faced with an endless succession of parents will naturally—and quite reasonably, I might add—draw the conclusion that no one really loves him, that there is no one for whom his well-being is a paramount concern. For a steward-parent, to have one's child feel unloved is the ultimate failure in stewardship, and the steward-parent will go to great lengths and make great personal sacrifices to prevent this from happening.

The family should be a source of psychic energy for a child, not a black hole that devours that energy. A family structure that—because of its stability—is one that a child can rely on, can even take for granted, should therefore be our ideal.

In making these remarks I do not mean to suggest that a change in parents is never a good thing for a child. Indeed, if a parent is extremely abusive to a child, removal of the parent will almost always benefit the child. Likewise, if parents are extremely abusive toward each other, removal of one parent might be in the best interests of their children. What I am suggesting is simply that in the typical family, children are significantly better off having the same two parents for all of their childhoods.

If I am right about the importance of parental stability, it follows that the parents in our Model Family should be bound by love. Love is probably the only "glue" strong enough to keep two people together through the nearly two decades required to raise their children—and even with love, there are no guarantees.

Not only should the parents in our Model Family be in love, but the love in question should involve a deep level of commitment. They should be prepared to stay together, through thick and thin, despite the changing circumstances of their lives in the coming decades, until their children are of age. They should stand ready to sacrifice, if necessary, much of their own freedom and happiness to fulfill this commitment.

To some ears, this will sound like a lot to ask: To sacrifice one's freedom and happiness for the sake of one's children. But the reader must remember that the present discussion is based on the stewardship model of parenting. A steward-parent knowingly assumes a number of obligations when he becomes a parent; and when it comes time to fulfill those obligations, he does his duty. If he didn't feel comfortable with this level of obligation, he wouldn't have become a parent in the first place.

Love and Marriage

The reader might conclude from the above discussion that in our Model Family, the parents will be married. Such a conclusion would be incorrect, for the commitment I have described is significantly *greater* than that required by the institution of marriage as it now exists in America.

This was not always the case. There was a time, before the no-fault divorce revolution in the 1970s, when marriage meant something. In particular, marriage was taken to be a contract, the breaking of which carried significant penalties for the "guilty" spouse. There might have been an unequal division of the property of the married couple, with the "guilty" spouse getting the smaller portion. The "guilty" spouse might also have been ordered to make alimony payments, possibly for life, to the "innocent spouse." With the advent of no-fault divorce, the notion that marriage involves a serious contract was abandoned. These days, either party to a marriage contract can break it on a whim and suffer no penalties for doing so. The courts no longer are interested in placing the blame for a failed marriage and are no longer interested in punishing the "blameworthy" party.

Stated bluntly, in America today there is little difference, as far as the level of commitment is concerned, between living with and marrying another person. In either case, you can walk out of the relationship on a whim and pay almost no price for doing so. (Indeed, when a man walks out of a marriage on a whim, he might benefit financially from doing so: He will no longer have to support his wife.)

In America today, when two people agree to marry, they are *not* making a serious promise to stay together for the nearly two decades it would take to raise a child. Thus, in our Model Family, the parents, rather than being married in the modern sense of the word, would be married in the pre-no-fault-divorce sense of the word. They would be sufficiently committed to remaining together that they would be willing to be penalized for failing to fulfill their commitment.

Some might reply to the above comments about marriage in the Model Family by arguing that people can intend to stay together without getting married. Indeed, it might even be argued that a marriage license is nothing but an insignificant piece of paper: If people are willing to stay together for a period of decades, a marriage license is superfluous; if they are not willing to stay together for a period of decades, a marriage license cannot make them do so.

In response to this suggestion, I must admit that thanks to no-fault divorce laws, a marriage license *is* a fairly insignificant piece of paper.[7] But as I have argued, in our Model Family, the parents will be married not in the modern sense of the word, but in the pre-no-fault sense of the word. *This* sort of marriage commitment has teeth and can therefore encourage people to stay together who might otherwise part.

More to the point, though, there is something paradoxical about two people who say that they intend to stay together for the nearly two decades it will take to raise a child, but who say they don't want to get married. We will naturally doubt the seriousness of their intentions. By way of analogy, suppose someone told you he was seriously interested in buying the house that you had for sale, but kept refusing to sign a purchase contract. You would soon come to doubt that his intentions were as serious as he claimed.

Here, in a nutshell, is the argument for married parents. If two people are unwilling to marry (in the pre-no-fault sense of the word), we can reasonably doubt their willingness to stay together for the next two decades. If we can reasonably doubt their willingness to stay together for the next two decades, we can reasonably doubt their effectiveness as parents, inasmuch as a child benefits from unhindered access to both his parents throughout his childhood. Therefore, the parents in our Model Family will be not merely living together, but married—and married in the pre-no-fault-divorce sense of the word.

Why Marriage?

Allow me, at this point, to make some observations about marriage. Why should society have an institution like marriage (in the pre-no-fault sense)? The state doesn't stick its nose into people's business when they decide to date. Why should it stick its nose into people's business when they decide to marry?

Marriage involves a contract between individuals, a sort of reciprocal promise. And typically marriage involves the special kind of contract that philosopher Thomas Hobbes referred to as a *covenant*.[8] A Hobbesian covenant is a contract in which one party promises to fulfill his end of the bargain immediately, while the other party promises to fulfill his end of the bargain at some future date.

To better understand the nature of a covenant, consider two different ways in which I can buy a book from you. On the one hand, we might agree to a trade in which you hand me the book at the same time as I hand you a sum of money. Since the parties to this contract will do what they have promised to do simultaneously, the contract is not a covenant. On the other hand, suppose that we agree that if you give me the book today, I will give you a certain sum of money next week. In this contract there would be a period of time in which you had fulfilled your end of the bargain but I had not; and since such a period exists, this contract would count as a Hobbesian covenant.

One of the core functions of government is to enforce the contracts into which people enter; and of the two sorts of contracts just described, it is clear that the contracts that will most be in need of enforcement are those that are covenants. Covenants, after all, are much more open to abuse than other sorts of contracts.

Now let us examine marriage as it traditionally existed. In

the past, the standard marriage contract (which of course was an unwritten contract) called for the woman to stay at home and raise the children while the man worked. The same contract called on the man to support the woman not just when she was raising their children, but till death parted them. What this meant was that the woman was called on to fulfill the greater part of her end of the marriage contract in the first decades of their marriage, whereas the man was called on to fulfill the greater part of his end of the marriage contract a few decades hence. Thus, the standard marriage contract was a covenant.

Notice, too, that it was a covenant that put women at risk. By staying at home to raise children, a woman was typically sacrificing her ability to become a self-supporting individual. If she went on the job market when her children were grown, chances are that she would find only marginal employment. She would spend her later years in poverty. The man, on the other hand, by going out and making a living, was likely to be at his peak earning power when his children were grown. An unscrupulous male might be tempted to enter into a marriage contract, only to default when, after the woman had finished raising his children, it came time to fulfill his promise to continue to support her.

Thus, a case can be made that the state, whose job it is to enforce contracts in general and covenants in particular, was well within its proper role in enforcing marriage contracts. The traditional way it did this was to make divorces hard to get; and when it allowed them, it typically forced the man (if he had been the "guilty spouse" in the divorce) to support the woman in her old age by means of alimony payments. It forced him, in other words, to live up to his end of the bargain.

Notice that by institutionalizing marriage and by penalizing those who violated the marriage contract, the state made it much less risky for women to stay at home and raise their children. In so doing, it benefited women, who might otherwise have found themselves on the losing end of their marriage contract. At the same time, it benefited the children of these women—if, at any rate, we think that children benefit from the full-time attention of a mother.

Also, notice that by enforcing the marriage contract, the state benefited children in a second way. By making it "expensive" for people to back out of a marriage contract, the state gave people an incentive to stay together, and this in turn increased the chance that children would spend their childhoods with the same two parents. If we think that children generally benefit from parental stability, this feature of the institutionalization of marriage was child-friendly.

I don't know whether the people who first "invented" marriage went through the reasoning processes described above and, in particular, whether they took into account the interests of women and children when they did so. The origins of marriage are, after all, lost in the mists of time. One thing that is clear, though, is that *if the institution of marriage did not exist, advocates of the stewardship model of parenting would probably want to invent it.*

The above argument has a sexist ring to it. Why, one might ask, must it be the woman who stays at home with the children? Why not the man?

Although in traditional marriages it was assumed that the woman would stay at home with the children, readers should realize that a modern father who decides to stay at home with the children while his wife goes off to work is open to the same sorts of risk that stay-at-home mothers faced in days gone by. In particular, by the time the children are grown, his wife will likely be at the peak of her earning power, while he, having spent the previous two decades baking cookies and wiping noses, will not be a prime candidate for the job market. By institutionalizing marriage, the state is protecting him in much the same way as it protected his grandmother.

While we are on the topic of marriage, let us take a moment to consider the ongoing movement to allow homosexual marriage. Let us consider, in particular, the extent to which the above rationales for the institution of marriage apply to homosexual couples.

It might be proposed, at the outset, that none of the above rationales apply to homosexuals. Notice, after all, that the rationales given revolve around the concept of parenthood. Marriage takes the risk out of one parent staying home with the children, and marriage increases the chance that a child will have the same two parents as he grows up. But, some might argue, homosexual couples are by nature incapable of becoming parents. Therefore, it looks like it would be difficult to justify homosexual marriage the way we justified heterosexual marriage.

This line of reasoning has some fairly obvious problems. In the first place, it is simply not true that homosexual couples are incapable of becoming parents. They can, to begin with, adopt. (Although adoption by homosexuals was long frowned on, if not forbidden, by adoption agencies, such adoption is becoming increasingly possible.) It is also possible for a homosexual couple to "make a child of their own." One member of a lesbian couple, for instance, can become pregnant through artificial insemination. Likewise, one member of a gay couple can father a child if they can find a "contract mother" who agrees to turn the baby over to them once it is born. Finally, a homosexual couple might find itself in the possession of a child because of a heterosexual relationship in which one member was formerly involved.

Thus, it is possible for a homosexual couple to find itself with one person at home raising children while the other person works. The marriage contract of such a couple might be a Hobbesian covenant like those of heterosexual marriages, and as such might be amenable to state enforcement.

Another problem with the above argument against homosexual marriage is that it applies equally well to *heterosexual* couples that, because of medical problems or age, are incapable of having children. If we think that the only couples that should be allowed to marry are those who either have or could have children, it would follow that these sterile couples should not be allowed to marry. How many opponents of homosexual marriage would favor such a restriction on heterosexual marriage?

Premarital Sex

There was a time when society not only expected people to get married before they had children, but expected them to get married before they had sex. If you were caught having sex before marriage, you were at least publicly humiliated and possibly even jailed. Above I have argued that the expectation that people marry before having children is justifiable in a society that wants to do right by its children. What about the expectation that people marry before having sex?

It might be suggested that the societal prohibition against premarital sex was nothing more than prudery. This suggestion, however, fails to recognize that there was a time—before effective means of birth control had been invented—when to have sexual relations was, for most people, to run a significant risk of making a baby. Under such circumstances, a society that cared about the well-being of its children and thought (correctly, I have argued) that children fare best when raised by married parents would naturally frown on premarital sex. In other words, the societal prohibition against premarital sex, rather than being an example of puritanical silliness, was arguably a justifiable prohibition for a society that valued the well-being of its children and lacked effective means of birth control.

This line of reasoning, to be sure, is not entirely relevant to today's society: Effective means of birth control are widely available and widely used. It is now possible to have premarital sex without running a significant risk of making a baby.

What about those cases in which unmarried people have sex but fail or refuse to use effective birth control? We might be tempted to say that as long as such sex takes place between two consenting adults, it is no one's business but theirs. We should realize, though, that if we care about the well-being of children and think that children are wronged by being born into bastardy, we have as much reason to censure unprotected premarital sex as our ancestors did.

How Many Children?

So much for the parents in our Model Family. What about the children? In particular, how many children will there be in the Model Family?

The issue of family size is, thanks to medical technology, almost completely under the control of the parents. They can, without much difficulty, stop at one child if they choose. Or they can keep making children until they have a baker's dozen.

It might be suggested at this point that there is no such thing as the "ideal" number of children for a family to have: Parents should be free to make as many as they want. The problem is that if we are operating on the stewardship model of parenting, there will indeed be such a thing as an ideal family size. It is reasonable to suppose that parents' ability to act as stewards for the children they bring into existence is not unlimited, and that with each additional child that comes along the job of stewardship becomes that much more difficult.

The nature of this problem becomes readily apparent when we consider very large families. Consider, then, a family with thirteen children. Only under the most unusual circumstances could the parents in such a family "do right" by each and every child— that is, develop a close personal relationship with each child, pay careful attention to each child's needs and wants, discover and develop each child's talents, and so forth. Usually in such cases, the parents would have to settle for giving their children a much lower level of care than, say, a two-child family would receive. They would probably feel themselves successful if they did nothing more than meet the immediate physical needs of their children.

In some cases, the parents of large families, because they have taken on so much work, recruit their own children to share the burden of raising children. The twelve-year-olds raise the five-year-olds so that the parents can take care of the babies. Unless we think that the most profitable way to spend a childhood is in raising children, we will not regard this use of children as effective stewardship.

A couple that has thirteen children will, almost without exception, be like a person who has agreed to act as steward for the lands of thirteen of his neighbors. Whereas he probably could have done an excellent job caring for the lands of one neighbor, and done an adequate job caring for the lands of, say, three of his neighbors, the attempt to care for the lands of thirteen of his neighbors will likely mean that none of his neighbors gets his lands taken care of. The fact that someone has taken on a lot of stewardship does not make him a good steward; what is much more important than the quantity of his stewardship is the quality of his stewardship. A good steward—of either land or children—will not take on more stewardship than he can handle.

I will not be so bold as to suggest an actual number for the "ideal" family size. Indeed, the number itself won't be fixed, but will vary depending on the circumstances of parents. Two energetic, affluent parents (only one of whom works) will typically be able to take care of the needs of more children than two aging, listless parents, both of whom are employed.

By the 1990s, medical technology had brought a new dimension to the issue of family size. Thanks to in vitro fertilization, it became increasingly possible for women not only to have large families, but to have them in one fell swoop. It is one thing for parents to have a family of, say, four children sequentially, allowing a few years to pass between the birth of each. It is quite another thing to give birth to quadruplets and to have to meet the needs of four newborns (and, subsequently, four infants and four toddlers and four teenagers) all at the same time. It is an undertaking that only the hardiest and most devoted of parents could succeed in.

Some of those undergoing in vitro fertilization are not prime candidates for multiple-parenthood. Consider, for example, the 55-year-old woman who, in 1998, used in vitro fertilization to become the mother of quadruplets.[9] Will a 55-year-old be up to the strain of this undertaking? Perhaps…with sufficient help. It is therefore worth noting that the woman in question was a single mother. One suspects that it will not be long before this woman comes to realize the advantages of sharing the burdens of parent-hood with a second parent.

"Family Values"

Allow me to recapitulate. Our Model Family will, according to the above argument, be headed by a woman and a man who are married, not in the no-fault sense of the word but in the traditional sense. This is a conclusion that would be agreeable to advocates of what have become known as "family values."[10]

Family values have gotten bad press in America. Many would have us believe that family values are the by-product of religious superstition and that only someone besotted by religion would hold such values. It is therefore important to realize that in my above "derivation of" a Model Family, I did not once invoke the Bible or religious ethics. What I did invoke, time and again, was the notion of doing what's best for children. My basic argument is that if a society places children at the top of its list of priorities, that society will advocate something very much like "family values."

The alternative to family values can perhaps best be described as "parental values." According to parental values, parents' interests come ahead of their children's interests. According to parental values, there is nothing at all wrong with quickie divorces, with women having and raising children out of wedlock, with men impregnating women and then wandering off. It is true that children may be harmed in the cases just described, but (according to "parental values") so what? Parents must be allowed to live their lives as they please, even though their children suffer as a result. It quickly becomes apparent that whereas "family values" are based on the stewardship model of parenting, "parental values" are based squarely on the ownership model of parenting.

It used to be taken for granted that children did best in the sort of family setting I have described above. It also used to be taken for granted that things that weakened or destroyed the family, like easy divorce, were evil. By the 1990s these ideas could no longer be taken for granted: One had to argue in support of views about the family that, in the 1950s, had been regarded as common sense.

In the process of writing this book, I have discussed family structures with college students. One of my most startling discoveries in these discussions is the extent to which they reject the "traditional family" in their life plans. They seem to have experienced, in their own lives, an allergic reaction to the traditional family. They regard it as the source of numerous evils. A surprising number of them plan to avoid, in their own lives, as many of the trappings of the traditional family as they can. They speak of having their children outside of marriage, or in group settings, or with people who are friends but not lovers.

Of course, college students are often surprised by the extent to which their plans in college are changed by exposure to the "real world." Nevertheless, the views of my students are disturbing, for notice that for the traditional family to be abandoned as America's model does not require an act of Congress. It requires only that an ever-increasing number of young people, in planning their own lives, abandon it.

Some readers will, at this point, deride me for holding up the standard family structure of the 1950s, or something close to it, as the model for today's Americans. They will point out that the families of the 1950s had their problems, but that many of these problems were hard to detect because family members worked so hard to suppress them. In particular, they might argue that the tensions that arose in a loveless marriage maintained "for the sake of the children" were unhealthy, for both parents and children. Or they might argue that it is hypocritical and/or counterproductive to raise children to be innocent.

In reply to these criticisms, I readily admit that families of the 1950s were not perfect. I will follow this admission, though, with the observation that from the mere fact that an option is imperfect, it does not follow that it is an option we should reject. In this life we are commonly called on to choose among many options, all of which are imperfect. In such cases, the sensible thing to do is to pick the option that is least imperfect.

A thoughtful person, rather than dwelling on the shortcomings of families back in the 1950s, will instead compare these shortcomings with those of modern families. It may indeed have been "unhealthy" to be a child in a family in which the parents were staying together for the sake of the children. But how healthy is it to experience the trauma of having one's parents divorce and, in the aftermath, to be partially deprived of access to one parent? And how healthy is it to be raised by a single mother who must work to support her child (since the child's father disappeared shortly after the reproductive act that brought the child into existence) and who, as a result, has little time or energy to devote to her child?

Despite their problems, the families of the 1950s had a great deal to recommend them. A case can be made that by casually discarding the 1950s model of parenting,[11] we have thrown away something very valuable and have, in many cases, grievously harmed our children in the process.

Changing Values

Let me conclude this chapter by commenting on an important change that has taken place in American values in the second half of the twentieth century and on the impact this change has had on children.

When it comes to personal value systems, we can distinguish between those that are competitive and those that are cooperative. A *competitive value system* equates success with victory in competitive endeavors—with advancing one's interests by "defeating" one or more other human beings. A *cooperative value system*, on the other hand, equates success not with defeating other human beings but with helping them—not with advancing one's own interests but with advancing those of other people. Someone holding a competitive value system might count himself successful because he beat out other candidates for a job or because he won a tennis match. Someone holding a cooperative value system, on the other hand, might count himself successful because he helped a friend get a job or because he spent the afternoon helping someone improve his tennis game.

If a person had a purely competitive value system, winning would be everything; if a person had a purely cooperative value system, helping would be everything. Most people, of course, have value systems that are neither purely competitive nor purely cooperative, but that involve a mix of competition and cooperation.

Which value system is better, one that primarily values competition or one that primarily values cooperation?

At the individual level, a case can be made that what is best is a mixed value system in which each person values both competition and cooperation. Notice, after all, that an extreme version of the competitive value system would result in a predatory egoist who would let nothing stand between him and (competitive) success, and an extreme version of the cooperative value system would produce a human doormat. An intensely competitive person would probably benefit from learning to cooperate, and an intensely cooperative person (an oxymoron?) would probably benefit from learning to compete.

At the societal level, a case can also be made that a mixed value system is best—that society benefits from the presence in it of both people who lean toward competition and people who lean toward cooperation. Certainly we benefit from the efforts of competitive people: We might enjoy watching them compete, or benefit from the fruits of their competition, as when competition between two drug companies results in a wonder drug appearing much sooner than it would have if competitive instincts had not been at work. We also benefit from the efforts of cooperative people who undertake activities which, though valuable, don't "pay" and hence are unlikely to be undertaken by competitive individuals.

As far as ethics is concerned, there is little need to defend cooperative value systems: Indeed, much of ethics is concerned with getting people to take the interests of others into account when they act. What needs defending, if anything does, are competitive value systems. Most ethicists, however, have no problem with a person acting to benefit his own interests, as long as he doesn't trample the rights of others in doing so. In short, both the cooperative and competitive value systems are ethically justifiable.

When it comes to families, a case can be made that children benefit from having a parent whose value system leans toward cooperation. Children need lots of nurturing, and a cooperative person will typically have a well-developed nurturing instinct. Even more importantly, a person with a cooperative value system is more likely to feel that staying at home and taking care of children is a worthwhile way to spend one's days. A person with a competitive value system, on the other hand, would probably find life at home with the children to be profoundly unsatisfying.

Children also benefit, however, from the presence in their lives of a person with a competitive value system. The competitive parent will encourage his children to try new things, to take chances, and to realize that the only thing worse than failure is to avoid failure by not even trying to succeed. A competitive parent is also desirable when it comes to meeting the material needs of a child: The job market tends to pay competitive people more highly than it pays cooperative people, and hence competitive people tend to be more effective as breadwinners.

In the old days—before the women's movement—both the competitive and cooperative value systems were present in most American families: The father typically had a competitive value system and the mother a cooperative value system. And it was no accident that the value systems were divided along sexual lines: Men were typically raised to value competition while women were typically raised to value cooperation.

The women's movement is best remembered for smashing the legal and traditional barriers that kept women from engaging in certain occupations and pastimes. In the process of smashing these barriers, though, the women's movement brought about a second important change in America, a change in people's value systems. In particular, it encouraged women to forsake their traditional cooperative value system (the one described above) in favor of a competitive value system. Women began to want what men want: power, pay, and a position in the hierarchy. They began to look down on those who contented themselves in helping others and in particular began to look down on any woman whose main goal in life was to stay at home and take care of her husband and children. (That, after all, is the crassest form of cooperative behavior.) To be a success, they argued, you must compete, and that means going out and getting a job. Let your husband and children look out for themselves.

Some feminists have implied that those women who valued cooperation did so as the result of the evil machinations of men, who for centuries have tricked women into playing the role of mild-mannered helpmate while they, the men, enjoyed the good things in life (namely, power, pay, and a position in the hierarchy). "Winners compete, suckers cooperate" was, unfortunately, one of the unpublished mottos of feminism.

I am not alone in pointing to the value-reversal that the women's movement helped bring about. Anthropologist Judith Posner points out that the same feelings of inadequacy that Betty Friedan documented in *The Feminine Mystique* and that sparked the women's movement are present in women who have forsaken life as a housewife for life as a corporate officer. "Much to my surprise," she tells us, "I found that [Betty Friedan's] thoughts and comments about women in the sixties were strangely applicable to women in the eighties."[12] What went wrong? Here is Posner's diagnosis:

> Mindlessly…we have followed the prescriptions of the work mystique and mistakenly treated them as a necessary part of feminist ideology. We have accepted the notion that *occupational and income status is the true indicator of independence and self-worth*. We have *reinforced the trivialization of housework and mothers' work*.[13] [Italics in the original.]

In short, "women have been co-opted by their own feminist rhetoric which follows the masculine ideal of basing one's societal value on a paycheck."[14] We are left with the following bit of irony: "In shaking off the shackles of a male-dominated, sexist society which asserts that women should remain barefoot and pregnant, [feminism] now prescribes that women should participate in the very same patriarchal culture which demeaned them in the first place."[15]

Feminists might point out that women paid a price by being cooperative, and this is no doubt true. We should keep in mind, though, first, that cooperation has its rewards, and second, that those who compete also pay a price—sometimes a terrible price—to do so. It is far from clear who, in our society, has it better off, the woman who stays at home and takes care of her children (and does so because in her heart of hearts it is what she truly wants to do) or the man who has risen to the highest levels of the corporate world. It is true that the man has more income and power than the woman, and has a higher place in the hierarchy of competitors, but the woman has likely experienced rewards that the man can only dream of.

If those at the top of the competitive hierarchy were happy, well-adjusted individuals, there might be reason for us to strive to become like them. In many cases, though, they are anything but happy. To want to be like them is an act of insanity.

To the extent that feminism sought to lead women away from a purely cooperative existence, it deserves our applause. It is, as we have said, difficult to distinguish between a purely cooperative person and a doormat. The problem is that feminism went far beyond this: Rather than exhorting women to become somewhat more competitive while preserving many of their cooperative values, it exhorted them to largely abandon cooperation in favor of competition.[16] The end result was a plethora of competitive individuals in our culture and a dearth of cooperative individuals—too much battle for survival and too little nurturing. And this change in value systems had tragic consequences for children: All too often they found themselves parented by two competitive individuals, when what they needed was some heartfelt nurturing.

It is, to be sure, unfair to put the blame entirely on women: As women abandoned their nurturing roles and cooperative value systems, it was possible for men to take them up. The problem is that most men didn't. And as a result, the children of America ended up paying the price for the decline of cooperative values. Instead of being allowed to spend their days in intimate contact with a parent, many children spent their early days at day-care centers in the company of a succession of strangers.

In summary, feminists are to be praised for fighting to re-move the legal and traditional barriers that blocked men and women from trying to break out of their traditional sex roles if they thought they would be happier in a different role. But after these barriers had fallen, a new barrier arose, one erected by a subgroup of feminists who branded those women who chose to stay in their traditional roles as traitors to the cause of women. This new barrier is arguably as indefensible and destructive as the old ones were.

Different women have different personalities and different needs. Trying to make all women conform to one mode of living will necessarily result in some people living lives that simply don't fit them. It was a mistake to assume, as our culture did in the 1950s, that all women were nurturers and should stay at home and nurture. This malignant doctrine meant that some women who would have been perfectly happy with business careers were miserable as housewives. It is likewise a mistake to assume, as some feminists now seem to, that no women are nurturers, and therefore that no women should be content staying at home and raising families. The result of this unfortunate doctrine is that there are, in America today, women who would have enjoyed a blissful existence as housewife, but who instead are living what is for them a hellish existence trying to climb the corporate ladder.

And of course these same comments apply to men. I for one am particularly glad to live in a culture which, thanks in part to the women's movement, allowed me to develop my nurturing in-stincts. I have changed my share of diapers, cooked my share of breakfasts, and baked more than my share of birthday cakes. I have sat up with sick kids and acted as chauffeur. Some of these activities were less than pleasant; yet they all had their rewards, the most significant being *the knowledge that I was there for someone when he needed me—the knowledge that I had made an important difference in someone else's life.* Had I been raised in my father's generation, I would not have done these things and would not have reaped these rewards. The personal loss would have been considerable—and sadder still, I probably wouldn't even have recognized the magnitude of my loss.

Many Americans in my generation have apparently concluded that the way to attain personal happiness is to pursue your own interests. Be an individual, and get what you, as an individual, want. No need to sacrifice. No need to make your own desires subservient to those of someone or something else.

The logic that leads them to this conclusion is clear: If not getting what you want makes you unhappy, does it not follow that the best way to become happy is to take aim squarely at what you want and get it, even though doing so entails a cost to others? If you make yourself the number one person in your life, surely you will be more likely to find happiness.

There was a time when I was seduced by the logic of this argument. One of the most significant discoveries of my adult life has been the extent to which I am able to attain happiness, not by pursuing my own interests but by making my interests subservient to the interests of other individuals. There was a time when I sought happiness through a self-centered sort of individualism; I now think that one important step in the attainment of happiness is a conscious blurring of the boundaries of self—a willingness to view myself as part of something bigger, as a cog in a larger machine.

Some look at steward-parents and remark on the sacrifices they make on behalf of their children. What they fail to realize is that these "sacrifices" are not painful if the person making them identifies his own interests with those of his children. Indeed, they can be a source of intense satisfaction.

CHAPTER 11

HAVING CHILDREN

Before ending my examination of the ethics of parenting, allow me to ask one last question: Why have children?[1]

The answer to this question used to be fairly straightforward: People had children because they didn't really have the option of not having them. Before the invention of effective means of birth control, the only way to avoid having children was to avoid having sex. For most people the cost of avoiding pregnancy (i.e., a sexless existence) was too high to pay: They could not "afford" it. For these people, the question "Why have children?" turned into the question "Why have sex?"; and this last question was one they could easily answer.

Even after the invention of effective birth control, the cost of not having children remained substantial. The cost was no longer a price paid in terms of a sexless existence, but a price paid in terms of social opprobrium. Couples were expected to marry, and married couples were expected to have children unless a medical condition prevented it. (And if a medical condition *did* prevent it, the couple in question was regarded as pitiable.) Married couples who by choice did not have children were thought to be selfish. Their behavior was regarded as puzzling by most: Why get married if you don't want to have children?

In the 1950s, which I have characterized as the Golden Age of Childhood, parents were prolific.[2] The three-child family was considered ideal, and families larger than this were not uncommon, even among college-educated women. By 1957 the average mom had 3.7 children, and only 7 percent of women of child-bearing age did not have children. This marked the high point of American fertility, though, and by 1976 the average mom had but 1.74 children. The number of childless women had also risen: In 1976, 15.6 percent of women 30 to 34 years old were childless, and by the middle of the 1990s this number had reached 26.7 percent.[3]

In Europe the decline in the number of children per family was even more dramatic, triggering a population implosion.

In the last four decades there has been a revolution in women's thinking about procreation. Women who once would have been called child*less* now prefer to be called child*free*: It was not nature or circumstances that kept them from having children, but a conscious decision not to have them.

For modern Americans the "costs" associated with a childfree existence are negligible. You no longer have to give up sex: Birth control products are both inexpensive and convenient. And society, while not completely understanding of couples who choose not to have children, is at least likely to keep its disapproval to itself. This means that today, the question "Should I have children?" is much harder to answer than it used to be. Indeed, it has been called "the predominant issue in the lives of many women of childbearing age today."[4]

Costs and Benefits

So why do people have children? The obvious answer is that people believe that the benefits they will derive from having children will outweigh the costs. There are two problems with this answer.

The first is that most potential parents don't do the sort of costs and benefits analysis just described. To the contrary, most people decide to have children simply because it feels like the right thing to do: They use their hearts rather than their heads in making this decision.

The second problem is that if people were actually to carry out the costs and benefits analysis in question, they would in many cases find that the benefits they can reasonably expect to derive from having children do not outweigh the costs. Having children is, for a good many people, "a losing proposition," and one they will enter into only if they allow their hearts to overrule their heads.

In defense of this last claim, let me describe some of the benefits and costs of having children, after which I will return to the question of whether the benefits outweigh the costs.

The Benefits of Having Children

The benefits of having a child can begin before the child is born. For a woman, pregnancy can be "the ultimate feminine experience."[5] Some women also point out an incidental benefit of pregnancy: You can go off your diet.

Once the baby is born, parents experience a variety of benefits. One author points to the following: Children can give and receive affection, can offer new perspectives to parents, can teach parents about themselves, can offer comic relief, can force parents to think about the future, can keep parents "on their toes" and help them remain open to change, and can help parents develop self-discipline.[6] Another author includes the following among the benefits of having children: having someone to pass on values, talents, family heirlooms, and memories to; increasing the chances of someday becoming a grandparent; pleasing your parents; and feeling part of a family-centered society.[7] This same author adds that in having a baby, a woman can prove her true womanhood or that she is a "grownup."[8]

Many parents are doubtless moved to have children in order to obtain the loving relationship that goes with parenthood. While an adult might reject your love, a child will not—at least not for the first decade of his life. For this reason, children are ideal as "love objects." And besides being lovable, children are incredibly loving. Rare is the child who doesn't shower his parents with an utterly unconditional form of love. The relationship between parent and child is in many respects the most perfect relationship a human can have, full of love and trust. To my mind, this relationship is the single most important benefit to be derived from parenting.

Some people have children because they want to "feel needed." Make a baby and you most definitely will be needed: Without your efforts the baby you have made will be in deep trouble.

Other people have children because they seek admiration. Children find their parents to be astonishingly smart and wonderful—at least they do when they are young. Parents are like gods to their children, and parents know it. They bask in the astonishment of their children.

And of course, with parenthood come moments of pride. Pride at watching a baby take its first step or utter its first word. Pride at watching a child throw a strike in Little League or play the piano at a recital. Pride at having your child bring home a perfect report card.

Making a baby is for many people the ultimate creative act. You are not only bringing a human being into existence, but you are shaping him day by day. The sense of accomplishment you get from raising a child is like the sense of accomplishment you might get from building a house from the ground up all by yourself—only better.

Children can also confer a kind of immortality on their parents. In most cultures, having a boy will preserve the family name. And whether a couple has a girl or a boy, they will be preserving their genetic identity for posterity.

Besides enabling parents to "cheat death," children also enable parents to have a second chance at life. They can, to begin with, create for their child the childhood they wish they themselves had had. Indeed, some have suggested that this is one of the main reasons women have children.[9] And as children grow, parents can, by carefully controlling their children's lives, vicariously live their own version of a perfect life. They can, through their children, avoid the mistakes of their own lives and accomplish the things they were unable to accomplish in their own lives.

For some parents, having control over the details of their child's life is itself a source of pleasure. Here, at last, is another person, every aspect of whose life they can control. They experience an intoxicating sense of power—power over the life of another human being.

Another advantage of having children is that their labor can be exploited. (This is most easily done in Third World countries; in developed countries children generally cost more to raise than they would bring home in wages.) And when their children are adults, parents might also exploit their labor by "requiring" their children to care for them in their old age, or at least provide them with companionship.

Some people have children in an attempt to salvage a failing relationship. Others have children in an attempt to avenge a failed relationship: When a couple breaks up, the woman might become pregnant by her new lover, or the man might impregnate his new lover to prove something (it isn't at all clear what) to her or his former lover.

People may have children for financial reasons. It used to be possible for a woman on welfare to increase her income by having children. There have also been cases in which people had children in an attempt to win a monetary prize: Remember, for example, the Millar Stork Derby mentioned in Chapter 1. Some governments also provide monetary incentives for their citizens to have children.

Many babies are made in an effort to please God, who commanded us, after all, to go forth and multiply.[10]

What is striking about the above "benefits" of having children is that many of them are benefits for the parent that come at the expense of the child. For this reason, many of the above-cited "benefits" of making a baby are not benefits that the steward-parent will seek. Indeed, as we shall see below, steward-parents will have a particularly difficult time trying to justify their decision to make a baby.

The Costs of Having Children

So much for the benefits of having children. Let us now turn our attention to the costs associated with having them. These costs—both monetary and nonmonetary—are enormous.

Consider first the price parents must pay before their baby is born. In a typical pregnancy there are medical expenses before the delivery (e.g., the cost of prenatal checkups), but these are usually minor compared to the other predelivery costs. The woman, because of her pregnant condition, might have to stop working or cut back her hours of employment, and this can mean a significant loss of income. And of course, besides these monetary costs associated with pregnancy, there are numerous nonmonetary costs. The woman will likely be in considerable discomfort during her pregnancy and possibly even in pain. Her sleep will be affected, as will her eating. She will lose much of her freedom. She will (if she is a caring individual) give up various recreational activities, including smoking and drinking. Her husband (or these days, the man in her life) might also pay a price during pregnancy, although not as great as that paid by the woman. He might, for example, find his sleep affected by the fact that hers is, or he might give up various recreational activities so he can be more helpful to her.

The above comments, to be sure, apply to the *typical* pregnancy. If a woman has trouble becoming pregnant, the cost to her of having children will likely be higher still. She might have to resort to in vitro fertilization treatments, which are both expensive and bothersome. Or she might have to suffer through several miscarriages in her attempt to become a parent.

At the end of the pregnancy, the process of giving birth will involve expense, but also exquisite pain for the pregnant woman.

E. E. Le Masters, author of an important study of the effects of children on families, uses the word "crisis" to describe the addition of a child to a family,[11] and this is no exaggeration. As soon as the newborn comes home, the household will experience a major disruption. It may be necessary for the parents to move to larger quarters or alter their current quarters. The parents will find themselves faced with a number of new expenses: They will learn, among other things, the price of disposable diapers. They will also not only learn how to change these diapers, but will change more of them than they would have imagined possible. At times their baby will cry and refuse to be consoled. They will feel frustrated. They will lose sleep. Their nerves will be frayed. They will quickly discover how many of the things that they used to enjoy doing are difficult or impossible to do with a baby along: They will lose their freedom. The former tranquility of their existence will be shattered. Regular sexual relations will be difficult. If the woman stays home with the baby, her income will be lost to the family—this is the so-called "opportunity cost" of parenting. Indeed, to stay at home with the child, she may find that she has to give up the career she dreamed of having, and with it all the fulfillment that can come from a career.

And if both parents continue to work full-time after their baby is born (and allow someone else to spend his or her days with the baby), they won't give up income or careers, but they will deprive themselves of many of the pleasures associated with "being there" as the child grows up. Most importantly, their status as absentee parents will undermine their chances of having an intense, loving relationship with their child—which relationship, I have suggested, is probably the greatest single benefit to be derived from parenting. I will have more to say about absentee parents below.

Some would have us believe that mothering is not a "real job" and that it is the refuge of those who cannot cope with the demands of "real jobs." Mothering may not be a "real job" in the sense that you don't get counted in employment statistics, but it certainly is a real job in every other sense of the word. Indeed, it is in almost every respect far more demanding than any "real job." The hours, for one thing, are longer: The typical mother is on call 24 hours a day, seven days a week. Her routine involves much menial work, including cleaning up her baby's various bodily emissions.

In a "real job" there is generally a set level of expectations and a set system of rewards. The rule is, "You do X, you get Y as a reward." This is not the case with mothering. You can do a spectacular job and get not even a "thank you" in return.

Furthermore, in most "real jobs" there is a certain level of decorum and restraint. Harassment of employees is generally forbidden, and employers who engage in it are open to a lawsuit. On the other hand, a mother's boss (i.e., her child) is typically extremely demanding and given to outbursts of temper. As the child's linguistic abilities develop, so might his tendency to shower his poor mother with threats and profanity. Should a misguided mother attempt to bring a harassment lawsuit against her child, she would be laughed out of court.

Consider, then, the comments of one mother who had experienced both a "real job" and motherhood:

> Since I decided to have a child, I felt it was my responsibility to raise it. But I discovered it takes a great deal of patience to raise a baby and the ability to carry on without any positive rewards, at least no immediate ones. At work, I was always receiving praise. I was often taken out to lunch by my employer, or given flowers. But I received none of these things as a full-time mother. Instead, I found boredom, less money, no adult stimulation, and no appreciation.[12]

Mothering, then, is like working in a menial capacity for an abusive employer who pays nothing and gives you virtually no time off. Mothering may not be a "real job," but it is arguably one of the hardest jobs on earth. Indeed if mothering were a "real job," the government would soon outlaw it, the way it has outlawed sweatshops.

It is doubtless true that some people choose to be stay-at-home parents because they cannot stand the pressures of the workplace. We should not forget, though, that there are also people who go to work because they cannot stand the pressures of parenting. For these people—and there are many of them—the workplace represents a refuge from family.

One might think that as children grow up, the level of stress experienced by their parents would diminish, and thus the "costs" associated with parenting would decline. Such is not the case. According to Louis Genevie and Eva Margolies in their groundbreaking *Motherhood Report*, the level of stress remains constant until children leave home. What changes as the child ages are the sources of the stress.[13]

In the beginning it is stressful for parents to constantly have to change a child's diapers. When the child outgrows diapers, this source of stress disappears—only to be replaced by the stress that comes from having to change the sheets of the bed that the now-diaperless child wets. Similarly, when a child is too young to speak, his parents will experience the stress of not understanding what it is that their child wants. When the child finally develops the power of speech, his parents will experience a new source of stress: He will make them fully aware of what it is that he wants, and they will have to spend considerable energy repeatedly saying No to those requests that are unreasonable. By the time junior high rolls around, the child's ability to speak might have developed into a talent for sarcastic speech. He may not spare any effort in conveying to his parents how low his opinion of them is. The same parents that in his first decade of life he thought were gods, in his second decade of life he thinks are buffoons.

The parents of a teenager might find themselves the targets of emotional warfare, with "the enemy" possessing an abundance of time and energy to devise new ways to make their lives miserable. Indeed, there are times when the parents of a teenager might find themselves wishing that their child would treat them with the same courtesy and respect as he treats utter strangers.

Teenagers typically build walls between themselves and their parents. According to the *Motherhood Report*, four out of ten mothers cited feelings of rejection as the darkest side of motherhood.[14]

As a child ages, the financial burden imposed on his parents will grow. On becoming a toddler, a child will need toys. A few years after that, he will need more and better toys, he will need to see movies, and he will need music lessons or gymnastics lessons. By his teens the child will discover the joy of eating and the family's food budget will balloon. The child will want to dress like his peers and will be willing to spend vast quantities of his parents' money to attain "the look." Later the child will learn to drive a car, and his parents will be expected to insure him. Then comes college, which can be enormously expensive.

And after college, do the parents' financial obligations come to an end? Not at all. There will be weddings to plan and finance. There will be young adults who need a helping hand financially or who need to be bailed out of the trouble they get themselves into. Or in some cases, there will be young adults who, despite their parents' efforts, find themselves unemployable (or at least not desiring employment) and who expect to keep their old bedroom.

Throughout it all, there is worry, worry, worry. Worry when trying to become pregnant. Worry during the pregnancy. Worry during the delivery. Worry about the baby. Worry about the toddler. Worry about big things and little things. Worry about how your child is doing in school, in sports, socially, in all areas. Worry that some catastrophe will befall your child, either ending his life or putting him in the hospital.

Even when it is clear that a parent's child has grown up successfully, that parent can look forward to worrying about the well-being of his grandchildren.

But won't successful adult children be a source of comfort in their parents' old age? If parents are lucky—but most parents aren't. For them, there are few "psychological rewards" to be derived from being the parent of an adult child.[15]

When do the worries of the parent finally come to an end? At his or her funeral.

Notice that the costs of parenting will depend upon the circumstances of the parents. For poor people the financial costs of parenting will likely be greater than for rich people. Even if poor people spend less money on their children than rich people, they are likely to feel the pinch of their expenditures more than rich people do. Likewise, for old, tired parents, the (nonfinancial) costs of parenting are likely to be higher than they are for young, energetic parents: It "costs" an old, tired parent considerably more to pick up his child's toys for the hundredth time than it costs a young, energetic parent. Furthermore, realize that for older people, parenting can be hazardous to one's health. It is one thing to lug around twenty pounds of baby when you are twenty-five years old; it is quite another thing to do the lugging at age forty. One psychologist sums up the predicament of older parents in these terms: "A lot of older parents are more psychologically sophisticated, have read all the books on child rearing, have handled their careers, are more financially secure. And they think...that they are better prepared. But their bodies just don't go along with those plans."[16] The result? Backaches, slipped disks, broken coccyges, and injured knees.

Also, the costs of parenting can depend upon the number of children that parents already have. When parents have a second child, their costs are in some ways lower: They don't, for example, have to buy a crib like they did when they had their first child. But in other respects, their costs can be higher: Parents of a single child don't have to spend time and energy breaking up sibling quarrels; parents of multiple children do.

In most relationships, as I have suggested above, mothers bear a disproportionate part of the costs of parenting. In most relationships, after all, mothers are the "primary parent." These mothers, as quoted by Genevie and Margolies, spell out the costs of parenting in no uncertain terms:

> Twenty-four hours a day, 365 days a year...the children's constant demand for attention...there are times when I am so tired but must push on for them, while their crying, fighting, and disobedience tears at my nerves. Sometimes I feel like screaming if anybody says 'Mommy' one more time....The demands are endless.[17]

> There are times when I feel like a 'prisoner' in my home—really tied down—unappreciated. I often feel that I am losing myself—

my own time no longer exists. I did not realize how my whole life would center around the children. I can't do anything without considering them first.[18]

Another mother, in discussing the motherhood experience, mentions "this drowning feeling" that mothers get and adds that sometimes she feels as if she is "going to go under."[19] Some might be tempted to classify the mothers who made the above remarks as jaded. Genevie and Margolies, however, present an impressive body of evidence to suggest that they are not so much jaded, as realistic in their assessments of the costs of mothering.

Easy Parents, Difficult Children

The above discussion of the costs and benefits of having children is flawed in one important respect: It is concerned with the costs and benefits experienced by the "average" parent who makes the "average" baby. Most parents and babies, though, are not "average," and this can radically affect the outcome of our analysis of the costs and benefits of having children.

Consider first parents. Parents can be divided into those who are easy and those who are difficult; and by "easy" and "difficult," I mean *easy to please* or *difficult to please*.

A parent who is easy will thrill at his baby's first word and at his baby's first step. He will look forward to changing his child's diaper as a moment of unusual closeness with the child. As his child grows older he will attend his child's every violin recital, and cry tears of joy as he listens to his child scratching out crude melodies. He will go to every Little League game his child plays in and be thrilled whenever his child comes up to bat, no matter what the outcome. (Indeed, he will even experience a happy, inner glow watching his child warm the bench.) And when his child is grown he will proudly tell anyone who wishes to listen about his child's career as a burger flipper in a local fast-food restaurant.

A parent who is difficult, on the other hand, will rarely thrill at his child's accomplishments. He will miss his child's first step because he's watching a football game on television. He will become physically ill in the act of changing his child's diapers. He will tend to develop migraine headaches at his child's violin recitals. He will occasionally attend his child's Little League games, but will do so out of a sense of duty, and during the game will find himself wishing he could instead be out on the fairway. And he will be disappointed with his child's ultimate career choice, even if it turns out to be in a respected profession. One apparently difficult parent summed up her own views on the joys of parenting in the following terms: "The greatest joy is getting them all into bed by 8:00 P.M."[20]

What determines whether a parent is easy or difficult? To a large extent, his personality. Some people, it seems, are constitutionally incapable of enjoying the primary benefits of parenthood.

We should note that even a person who is capable of enjoying parenthood might, because of his or her circumstances in life, be a difficult parent. Consider, for example, a divorced woman who must, in order to support herself and her child, work long hours at a demanding job. Such a woman might find herself with precious little time and energy with which to enjoy motherhood.

In the same way as parents can be easy or difficult, children can be easy or difficult, and here by "easy" or "difficult" I mean *easy or difficult for their parents to get along with*.

A truly easy child will give its mother no problems during pregnancy. Its birth won't be particularly difficult or painful. It will start sleeping through the night when it is one week old, if not sooner. Indeed, it will spend most of its first year of life sleeping, and when it is not sleeping, it will smile at everyone, while making happy, gurgling sounds.

As a toddler, the easy child will be active, but not overly active. He will use the word No in a restrained fashion, if at all. And as he grows, his personality will become ever more pleasant. He will aim to please his parents and the adult world in general. He will care about the feelings of those around him and will be unstinting with his love. He will not fight with his siblings, but will instead offer to help his parents care for them.

His teen years will be marked not by rebellion, but by a smooth transition into adulthood. With each passing year he will grow wiser and more responsible. Awards of various kinds will be showered on him.

Throughout his childhood this easy child will have shown himself to be a talented individual and will have worked hard to develop these talents. He will also have taken his education quite seriously and will have nearly perfect report cards to show for it. As a result of all this effort, he will be wonderfully ready, on reaching adulthood, to embark on some particularly meaningful and profoundly remunerative career.

And as the parents of this easy child age, they will find their adult child to be the source of enormous pride and comfort. When it comes time for them to die, he will be at their bedside, a pillar of strength in their time of need.

A truly difficult child, on the other hand, will have caused his mother anguish during the pregnancy and delivery. He will have emerged from the womb screaming and will not have stopped screaming until...well, he will never really have stopped screaming.

This difficult child will not sleep through the night for months and will spend his (numerous) wakeful hours in a state of distress, crying and spitting up food. As a toddler he will become his parents' worst nightmare, destroying household objects at will and refusing to take No for an answer. His behavior will make his parents prisoners in their own home, unable to take him into public for fear of his noisy tantrums, and unable to find a sitter willing to sit for him.

When he is of school age, this difficult child will refuse to learn and be a constant source of grief not only for his teachers but for the other students as well. His parents will come to dread calls from the school principal. And at home the difficult child will behave barbarously toward his siblings, so much so that his parents dare not leave him alone in the same room with them.

In his teenage years the difficult child will stop going to school and devote himself instead to partying. He will destroy his parents' cars on numerous occasions, despite the fact that he doesn't yet have a driver's license. He will not only refuse to help do housework but leave messes wherever he goes, thereby increasing the housework for others to do. He will periodically get into trouble with the law. He will make various efforts to corrupt his siblings, by trying to induce them, for example, to take drugs. He will impregnate various girls and take no responsibility for what he has done; or, if the difficult child is a girl, she will get pregnant herself and foist the resulting child on her parents so that her own life of partying is not disrupted.

A particularly difficult child may even commit suicide, pausing only to leave a note accusing his parents (who may in fact have been wonderful parents) of having made his life unlivable. Anything to increase their anguish.

In his dealings with his parents the difficult child will point out in no uncertain terms how much he hates them and what failures he takes them to be. He will use horribly offensive language in making reference to them. He will physically abuse his parents—and might, in the case of an extremely difficult child, attempt to kill them.

As an adult this difficult child will refuse to leave home. And when finally forced out, he will cut off communications with his parents—unless he needs money or needs to be bailed out of jail. If his parents, now aging, ever need his help, they will know better than to ask, since his response will be to rebuke them.

Parents of a difficult baby can always cling to the hope that their baby will change in time. By the time the difficult baby is a difficult adult, though, parents will have little left to hope for. They must live with the disappointment of having raised a child who did not live up to their expectations as well as the haunting (and quite possibly incorrect) feeling that they are somehow to blame for their child's failings.

It is important to keep certain things in mind when discussing difficult children.

First, in many cases they are not difficult "on purpose." To the contrary, some children cannot help but be difficult. Certainly this is the case when a child gives his parents trouble while still in the womb or while just a baby. Likewise, if a child is born with massive birth defects, he will be a difficult child through no fault of his own: As long as he is alive, he will sap the time, patience, emotions, and finances of his parents.

Second, we should keep in mind that just because a child is difficult does not mean that his parents won't love him. Indeed, Genevie and Margolies point to the tendency of the mothers of difficult children to say, in effect, "I love my child; I just don't like him." Of course, the fact that parents love their difficult child can serve to increase the anguish they experience because of him.

Third, a difficult child will possess the ability to transform what we have listed above as *benefits* of having children into costs. Thus, suppose you had a child so you could transmit your values to him; a difficult child not only will refuse to be indoctrinated with your values, but will adopt values diametrically opposed to your own. (According to the *Motherhood Report*, having your children abandon your values is a prime source of parental suffering.)[21] Or, suppose you had a child so that your family name wouldn't die with you; a difficult child might spite you by changing his last name, or by giving his children his wife's last name. Or suppose you had a child so that he could follow in your footsteps (and thereby allow you to vicariously "live again"); a difficult child might, as soon as he determined where your footsteps lay, start walking vigorously in the opposite direction.

Fourth, whether a child is difficult or easy is, to a certain extent, "in the eye of the beholder." A child who would be considered difficult by one set of parents might be considered easy by another. Suppose, for example, a child stubbornly insists on spending all his free time practicing cello. Such a child might be a nightmare for parents whose goal it was, say, to raise the next Ty Cobb. They might complain about the child's obstinacy and about the ruination of their dreams for the child. This same child might be the ideal child of another set of parents whose own child, much to their dismay, steadfastly refuses to practice his cello and instead sneaks off to play baseball with his friends.

When the personalities of children clash with those of their parents, it increases the chance that parents will find their children difficult. A messy parent might be understanding of a messy child; a particularly tidy parent, however, might find life with a messy child to be a trying experience. Boisterous parents might get along splendidly with a boisterous child; quiet parents probably wouldn't.

Then again, parents can find a child to be difficult, not because the child's personality differs from theirs, but because it resembles theirs. Suppose, for instance, that a parent was a lifelong procrastinator who felt that he had failed miserably in life because of his tendency to procrastinate. Such a parent might anguish over his child's tendency to procrastinate.

To a large extent, then, what determines whether a child is easy or difficult is not so much that child's personality as the "fit" between that child's personality and those of his parents.

Ever More Difficult

It is quite likely that in America today, the percentage of difficult children is higher than it was a generation ago. Allow me to explain some of the factors that I think lie behind this change.

Whether a child is easy or difficult is subjective: It is, as I have suggested, in the eye of the beholder. Thus, if parents become harder to please, there will be an increase in the number of children regarded as difficult (and therefore in the number of children who *are* difficult), *even if the children themselves remain unchanged.*

A case can be made, though, that parents *have* become harder to please in the last few decades. Behavior in children that once would have been shrugged off as "boys being boys" is these days much less likely to be tolerated. Similarly, whereas parents of the 1950s might have expected their children to play when not in school, today's parents often have considerably loftier expectations for their children: A child's "free time" might be taken up with participation in organized sports, music lessons, gymnastics lessons, Japanese lessons, or other structured activities. Of course, the more a parent expects of his child, the easier it is for a parent to be displeased by his child.

To understand why parents have become "more difficult," consider some of the changes that have taken place in families in the last several decades. Presumably a parent's tolerance for "childish behavior" depends on how much time and energy he has: The less time and energy, the more problems this behavior will create for him. In the 1950s the typical child had two parents, one of whom (usually the mother) was a full-time parent. That full-time parent could devote whatever energy she had to her children; it was not dissipated at a "real job."

Many modern families, by way of contrast, are headed by a single woman, and that woman may be forced to work. As a result, when she is at home she is likely to be tired and cranky and therefore unlikely to have much tolerance for "boys being boys." And even if this one parent does not have to work but can instead spend her days with her children, the process of doing so is likely to wear her to a frazzle: There is, after all, no other parent to whom she can "hand off" the child when she runs out of energy.

Even when a modern family has two parents, there is a good chance that both of them work. As a result, both parents will tend to come home tired and not be in the mood for childish behavior.

Suppose, finally, that a modern child is lucky enough to have two parents, one of whom is a stay-at-home parent. Chances are that this parent is older than the average mom or dad of 1950. With increasing age comes a decline in energy. Older parents are less likely to be tolerant of childish behavior than younger parents.

The factors just cited, besides tending to make children "more difficult" in the eyes of their parents, will also affect the extent to which parents discipline their children. Notice, after all, that to discipline a child requires considerable effort. It is easy to state a rule, but it takes considerable time and energy to deal with the child's repeated attempts to test the exact limits of the rule. Likewise, it is easy to punish a child by telling him to go to his room for an hour, but it takes somewhat more time and energy to make sure that the child stays put in his room for the full hour. It is easy to tell your teenager to be home by midnight "or else," but almost impossible (for many middle-aged parents) to stay up until midnight to make sure the command has been obeyed: The spirit may be willing, but the flesh is weak.

It will be quite difficult for a single parent to spend the time and energy required by an ongoing program of child discipline. Notice, in particular, that when this parent gets tired of enforcing "the law," there will be no other parent to take over. As a result, the single parent might be tempted to relax his or her standards of child discipline.

Likewise, the demands placed on parents, both of whom work full-time, will be considerable. Parents who spend their days at demanding jobs might not have the time, energy, or desire to discipline their children: When they come home from work they will want to relax, not argue with the kids. If these parents set aside "quality time" for their children, they will want to spend it not punishing the children for their transgressions but playing with them. And of course when both parents work, it means that someone else will be taking care of their child during the day, and if this "someone else" has many other children to care for, he will have a limited amount of time and energy to devote to the behavioral problems of one particular child.

In short, there is reason to think that today's parents spend considerably less time and energy disciplining their children than was the case in decades past. Research confirms this view: For instance, in 1962 spanking was the favored disciplinary technique of 59 percent of parents, with limiting TV, scolding, and sending to bed coming in as the favored disciplinary techniques of 38 percent, 17 percent, and 8 percent of parents, respectively. By 1992 spanking was the favored disciplinary technique of only 19 percent of parents; and the number of parents who favored limiting TV, scolding, and sending to bed had dropped to 15 percent, 15 percent, and 2 percent, respectively. What were parents doing to discipline their children? "Time out," favored by 35 percent of parents, was the most popular disciplinary technique.[22]

No matter what we might think of the appropriateness of the child-discipline techniques of days gone by—and I myself think it is a mistake for parents to spank children—the above comments make it clear that the penalties for juvenile misbehavior are likely to be far less serious today than they were in past decades. Parents are increasingly favoring "soft" forms of discipline. Furthermore, a case can be made that the most popular disciplinary technique, a "time out," doesn't involve much discipline at all. Suppose, for example, that in a time-out a child is sent to his room. This room, rather than being the moral equivalent of a jail cell, may well be what is, from a child's point of view, a garden of earthly delights. He might have a television in his room, so that sending him there is not tantamount to limiting television privileges; he might have a telephone (or a computer with a modem) in his room, so that sending him there is not tantamount to cutting off his ability to converse with friends; and his room might be a treasure trove of wonderful toys. A child might not find it particularly troubling to be "sentenced" to spend an hour in his room; indeed, the real question is, What could possibly have induced him to leave such a wonderful place to begin with?

The decline of child discipline is significant if we think—as I do—that a disciplined child is more likely to be "easy" than an undisciplined child. A disciplined child, after all, is more likely to consider the consequences of his actions—and in particular is more likely to consider the consequences his actions have for others—than is an undisciplined child. A disciplined child is therefore less likely to be a "pain in the neck" to his parents and the other people he associates with than is an undisciplined child. Thus, there is reason to think that today's children, because of the relative lack of parental discipline, would be harder for their parents to get along with than were the children of the 1950s—*even if parents had not raised their standards of what counts as appropriate childhood behavior.*

Children, because they are not disciplined, grow less willing to please their parents at the same time as parents, with less time and energy, grow harder to please: It is hardly surprising that there would be a surge in the number of "difficult children" in America.

A Digression: Ritalin in America

What does a country do when it finds itself with an increasing number of difficult children but a decreasing ability (or desire) on the part of adults to use behavior-modification techniques to deal with these children? In the case of America, parents have resorted to behavior-altering drugs. The use of Ritalin in America, for example, has skyrocketed, rising by about 130 percent between 1990 and 1994. About 3.5 percent of children between ages 5 and 14 take it regularly. Furthermore, the rise of Ritalin appears to be primarily an American phenomenon: Ritalin use in the United States is at least five times higher than in the rest of the world.[23]

The thing to keep in mind about attention deficit disorder (ADD),[24] the malady that Ritalin is supposed to treat, is that its diagnosis is quite subjective. For instance, one symptom is fidgeting. How much fidgeting is too much fidgeting? Enough fidgeting to be a problem. A problem for whom? A problem for a child's parents and teachers. Notice that different adults, in different situations, will have different tolerances for fidgetiness in children. Fidgetiness that might drive one adult to distraction might not bother another who has more patience about this sort of thing.

Other symptoms of ADD include climbing excessively, having difficulty playing quietly, and talking excessively. These are all subjective symptoms. For some parents, a child who talks at all might be regarded as a child who talks excessively.

For the owner-parent to put his child on Ritalin requires no justification: If it makes the parent's life better, that is justification enough. For the steward-parent, though, the decision to put a child on Ritalin will in many cases be difficult to defend.

It might be argued, at the outset, that a steward-parent would *never* put his child on Ritalin. Indeed, some might compare parents who put their children on Ritalin with the nurses of days gone by who gave laudanum to the babies in their care. Both the nurse and the Ritalin-giving parent are drugging their children to make their own days more pleasant.

This comparison, however, is unfair. For one thing, the nurses who gave laudanum were benefiting at the expense of the child. Consider, however, those cases in which a child is extremely hyperactive, so much so that he becomes a social outcast and is essentially unteachable. Suppose, too, that efforts to calm the child's hyperactivity through behavior-modification techniques are in vain. In such cases, Ritalin would be undeniably beneficial to the child. Thanks to Ritalin, he can live a fairly normal life and has a good chance of successfully completing his education. In such cases, it would be as wrong for parents to withhold Ritalin from a child as it would be to withhold antibiotics from him if he had a dangerous infection.

Other cases in which parents give their children Ritalin are not this clear-cut. Suppose, for example, that without Ritalin a child has a fairly normal life and is doing adequately in school; suppose that his parents give him Ritalin so that he is a bit less of a handful than he would otherwise be. That such cases exist is suggested by the fact that many doctors prescribe Ritalin without taking the time necessary to do a complete diagnosis of ADD. It is also suggested by the fact that many parents are reluctant to take No for an answer to their request for Ritalin: These parents "doctor shop" until they find a doctor who agrees with their own assessment that their child needs the drug.[25]

Parents might defend giving children Ritalin in such cases by arguing that as long as a child is not harmed by taking the drug, his parents are doing nothing wrong in giving it to him. It is true that they benefit, but not at the child's expense. Those offering this argument might go on to suggest that old-fashioned (i.e., nonpharmaceutical) forms of behavior modification are outmoded and that Ritalin is nothing more than behavior modification in pill form.

This is a promising argument, but for a number of reasons I

hesitate to endorse it.

First, although Ritalin looks safe from a medical point of view, it will be some time before we can be absolutely confident that it is a drug which, when used in children, is without long-term negative consequences. It may be reasonable to expose a child to a certain level of medical risk to, say, save his eyesight, but is it likewise reasonable to expose a child to medical risk simply so that your days will be more tranquil?

Second, even if Ritalin itself proves to be utterly safe from a medical point of view, there are dangers in using it to treat behavior problems, inasmuch as it might signal the child that in this world, when you do not "fit in," using drugs can help you. It will be interesting to see, as the decades pass and today's Ritalin Youth grow up, whether they will be more likely to abuse drugs as adults. (Early indications, by the way, suggest that they will not.)[26]

Third, if a goal of the steward-parent is to raise a child "to be free"—and in Chapter 9, I argued that this is a primary goal of steward-parenting—then steward-parents will not treat Ritalin as a functional equivalent of traditional behavior-modification techniques. One thing that behavior-modification techniques can do that Ritalin can never do is help the child gain self-control—that is, help a child master himself and his impulses. Ritalin apparently functions by suppressing a variety of impulses the child would otherwise have, for example, the urge to talk. Consequently, the child needn't learn how to control the urge to talk: The urge seldom arises. Traditional behavior-modification techniques, on the other hand, do nothing to suppress urges; they do, however, teach the child how to fight urges that arise, and help teach him to become master of himself.

Fourth and finally, I am bothered by the thought that when you modify a child's behavior by giving him Ritalin, you are in an important sense failing to respect the child as the person he is.

To better understand this last point, suppose that someone you dealt with daily—maybe your spouse, maybe a coworker—were discovered to have been sneaking a personality-altering drug into your daily cup of coffee—something like Prozac, we can imagine, although I don't know whether you could successfully slip this drug to someone in coffee. Suppose that the reason he did it was to make you more cheerful, so that his daily dealings with you would be less stressful. How would you react on discovering his scheme? Most people would not thank the drugger. In fact, lots of people would press charges. And even if the drug did you no physical harm whatever—even if you admitted that you had been rather happy during your months of unknowingly being drugged—you might nevertheless argue that your "person" had been violated in a very important way: Your normally cantankerous personality had been, for lack of a better word, "kidnapped."

Here is another way to explain what is involved in "respecting a person." Consider what totalitarian countries do with political nonconformists. In some countries they are jailed; in other countries (e.g., the old Soviet Union) they are locked in psychiatric wards and treated with various psychotropic drugs. Most people agree that, while both these ways of treating political nonconformists are outrageous, the latter treatment is worse than the former. Jail respects the person's mind, but not his freedom; psychiatric wards (used for political purposes) respect neither the person's mind nor his freedom. Thus, jails respect persons in a way that psychiatric wards do not.

Of course, parents who give a child Ritalin typically do not do so on the sly. And no one would hold parents who give Ritalin to somewhat-troublesome children to be the moral equivalent of Soviet jailers. I introduced the previous examples only to make it clear that in many cases, respect for a person will preclude us from chemically altering that person's personality, even though it may be in our own interests to do so. A steward-parent will be intently concerned with respecting his child's person, and he will not mind the fact that behavior-modification techniques will take much more time and energy than will a daily dose of Ritalin. Indeed, he will exhaust conventional means of behavior modification before resorting to medication. He will think long and hard before putting his child on Ritalin, and the key question he will ask himself in making this decision is, Am I doing this for the child or for myself?

In America today, parents who want to keep their rambunctious children off Ritalin face an uphill battle. Although these parents may be willing to "go the extra mile" that it takes to keep their child under control without the use of behavior-modifying drugs, they might find that the teachers at their child's school are not quite so patient. They might get a request from the school to come in and talk, and when they arrive they might find themselves confronting not just the child's teacher, but his counselor, his principal, and the school psychologist as well, all of whom push the parent to accept that his child is behaviorally disabled and to get help (i.e., Ritalin) for him.[27] It is difficult for typical parents to battle against these "experts," and when they do, those at the school, rather than taking the parents' arguments seriously, might dismiss them as a form of parental denial.

It is worth noting, by the way, that these "experts" can hardly be regarded as disinterested parties. If a troublesome child is put on Ritalin, it will benefit them in two ways. First, their job of dealing with the child will be made easier, and second, they stand to receive a $420 federal bounty when the child is categorized as "disabled."[28]

To understand the obstacles that confront the Ritalin-resistant parent, consider the plight of Beth Wolt, whose son Marty was, putting it mildly, a difficult child.[29] Ms. Wolt struggled against school administrators' recommendation that Marty be put on Ritalin. In the end she gave in to their demands. Marty's behavior improved dramatically, but the price of this improvement was the extinction of much of her son's admittedly boisterous personality. Ms. Wolt described the change in these terms: "He wasn't there. He did everything he was supposed to do. But his personality was gone."

Ms. Wolt took her son off Ritalin without telling his teachers that she was doing so and—surprise—his good behavior in school continued. Ms. Wolt decided that what Marty needed was not Ritalin, but industrial-strength behavior modification.

And how did Marty turn out? At the time of this writing he was in eleventh grade and doing fine. He had outgrown most of his troublesome behavior.

Some might respond to this tale by pointing out that Marty would probably have turned out fine if given Ritalin, and that a Ritalin-suppressed Marty would have meant less grief for his teachers, his mother, and possibly even for Marty himself. This may be true, but it misses the point: Ms. Wolt took the steps she did because she respected Marty's person and because she realized that Marty's personality, as difficult as it might be, was an important part of his person. Fate had given Ms. Wolt a difficult child to raise, but as a steward-parent, she rose to the challenge he presented rather than taking the easy way out.

In America today, boyhood (and I say "boyhood" on purpose, since an estimated 80 to 90 percent of ADD cases are boys)[30] has been pathologized—more precisely, boyish behavior has been classified as a form of mental illness, whose treatment consists of daily doses of Ritalin. By treating these boys with Ritalin we make them behave "better"—that is, more like girls.

A case can be made, though, that in eradicating boyish behavior we run the risk of eradicating some of the desirable traits that might ultimately grow out of boyish behavior. We might make it less likely, for example, that boys grow up to be men who think for themselves, who sometimes don't take No for an answer, and who sometimes fight the system. Crush the spirit of the boy, and you run the risk of producing a dispirited man. Says Beth Wolt of her son: "They never crushed him."[31]

One last thought about the drugging of America's children: In the 1990s there was a sharp rise in the number of *infants* who were on psychotropic medications.[32] This trend is alarming for a pair of reasons. First, there is no scientific evidence to show that these drugs are safe for infants to take; most of the prescriptions for them involve "off label" uses of drugs, and in some cases these prescriptions ignore warnings *against* using the drugs in children younger than six.[33] Second, although it can be argued that it is abnormal for a fourteen-year-old to be fidgety and easily distracted, such behavior in two-year-olds is entirely normal and probably even developmentally desirable.

It is not difficult to imagine an America in the not-so-distant future in which a significant number of children spend their entire childhoods—at the behest of their parents and with the complicity of their doctors—in a drugged state of mind. The parents will be spared much of the stress that comes from raising an unruly child, but at what cost to their children? And at what cost to society?

Costs and Benefits, Concluded

So, do the benefits of making a baby outweigh the costs? It depends in large part on whether the baby you make is (according to your standards) a difficult child or an easy one, and on whether you yourself are a difficult or easy (to please) parent. A difficult parent will probably find the ratio of benefits to costs to be shockingly low, even if he is blessed with an easy child. An easy parent, on the other hand, might find the ratio of benefits to costs to be acceptable, even if his child turns out to be difficult.

What about the "average" parent? Well, he will find that the benefits of parenting, as described above, tend to be intangible, whereas the costs tend to be painfully tangible. It is far from obvious that for the "average" parent the benefits derived from raising the "average" child will outweigh the costs.

Before ending our discussion of the costs and benefits of parenting, let us return to a topic raised briefly above: "absentee parents." Consider those cases in which parents are absent from their child for much of the day because they both hold full-time jobs. For such parents it is far less likely that the benefits of parenthood will outweigh the costs than it is for other parents.

Notice, after all, that career parents will miss out on many of the intangible benefits of having children. One such benefit is sharing in your child's little triumphs. If you work full-time, you are unlikely to be there when he takes his first steps, utters his first word, reads his first word, hits his first home run, and so on.

Of course, by working full-time you also miss his many little "disasters"—his skinned knees, his crying fits, his soiled diapers. It might be suggested that the trade-off is worth it: Yes, you missed his first steps, but you also missed thousands of dirty diapers.

This suggestion sounds plausible—until we think about how it is that intense, loving relationships are formed. Such relationships come into existence not merely because two people have shared some good times, but because they have shared some bad times as well. The real test of a loving relationship is whether one person is there when the other person needs him. If he is, the relationship is strengthened; if not, the relationship might founder.

This means that parents who work full-time will have a difficult time forming an intense, loving relationship with their children simply because they won't, in many cases, be there for their children in their children's time of need. It will be someone else who changes his diaper, kisses his skinned knee, or comforts him when he is frightened.

I am by no means saying that a child won't come to love his parents as the result of spending a half-hour of "quality time" with them each day. The danger is that the intensity of this love will be a pale shadow of what it might have been if the child and his parents had spent extensive amounts of time together. The number of intimate moments shared would have been far greater, as would the number of times the parent was there for the child in his time of need. What is particularly sad is that in some cases, absentee parents won't have a clue that their relationship with their child could have been dramatically different if only they had put child ahead of career.

When it comes to our relationships with adults, we realize these things. If, for example, a man wished to develop an intense, loving relationship with a woman (as opposed to, say, merely wishing to have sex with her), it simply would not do to devote a half-hour of quality time to her each day. To the contrary, he would want to share as many moments with her as possible. He would want to have fun times with her, but he would also realize the importance of being there for her when she needed him. If she came to him in tears, he would be an absolute fool (if he wished to develop an intense, loving relationship with her) if he suggested that she take her problems to her mother or to her girlfriend instead of sharing them with him.

Why would absentee parents have children—maybe even lots of them—when their absenteeism undermines their ability to form intense, loving relationships with the children they have? This question is difficult to answer until we realize that many absentee parents don't *want* to have intense, loving relationships with their children. To the contrary, they have children in order to practice what economist Thorstein Veblen called "conspicuous consumption." Stated differently, children are, for some couples, the ultimate fashion accessory: They are possessions that complete the "look" of the family, much the same as a spacious home and a Lexus in the driveway do. In such cases, as one demographer put it, "children have become the priciest of baubles."[34] Or, as one absentee parent put it, "[My daughter] was really like a little doll that I could show off."[35]

Of course, those favoring the stewardship model of parenting will be reluctant to think of their children in these terms.

Are Parents Happy?

Let us set aside our discussion of the costs and benefits of parenting and instead turn to a simpler question: Does parenting tend to make people happy? If it does, then we will have a satisfying and conclusive answer to the question of why people become parents: They become parents because doing so makes them happy. No more would need to be said on the subject.

Fortunately for us, a fair amount of research has been done into the effects that parenthood has on people's happiness. The research in question shows that for a good many people it is counterproductive to seek happiness by becoming a parent.

There is, to begin with, a body of psychological research to suggest that when all things are considered, children are a source of unhappiness for their parents. Several studies have measured the happiness of parents at various points in their marriage.[36] The data, when plotted, makes a lovely U-shaped curve, starting out high before children come along, dropping to its nadir when the children are teenagers, and recovering to its original level of happiness only when the nest is empty. The simple truth is that it is hard to be happy when you are exhausted, worried about your finances, deprived of your free time and freedom, and constantly subject to emotional harassment.

But can't having a baby increase the happiness of parents by helping to cement the relationship between a man and a woman? Perhaps, but it also causes a great deal of stress: Having a baby is twice as likely to change a woman's marriage for the worse as it is to change it for the better.[37]

What about the "empty nest" syndrome, that feeling of lone-liness that parents get when their children grow up and leave home? Researchers had a hard time finding it: The primary feel-ing experienced by mothers when their children left the nest was a sense of relief.[38]

Another way to assess the overall impact that parenthood has on a person's happiness is to ask those who have experienced what parenthood has to offer the following question: If you had it to do over again knowing what you know now, would you be-come a parent?

In 1975, columnist Ann Landers asked her readers this ques-tion. Fifty thousand replied, and of them, 70 percent said they would not have children if they had it to do over again.

To be sure, there is probably less to Landers's survey than meets the eye. In her survey, after all, the sample was "self-selecting," so there is a danger that a disproportionate number of unhappy parents wrote in.

Another, more scientific attempt to ask the "if you could do it over again" question was made by Genevie and Margolies. Their survey was based on a random sampling of 1,100 mothers in the United States.[39] When they asked these mothers whether they would have children if they could relive their lives knowing what they know now, only 4 percent said that they probably or definitely wouldn't have children. Fully 81 percent said they would definitely have children again.

These last numbers are pretty much in line with the numbers produced in a 1975 survey by *McCall's* and a 1978 survey by *Better Homes and Gardens*, both of which found that one in ten mothers would choose not to have children if they could relive their lives.[40]

One is tempted, on the basis of these numbers, to conclude that parenthood is a generally positive experience for parents, in terms of their happiness. Otherwise, why the willingness to do it all over again? Such a conclusion might not be warranted, though. Notice, in particular, that for a woman to admit that she would not have children if she had it to do over again is tantamount to admitting that at some level she wishes that her children had never been born. This is more than most mothers—even the mothers of extremely difficult children—can bring themselves to do. Furthermore, there is a difference between saying you would have children if you had it to do over again—knowing full well that you *don't* have it to do over again—and actually choosing to have children, knowing what you know now, if you in fact *did* have it to do over again. Along these lines, if you asked a soldier whether, knowing what he knows now, he thinks that the pain suffered in boot camp was worth it, he might answer that it was. If you asked this same soldier whether he would like to go through boot camp again starting tomorrow, he would probably reject the offer.

Another statistic turned up by Genevie and Margolies suggests that many women are less than happy in their role as mother: They found that about one in four women had very positive feelings about motherhood, that about one in five had predominantly negative feelings about it, and that the remaining mothers (about 55 percent of the sample) were ambivalent.[41] For most mothers, motherhood brings a mixed bag of joys and sorrows.

We may quibble about what, if anything, the above findings

show, but one thing is certain: We are woefully mistaken if we think that babies will bring joy to whoever makes them. For a good many people, becoming a parent is a big mistake, if what they want is to maximize their lifetime happiness.

Perfect Children

When people are considering whether or not to have children, they tend to base their deliberations on the assumption that theirs will be not just an easy child, but a perfect child. According to Genevie and Margolies,

> The majority of women of all ages and educational backgrounds (about 70 percent) were neither realistic nor pessimistic but extraordinarily illusionistic in their visions of what motherhood would be like. Their unrealistic fantasies ran the gamut from slightly romanticized notions to fantasies of perfection: perfect children, perfect mothers, perfect families.[42]

In his study of the effects of children on families, E. E. Le Masters concluded that women's fantasies of motherhood are the real "romantic complex" in our culture.[43]

So do most people end up having perfect children? Of course not. In defense of this claim, we need only remember that for nearly all parents there is something about their child that they would change if they could; if their child were perfect, there would be no need for change.

And for many parents, their children will not only have *some* imperfections, but *many* imperfections. If we asked these parents whether there was anything they would change about their children if they could, they might (if they were in a forthright frame of mind) produce for us a rather lengthy list of possible "improvements" in their child, including such things as keeping his room neater (or not being such a "neat freak"), taking showers more often (or less often), trying harder in school (or being less compulsive about getting good grades), and so on.

Why do parents tend to believe that their child will be perfect? In part because they have been deceived by their friends and by society. The children of their friends will, in many cases, appear to be nearly perfect. This appearance, of course, is utterly misleading. Most parents present the world with a distorted view of their children: They brag about their children's strengths and hide their weaknesses. Thus, other adults are almost certain to hear about their son's *A* in math, but are far less likely to hear about the horrid mess in his bedroom. When other adults are present in the house, their child's stereo is likely to be played at levels that are almost inaudible; when the other adults depart, up goes the stereo. For every tantrum a child throws in public, he is likely to throw twenty in the privacy of his own home; for while he doesn't care what his parents think of his behavior, he might be acutely sensitive to what passing strangers might think of it.

Even when people spend long periods with a friend's child, they might not come away with a picture of the child as he really is. The child in question might behave far better for them than he behaves for his own parents. He might pick up after himself, carry his dinner dishes from the table without being asked, and say "please" and "thank you," things he would never dream of doing with his own parents.

When prospective parents turn to television, they again find either perfect children or children whose imperfections are endearing and amusing. Children who appear on television programs almost without exception have "hearts of gold," even when they misbehave. The picture is a pretty one, but as is the case with much on television, it is a picture that bears little resemblance to reality.

Personality Problems

Even when parents are aware of the imperfections in other people's children, they tend to think that they will be unlike other people in this respect. The child they make, after all, will possess a superior genetic makeup—namely, their own. More importantly, the

child they make will be raised by them; and by carefully controlling its environment, they feel confident that they can raise it to
be a perfect child. Speaking of the mind-set of potential mothers, Genevie and Margolies have this to say: "Unlike other 'imperfect' mothers they had seen—mothers who lost their tempers,
mothers who were frazzled at the edges—they would be perfect,
creating perfect children by virtue of their perfect mothering."[44]

There are a number of problems with this plan.

First, realize that for most people the key factor in determining whether their child will, in their eyes, count as perfect is
his personality. A child with an offensive personality—one who
is selfish, rude, and ill-tempered—might be a pain to live with,
regardless of what admirable qualities he may possess. On the
other hand, a child with a terrific personality might well count as
perfect in their eyes, even though the child might have a number
of non-personality-related imperfections, for example, birth defects.

This suggests that if parents could determine their child's
personality, either by determining his genetic makeup or by controlling his environment, then it might be in their power to produce perfect children at will. The problem is, first, that a child's
personality does not appear to be a function of his genetic makeup,
and second, that the ability of parents to determine their child's
personality by controlling his environment appears to be somewhat limited.

As far as genetics is concerned, consider this: It is entirely
possible for the same two parents to produce offspring whose
personalities vary considerably, despite the fact that these offspring come from the same genetic stock. It is common for parents with more than one child to spend time scratching their
heads in puzzlement over the personality differences between their
children. Or, if this isn't convincing, consider those cases in which
parents give birth to identical twins who, despite their genetic
identity, develop different personalities. There is strong evidence,
in other words, that a child's personality is only weakly linked to
his genetic makeup, so even if you could control a child's genetic
makeup, you couldn't count on thereby controlling his personality.

What about controlling a child's environment? Will this

enable us to control his personality? Nope. Again, I can point to the common situation in which the same two parents raise several children "in the same way," only to have the children turn out differently.

Of course, in such cases it might be argued that the children in question aren't really raised "in the same way." After all, even when children are raised by the same parents, they will likely experience significantly different environments while they grow up. Notice, in particular, that the younger children will experience one important environmental factor that the oldest child didn't: the presence in the household of an older sibling.

This point is well taken, but consider again the Dionne quints, whose story was told in Chapter 2. Not only were these quints genetically identical, but they were probably raised as much alike as it would be possible to raise children: Their childhood was spent in a "laboratory" setting and was constantly monitored by psychologists. Nevertheless, there were significant personality differences between the quints. This suggests that even if parents tried to control their child's environment in minute detail, there is no guarantee that theirs would turn out to be a perfect child, personality-wise.

This is not to say that environment has *no* effect on personality. Parents can, I think, "shape" their child's personality by controlling his environment. There is, however, a sizable difference between *shaping* a child's personality and *determining* a child's personality. Thus, if the parents of a child given to emotional outbursts use behavior-modification techniques to deal with these outbursts, the number of such outbursts is likely to diminish with the passing years, but might never drop to the level that the parents had hoped for. Likewise, when two gregarious parents find themselves in the custody of a shy child, there are a number of things they can do to encourage the child to "open up," but despite their efforts the child might never be the extrovert they had expected him to be.

To better appreciate the absurdity of attempts to determine a child's personality, consider the difficulties we adults encounter in trying to determine *our own* personalities. To a large extent our personalities are beyond our control.

Consider, for example, the plight of bashful people. A bashful person might experience much pain because of his bashfulness and might sincerely wish he could overcome this character trait. Could such a person, by an act of the will, change his personality and become an outspoken extrovert? Probably not.

Personality is a powerful thing; it holds us captive. Because of it, something that is easy for others to do—for example, flirting with members of the opposite sex—might be overwhelmingly difficult for a bashful person to do; and conversely, something that is difficult for others to do—such as parachuting—might be easy for a bashful person to do. Realistically speaking, the best our bashful individual could hope for is that, as the result of conscious effort, he becomes, with the passage of time, more outgoing. No matter how hard he tries, it is unlikely that he will ever become a social butterfly.

If it is difficult to change your own personality, it is more difficult still to change someone else's personality. Parents should keep this fact in mind in their dealings with their child. To some extent they should take his personality to be a "given": It is the raw material with which they must work in their attempts to raise their child. They might succeed in shaping their child's personality but it is unlikely that they can supplant it. They must do their best to "work around" the personality. Their goal should be not to produce the child with the best personality, but the best child they can, given the limitations of his personality.

Another thing to keep in mind about the personalities of children is that it is ludicrous, in most cases, to talk about a child's personality. Instead, one must speak of a child's personali*ties*— the various personalities he has at various stages of his life. It is not only possible, but is unfortunately rather likely, that the loving, inquisitive four-year old will, ten years later, be neither loving nor inquisitive—indeed, that his personality will have undergone a Jekyll-and-Hyde transformation. Rare is the child who retains the same personality throughout childhood. As a consequence, those parents who are fortunate enough to find themselves living with a perfect baby should not count on their child remaining perfect throughout his childhood. In particular, they should not count on someday being the parents of a perfect teenager.

Consequently, even if a child's *ultimate* personality were determined by his genes and upbringing, this would be of little comfort to parents who, after all, spend time with the child in those decades *before* he comes into possession of his "ultimate personality."

Genevie and Margolies looked into the question of whether, by providing "quality parenting," mothers could control how easy or difficult their children were. They found no apparent connection between the quality of the mothering children receive and how difficult or easy they turn out to be: It is possible for truly second-rate parents to have what are uncommonly easy children, and for what are in all respects wonderful parents to end up with difficult children. How difficult your children are would appear to depend, as one mother observed, on "a roll of the dice."[45]

Indeed, there is reason to think that it is not the quality of mothering that determines whether a child is difficult or easy; to the contrary, *it is whether a child is difficult or easy that determines the quality of mothering he receives.* According to Genevie and Margolies, mothers quite understandably had better relationships with and were better mothers to easy children. They concluded that "it is as much the child who makes the mother as it is the mother who makes the child."[46]

Because parents often fail to take account of the possibility that their children will (despite their efforts) possess substantially different personalities than they do, parents' plans for making their children happy often go awry. Consider, for example, parents who strive to make their children happy by creating for them the childhoods they wish they themselves had had. Such attempts often fail to take into account the fact that these children, because their personalities differ from those of their parents, might not be particularly happy living their parents' dream childhood. A man who, as a child, might have wanted more than anything to have a father who was interested in, say, science—who would do chemistry experiments with him and take him to museums—might be profoundly disappointed when he finds that his own children want not to do experiments or go to museums, but to go skating or bowling, activities he abhors.

It is one of parenting's ironies that the child for whom you might have been the ideal parent, in terms of a matching of personalities and interests, is the offspring of another parent, whose own personality and interests are uniquely mismatched to those of his child.

The Helen Nearing Game

In her book *The Childfree Alternative*, Kate Harper interviewed Scott and Helen Nearing, the famous back-to-nature radicals. When Harper asked Helen Nearing about her decision not to have children, she replied: "I'm very glad, when I see some children, that I don't have *them*. As we have traveled through the United States, and we have done it plenty, I would say that there have been about a dozen children I would like to have had, out of the thousands I've seen."[47] A dozen out of thousands—the odds are not attractive.

This suggests a game that prospective parents can play when deciding whether or not to make a baby. Rather than assuming (unrealistically, as we have seen) that their child will be perfect, they should assume that, despite their genetic makeup and despite the effort they put into parenting, theirs will be a child drawn at random from the children they have known or observed. Thus, there is a chance that their child, as a baby, will be a bundle of joy, but there is also a chance that their child will be born with missing arms. As an infant there is a chance that their child will like to be cuddled and be read bedtime stories, but there is also a chance that he will be prone to tantrums and will not take No for an answer. In high school there is a chance that their child will be a straight-*A* student, but there is also a chance that their child will get pregnant and drop out of school. As an adult there is a chance that their child will make a respectable living, but there is also a chance that he will be unemployed or become a criminal. Basically, the question they should ask themselves—much as Helen Nearing did—is, What percentage of actual children would they like to parent?

Exceptionally easy parents might answer that they would want to parent almost any child alive. Exceptionally difficult parents—like, perhaps, Helen Nearing—might want to parent only, say, one percent of the children now alive. And many "average" parents will, if they think long and hard about it, come to the conclusion that they would *not* want to be parents to *most* of the children now alive. For these people, parenthood does not look like a winning proposition.

In the Dark

In this book I have repeatedly compared the role of the steward-parent to that of the land steward. At this point, one striking difference between them becomes apparent.

Notice that when your neighbor comes to you and asks if you will take care of his lands while he is on a trip, you can make some important determinations before deciding whether or not to undertake this obligation. You can, most importantly, consider whether the land you are being asked to take care of is "difficult" land (e.g., a piece of semiarid land where crops can be grown only by intensive effort) or "easy" land (e.g., a piece of prime farmland where crops spring out of the ground and flourish "as if by magic"). If the land would be extremely difficult for you to take care of, it would be completely understandable if you turned down your neighbor's request.

Prospective parents, on the other hand, do not have the luxury of knowing ahead of time whether their child will be difficult or easy. As the above discussion shows, they are to a large extent "in the dark" about how rewarding their life as a parent will be. It could be that they will experience parental bliss from day one; or it could be that—due to circumstances beyond their control—

parenthood will be a hellish experience from which they can escape only by dying.

Taking on the responsibilities of parenting, then, is like agreeing to take care of someone's lands without knowing ahead of time whether these lands will be difficult or easy to take care of. It might be foolish for you to undertake such an obligation, but if you freely undertake it, your obligation will in no way be diminished if it turns out that caring for the lands demands incredible amounts of unrewarding labor. You will, if you are an ethical person, see the job through, even though it will cost you considerably to do so.

In like fashion, someone who becomes a parent should do so hoping for the best—an easy child who is a delight to parent—but prepared for the worst. If fate deals him a difficult hand, he will not, if he is a moral person, "discard" the hand, but will play it out to the best of his ability.

The above analogy should also make it clear how awesome is the obligation undertaken when someone becomes a parent. It is precisely because of the magnitude of this obligation that it is disturbing when people undertake it lightly. One assumes, in such cases, either that the parents in question don't understand the magnitude of the obligations consequent to parenting, or that they understand the magnitude of these obligations but have no intention of fulfilling them. In either case, they are not operating on the stewardship model of parenting.

Climbing Everest

In many respects, the question of whether or not to make a baby is like the question of whether or not to climb Mount Everest.

Notice that undertaking an expedition to climb Everest is quite expensive. Climbers can expect to experience considerable physical discomfort during the climb. All this is done for a reward that is ephemeral—the thrill of standing on a cold, windy mountaintop for a few minutes, or maybe not even that.[48] And yet, despite all this, there are people who climb Everest. Why climb Everest then? George Mallory gave what is arguably the best answer to this question: "Because it is there."[49] The decision to climb Everest is not one, it would seem, that can "rationally" be defended.

In much the same way, making a baby is quite expensive; those making one will experience physical discomfort; and yet the joys of parenting are largely ephemeral, especially if one finds oneself the parent of a difficult child. In the last analysis, the decision to make a baby, like the decision to climb Everest, is probably one that, for most people, cannot be "rationally" defended.

The reader may protest that it is unfair to compare having children with climbing Everest. I entirely agree. If anything, the decision to have children is *harder* to justify rationally than the decision to climb Everest. The cost of climbing Everest—recently $65,000[50]—is a fraction of the cost of having and raising a child. And the discomforts involved in an attempt on Everest are probably less than the discomforts involved in pregnancy and in raising a child. Notice, for one thing, that the discomforts involved in an attempt on Everest last only for a few weeks, whereas the discomforts of pregnancy last for several months, while those associated with raising a child (midnight feedings, changing diapers, being the object of sarcasm, etc.) last for decades. As far as outright pain is concerned, the pain experienced by the typical climber of Everest is likely to be insignificant compared with that of a woman giving birth. But, you say, people sometimes die trying to climb Everest; and when they don't die, they are sometimes disfigured by frostbite. Before we make too much of this point, though, we should call to mind that women sometimes die in childbirth[51] and that childbirth is, for nearly all women, a disfiguring experience, in the sense that it changes their bodies in ways that for them are undesirable.

And what about the joys of childbirth and parenting? Aren't they more intense than the joys of conquering Everest? Sometimes...for some people.

Mountain climbing is not for everyone. The experience of standing on a cold, windy mountaintop might induce a state of ecstasy in some people, but will leave other people...well, cold and windblown. In much the same way, having children is not for everyone. As the above discussion shows, parents with certain personality types are likely to derive far more pleasure from parenting than parents with other personality types. When considering the benefits of parenting, prospective parents would do well to keep this in mind.

Although the decision of whether to make a baby is in many respects on a par with the decision of whether to climb Everest, we nevertheless find far more people having children than climbing Everest? Why should this be?

In part because most of the cost of climbing Everest must be paid up front: You must raise a significant amount of money before you can embark on a Himalayan expedition. If parents had to pay the cost of raising a child *before* they could make a baby, we would expect birthrates to fall dramatically.

A more significant factor is this: Although people lack an instinctual urge to climb mountains, they share an instinctual urge to have children. The urge is stronger in some people than in others, but it is nevertheless an urge both powerful and widespread.

Human beings are biologically programmed to have children. It would be astonishing if it were otherwise, for a species that does not feel driven to procreate generally doesn't last long as a species.

Consider your direct ancestors. As far as life's options are concerned, you differ from them—and they differ from each other—in countless respects. Some of them got married, and some did not. Some of them went to college, and some did not. Some of them were honest, and some were not. Some learned how to write their names, and some did not. Some scaled significant mountain peaks, and some did not. But there is one of life's options that every one of your direct ancestors had in common: Each of them made a child. Otherwise, you wouldn't be here now.

One way in which our biological programming to have children expresses itself is in sexual urges. In the old days, before effective means of birth control existed, this urge alone pretty much guaranteed that babies would come into existence. But for us to survive as a species, it isn't enough that babies come into existence. The babies in question must also be cared for and raised for at least a decade—must, that is, be parented—or they won't survive childhood and therefore won't themselves go on to reproduce, and our species will become extinct.

Suppose that our species possessed a powerful urge to have sex, but was utterly lacking in the urge to parent. We might, under such circumstances, look on the children we made simply as an unpleasant aftereffect of sex, rather like most people look on a hangover as an unpleasant aftereffect of drinking alcohol: It would no more occur to us to care for the children we made than it would occur to us to "care for" our vomit. Indeed, rather than caring for our children, our reaction might be to dispose of them.

For us to survive as a species, then, it is important that our urge to have sex is accompanied by an urge to care for and raise the babies that our having sex produces. The suggestion, in other words, is that we are programmed to respond positively to the babies we make—to take joy in them—and that part of what is involved in the urge to have children is a desire to experience this particular joy.

In different people, these two urges, the urge to have sex and the urge to parent, are present in differing degrees. In some people the urge to have sex is more powerful than the urge to parent, and in other people the urge to parent is more powerful than the urge to have sex. Along these lines, notice how different people react when a baby is brought into a room. Some people immediately go up to the baby, smile at it, and make cooing noises. These people react to the baby—as one woman I know put it— by going "all gooey" inside. Other people react to the baby by keeping their distance or by carrying on as if the baby weren't present at all.

Our sexual urges are biologically "hardwired" into us. They are the result of hormone production that is utterly beyond our control. Our urge to parent, on the other hand, does not appear to be "hardwired" into us to the same extent: For most people, the urge to make and raise children would appear to be easier to resist than the urge to have sex. Notice, too, that the urge to make children can, for most people, be satisfied for life by having a child or two; the urge to have sex, on the other hand, is not so easily satisfied.

Besides these biological urges, there is a layer of societally-programmed urges as well. If you are raised in a society in which you are repeatedly told what a wonderful thing it is to have children—or, alternatively, that it is your duty to have children, regardless of whether it is wonderful or not—then the easiest thing for you to do, unless you are a cultural rebel, is to have children. My guess is that this societal programming, though powerful, is never as powerful as the biological programming. There is also reason to believe that this societal programming has grown less powerful in recent years, as society has grown more accepting of those who choose to remain childfree.

One last comment on the urge to procreate: Notice that for a couple to have children it is not essential that *both* partners experience a strong urge to do so. If one partner has a very strong urge and the other partner is neutral with respect to the idea, then there is a very good chance that a baby will be created. Thus, in the case of many of the couples that I've encountered, it was one partner—typically the woman—who was the driving force behind procreation.

In summary, I would argue that the reason most people have children is not because it makes rational sense to do so, not because they have thought the issue through and have come to the conclusion that the benefits of parenting will, for them, outweigh the costs, and not even because there is reason to think that they will enjoy being parents, but because people experience a compelling urge—one that has been in some sense programmed into them—to have children.

That the question of whether or not to have children is typically decided in a "semi-rational" fashion is not unusual. Many important decisions are made in this way. How many of us, for example, did a costs and benefits analysis before deciding whether or not to marry a certain person? In most cases it is a decision we made with our hearts rather than with our heads.

Of course, it is one thing to make a decision in an off-the-cuff manner when ourselves and other consenting adults are the ones primarily affected by it; this is the case in the decision to marry. It is quite another thing to make a decision in an off-the-cuff manner when the life of an "innocent bystander" will be profoundly affected by our decision, and this is what happens when two people become parents without having given serious consideration to whether they are in fact well-suited to parenthood by their personality and their lifestyle and their circumstances. The innocent bystander is the child they create.

The mere fact that a person experiences a strong biological urge does not make him morally justified in acting on that urge. Indeed, one of the hallmarks of being a moral person is the ability to suppress biological urges. Thus, a moral man, when he experiences a strong urge to have sex with a certain woman, does his best to suppress it or at least express it in a socially acceptable way. He does not react to the urge by forcing himself on her, even though doing so would relieve his urge. Similarly, a moral person, on having his car hit by another driver, might experience a strong evolutionarily-programmed urge to wreak physical havoc on the offending driver. His adrenalin might be flowing and his nostrils might be dilated, but if he wishes to do the right thing, morally speaking, he must suppress his urges and instead speak calmly to the other driver until the police arrive.

In much the same way, the mere fact that you have a strong urge to become a parent does not in and of itself mean that you are morally justified in becoming one. To the contrary, it is arguably one of those urges that morality requires you to "properly channel." Thus, if you would make a poor parent, then your moral duty might be to suppress your urge to parent even though doing so causes you pain.

No Regrets

One reason people have children is to eliminate a disturbing fear that afflicts them: namely, the fear that if they choose *not* to have children, they may someday—when it is too late to have them—be haunted by a feeling of intense regret, a feeling that would last until they died. The easiest way to deal with this fear is to go ahead and have a child.

What lots of people ignore when deciding to have children is that the opposite regret is also possible: If you go ahead and make a baby, you may someday be overwhelmed by an intense feeling of regret—regret that you *made* a baby. You may find that you do not like parenthood or do not like the particular child fate has dealt you. You may wish you had never made a baby, and you may regret until the day you die your decision to make one.

Thus, when people are considering parenthood, there are two mistakes they can make. The first is the mistake of not becoming a parent and then living to regret the decision. The second is the mistake of becoming a parent only to discover that parenthood is not their cup of tea. Parents tend to give the possibility of making the former mistake greater weight, in their decision-making, than the possibility of making the latter mistake. "When in doubt, make a child," seems to be the rule of thumb.

Why do prospective parents tend to downplay the costs associated with a parental disappointment? One reason is that they tend to assume—in many cases incorrectly, as we have seen—that theirs will be a uniquely likable child and that they will therefore not be disappointed by parenthood. A second, more sinister reason is that parents realize that if they *do* end up regretting having a child, there are steps they can take to "cut their losses." They can relinquish their parental rights—they can, that is, give the child away. Or they can take less radical steps to ameliorate the consequences of their bad decision-making. They might, for example, take steps to distance themselves from their child. They might ignore it. They might turn it over to babysitters. They might send it off to boarding school.

Stated differently, if you regret having a child, you can easily lessen the costs of your mistake by shifting these costs onto the child. On the other hand, if you regret *not* having had children, there is no one onto whom to shift the costs of your mistake; you must bear these costs yourself. Of course, the process of shifting costs onto a child will, in many cases, result in the child having a second-rate childhood. Thus, the decision to have children "when in doubt" makes sense only if we are willing to ignore the interests of children in order to further the interests of their parents, and this is something steward-parents will be unwilling to do. Only an owner-parent would be motivated to have a child by the fear of someday regretting not having had children.

Special Problems for Steward-Parents

For owner-parents, the question of whether or not to have children is relatively easy to answer: Owner-parents might have children because they need help around the farm, because they need to feel needed, or because they want a second chance at life and hope to live vicariously through the child they bring into existence. Indeed, an owner-parent no more needs to justify his decision to make a baby than he needs to justify his decision, say, to buy a boat on a whim: The fact that he feels like doing it is justification enough.

For steward-parents, on the other hand, the question of whether or not to have children is much more difficult to answer.

Notice, in the first place, that for the steward-parent, the costs-to-benefits ratio of having children will be less favorable than for the owner-parent. This is because the steward-parent will be expected to take better care of his children than the owner-parent and will therefore experience higher costs, both financial and emotional, than the owner-parent. Furthermore, the steward-parent will be less able than the owner-parent to "extract value" from his child by, say, having him spend his childhood at a factory instead of in school. If it is hard for an owner-parent to rationally justify having children, it is harder still for a steward-parent.

But aside from the issues raised by the costs and benefits analysis, the steward-parent faces a moral issue that the owner-parent does not. To better understand the nature of this moral issue, let us again consider the land-stewardship analogy.

In the case I described, a person is approached by a neighbor who is going away on a trip. The neighbor asks him to care for his lands while he is gone. If the person accepts the request and takes on the duties of stewardship, he does so to help out another person in need. He is acting altruistically, making a personal sacrifice to benefit another.

We can even imagine a land steward acting more altruistically than this. Rather than waiting for people to seek his help, he might seek out people who could benefit from his services as land steward. He might, for example, put an ad in the paper declaring his willingness to take care for free of the lands of anyone going on an extended journey.

Notice, however, that when a steward-parent accepts the responsibilities of parenting by making a child, he is not helping out another person who came to him asking for help. Nor is he seeking out people who might need his help and then helping them. Before he became a parent, there was no person who needed his help.[52] What the steward-parent is doing, then, is bringing into existence a person who *will* need his help. He is rather like a farmer who forces his neighbor to go on extended journeys, but who offers to care for his lands until his return. It would be difficult for a farmer to justify such behavior. Is it possible for the steward-parent to morally justify parallel behavior?

It would clearly be wrong for a steward-parent to have children if there was good reason to think that the children in question would lead undesirable lives. Suppose, for example, he knew that because of some ecocatastrophe, life on earth would, during the life of any child he made, become increasingly unendurable. Or suppose he knew that, because of a genetic defect in him, any baby he made would live a life of misery. In such cases, if he went ahead and made a baby, we would have to conclude that he was doing so to meet his own needs, not to meet the needs of his child—we would have to conclude, in other words, that he was not a good steward-parent.

Thus, a *necessary* condition for a steward-parent to be justified in making a baby is that there be reason to think, at the time he makes one, that the baby in question will have a life that is, on balance, a desirable life—that it will be a life which, from the baby's point of view, is better lived than not lived. If there is reason to think that the baby he made would, reflecting back on his or her life as an old man or old woman, be inclined to say, "Better that I hadn't been born," then the steward-parent will have a difficult time justifying having made the baby in question.

Although ability to provide a child with "a life worth living" may be a *necessary* condition for a steward-parent to make a baby, is it also a *sufficient* condition? In other words, is the mere fact that a steward-parent reasonably believes that he can provide any baby he makes with "a life worth living" an adequate justification for making a baby? This question is much more difficult to answer, but I believe that it can be answered in the affirmative.

In Chapter 7, I mentioned that being a steward-parent does not mean utterly ignoring one's own interests. To the contrary, there will be plenty of cases in which the interests of a child and his steward-parents can simultaneously be served, and in such cases, steward-parents should not shy away from serving their own interests. Thus, a case can be made that when a person finds himself wanting a child and subsequently satisfies that desire by bringing a child into existence, he can claim to be operating on the stewardship model of parenting, *as long as it is reasonable to think that this person can provide the child he brings into existence with a life that is on balance quite worth living*. Both he and the child he creates will, under such circumstances, benefit from the act of creation.

The condition just cited, it should be noted, will not be easy to meet, and anyone who is not willing to devote himself to the task of parenting will be unlikely to meet it.

In this chapter I have laid out the case against having children. I have suggested that there are people—those I have called "difficult parents"—for whom having children is probably a counterproductive act: For them, the costs of parenthood will likely far outweigh the benefits. I have suggested that even those who would be "easy parents" should think twice before having children: There is no guarantee that the child they have will be an "easy child." I have suggested that many common motives for having children are "impure"; in particular, from the mere fact that someone experiences an intense biological urge to have children, it does not follow that he or she is doing something morally permissible in giving in to this urge.

In America today, many children come into existence not because parents, after much thought, conclude that they are up to the burdens of parenthood and can do right by their children; rather, they come into existence because their parents are uniquely thoughtless with respect to procreation. Their heads are filled with unwarranted assumptions about themselves, about their prospective children, and about what parenting will be like. The law gives them the right to make babies, and it is a right they exercise to the fullest, often with disastrous consequences both to themselves and to the children they bring forth.

EPILOGUE

In this book I have encouraged readers to think about the place that children have had and should have in the world.

I began with a rather horrific discussion of the uses to which past generations have put their children. I described the gradual improvement in the lot of children that has taken place in recent centuries and that, I suggested, reached its zenith—in America, at any rate—in the 1950s. I described the decline in the concept of childhood that has taken place since that time, and I offered my own rather pessimistic views on the prospects for a return to the Golden Age of Childhood.

I went on to ask a significant ethical question: How would we treat our children if our primary concern was their well-being? The answer to this question is that we would treat them as if we were their stewards, doing our best to care for them and nurture them. Our success as stewards could be measured by checking to see, when they emerged from our care as young adults, whether they are relatively happy, whether they are well-adjusted to their social environment, and—perhaps most importantly—whether they are free, in the sense of having open to them a number of meaningful choices about what they will do with their lives.

I argued that such stewardship required parents to make a substantial sacrifice of their own freedom, time, and resources. It might even mean making what some of today's Americans would regard as supreme sacrifices: staying married to the same person for the two decades that it would take to raise one's children, and putting one's dreams of a meaningful career on hold at least until one's children are in school.

I suggested that many of those Americans who decide to become parents do not really think the matter through carefully.

To the contrary, they become parents because they imagine, quite implausibly, that theirs will be a perfect child and will therefore be easy to parent. Or they become parents because doing so will satisfy a deep urge they find in themselves; of course, if satisfying this urge would condemn the children they create to an unsatisfactory childhood, then they are morally blameworthy for selfishly giving in to the urge.

But isn't it selfish *not* to have children? Isn't it selfish to spend your life trying to make yourself happy rather than bringing children into the world and trying to make them happy? An interesting question, and one that is ambiguous.

By "selfish" someone might mean selfish *to our species*: "Suppose everyone decided to spend his adult life unencumbered by children. Our species would die out. You owe it to your species to have children." This line of argument, however, is not particularly plausible. To begin with, it is unlikely that *everyone* will decide to live a childless existence, so there is little danger of our extinction as a species. And even if extinction were a genuine danger, there are those who would argue that although it is possible to owe something to *a member of* your species, it makes no sense to talk of a debt to *your species itself*. They might add that the universe got along just fine before our arrival as a species a few million years back, and that it would get along just fine without us.

Or, by "selfish" someone might mean something more personal: A selfish person is one who looks out for his own interests and cares not a whit about the interests of others. A selfish person is one who never gives to charity or does an altruistic act. Are childless adults selfish in this sense? Not necessarily. Notice, to begin with, that it is far from clear that by having children you are engaged in an altruistic act. In particular, suppose that because you are impoverished or because of your temperament, chances are that any child born to you would not have a joyous existence, but would instead experience a miserable start to a miserable life. In such a case, the selfish thing to do would be *to* have children.

It can also be argued that what is selfish (in the "personal" sense of the word) in this overpopulated world, is not the decision to remain childless, but the decision to have children.

Having heard all this, the reader can reasonably ask, Am I trying to talk people out of having children? Well, yes...in a way. What I am suggesting is that a lot more people should have a lot fewer children—or none at all. In particular, people who want to be free to live their lives as they wish and avoid responsibility would do well to avoid having children, for both their own sake and the sake of their prospective children—as should those who lack the time and resources to fulfill their responsibilities as parents and those temperamentally unsuited to parenthood.

In Chapter 8 we did an ethical thought experiment involving reincarnation. The question, stated simply, was this: If you knew that you were going to die and be reincarnated, and if you had the ability to select the parents you would be reborn to, what sort of parents would you select? On asking this question, it quickly becomes apparent that some characteristics are desirable in a parent and others are not. Indeed, there are some people that virtually no one—not even they themselves—would want to have as a parent, if they had any say in the matter. And yet we find many of these individuals not only having children but having large families, thus repeatedly inflicting themselves on innocent children.

It is, to be sure, a chilling question: Would you want to have yourself as a parent? And for just that reason it is a question that all-too-many people do not ask themselves.

There is, to be sure, a danger in encouraging people to think long and hard before deciding whether to have children.

Notice, after all, that thoughtfulness is presumably a desirable feature in parents. To succeed as a parent (as a steward-parent, at any rate) requires an ability to plan ahead as well as an ability to learn from one's mistakes. Thoughtless people—those incapable of planning or learning from their mistakes—are likely to make second-rate parents whose children might survive but almost certainly will not thrive.

Thoughtful people, however, are most likely to take to heart the advice to think long and hard about whether to have children; and after contemplating the matter, they will in many cases conclude that they should not. Thoughtless people, on the other hand, are unlikely to act on the advice and as a result will probably be unaffected by it.

This, to my mind, is another cruel irony of parenting: In many cases, those people most likely to take the responsibilities of parenting seriously are least likely to become parents, while those people least likely to take the responsibilities of parenting seriously are most likely to become parents.

Parenthood (under the stewardship model of parenting) involves a serious and decades-long commitment. It should not be undertaken lightly. It should not be undertaken on a whim, any more than an ascent of Mount Everest should be undertaken on a whim. (The average person would think twice before undertaking an ascent of Mount Everest; and yet, as I have suggested, an attempt on Mount Everest is, in many respects, child's play compared to fulfilling the obligations of steward-parenthood.) Ideally, parenthood should be undertaken only by those who are ready to make considerable personal sacrifices.

And what about those who want lives without sacrifice? Who want to live without commitment? Who want to put their careers ahead of everything? Who want to put personal development first? They should do so, but at the same time they should realize that all these things are incompatible with the stewardship model of parenting. They would do well, both for their own sake and for the sake of childkind, to remain childless—or, as one might say, childfree.

In today's world a childfree existence is far less painful than it used to be. People can have sex to their heart's content and still remain childfree—this was not always the case. Childfree individuals are less open to social criticism than was the case a generation ago. And while it is true that in a childfree state they will miss out on the benefits of parenting, one suspects that many of these freedom-loving individuals would not delight in parenting: For them, the costs of parenting would likely outweigh the benefits.

Notice, too, that there is a way for people to obtain many of the benefits of parenting with a fraction of the costs: They can get a pet. Pets need you. Treated well, they will love you unconditionally. They will bond with you. In having a pet you can experience many of the joys of having an infant, without having to worry about the infant becoming a sarcastic teenager and without having to pay for college.

Many potential parents would do well to keep these words of advice in mind: Cats make wonderful pets. So do dogs.

NOTES

Prologue

1. U.S. Department of Education, National Center for Education Statistics, *Youth Indicators 1996*, Ind. 8.

2. "Nothing to get excited about...," *The Economist* (March 30, 1996), p. 52.

3. Myriam Marquez, "Honor-roll mom not good enough," *Dayton Daily News* (May 4, 1998), p. 10A.

4. For more on this period of Bergman's life, see Donald Spoto's *Notorious: The Life of Ingrid Bergman* (New York: Harper Collins, 1997), pp. 292-97.

5. *Youth Indicators 1996*, Ind. 4.

6. *Youth Indicators 1996*, Inds. 3 and 4.

7. *Youth Indicators 1996*, Ind. 11.

8. U.S. Bureau of the Census, *Current Population Reports*, ser. P20-469, "Marital Status and Living Arrangements: March 1996."

9. *Youth Indicators 1996*, Ind. 19.

10. *Current Population Survey, June 1995*.

11. Of married couples with children under six, 62 percent were two-income families; of married couples without children under six, only 54 percent were two-income families. [U.S. Bureau of the Census, *Current Population Reports*, ser. P20-509, "Household and Family Characteristics: March 1997," MC1.]

12. In 1950, only 4 in 1,000 children between 14 and 17 years of age were arrested; by 1993, that number had skyrocketed to 130 per 1,000. [*Youth Indicators 1996*, Ind. 58.]

13. Nadine Joseph, "Just 'a Little Munchkin'," *Newsweek* (May 6, 1996), p. 38.

14. Keith Naughton and Evan Thomas, "Did Kayla Have to Die?" *Newsweek* (March 13, 2000), p. 27.

15. In giving the seventeenth century as the important turning point in the history of childhood, I am following in the footsteps of social historian Philippe Ariès. Some historians of the family would argue with this choice, but realize that my project in these pages is not so much to establish the exact moment at which childhood was "invented," as to establish that it *was* invented—i.e., that there was a time when children were treated with nothing like the care and respect that they enjoyed in the middle of the twentieth century.

Chapter 1: The Uses of Children

1. Lloyd deMause, "The Evolution of Childhood," in *The History of Childhood*, ed. Lloyd deMause (New York: The Psychohistory Press, 1974), p. 27.

2. Pierre Berton, *The Dionne Years: A Thirties Melodrama* (New York: W. W. Norton & Company, 1977), pp. 68f.

3. Ivy Pinchbeck and Margaret Hewitt, *Children in English Society* (London: Routledge & Kegan Paul, 1969), I:45.

4. C. John Sommerville, *The Rise and Fall of Childhood* (Beverly Hills, Cal.: Sage Publications, 1982), p. 100.

5. Pinchbeck and Hewitt, *Children in English Society*, I:75.

6. Sommerville, *The Rise and Fall of Childhood*, p. 101.

7. Pinchbeck and Hewitt, *Children in English Society*, II:350.

8. Sommerville, *The Rise and Fall of Childhood*, p. 48.

9. Sidney Painter, *William Marshall: Knight-Errant, Baron, and Regent of England*, p. 14, as cited by deMause, "The Evolution of Childhood," p. 33.

10. Sidney Painter, *William Marshall: Knight-Errant, Baron, and Regent of England*, p. 16, as cited by deMause, "The Evolution of Childhood," p. 33.

11. Saint Justin Martyr, *Writings*, p. 63, as quoted by deMause, "The Evolution of Childhood," p. 28.

12. deMause, "The Evolution of Childhood," p. 44.

13. Suetonius, *The Twelve Caesars*, trans. Robert Graves (New York: Penguin Books, 1976), p. 131.

14. Paulus Aegineta, *Aegineta*, pp. 379-81, as quoted by deMause, "The Evolution of Childhood," p. 46.

15. deMause, "The Evolution of Childhood," pp. 44f.

16. Reuters News Service, July 17, 1995.

17. "Privacy and Paedophilia," *The Economist* (August 3, 1996), p. 46.

18. Valerie Reitman, "Japan's New Growth Industry: Schoolgirl Prostitution," *The Wall Street Journal* (October 2, 1996), p. A8.

19. Tuchman, Barbara, *A Distant Mirror: The Calamitous 14th Century* (New York: Alfred A. Knopf, 1978), p. 111.

20. deMause, "The Evolution of Childhood," pp. 47, 49.

21. Nicolau Barquet and Pere Domingo, "Smallpox: The Triumph over the Most Terrible of the Ministers of Death," *Annals of Internal Medicine* (October 15, 1997), p. 640.

22. Lance Morrow, "When One Body Can Save Another," *Time* (June 17, 1991), pp. 54-58.

23. "For the Sake of Some Umbilical Cells…," *Time* (June 17, 1991), p. 58.

24. For the details of Dickens's childhood, I am relying on Michael Allen's *Charles Dickens' Childhood* (London: Macmillan Press, 1988), unless otherwise noted.

25. John Foster, *The Life of Charles Dickens* (n.p.: Chapman & Hall, 1872-74), 1:31-33, as quoted by Allen, *Charles Dickens' Childhood*, p. 81.

26. John Foster, *The Life of Charles Dickens* (n.p.: Chapman & Hall, 1872-74), 1:31-33, as quoted by Allen, *Charles Dickens' Childhood*, pp. 82f.

27. Charles Dickens, *David Copperfield* (New York: New American Library, 1962), pp. 284f.

28. "The First Report of the Commission on the Employment of Children and Young Persons in Mines," *Parliamentary Papers* (1842), XVII:75, as quoted by Pinchbeck and Hewitt, *Children in English Society*, II:354.

29. R. Ayton, *A Voyage Round Great Britain*, II:155-60, as quoted by Ivy Pinchbeck, *Women Workers and the Industrial Revolution* (London: George Routledge & Sons, 1930), p. 243.

30. Pinchbeck and Hewitt, *Children in English Society*, II:401f.

31. Ibid., II:354.

32. "Report on Mines" of the Children's Employment Commission, XVII:75, as quoted by Pinchbeck, *Women Workers and the Industrial Revolution*, p. 249.

33. Pinchbeck and Hewitt, *Children in English Society*, II:401f.

34. Ibid.

35. Ibid., II:354.

36. Ibid., II:354f.

37. Ibid., II:407f.

38. Ibid., II:403.

39. Ibid., II:407f.

40. Ibid., II:404.

41. Karl Marx, *Capital: A Critique of Political Economy* (New York: The Modern Library, 1906), p. 431.

42. Pinchbeck and Hewitt, *Children in English Society*, I:250, 311.

43. David Porter, "Considerations on the present state of chimney sweepers...," in *Improving the Lot of the Chimney Sweeps: One Book and Nine Pamphlets*, ed. Kenneth E. Carpenter (New York: Arno Press, 1972), p. vi.

44. Ibid., p. v.

45. Jonas Hanway, "A sentimental history of chimney-sweepers...," in *Improving the Lot of the Chimney Sweeps*, p. 31.

46. Ibid., pp. 19-22.

47. Robert Steven, "The trade of chimney-sweeping exhibited in its true light...," in *Improving the Lot of the Chimney Sweeps*, pp. 7f.

48. "Twenty-First Report of the committee of the Society for superseding the necessity of climbing boys...,"in *Improving the Lot of the Chimney Sweeps*, pp. 18f.

49. Porter, "Considerations on the present state of chimney sweepers...," pp. 61f.

50. Ibid., p. 63.

51. Stephen Lushington, "The reply of Dr. Lushington, in support of the bill for the better regulation of chimney-sweepers and their apprentices...," in *Improving the Lot of the Chimney Sweeps*, p. 25.

52. Steven, "The trade of chimney-sweeping exhibited in its true light...," p. 5.

53. Hanway, "A sentimental history of chimney-sweepers...," p. 54.

54. "Twelfth Report of the committee of the Society for superseding the necessity of climbing boys...," in *Improving the Lot of the Chimney Sweeps*, p. 13.

55. Steven, "The trade of chimney-sweeping exhibited in its true light...," p. 3.

56. "Twelfth Report of the committee of the Society for superseding the necessity of climbing boys...," p. 13.

57. Steven, "The trade of chimney-sweeping exhibited in its true light...," p. 14.

58. "Twenty-First Report of the committee of the Society for superseding the necessity of climbing boys...," pp. 10f.

59. Steven, "The trade of chimney-sweeping exhibited in its true light...," pp. 13f.

60. Lushington, "The reply of Dr. Lushington...," p. 28.

61. Samuel Roberts, "...An address to British females of every rank and station, on the employment of climbing boys in sweeping chimneys...," in *Improving the Lot of the Chimney Sweeps*, pp. 16f.

62. Steven, "The trade of chimney-sweeping exhibited in its true light...," p. 15.

63. Ibid., p. 16.

64. Lushington, "The reply of Dr. Lushington...," p. 25.

65. Ibid., p. 27.

66. "Twelfth Report of the committee of the Society for superseding the necessity of climbing boys...," p. 13.

67. Hanway, "A sentimental history of chimney-sweepers...," pp. 77f.

68. "Report of the committee of the Society for superseding the necessity of climbing boys...," in *Improving the Lot of the Chimney Sweeps*, p. 25.

69. Porter, "Considerations on the present state of chimney sweepers...," p. 35n.

70. John Harding, as quoted by Steven, "The trade of chimney-sweeping exhibited in its true light...," p. 8.

71. "Report of the committee of the Society for superseding the necessity of climbing boys...," pp. 25f. See also "Twelfth Report of the committee of the Society for superseding the necessity of climbing boys...," p. 14, and "Twenty-First Report of the committee of the Society for superseding the necessity of climbing boys...," pp. 12f.

72. "Twenty-First Report of the committee of the Society for superseding the necessity of climbing boys...," pp. 12f.

73. Porter, "Considerations on the present state of chimney sweepers...," pp. 35f.

74. Hanway, "A sentimental history of chimney-sweepers...," p. 27.

75. Steven, "The trade of chimney-sweeping exhibited in its true light...," p. 5.

76. Porter, "Considerations on the present state of chimney sweepers...," p. 37.

77. Ibid., pp. 39f.

78. Ibid.

79. Steven, "The trade of chimney-sweeping exhibited in its true light...," pp. 6f.

80. Porter, "Considerations on the present state of chimney sweepers...," p. 40.

81. Steven, "The trade of chimney-sweeping exhibited in its true light...," p. 2.

82. Hanway, "A sentimental history of chimney-sweepers...," p. 25.

83. Ibid.

84. Ibid., pp. 2, 10.

85. Pinchbeck and Hewitt, *Children in English Society*, II:360.

86. Lushington, "The reply of Dr. Lushington...," p. 15.

87. Steven, "The trade of chimney-sweeping exhibited in its true light...," p. 1.

88. Hanway, "A sentimental history of chimney-sweepers...," pp. 82f.

89. Some of these techniques are described in the "Report of the committee of the Society for superseding the necessity of climbing boys..." and the "Twelfth Report of the committee of the Society for superseding the necessity of climbing boys...."

90. See the Appendix to the "Fourteenth Report of the committee of the Society for superseding the necessity of climbing boys...," in *Improving the Lot of the Chimney Sweeps*.

91. Steven, "The trade of chimney-sweeping exhibited in its true light...," p. 21.

92. Ibid., p. 18.

93. Roberts, "...An address to British females...," p. 11.

94. One cannot help but wonder, Did Charles Dickens ever employ a climbing boy? And if he did, what thoughts, if any, went through his mind?

Chapter 2: Child Stars

1. In my account of Velluti and the other castrati, I am relying, unless otherwise noted, on Angus Heriot's *The Castrati in Opera* (New York: Da Capo Press, 1974).

2. Ibid., p. 191.

3. Ibid., pp. 192f.

4. Lord Mount Edgcumbe, as quoted by Heriot, *The Castrati in Opera*, p. 195.

5. Lord Mount Edgcumbe, as quoted by Heriot, *The Castrati in Opera*, p. 196.

6. Charles De Brosses, as quoted by Heriot, *The Castrati in Opera*, p. 14.

7. Desmond Shawe-Taylor, "A Castrato Voice on the Gramophone," an Appendix to Heriot, *The Castrati in Opera*, pp. 225-27.

8. Heriot, *The Castrati in Opera*, p. 13.

9. Ibid., pp. 38f.

10. For more on castration techniques as well as the effects of castrations on the sexuality of males, see N. M. Penzer's *The Harem* (London: Spring Books, 1936), pp. 142-48.

11. Johann Wilhelm von Archenholz, *A Picture of Italy*, trans. Joseph Trapp (London, 1791), as quoted by Heriot, *The Castrati in Opera*, p. 47.

12. Heriot, *The Castrati in Opera*, p. 63.

13. "High Note," *The Wall Street Journal* (January 14, 2000), p. W11.

14. Alexander Wheelock Thayer, *The Life of Ludwig van Beethoven* (New York: The Beethoven Association, 1921), I:58.

15. Ibid., I:61.

16. Louise Lee, "Classical-Music World Uses Child Prodigies to Orchestrate Gains," *The Wall Street Journal* (July 23, 1996), p. A1.

17. Ibid.

18. Ibid.

19. Ibid.

20. Gelsey Kirkland and Greg Lawrence, *Dancing on My Grave* (New York: Doubleday & Company, Garden City, 1986), p. 27.

21. Ibid., p. 33.

22. George Balanchine, "Notes on Choreography," as quoted by Kirkland and Lawrence, *Dancing on My Grave*, p. 34.

23. Nike has since designed a high-tech ballet shoe that would reduce the foot injuries and suffering experienced by ballerinas. The ballet world has shown little interest in them. Says one dancer, "Ballet isn't about health. It's an art form." The dancer in question not only refuses to wear them, but won't recommend them to her students. [Michelle Higgins, "The Ballet Shoe Gets a Makeover…," *The Wall Street Journal* (August 18, 1998), p. A1.]

24. Kirkland and Lawrence, *Dancing on My Grave*, p. 35.

25. Ibid. p. 51.

26. Peter Plagens,"Even a Kid Could Do It," *Newsweek* (June 3, 1996), p. 70.

27. For an account of Shirley Temple's childhood, see Anne Edwards's *Shirley Temple: American Princess* (New York: William Morrow & Company, 1988).

28. Ibid., p. 28.

29. Leonard Mosley, *Zanuck*, p. 162, as quoted by Edwards, *Shirley Temple: American Princess*, p. 88.

30. For the details of the Dionne quints' childhoods, see Pierre Berton's *The Dionne Years: A Thirties Melodrama* (New York: W. W. Norton & Company, 1977) or Jean-Yves Soucy's *Family Secrets: The Dionne Quintuplets' Auto-*

biography (New York: Berkeley Publishing, 1997).

31. "Preemie Rights," *The Wall Street Journal* (September 1, 1998), p. A1.

32. A. R. Dafoe, in an address delivered to the New York Academy of Medicine on December 13, 1934, as quoted by Berton, *The Dionne Years: a Thirties Melodrama*, p. 76.

33. Berton, *The Dionne Years: A Thirties Melodrama*, p. 123.

34. Lotta Dempsey, "What Will Become of Them?" *Chatelaine* (June 1937), as quoted by Berton, *The Dionne Years: A Thirties Melodrama*, p. 131.

35. James Brough, *We Were Five* (New York: n.p., 1965), as quoted by Berton, *The Dionne Years: A Thirties Melodrama*, p. 205.

36. David Crary, "Dionnes say father abused them," *Dayton Daily News* (September 26, 1995), p. 5A.

37. "The surviving Dionne quintuplets...," *The Wall Street Journal* (March 9, 1998), p. A1.

38. Edwards, *Shirley Temple: American Princess*, p. 92.

39. Ibid. p. 98.

40. Tom Gliatto, "Out of Pocket...," *People Weekly* (September 6, 1999), p. 68.

41. "Independence Day...," *People Weekly* (March 17, 1997), p. 111.

42. Ron LaBrecque, *Special Effects: Disaster at Twilight Zone* (New York: Charles Scribner's Sons, 1988), pp. 9-15.

43. Ibid., p. 54.

44. Ibid., p. 281.

45. At the time of this writing, the foundation maintained a web site at www.minorcon.org.

46. For an excellent introduction to the modeling business and the perils that await child models, see Michael Gross's *Model: The Ugly Business of Beautiful Women* (New York: William Morrow and Company, 1995).

47. Ibid., p. 402.

48. Ibid., p. 367.

49. Ibid., p. 142.

50. Ibid., p. 350.

51. Ibid., p. 351.

52. Ibid., p. 2.

53. "Racier Ads to Be Reserved for Europe, Klein Says," *The Wall Street Journal* (December 20, 1995), p. B2.

54. Wendy Bounds, "An Aspiring Model at 15," *The Wall Street Journal* (October 12, 1995), p. B1.

55. Ibid.

56. Gross, *Model: The Ugly Business of Beautiful Women*, p. 487.

57. The best account of the present state of women's gymnastics is Joan Ryan's *Little Girls in Pretty Boxes: The Making and Breaking of Elite Gymnasts and Figure Skaters* (New York: Doubleday & Company, 1995).

58. Merrell Noden, "Dying to Win," *Sports Illustrated* (August 8, 1994), p.

54.

59. Ryan, *Little Girls in Pretty Boxes*, p. 94.

60. Ibid., p. 35.

61. Ibid., p. 154.

62. Ibid., p. 10.

63. Ibid., p. 153.

64. Ibid., p. 148.

65. Ibid., pp. 79f.

66. Ibid., p. 150.

67. Ibid., p. 72.

68. Ibid., p. 22.

69. Noden, "Dying to Win," p. 60.

70. Ryan, *Little Girls in Pretty Boxes*, pp. 164ff.

71. Ibid., p. 119.

72. Ibid., p. 155.

73. The authoritative account of Tracy Austin's life is her *Beyond Center Court: My Story* (New York: William Morrow and Company, 1992).

74. Ibid., p. 15.

75. Ibid., p. 88.

76. Ibid., p. 36.

77. Richard Stengel, "Fly till I Die," *Time* (April 22, 1996), p. 38.

78. Quoted in Stengel, "Fly till I Die," p. 35.

Chapter 3: What Price Childhood?

1. Susan Reed, "Losing Her Grip," *People* (May 30, 1994), p. 84.

2. Benjamin Franklin, *Autobiography* (New York: The Modern Library, 1944), pp. 15ff.

3. Michael Argyle, *The Psychology of Happiness* (London: Methuen & Company, 1987), p. 93.

4. If material desires cause unhappiness, and if the satisfaction of material desires simply leads to the creation of new material desires, does it follow that happiness is unattainable? Not necessarily. There is, after all, another way to "deal with" material desires than by satisfying them: One can instead "overcome" them—i.e., learn not to have material desires. This sort of thinking is central to Buddhism.

5. Felicia Paik, "When Too Big Isn't Big Enough," *The Wall Street Journal* (May 1, 1998), p. W10.

6. Ryan, *Little Girls in Pretty Boxes*, p. 136.

7. Ibid., p. 8.

8. Ibid., pp. 229f.

9. Edwards, *Shirley Temple*, p. 226.

10. Eliot Berry, *Topspin: Ups and Downs in Big-Time Tennis* (New York:

Henry Holt and Company, 1996), pp. 142f.

11. "Tennis—Capriati sobs after comeback hits dead end," Reuters World Report, January 13, 1997.

12. Berry, *Topspin*, pp. 97f.

13. Ibid., pp. 133f and 309.

14. Ryan, *Little Girls in Pretty Boxes*, p. 155.

15. Berry, *Topspin*, p. 28.

16. Eric Siegel, "Double Fault," *The Baltimore Sun* (August 1, 1982).

17. Joe Cook, "Tennis academy plan for little Nasties," *Financial Times* (March 20/21, 1999), p. 2.

18. Berry, *Topspin*, p. 308.

19. I mentioned Bela Karolyi's away-from-home training program for gymnasts in Chapter 2. Tennis prodigies might be sent to the Nick Bollettieri Tennis Academy, and promising young skiers might be sent to the Rowmark Academy.

20. I am not alone in offering such an argument. Joan Ryan, for example, argues along similar lines in *Little Girls in Pretty Boxes*.

One could, of course, easily broaden this proposal to include other "childhood professions"; in what follows, though, I will focus my remarks on girls' gymnastics.

21. A teaching "certificate" is really a license to teach, since if you lack one, most state governments will not allow you to teach in public schools.

22. Viviana A. Zelizer, *The Priceless Child: The Changing Social Value of Children* (New York: Basic Books, 1981), pp. 85f.

23. Ibid., p. 88.

24. Ibid., pp. 89-93.

25. Ibid., p. 94.

26. Austin, *Beyond Center Court*, p. 114.

27. Sally Jenkins, "The Sorry State of Tennis," *Sports Illustrated* (May 9, 1994), pp. 81-85.

28. Ibid., p. 78.

Chapter 4: The Invention of Childhood

1. Philippe Ariès, *Centuries of Childhood* (New York: Random House, 1962).

2. Ibid., 128.

3. Ibid., 353.

4. Tuchman, *A Distant Mirror: The Calamitous 14th Century*, p. 50.

5. Unless otherwise noted, I am relying on Edward Shorter's *The Making of the Modern Family* (New York: Basic Books, 1975) in my account of childhood in Europe.

6. C. Viry, *Mémoire statistique du département de la Lys* (Paris, 1812), p. 57, as quoted by Shorter, *The Making of the Modern Family*, pp. 57f.

7. Shorter, *The Making of the Modern Family*, p. 58.

8. Ibid., p. 55.

9. Ibid., p. 173.

10. Shulamith Shahar, *Childhood in the Middle Ages* (London: Routledge, 1990), p. 55.

11. Samuel X. Radbill, "Pediatrics," in *Medicine in Seventeenth Century England*, ed. Allen G. Debus (Berkeley: University of California Press, 1974), p. 248.

12. Shorter, *The Making of the Modern Family*, p. 179.

13. Radbill, "Pediatrics," p. 252.

14. Dr. Jean-Emmanuel Gilibert, *Anarchie médicinale*, III, pp. 290f, as quoted by Shorter, *The Making of the Modern Family*, p. 197.

15. It would be nice to think that such behavior was a thing of the past, but in the late 1990s America witnessed a number of cases in which young women covertly gave birth to babies and then "trashed" them.

16. Radbill, "Pediatrics," p. 244.

17. Ibid.

18. Bartholomew Batty, *The Christian Mans Closet*, as quoted by deMause, "The Evolution of Childhood," p. 42.

19. Shahar, *Childhood in the Middle Ages*, pp. 1ff.

20. David Hunt, *Parents and Children in History* (New York: Basic Books, 1970), pp. 127-30.

21. Shorter, *The Making of the Modern Family*, p. 242.

22. In my account of childhood in America, I am, unless otherwise noted, relying on Viviana A. Zelizer's *The Priceless Child: The Changing Social Value of Children*.

23. Marion Delcomyn, "Why Children Work," *Forum*, as quoted by Zelizer, *The Priceless Child*, p. 71.

24. Peter Singer, *Animal Liberation* (New York: Avon Books, 1975), p. 234.

25. Shorter, *The Making of the Modern Family*, p. 204.

26. Richard Dawkins, *The Selfish Gene* (Oxford: Oxford University Press, 1976), p. 117.

27. Shorter, *The Making of the Modern Family*, p. 174.

28. Ibid., p. 265.

29. Zelizer, *The Priceless Child*, pp. 62f.

30. Shorter, *The Making of the Modern Family*, pp. 260f.

Chapter 5: Childhood's End?

1. Neil Postman, *The Disappearance of Childhood* (New York: Delacorte Press, 1982), p. 134.

2. Dona Schneider, *American Childhood: Risks and Realities* (New Brunswick, N J: Rutgers University Press, 1995), pp. 170-80.

3. Kevin J. Strom, "Profile of State Prisoners under Age 18, 1985-97," a

special report issued by the Bureau of Justice Statistics of the U.S. Department of Justice, February 2000, p. 1.

4. Gerald F. Seib, "Youthful Crimes: Do They Justify Death Penalty?" *The Wall Street Journal* (June 16, 1999), p. A 28.

5. Schneider, *American Childhood: Risks and Realities* , p. 67.

6. Between 1950 and 1992, the birthrate for women aged 15 to 19 declined by 37 percent, from 81.6 to 51.8 per 1,000. [*Youth Indicators 1996*, Ind. 6.] During that same period, the birthrate for *unmarried* women aged 15 to 19 rose by 254 percent, from 12.6 to 44.6 per thousand. [*Youth Indicators 1996*, Ind. 7.]

7. Schneider, *American Childhood: Risks and Realities* , p. 70.

8. June Kronholz, "Reading, Writing and Miranda Rights...," *The Wall Street Journal* (September 20, 1999), p. A1.

9. Massad Ayoob, "Arm Teachers to Stop School Shootings," *The Wall Street Journal* (May 21, 1999), p. A12.

10. To be fair, many of the students at the university at which I teach are nontraditional—i.e., older—students. It might be that at the time they graduated from high school they could do math at the twelfth-grade level, but that they have since seen their math skills wither away until they were at the sixth-grade level.

11. "Employers, Parents Differ on High-School Diploma," *The Wall Street Journal* (January 8, 1998), p. C18.

12. June Kronholz, "U.S. 12th-Graders Rank Near Bottom in Math, Science," *The Wall Street Journal* (February 25, 1998), p. B2.

13. The suicide rate rose from 0.3 per 100,000 in 1960 to 0.9 per 100,000 in 1992. *Youth Indicators 1996*, Ind. 51.

14. National Center for Health Statistics, *Monthly vital statistics report,* vol. 45, no. 11, supp. 2, table 7.

15. Marie Winn, *Children without Childhood* (New York: Pantheon Books, 1983), pp. 199-204.

16. Postman, *The Disappearance of Childhood*, p. 93.

17. Winn, *Children without Childhood*, pp. 160f.

18. Shiela Muto, "From Here to Immodesty: Milestones in the Toppling of TV's Taboos," *The Wall Street Journal* (September 15, 1995), p. B1.

19. "Saturday Night Fever," *The Wall Street Journal* (October 9, 1998), p. W13.

20. "And toot to you, too," *The Economist* (January 6, 1996), p. 23.

21. Geraldo Rivera, "I Was Going to Hell," *Newsweek* (July 15, 1996), p. 48.

22. Dorothy Rabinowitz, "Kids After School...," *The Wall Street Journal* (April 17, 1998), p. W13.

23. "'Snuff TV': Some Very Harsh Realities," *Newsweek* (December 23, 1996), p. 60.

24. "NYTV Blue," *The Economist* (November 18, 1995), p. 30.

25. While we are on the topic of obscenities, it is worth noting that it is a bit of a mystery why obscenities exist. Obscenities always have nonobscene

synonyms—i.e., other words that mean the same thing but are not obscene. That one word should be obscene while its synonym is not is purely a matter of social convention; it would make as much sense for the first word to be socially appropriate and the second word to be labeled obscene. In a sense, then, obscenities are "created" by adults; and of course if adults did not create obscenities in the first place, they wouldn't have to conceal them from children.

It also looks as if today's young adults, in their freewheeling use of obscenities for the sake of using obscenities—in some cases, they appear not even to realize that the f-word is regarded by some as obscene—might be engaged in a bit of self-defeating behavior: Once obscenities become socially acceptable through constant use, they will no longer be obscene. Obscene language is possible only in a polite society.

26. Sara Mosle, "The Outlook's Bleak," *The New York Times* (August 2, 1998), sec. 2, p. 34.

27. "X-Rated," *The Wall Street Journal* (January 14, 2000), p. W11.

28. Sam Walker, "The Super Bowl...," *The Wall Street Journal* (January 25, 2000), p. A1.

29. Edward Felsenthal and Jared Sandberg, "High Court Strikes Down Internet Smut Law," *The Wall Street Journal* (June 27, 1997), p. B1.

30. I recently had my first encounter with violent video games. I was in an electronics store that had a video-game display on which potential customers could try out games before buying them. I took the controller and started pushing buttons—I had no idea what buttons did what or what I was supposed to do. Moments later, a man and a woman started fighting on the screen before me. I wasn't sure whether I was the man or the woman.

After randomly pushing buttons, I discovered not only that I was the man, but that by pushing a certain button, I could make him jump and kick. The woman approached, I pushed the button, and delivered a kick to her head that laid her flat. I was horrified and felt like apologizing—but to whom? A boy who had been standing behind me waiting for his turn summed up his own feelings: "Nice kick!"

31. Barbara Kantrowitz and Pat Wingert, "Learning at Home: Does It Pass the Test?" *Newsweek* (October 5, 1998), p. 66.

32. Sue Shellenbarger, "Tight Labor Market Is Putting Squeeze on Quality Day Care," *The Wall Street Journal* (October 21, 1998), p. B1.

33. In my discussion of the price changes that have taken place this century, I am relying on the data provided by W. Michael Cox and Richard Alm in "Time Well Spent: The Declining *Real* Cost of Living in America," *1997 Annual Report of the Federal Reserve Bank of Dallas*.

34. Indeed, even from an adult's point of view, the labor-cost of an item should be of considerable interest. As Thoreau noted in *Walden*, "the cost of a thing is the amount of...life which is required to be exchanged for it."

35. Two conspicuous examples of services that cost more in labor terms than in days gone by are university education and medical care. Perhaps the

increased labor-cost of medical care is justifiable inasmuch as the quality of medical care has increased so much: What would have counted as medical miracles a few decades ago are taken for granted. It would be hard to make similar claims for the quality of university education.

36. Winn, *Children without Childhood*, p. 209.

Chapter 6: The Resurrection of Childhood?

1. Psychologist Peter Neubauer, as quoted by Winn, *Children without Childhood*, p. 199.

2. Female altruism, on the other hand, traditionally took a somewhat different form: Women used to forsake careers so they could care on a full-time basis for the needs of their families.

Both women and men gained something and lost something in accepting traditional roles. As we have seen, women, in accepting "protection" from men, generally gave up some of their freedom; and men, in accepting the role of "protectors" of women, gave up some of their freedom (since "protecting" women generally involved, for example, being gainfully employed) and possibly even their lives (in, for example, time of war). Whether women or men came out ahead in this bargain is debatable, although seldom debated anymore, the standard belief being that women got the worse end of the deal.

3. Jean Jacques Rousseau, *Emile, or Education*, trans. Barbara Foxley (New York: E. P. Dutton & Company, 1911), p. 43.

Chapter 7: Models of Parenting

1. This statement is potentially misleading. A steward-parent *will* have rights with respect to his child: He will, for example, have the right to determine how his child is raised. What he will deny is that he has certain rights that the owner-parent will take for granted, e.g., the right to live off his child's labor.

2. There is nothing magical about the age eighteen. Indeed, there is reason to think that some people become "adults" before they are eighteen and that other people never really achieve "adulthood."

3. For an outspoken defense of the liberation model of parenting, see Richard Farson's *Birthrights* (New York: Macmillan Publishing, 1974).

Chapter 8: Choosing a Model of Parenting

1. Singer, *Animal Liberation*, p. 234

2. "Fluffy and Mommy," *The Wall Street Journal* (January 19, 1998), p. A14.

3. John Locke, *Second Treatise of Government*, ed. C. B. Macpherson (In-

dianapolis: Hackett Publishing Company, 1980), sec. 27.

4. For Aristotle's discussion of slavery, see bk. I, ch. 3 of his *Politics*.

5. A cow may not have hopes and ambitions, and it may not be able to make plans, but it can feel—pain, for instance—and it can experience fear.

6. Readers who wish to consider further the argument that it is wrong to treat animals as property (and eat them for lunch) are encouraged to take a look at Peter Singer's *Animal Liberation*.

7. Some, on hearing about the reincarnation scenario, might respond by pointing out that such a scenario is not just unlikely (which I readily admit), but that it is *impossible*. They might point out, in particular, that it makes no sense to say that the baby I am reborn as is really *me*. If we assume that the baby has a "fresh" body (i.e., that its body is composed of none of the matter from my body) and that it comes with a "fresh" mind (i.e., that it has none of my memories), then it will no more be me than my next-door neighbor is me.

If I had asked readers to pick parents for a child that had *nothing whatever to do with them*, I would have avoided the above difficulty, but the answers readers gave might not have been terribly useful: It is one thing to pick parents *for someone else*, whose pains and pleasures you won't have to experience personally; it is quite another thing to pick out your own parents, since you yourself will have to live with the consequences of your choice. By describing the child that is reborn as being *them*, I hope to increase the chance that readers will take the experiment seriously.

The reincarnation scenario is an adapted version of a Rawlsian "veil of ignorance." John Rawls, in his *Theory of Justice* (Cambridge, MA: Harvard University Press, 1971), uses a veil of ignorance to discover principles of justice; I use a veil of ignorance to discover principles of good parenting.

8. You can, if you choose, be an unplanned pregnancy. Could you also be born to a virgin? An interesting question, and one that I will do my best to dodge.

9. One Arceli Keh accomplished this feat in 1996.

10. In considering cases like these, we become aware that our use of the reincarnation scenario is, in a sense, circular. In order for us to be able to conclude that someone has been "corrupted" by his upbringing, we must already know what is involved in a proper upbringing; and this is problematic inasmuch as we are using the reincarnation scenario in part to determine what counts as a proper upbringing.

This circularity should not trouble the reader, though. I freely admit that the reincarnation scenario would be utterly useless to someone who had no notion at all of what is involved in good parenting. The scenario is designed for those who—like most of us—have an idea of what is involved in good parenting, but wish to clarify their views and rid them of internal inconsistencies.

Chapter 9: The Goals of the Steward-Parent

1. "ABC News Special," April 15, 1996.

2. Michael Argyle, *The Psychology of Happiness*, pp. 102-6.

3. Ibid., p. 93.

4. Ibid., pp. 97f.

5. Then again, if an owner-parent would get in legal trouble if he did not educate his child, it would make sense for him to educate. Likewise, if an owner-parent's plan for his child (e.g., to take over the family business) required that the child be educated to a certain level, it would make sense for him to educate. Notice that in these cases, when the owner-parent educates his child, he does so to promote his own interests, not those of his child.

6. In making the above remarks about cultural education, I am not assuming that *all* American children should be educated in "American culture." If, for example, the parents of an American child knew that their child (because of some bizarre set of circumstances) would spend his adult life running through the jungles of Brazil, it would be a colossal mistake to teach him American manners and customs. These would not serve him well in the jungles of Brazil. Of course, most American children will spend their lives in America rather than in the jungles of Brazil, so it makes sense for their parents to educate them in "American culture."

7. I have nothing against American parents teaching their child *both* English *and* Icelandic. Indeed, learning a second language at an early age can give a child interesting choices later in life—although it is far from clear that of the second languages they could have taught their child, Icelandic is the best choice.

8. Laura Purdy, *In Their Best Interest?: The Case Against Equal Rights for Children* (Ithaca: Cornell University Press, 1992), p. 45.

9. The third Anthony Ashley Cooper, as quoted by James L. Axtell, introduction to *The Educational Writings of John Locke* (Cambridge: Cambridge University Press, 1968), p. 45.

10. John Locke, "Some Thoughts Concerning Education" in *The Educational Writings of John Locke*, ed. James L. Axtell (Cambridge: Cambridge University Press, 1968), sec. 7.

11. Ibid., secs. 5, 15, 22.

12. Edmund Leites, "Locke's Liberal Theory of Parenthood," *Having Children: Philosophical and Legal Reflections on Parenthood* (New York: Oxford University Press, 1979), pp. 308f.

13. Locke, "Some Thoughts Concerning Education," sec. 36.

14. Ibid., secs. 78, 87.

15. Leites, "Locke's Liberal Theory of Parenthood," p. 310.

16. Locke, *Second Treatise of Government*, sec. 63.

17. Locke, "Some Thoughts Concerning Education," sec. 46.

18. Ibid., sec. 40.

19. Ibid., sec. 95.

20. Actually, Rousseau's comments in *Emile* apply primarily to boys, for Rousseau had different views on how to raise girls. Whereas boys should be

raised to be "strong and active," girls, he tells us, should be raised to be "weak and passive." [Rousseau, *Emile, or Education*, p. 322.]

21. Paul Johnson, *Intellectuals* (New York: Harper Perennial, 1990), p. 21.

22. Rousseau, *Emile, or Education*, p. 18.

23. Christina Hardyment, *Dream Babies: Three Centuries of Good Advice on Child Care* (New York: Harper and Row: 1983), p. 18.

24. Rousseau, *Emile, or Education*, p. 16.

25. Ibid., p. 17.

26. Ibid.

27. Ibid., p. 44.

28. Ibid., p. 54.

29. Ibid., p. 10.

30. Ibid., p. 41.

31. Ibid., p. 80.

32. Ibid., p. 147.

33. Ibid., p. 57.

34. Ibid., p. 53. To be fair to Locke, those parents who took Rousseau to heart and abandoned attempts to reason with children and instead allowed nature to be their teacher tended to produce children who were sadly deficient by almost any measure. [Hardyment, *Dream Babies*, p. 19.] Curiously, it appears that Rousseau had little interest in the outcome of these experiments and even secretly ridiculed those parents who took his advice on child rearing to heart. [Sommerville, *The Rise and Fall of Childhood*, p. 132.]

35. Rousseau, *Emile, or Education*, p. 58.

36. Ibid., p. 56.

37. Ibid., p. 84.

38. Ibid., p. 55.

39. Ibid., p. 48.

40. Ibid., p. 5.

41. Ibid., p. 57.

42. In saying this, I make it sound like I am an ethical relativist. Rest assured that I am not. I am an absolutist when it comes to *ethical* values, but as we shall see, there are many values that parents transmit to children that are not ethical in nature. It is with respect to these latter values that I lean toward relativism.

43. Charles Murray, *In Pursuit of Happiness and Good Government* (New York: Simon and Schuster, 1988), p. 114.

44. Ibid., pp. 117f.

45. Ibid, pp. 124-29.

46. This advice, I should note, will be counterproductive if it turns out that, contrary to what was assumed above, people have little control over what happens to them in this life—in particular, if the things that happen are fated to happen. Under such circumstances, it would be foolish to take responsibility for your mistakes and failings. By blaming yourself for things over which

you had no control, you would be setting yourself up for a lifetime of heart-break and frustration. I am doubtful, however, that a persuasive argument for fatalism is forthcoming.

47. W. Somerset Maugham, *Of Human Bondage* (New York: Vintage Books, 1956), p. 255.

Chapter 10: Reinventing the Family

1. Michele Ingrassia, "Endangered Family," *Newsweek* (August 30, 1993), p. 17.

2. Many of the remarks that follow could also apply to polyandrous marriages or even to group marriages. Polygamous marriages, however, would appear to be the most common alternative to monogamous marriages and so perhaps have best claim to our attention.

3. Some feminists, I realize, will argue that to be deprived of a father is a blessing, not a curse. For present purposes I will assume that children generally benefit from the presence of fathers. Shortly I will argue for the importance of fathers—and mothers too—in families.

4. David Popenoe, "Life without Father," in *Lost Fathers: The Politics of Fatherlessness in America*, ed. Cynthia R. Daniels (New York: St. Martin's Press, 1998), p. 41.

5. To be sure, the presence in a child's life of a parent of the same sex does not guarantee that the child will have a good gender-mentor. Indeed, suppose that a boy's father is "psychopathically masculine." The boy might fall under the spell of his father's notions of masculinity and be much the worse because of it. Such a boy would (in most circumstances) have been better off raised by women. This case is, however, atypical.

6. Tine Thevenin, *Mothering and Fathering: The Gender Differences in Child Rearing* (Garden City Park, New York: Avery Publishing Group, 1993), p. 2.

7. Fairly insignificant, but not entirely so. Studies show, for example, that even though the institution of marriage has been eviscerated, married couples are five times as likely to stay together as cohabiting couples. ["Nothing to get excited about…," *The Economist* (March 30, 1996), p. 52.]

Of course, as is always the case in such studies, it is difficult to know whether the couples in question stayed together because they got married or got married because they planned to stay together.

8. Thomas Hobbes, *Leviathan*, ch. 14.

9. Paula Story, "Woman, 55, gives birth to quads," *Dayton Daily News* (April 24, 1998), p. 5A.

10. To be sure, there are significant differences between the "family values" embodied in my Model Family and the "family values" that many conservatives espouse. We saw, for example, that it is difficult to argue that a family with two parents is better for children than a family with three or more par-

ents; some conventional advocates of family values might object to, say, polygamous marriages. Notice, too, that whereas some conventional advocates of family values might argue that big families are a good thing, I have argued to the contrary.

11. It is an overstatement to say that "we" have discarded the 1950s model of parenting. Many Americans have, but there are others of us who are raising our children pretty much like our parents raised us. Indeed, most of the families I know and socialize with are headed by couples who are not only married, but whose marriages are into their third decade. For these couples, the well-being of their children and of children in general is still a paramount concern. They make any number of sacrifices on behalf of their children and do so gladly. (Indeed, they are reluctant to speak of the things they do for their children as involving sacrifices.) They read the newspapers and shake their heads about the state of affairs. They worry that their children's children—their grandchildren—will be the victims of lowered standards of parenting.

12. Judith Posner, *The Feminine Mistake: Women, Work, and Identity* (New York: Warner Books, 1992), p. 10.

13. Ibid., pp. 19f.

14. Ibid., p. 9.

15. Ibid., p. 13.

16. Perhaps this was a conscious strategy: It might have been felt that the only way to get women to become somewhat more competitive was by exhorting them to become intensely competitive. If so, the strategy backfired.

Chapter 11: Having Children

1. There are two ways in which parents can choose to "have children": They can have babies and raise the babies they have, or they can adopt children that other people had. In most of the following remarks, I will focus my attention on parents who "have children" in the first of these two senses. Nevertheless, many of my remarks will apply equally well to adoptive parents.

2. Susan S. Lang, *Women without Children: The Reasons, the Rewards, the Regrets* (New York: Pharos Books, 1991), pp. 35f, 42.

3. U.S. Bureau of Census, *Current Population Surveys, June 1976 and 1995.*

4. Marian Faux, *Childless by Choice: Choosing Childlessness in the Eighties* (Garden City, New York: Anchor Press/Doubleday, 1984), p. 6.

5. Louis Genevie and Eva Margolies, *The Motherhood Report: How Women Feel about Being Mothers* (New York: Macmillan, 1987), p. 102.

6. Merle Bombardieri, *The Baby Decision: How to Make the Most Important Choice of Your Life* (New York: Rawson, Wade Publishers, 1981), pp. 223f.

7. Lang, *Women without Children*, pp. 218f.

8. Ibid., p. 182.

9. Nancy Chodorow, *The Reproduction of Mothering* (Berkeley: University

of California Press, 1978), p. 57.

10. A cynic, on hearing of such religions, might offer the following analysis of the situation. If you were going to design a religion from scratch, two features you would want to include would be, first, a directive that parents have many children, and second, a directive that parents raise their children in the religion in question. It would be one of the easiest ways for the religion to grow.

Someone less cynical than this might argue not that religions are designed so that they will grow, but that there is a kind of natural selection at work: The religions that (through no conscious design) foster large families endure and grow, while those that do not ultimately face extinction.

11. E. E. Le Masters, "Parenthood as Crisis," in *Sourcebook in Marriage and the Family*, 3rd ed., ed. Marvin B. Sussman (Boston: Houghton Mifflin, 1968), p. 460.

12. Genevie and Margolies, *The Motherhood Report*, pp. 402f.

13. Ibid., p. 17.

14. Ibid., pp. 69f.

15. Lang, *Women without Children*, p. 169.

16. Caleb Solomon, "Warning: Little Kids Are a Health Hazard to the Older Parent," *The Wall Street Journal* (November 7, 1994), p. A1.

17. Genevie and Margolies, *The Motherhood Report*, p. 15.

18. Ibid., p. 31.

19. Ibid., p. 17.

20. Ibid., p. 55.

21. Ibid., p. 238.

22. Jonathan Kaufman, "At Age 5, Reading, Writing and Rushing," *The Wall Street Journal* (February 14, 1997), p. B1.

23. LynNell Hancock, "Mother's Little Helper," *Newsweek* (March 18, 1996), p. 52.

24. I am using the term "ADD" to refer to all attention deficit disorders, including attention deficit hyperactivity disorder.

25. Hancock, "Mother's Little Helper," p. 52.

26. According to a study funded by the National Institute of Mental Health and the National Institute on Drug Abuse, boys with ADD who were not treated with stimulants had a significantly greater chance of abusing drugs and alcohol when they got older than boys who were treated.

27. G. Pascal Zachary, "Boys Used to Be Boys, But Do Some Now See Boyhood as a Malady?" *The Wall Street Journal* (May 2, 1997), p. A1.

28. Ibid.

29. Ibid.

30. Ibid.

31. Ibid.

32. Julie Magno Zito, et al., "Trends in the Prescribing of Psychotropic

Medications to Preschoolers," *Journal of the American Medical Association* (February 23, 2000), p. 1025.

33. Joseph T. Coyle, "Psychotropic Drug Use in Very Young Children," *Journal of the American Medical Association* (February 23, 2000), p. 1059.

34. Karl Zinmeister, "The American Dream: The Family's Tie," *Current* (February 1987), p. 12.

35. Ellen Joan Pollock, "Dual-Career Couples, Those '70s Pioneers, Two Decades Later," *The Wall Street Journal* (July 15, 1998), p. A8.

36. Argyle, *The Psychology of Happiness*, pp. 19ff.

37. Genevie and Margolies, *The Motherhood Report*, p. 16.

38. Ibid., p. 180.

39. Ibid., p. xix.

40. Lang, *Women without Children*, pp. 229f.

41. Genevie and Margolies, *The Motherhood Report*, pp. xxv-xxvi.

42. Ibid, p. 5.

43. Le Masters, "Parenthood as Crisis," p. 461.

44. Genevie and Margolies, *The Motherhood Report*, p. 10.

45. Ibid., p. 72.

46. Ibid., p. 206.

47. Kate Harper, *The Childfree Alternative* (Brattleboro, VT: The Stephen Greene Press, 1980), p. 74.

48. Conquering Everest doesn't necessarily generate a thrill. One climber describes his successful ascent in the following terms: "Reaching the top of Everest is supposed to trigger a surge of intense elation...[but] any impulse I might have felt toward self-congratulation was extinguished by overwhelming apprehension about the long, dangerous descent that lay ahead." [Jon Krakauer, *Into Thin Air: A Personal Account of the Mount Everest Disaster* (New York: Villard Books, 1997), p. 181.]

49. Krakauer, *Into Thin Air*, p. 5.

50. Ibid., p. 24.

51. Admittedly, the chance of dying while climbing Everest is far greater than the chance of dying while giving birth: The ratio of people who successfully climb Everest to people who die trying is four to one. [Krakauer, *Into Thin Air*, p. 275.]

52. The above remarks, it should be noted, do not apply in those cases in which a steward-parent *adopts* a child who needs a parent.

INDEX